THE MYTHOLOGY OF ALL RACES

VOLUME I

GREEK AND ROMAN

Volume I. *Greek and Roman*
William Sherwood Fox, Ph.D., Princeton University.

Volume II. *Teutonic*
Axel Olrik, Ph.D., University of Copenhagen.

Volume III. *Celtic, Slavic*
Canon John A. MacCulloch, D.D., Bridge of Allan, Scotland.
Jan Máchal, Ph.D., Bohemian University, Prague.

Volume IV. *Finno-Ugric, Siberian*
Uno Holmberg, Ph.D., University of Finland, Helsingfors.

Volume V. *Semitic*
R. Campbell Thompson, M.A., F.S.A., F.R.G.S., Oxford.

Volume VI. *Indian, Iranian*
A. Berriedale Keith, D.C.L., Edinburgh University.
Albert J. Carnoy, Ph.D., University of Louvain.

Volume VII. *Armenian, African*
Mardiros Ananikian, B.D., Kennedy School of Missions, Hartford, Connecticut.
George Foucart, Docteur ès Lettres, French Institute of Oriental Archæology, Cairo.

Volume VIII. *Chinese, Japanese*
U. Hattori, Litt.D., University of Tokyo.
(*Japanese Exchange Professor at Harvard University, 1915–1916*)
Masaharu Anesaki, Litt.D., University of Tokyo.
(*Japanese Exchange Professor at Harvard University, 1913–1915*)

Volume IX. *Oceanic*
Roland Burrage Dixon, Ph.D., Harvard University.

Volume X. *American (North of Mexico)*
Hartley Burr Alexander, Ph.D., University of Nebraska.

Volume XI. *American (Latin)*
Hartley Burr Alexander, Ph.D., University of Nebraska.

Volume XII. *Egypt, Far East*
W. Max Müller, Ph.D., University of Pennsylvania.
Sir (James) George Scott, K.C.I.E., London.

Volume XIII. *Index*

PLATE I

Aphrodite the Mother

On Aphrodite's left arm originally rested an infant, the fingers of whose little hand may still be seen on the drapery of its mother's bosom. The goddess is looking straight before her, not, however, with her vision concentrated on a definite object, but rather abstractedly, as if serenely proud of her motherhood. She seems to represent here that special development of the earth goddess who typified the kindly, fostering care of the soil, and reminds one of certain Asiatic images of the divine mother and child. From a marble statue of the fourth or third century B.C., found on the Greek mainland, and now in the Royal Ontario Museum of Archaeology, Toronto (*photograph*). See pp. 196 ff.

THE MYTHOLOGY OF ALL RACES

IN THIRTEEN VOLUMES

LOUIS HERBERT GRAY, A.M., PH.D., EDITOR
GEORGE FOOT MOORE, A.M., D.D., LL.D., CONSULTING EDITOR

GREEK AND ROMAN

BY

WILLIAM SHERWOOD FOX, A.M., PH.D.

ASSISTANT PROFESSOR OF CLASSICS
PRINCETON UNIVERSITY

VOLUME I

BOSTON
MARSHALL JONES COMPANY
M DCCCC XVI

Printed June, 1916

PRINTED IN THE UNITED STATES OF AMERICA BY THE UNIVERSITY PRESS
CAMBRIDGE, MASSACHUSETTS

BOUND BY THE BOSTON BOOKBINDING COMPANY

TO THE MEMORY

OF

HARRY LANGFORD WILSON

SCHOLAR · TEACHER · FRIEND

CONSULTING EDITOR'S PREFACE

THERE are many good books on the mythology of particular peoples or races, ancient and modern, and much material accessible in books of travel and works on ethnology and religion; for classical antiquity excellent dictionaries of mythology exist. There are also books of narrower or wider range on comparative mythology, besides many in which myth and custom have been pressed into the service of theories of society, civilization, and religion, or are adduced for the illustration of art and archaeology. But a comprehensive collection by competent scholars of myths from all quarters of the earth and all ages has not hitherto been attempted; for several important parts of the field, no satisfactory works exist in English, while in some there is none in any language. On the value of an undertaking like the *Mythology of All Races*, therefore, no words need be spent.

The intrinsic interest of the subject is very great; for better than almost anything else myths reveal men's first notions about their world and the powers at work in it, and the relations between men and those powers. They show what things in their surroundings early engaged men's attention; what things seemed to them to need explanation; and how they explained them.

For a myth is commonly an explanation of something, in the form of a story — what happened once upon a time, or what repeats itself from day to day — and in natural myths, as distinct from the invented myths of philosophers and poets, the story is not the artificial vesture of an idea but its spontaneous expression, not a fiction but a self-evident fact. The student of the mind of man in its uniformity and its variations therefore finds in mythology a great fund of instructive material. A comprehensive collection like the present lends itself also to comparative study of single myths or systems of myth among different and widely remote peoples, and this use of the volumes will be facilitated by a suitable analytical index.

It is one of the merits of this collection that it is made for its own sake, with no theory to maintain or illustrate. The contributors have been given free hand to treat their subjects by such methods as may be best adapted to the nature of the sources and the peculiarities of the mythology itself, without any attempt to impose upon either the material or the writers a schematic plan.

The names of the contributors are a sufficient guarantee of the thoroughness and trustworthiness of their work, while the general editor is himself a scholar of wide attainments in this field. The volumes will be amply illustrated, not for the sake of making picture books, but for the legitimate purposes of illustration — a feature which will add much to the usefulness as well as to the attractiveness of the series. Taken all in all, therefore, the *Mythology of All Races* may safely be pronounced one of the most important enterprises of this age of co-operative scholarship.

GEORGE FOOT MOORE.

HARVARD UNIVERSITY
March 20, 1916.

EDITOR'S PREFACE

THE theme of mythology is of perennial interest, and, more than this, it possesses a value that is very real. It is a document and a record — existing not merely in the dim past, but in the living present — of man's thought, of his ceaseless endeavour to attain that very real happiness which, as Vergil tells us, arises from "knowledge of the causes of things." Even in his most primitive stages of development man finds himself dwelling in a world filled with phenomena that to him are strange, sometimes friendly, often hostile. Why are these things so? Rightly mankind perceives that a phenomenon is not a Thing in Itself, an Absolute, but that it is an effect, the result of a cause. Now, the immediate cause may often be found; but then it will be seen that this cause is itself only a result of an anterior cause; and so, step by step, the search for ultimate Cause proceeds. Thus mythology is a very real phase — perhaps the most important primitive phase — of that eternal quest of Truth which ever drives us on, though we know that in its full beauty it may never be revealed to mortal eye nor heard by ear of man — that quest more precious than meat or raiment — that quest which we may not abandon if we will still be men.

Mythology is not, then, a thing of mere academic interest; its value is real — real to you and to me. It is the history of the thought of early man, and of primitive man today. In it we may find much to tell us how he lived, and how he had lived in the ages of which his myths recount. As affording us materials for a history of civilization mythology is of inestimable value. We know now that history is something more than a matter of dates and events. "Magna Charta was signed by King John at Runnimede in 1215." What of it, if that be all? The exact words of the document, the particular monarch who signed it, the precise spot, the specific date are of no worth in themselves. The real historical question is — What were the causes which led the English Barons, at a certain point in the development of the British Nation, to compel the King to sanction a document abridging the Royal prerogatives; and what have been the consequences, not merely to the subsequent evolution of the British Constitution, but to all States and Colonies thereby affected? So, too, we read mythology, not only for its specific statements — its legends of gods and of heroes, its theories of the world, and its attempts to solve the mystery of the destiny of each and every individual — but also, with a wider purview, for the light which it sheds upon the infancy and the childhood of the race to which we — you who read and I who write — belong.

Science; has mythology aught to do with that? Assuredly, yes. Mythology is science in its infancy. Does the geologist seek to determine how the earth came into being, how the mountains and the lakes were formed; does the astronomer essay to know the stars and their natures; do the zoologist and the botanist endeavour to explain why animals and trees are as they are — the maker of myth does even the same. The scientist today is the lineal descendant of the myth-maker of olden days. To say this is to honour both alike — both, with all the light at their command, have sought, and ever seek, the Truth. The hypotheses of the myths, do they differ in principle from the hypotheses of science? We think not. There is no real scientist who does not know that the hypotheses with which he needs must work and which seem thus far infallible in providing explanations for all phenomena in his field may some day be modified or even utterly destroyed by new discoveries. The Ptolemaic Theory is gone, the Atomic Theory is questioned. But no sane man will for that reason condemn hypotheses *in toto*, neither will he despise those who, in their day, held hypotheses then deemed irrefutable.

The connexion of mythology with religion is obvious, yet a word of caution is needed here. Mythology is not synonymous with religion, but only a part of it. Religion consists of at least three parts — the attitude of soul, which is religion *par excellence;* the outward act of worship, which is ritual; and the scientific explanation, which — in the very highest and noblest sense of the term — is myth; and these three — which we may call the attitude of soul, body, and mind — go together to make religion. Throughout our study of mythology we must bear constantly in mind that we are dealing with only one feature of religion — its causal aspect. We must not take the part for the whole, else we shall be one-sided and unjust in our appreciation of religion as a whole.

One attitude of mind is absolutely essential in reading mythology — sympathy — and almost as important a requisite is that, while reading it, its premisses must be granted. If we approach mythology with the preconception that it is false or nonsensical or trivial, it will be but waste of time to read it; indeed it will be better never to have read it, for reading in such a spirit will only embitter. It is, perhaps, not sufficiently recognized how important a factor one's attitude of sympathy is, not merely in regard to religion or psychology or philosophy, or any other "mental and moral science," but also toward the "exact sciences." If, for example, I make up my mind that spectral analysis is utterly impossible, the discovery of a new element in the gaseous emanation of a distant planet by such analysis will be to me nothing but folly. If, again, I reject the mathematical concept of infinity, which I have never seen, and which cannot be weighed or measured, then I shall of course deny that parallel lines meet in infinity; you cannot give me the precise location of infinity, and, besides, all parallel lines that I have ever seen are equidistant at all points from each other. This is a *reductio ad absurdum* of an attitude which is far too common in regard to mythology and religion. This does not, of course, mean that we must implicitly believe all that we read; but it does mean that we should approach with kindly hearts. With reverence, then, and with love we take up myths. We may smile, at times, at their *naïveté;* but we shall never sneer at them. Unblushing, sometimes, we shall find them, and cruel; but it is the unmodesty and the cruelty of the child. Myths may be moral or un-moral; they are not immoral, and only a morbid mind will see uncleanness in them.

No attempt has hitherto been made to collect the myths of the entire human race into a single series. Yet this is not so strange as it might appear at first. Scattered in many volumes both old and new, and in periodicals of many kinds and languages, it is an impossible task for one man to know all myths, or to master more than one or two specific mythologies or a few special themes in mythology as a whole. It is quite true that countless volumes have been written on the myths of individual peoples and on special mythic themes, but their assemblage into a single unit has not thus far been accomplished. This is the purpose of the present series of the *Mythology of All Races*, and this the reason for its being. Herein it differs from all other collections of mythologies in that the mythology of each race is not merely given a special volume or half-volume of its own; but, since the series is an organic entity — not a chance collection of monographs — the mythology of an individual race is seen to form a coherent part of mythology. Moreover, the mythology of one people will not infrequently be found to cast light upon problems connected with the mythic system of quite another people, whence an accurate and a thorough understanding of any individual mythology whatever demands an acquaintance with the mythic systems of mankind as a whole. On the other hand, by thus taking a broad survey, and by considering primarily the simple facts — as presented chiefly by travellers, missionaries, and anthropologists — we may hope to escape some of the peculiar dangers which beset the study of mythology, especially preconceived theories and prejudices, and the risk of taking for aboriginal what is really borrowed and *vice versa*. We shall advance no special theory of mythology which shall seek to solve each and every problem by one and the same formula; we shall aim to present the facts in the case — and the theories may safely be trusted to take care of themselves, being then wisely built on solid foundations.

We have not attempted to make an encyclopaedia of mythology, nor have we planned a mere reference book, which would have been, in many ways, an easier task. We have had constantly in mind not only the technical student — though he, too, if the editor's own experience be any criterion, will learn much — but the more general reader who desires breadth of understanding, and who would know what the childhood of our race has thought of the mysteries of nature and of life, and how it has endeavoured to resolve them. We have sought to be scientific — in the best sense of the term — but we have also sought to present a book that shall be eminently readable, that shall set forth myths as living entities, and that — because each writer knows and loves the mythology of which he treats — will fill the reader with enthusiasm for them.

Much of the material here given appears for the first time in the English language — Slavic and Finno-Ugric, Oceanic, Armenian, and African. No survey of American mythology as a whole has hitherto been written. Even where — as in Indian, Teutonic, and Semitic — English monographs exist, new points of view are presented. Taking our stand on the best modern scholarship, we venture to hope that many current misconceptions of mythology may be brought to an end. Thus, within recent years, the science of Greek mythology has been revolutionized by the discovery of the very simple fact that Homer is not its ultimate authority, that, indeed, he represents a comparatively late stage in its development;

so that we must give full consideration to the non-Homeric myths and see that here, too, there is the same underlying primitive stratum common to all the race of man. This modern scientific treatment of Classical mythology has its initial English presentation in our series. Perhaps, at first blush, we shall seem to lose much both here and elsewhere; we may, perchance, be disappointed when we find that the vaunted wisdom of Egyptians and of Druids was not so very profound; but if we must part with some false, though pretty, ideas, we shall find ample compensation in knowing Egyptians and Druids as they were. After all, which do we prefer — a fanciful picture of our friend, or his actual portrait?

Mythology may be written in either of two ways — presentational or comparative. In the former the myths of each people are presented separately; in the latter some special theme — the deluge-legend, the afterworld, or the like — is considered as it appears in myth throughout the world.

The utmost care has been taken in the choice of collaborators, and it is believed that to scholars their names will be in themselves sufficient warrant that the volumes will possess distinct scientific value. The ample bibliographies and references appended to the pertinent sections will enhance the technical worth of our series. In addition, we propose to give in our index volume not merely the names and subjects discussed in the various volumes, but also a topical arrangement by which the variant myths and mythic themes of the different peoples upon a given subject may be found readily and accurately.

The selection of illustrations will, it is hoped, meet with general favour. It would have been a very easy matter to present fancy pictures or to reproduce paintings of great modern artists. Instead of that, we have deemed it more in harmony with the purpose of the series to choose for each section pictures of the deities or of mythic incidents as delineated by the people who themselves believed in those deities or incidents. This will have the added advantage of extending some knowledge of the art of early times and the more primitive peoples, as well as of such highly developed arts as those of the Orient. Here the material necessarily runs unevenly. For some mythologies — as Greek, Indian, and American — there is truly an *embarras de richesses;* for others — notably Celtic, Slavic, and Armenian — where the mythic systems have vanished leaving scarcely a trace of artistry — whether because they never developed it in high measure, or because their pagan art was later destroyed — the artistic remains are lamentably meagre.

In the plan and arrangement of each volume and section full latitude has been given to its author. It is obviously impossible to build a single Procrustean bed into which any and every mythology must be forced to fit; such "consistency" would be mere pedantry, and, by its false implications, would defeat its own ends.

It will perhaps be well to stress the fact that there will be nothing in our series that can be, in Roman Catholic phrase, "offensive to pious ears." In this respect, the editor is happy to say, his duties of censor have been practically a sinecure.

In conclusion, a brief outline of our series may appropriately be given.

The first volume is on Greek and Roman Mythology, by Professor W. Sherwood Fox, of Princeton University, and is written from the point of view to which we have already referred.

The second volume, devoted to Teutonic Mythology, is by Dr. Axel Olrik, of the University of Copenhagen, and author of *Danmarks heltedigtning* ("The Epic Poetry of Denmark"), *Kilderne til Sakses oldhistorie* ("Sources for Ancient Saxon History"), and *Nordisk aansdliv i vikingetid og tidlig middelalder* ("Norse Intellectual Life in the Viking Period and the Early Middle Ages"). Teutonic Mythology is almost wholly that of the Old Icelandic Sagas, and without a knowledge of it Wagner's *Nibelungenring*, for example, is quite unintelligible. Curiously enough, there is little Teutonic mythology (except for survivals in popular customs and beliefs) outside of Iceland; but in that island a rich literature was composed, and the mythology of the ancient Teutons is one of the most fascinating that has ever been evolved.

The third volume is divided between Celtic and Slavic. The first part is from the pen of Canon John A. MacCulloch, Rector of St. Saviour's, Bridge of Allan, Scotland, and author of *The Childhood of Fiction*, *Religion of the Ancient Celts*, and other standard works. The vivid imagination and warm-heartedness of the modern Irish, the quick impetuosity of the Welsh, the "dour" fatalism of the Scotsman, all find expression in their ancient mythology. We think at once of King Arthur and the Knights of the Round Table when we speak of Celtic mythology, but we are only too dimly aware of the dire struggles between the Fomorians and the Tuatha dé Danann, and we are all too prone to forget the vast mythology of the peoples who occupied Gaul when Caesar conquered it, and who still dwell in Ireland, Wales, Brittany, and much of Scotland.

The Slavic section is written by Professor Jan Máchal, of the Bohemian University of Prague, and author of *Bohatýrsky epos slovanský* ("Heroic Epic of the Slavs"), *Bájeslovi slovanské* ("Slavic Mythology"), etc. No work in English exists on the mythology of the Slavic peoples; yet in a way they are second only to the Hindus as representing the oldest mythological concepts of our own Indo-European race. Slavic mythology also includes the concepts of the Baltic nations — the Lithuanians and ancient Prussians (who, it may be remarked, were Balto-Slavs, not Germans). Of all the European peoples, the Balto-Slavs were the last to be Christianized, and to the downfall of their paganism it retained a remarkably primitive form, beside which the Greek or the Teutonic seems well-nigh distinctly modern.

The fourth volume is devoted to the Finno-Ugric and Siberian peoples, and its author is Dr. Uno Holmberg, of the

University of Finland, Helsingfors, who has already written *Permalaisten uskonto* ("Religion of the Permians"), *Tsheremissien uskonto* ("Religion of the Cheremiss"), and *Lappalaisten uskonto* ("Religion of the Lapps"). The mention of the Finns at once brings to mind the great world-epic of the *Kalevala*, but the Finns are also distantly related to the Hungarians and the early Turks. Much has been written on the *Kalevala*, but little on any other portions of Finnish mythology. The Siberian portion of the volume, dealing with the very interesting and primitive theme of "shamanism," will be the first scholarly presentation of the subject in English.

In the fifth volume Captain R. Campbell Thompson, the author of *The Reports of the Magicians and Astrologers of Nineveh and Babylon*, *The Devils and Evil Spirits of Babylonia*, *Babylonian Letters*, *Semitic Magic*, and other works of high rank, discusses Semitic Mythology. By this we shall understand the mythology of the ancient Assyrians and Babylonians and the scanty traces of primitive Arabian religion before the coming of Muhammad. While many excellent treatises on this subject exist, we may point out a new feature — the rendering, for the first time, of practically all the Assyro-Babylonian myths into English verse. Moreover, by his repeated visits to the East, Captain Campbell Thompson has succeeded in interpreting a number of mythological ideas by modern beliefs and phenomena. We have, after due consideration, decided to omit an account of Muhammadanism, since it has no mythology in the strict sense of the term.

The sixth volume is composite, dealing with the closely kindred races of India and Persia. The Indian Mythology is written by Professor A. Berriedale Keith, of Edinburgh University, the author of the standard *Vedic Index of Names and Subjects* and editor and translator of the *Śāṅkhāyana* and *Aitareya Āraṇyakas* and of the *Taittirīya Saṁhitā*. Here we have the earliest religious records of the Indo-European race. Professor Keith traces the development of the Indian mythology from the Rigveda (about 1500 B.C.) to the present day. If in the Rigveda itself we find few myths, they appear in rich abundance in the later periods, and they possess a luxuriance of fancy that is peculiarly Oriental. The second portion of this volume, by Professor A. J. Carnoy, of the University of Louvain, and author of *Le Latin d'Espagne d'après les inscriptions*, *La Stylistique grecque*, and *The Religion of the Avesta*, deals with the mythology of the so-called "fire-worshippers," the followers of Zoroaster. No treatise at once scholarly and popular has yet appeared in English on this theme, which draws its sources not only from the ancient Avesta, but also from one of the great epics of the world, the *Book of Kings* of the Persian poet, Firdausi.

The first third of the seventh volume, by Professor Mardiros Ananikian, of the Kennedy School of Missions, Hartford, treats of Armenian mythology, of which practically nothing is known, except for a few works in the Armenian language, and a couple of short special monographs in French and German, although its myths are of peculiar interest, especially in relation to Iranian mythology.

The remainder of the volume is from the pen of Professor George Foucart, head of the French Institute of Oriental Archaeology at Cairo, and author of *La Méthode comparative dans l'histoire des religions*, who will discuss the extremely primitive mythology of the pagan Africans. Here, again, no English work exists which considers this subject as a whole.

The eighth volume is divided equally between Chinese and Japanese mythology. The first part, written by Professor U. Hattori, of the Imperial University of Tokyo, considers especially the mythology of Taoism, for the Buddhism of China is really Indian, while Confucianism is a system of ethics and has no mythology. The second portion, from the pen of Professor Masaharu Anesaki, of the same university, and author of *Buddhist Art in its Relation to Buddhist Ideals*, treats particularly of the curiously primitive mythology of Shintoism.

In the ninth volume Professor Roland Burrage Dixon, of Harvard University, and author of *Maidu Texts*, discusses, for the first time in connected form in English, the mythology of the Malayo-Polynesian and Australian peoples. The Australians are of particular interest as being among the most primitive of all living races, and their myths are equally elementary. On the other hand, Polynesian mythology competes in richness and poetic charm with the mythology of ancient Greece itself, as in the legend of Tangaloa, one of the great cosmic gods, or of Pele, the dread divinity of the Hawaiian volcanoes; while among the Malays we find a curious blending of aboriginal beliefs and of Hindu and Muhammadan influences and elements.

Two volumes, the tenth and eleventh, are devoted by Professor Hartley B. Alexander, of the University of Nebraska, and author of *Poetry and the Individual* and of numerous articles on the American Indians in the *Encyclopaedia of Religion and Ethics*, to the mythology of the American Indians. The first volume treats of the Indians north of Mexico, and deals with the very varied mythological systems of the Eskimo, the Algonquians, the Plains Indians, the Pacific Coast tribes, and the Indians of the Southern States, the Puebloans, etc. In the second portion — on Latin America — the highly developed religions of the ancient Aztecs, Central Americans, and Peruvians will be found to stand in striking contrast to the extremely primitive myths of the South American Indians generally. The collection of the South American mythologies will be, we should note, the first that has yet been written with any approach to completeness.

The twelfth volume again is divided into two parts. The first of these deals with the mythology of ancient Egypt, and has been written by Professor W. Max Müller, of the University of Pennsylvania, and author of *Asien und Europa* and *Egyptological Researches*. This will present the faith of the Nile-Land from the point of view of the most modern scholarship, and will go far toward dissipating some very common errors regarding that system. The remainder of the volume, written by Sir George Scott, formerly of the British Burmese Service, and editor of *The Upper Burma Gazetteer*, discusses the mythology of Burma, Siam, and Annam with the same vivid charm that characterizes his volume on *The Burman, his Life and Notions*.

LOUIS H. GRAY.

April 10, 1916.

AUTHOR'S PREFACE

THE purpose which has guided me throughout the preparation of this book has been to present and interpret a number of the typical myths of Greece and Rome as vehicles of religious thought; that is to say, in the discharge of their original function. It is to be assumed, of course, that the standard controlling both the choice of the legends and their interpretation is religion in its most comprehensive aspect, an aspect that is most satisfactorily defined by Professor Irving King (*The Development of Religion*, p. 7): "The religious attitude may be said to be a peculiar organization of mental processes about the final meanings of life as they are conceived by the individual or the social group." By accepting this definition one puts himself under bond, in spite of certain ethical and philosophical misgivings, to include with religion the beliefs and practices of magic, the Cain of the family of spiritual activities. This extension of the field of observation, added to the present writer's shortcomings and the natural restrictions of book-making, has perforce limited the choice of myths to a comparatively small fraction of those which are logically available. For the same reasons, as well as for several others equally obvious, the interpretations which I have offered are of necessity far from being exhaustive. If it is true, and I believe that it is, that most of the legends recorded on these pages have already secured a permanent place in literature, then so much is clear gain; but so far as the purpose of this volume is concerned their inclusion as pure literature is accidental.

Contrary to the usual practice of mythologists, I have narrated the stories of the local heroes before proceeding to the delineation of the divinities, an order which appealed to me as the logical one even before I learned that it was advocated by Gruppe. Doubtless the reader, too, will share this view when he realizes that the descriptions of the gods contained in the second part of the book are in reality composite portraits largely made up of individual characteristics casually revealed by the gods themselves as they play their parts on the stage of the local myths.

Although frankly recognizing the impossibility of being perfectly consistent in the matter of spelling Greek proper names in English, I have not utterly despaired of attaining a certain measure of uniformity. The Attic orthography of the great dramatists has been adopted as the standard, and names have been transliterated into English according to the mechanical method usually followed, the one exception being that *ch* and not *kh* is used as the equivalent of χ. The established English spelling, however, has been retained in personal names which in the course of centuries have become so much a part of the English language that alteration of their form would seem at the same time to disguise the personalities for which they stand (e. g. Achilles, Apollo, and not Achilleus, Apollon); and likewise in names of districts, cities, islands, and bodies of water to which frequent allusion is still made in English journalism and literature (e. g. Thrace, Athens, Cyprus, and Aegean, and not Thrake, Athenai, Kypros, and Aigaian).

Those who are acquainted with the remains of Greek and Roman art will recognize many familiar subjects among the illustrations, but at the same time they will find a number which have seldom, if ever before, been employed in a treatise on mythology. Of this latter class may be mentioned in particular the reproductions of the vase-paintings found within recent years at Gela, and of the bronzes and other objects in Boston and New York, and also the photogravure of the Aphrodite in Toronto. Sufficient new material of a high order is not yet at hand to permit one entirely to dispense with the older works of art which have served to illumine the writings of three generations of mythologists.

It would be ungracious of me to let pass this opportunity of publicly acknowledging my indebtedness, too great to compute, to a large number of scholars whose writings I have freely consulted and drawn upon as occasion required. To those who know the real worth of L. R. Farnell's *Cults of the Greek States* and Otto Gruppe's *Griechische Mythologie und Religionsgeschichte* a special mention of these works as having been of incalculable help to me will not seem invidious. I regret to say that, owing to the baffling delays of war-time, the first volume of A. B. Cook's *Zeus* did not come into my hands sufficiently early for me to profit by it to an extent of which it is truly worthy.

In conclusion, I desire to record my deep sense of gratitude to all those with whom I have been associated in this undertaking; to my colleagues Professors Edward Capps and A. C. Johnson for timely suggestions regarding the problems of organization; to another colleague, Professor G. W. Elderkin, for his expert advice relative to the vase-paintings; to the publishers for their quick sympathy with my aims, and their generosity in making it possible to provide the myths with adequate and artistic illustrations; and, principally, to the editor-in-chief of this series of volumes, Dr. Louis H. Gray, whose wide learning, clear judgement, and candid criticism have enriched this book, and whose unfailing courtesy has graced our mutual relations with a happy and inspiring informality.

W. SHERWOOD FOX.

PRINCETON UNIVERSITY,
April 21, 1916.

CONTENTS

ILLUSTRATIONS

FULL PAGE ILLUSTRATIONS

ILLUSTRATIONS IN THE TEXT

INTRODUCTION TO THE GREEK MYTHS

TO proceed immediately to the narration and discussion of the myths of Greece would be much like an attempt to construct a high road without a survey. We must first of all make certain that we know what a myth is, and such an endeavour to give sharp definition to our theme will naturally lead to an investigation of the special conditions which, like soil and weather to a plant, favour the germination and growth of myth. Then, granting that myth has some connexion with religion, we must inform ourselves as to the peculiar nature of the religion and the gods of Greece. By such a course we may perhaps be so fortunate as to reach a point of vantage from which we can gain a clear and comprehensive view of the unique character of the Greek myths. Once this has been gained, a series of pertinent questions will present themselves, and these we shall enumerate and discuss in their proper place and order.

1. What is Myth?—We wish it were possible to define myth satisfactorily by an epigram; to say with Marett, for instance, that it is "Animatism grown picturesque." But, unhappily, epigram is a definition only for those who know, and this circumstance limits us to the use of cold analysis.

For the purpose of ascertaining the elements of myth let us regard it from the points of view of (a) form, (b) time, (c) subject-matter, and (d) relation to fact.

(a) It is commonly stated that a myth, in order to be a myth, must be cast in narrative form. A little reflection, however, will show that to make this a hard and fast rule is tantamount to rejecting not only the epithets applied to the gods by their worshippers, but also the attributes accorded them by poet, priest, and artist. This we cannot consistently do (and, moreover, no writer on mythology ever does it, in spite of his insistence on literal narrative form); for an epithet, as a statement compressed into one word, and an attribute, as a symbol of a statement, are, after all, substantially narratives. The difference under debate is really one of length, and not one of essential quality. Where can we draw the line? The thunder-weapon put into the hands of Zeus by an artist is in kind, then, as much a myth as the whole elaborate tale of Prometheus.

(b) The statements of myth have a direct reference to the past or to the universal present; only so far as the universal present implies the probable continuity of a condition have they any reference to the future. That Hephaistos limped and that Hermes flew were, to the Greek, facts true for all time. Why the simple present was excluded from the temporal reference of the myths will be clear after we have examined the nature of their subject-matter.

(c) No reader of myth can have failed to notice that its themes are invariably drawn from the realm of the unverifiable, or at least from that which was incapable of demonstration at the time of the creation of the myth. The war of Troy was fought at so remote a period that none could debate or deny the allegations of myth that a quarrel over a woman was the cause of it; and the impossibility of refutation in this and other like instances was eagerly accepted as a proof of fact. Moreover, why spoil a good story by being too inquisitive and by applying to it the tests of workaday life? Typhon rebelled against Zeus, and Zeus punished him by heaping upon him the great mass of Aetna. Since nobody could explain the origin of the volcano from the known experience of mankind, why was it absurd to attribute it to the acts of beings greater than man? Apollo was invisible to the eye of flesh, according to the myths, yet he could both cause and heal the bodily ills of men and could inspire his priestesses to utter prophecies which the ears of men could hear. The sickness and the healing and

PLATE II

1

Zeus and Typhon

Zeus is approaching swiftly from the left and with raised right hand is about to hurl a thunderbolt at a monster with a bearded human head and a winged trunk terminating in two long serpent-like coils. The creature, probably Typhon, looks at the King of the Gods in great alarm and madly lashes about with his scaly body in a vain endeavour to escape from the doom awaiting him. From a Chalkidian *hydria* of about 650 B.C., in Munich (Furtwängler-Reichhold, *Griechische Vasenmalerei*, No. 32). See pp. xii, 8–9.

2

Medousa Beheaded

The unique feature of this vase-painting is that it represents the three Gorgons after the flight of Perseus with Medousa's head. The two immortal sisters are apparently just setting out in pursuit of the slayer, as their spread wings, bent knees, and swinging hands vividly indicate. The body of Medousa is about to fall inertly to the ground. From a black-figured *skyphos* of the late sixth century B.C., in Athens (*Catalogue des vases peints du musée national d'Athènes*, *Supplément par Georges Nicole*, Plate XI). See p. 34.

I

2

the prophesying were facts, and none could prove that any other than Apollo was responsible for them. To believe that he actually was responsible fed the fancy, and without fancy there was no zest in life. The souls of the departed were said to be gathered together in a dark realm beneath the earth. For to what other place could they have disappeared after burial or cremation? No god or hero was represented by a myth-maker as initiating any movement simultaneous with the narration of the myth. The reason for this is now obvious; such a statement would be so open to the scrutiny of contemporaries that criticism and the fear of criticism would destroy the illusion and the charm which the story might otherwise possess.

(d) The most generally recognized characteristic of myth is the fact that it is a product of the imagination, and so, popularly though erroneously, the mythical is regarded as the exact equivalent of the imaginary. Nevertheless, since the special function of the imagination is to create, it is not to be expected that all its creations must conform to the attested experience of mankind or to what we may estimate as probable. It is for this reason that most of the details of the myths relate to the improbable, but the probable and improbable alike were held to be true by the people among whom the legends had currency.

We may now sum up the results of our analysis with a working definition:

A myth is a statement, or a virtual statement as implied in a symbol, an attribute, or an epithet, accepted as true by its original maker and his hearers, and referring to the eternal nature and past acts of beings greater than man, and frequently to circumstances which are to us improbable or impossible.

2. *The Origin of Myth.* — It is no more possible to detail one and all the impulses, singly or in classes, which have given rise to myth than it is to discover and give the full tale of all the fountain-heads of a great river. Yet we find that we can

account for the origin of a river in a way which serves all practical purposes. Is it not within our power to explain the beginnings of myth to the same extent, even though the admission must be made that the task is infinitely more difficult, involving, as it does, all the subtleties of human nature and an almost inextricable tangle of theories?

The statement that the mainspring of all myth is personification and metaphor has too much of the weakness of epigram; it explains only after one has learned why personification and myth have any power at all. To say that every myth is an answer to a question of primitive man regarding some phenomenon of the universe gives a more satisfactory reason in that it implies a certain intellectual attitude in man. But even this does not go to the bottom of the matter, for it fails to show why the answers are cast as they are. It remained for the modern evolutionary biologist to supply a broad and fundamental explanation. Just as each human being between conception and maturity passes successively through all the stages of the biological development of the race, so all human minds at the same stage of racial progress act in virtually the same way, the slight variations which occur being due in large part to differences in external environment. It must be frankly confessed that this statement, like that of the theory of universal evolution, is not susceptible of proof in every instance; nevertheless, it stands as the best working hypothesis which the modern student of the folk-ways has been able to secure. No one ventures to assert that it is final.

How, then, does primitive man tend to think of the world? Investigators tell us that he cannot distinguish between life and no life. Knowing his own power to bring things to pass by means of calculation and will, he attributes these same faculties in varying degrees to everything in nature outside of himself. In other words, he endows everything with personality. To him the beast is the peer of man in astuteness and purposefulness, and tree, mountain, and sea are sentient beings.

Here metaphor plays its part. For example, the simple poetic statement, "The sun drives his car across the heavens," can under stress of emotion be stripped of its similitude and be cast in the categorical form, "The sun is a driver and he rides in a car across the heavens"; and belief in it as a truth can be engendered and fostered by allusions to that effect in art and ritual. From this illustration it may be gathered that the primitive mind demands objectivity in the expression of its thought. This is indeed true, and will explain the lack of abstractions in myth except when they are presented as concrete personalities.

Another characteristic of man in this immature stage is that he is unable to see the inherent connexion of things. He is, therefore, likely to be unduly sensitive to the startling phenomena of nature and to the unusual incidents of his social life; while his fancy, exaggerating these beyond all warrant, contrives impossible explanations of their origin along the same lines as his theories of the beginnings of the commonplaces of his existence. Here lies the reason for the mythic prominence of the lightning, the earthquake, beasts of prey, monsters of the sea, wars, tyrants, the rise and fall of dynasties, and the like.

In some quarters the belief now prevails that most myths have arisen from the misunderstanding of rituals, of worship and magic alike, whose first meanings have been forgotten; and it is asserted that a sincere attempt to clothe them with a definite import for the worshipper has been the immediate cause of myth. This is undoubtedly true in many instances. The stories of the Kouretes' defence of the infant Zeus and of Skiron's murder of travellers seem to belong to this class of legends. Akin to them are those which have obviously grown out of the misinterpretation of the cult-titles of divinities.

To avoid confusion we have thus far assumed that all myths are the spontaneous issue of the primitive mind. Unfortunately this is a theory which we cannot verify, although we are probably safe in saying that at least the germ of every true myth is of this order. On the other hand, we are unable thus to account for all the details with which the germs have gradually become encrusted. It is impossible to disbelieve that many a myth has been deliberately reshaped at some time or other to satisfy an exacting aesthetic or moral sense, or to secure the semblance of a religious sanction for a definite cause or for a course of action. It has been suggested that, for instance, the story of the dreadful end of the inquisitive sisters of Pandrosos was a priestly fabrication to frighten worshippers into submission to a rule of ritual; and one can scarcely doubt that the cycle of the Theseus myths contains many conscious additions, if not inventions. In this class we do not include the manipulations of myths in the hands of the poets, for in the popular view the work of these divinely inspired men enhanced rather than invalidated the truth of the stories.

If one would gain an insight into the sudden birth of myth from a mere nothing at times of high spiritual tension in a community, let him turn to the pages of *Thaïs* where Anatole France describes the weaving of the tissue of tales about the person of Paphnuce after he has become a holy man and taken his place upon the pillar, or to the lines in Noyes's epic, *Drake*, in which the great admiral, on learning of the sailing of the Armada, unconcernedly picks up a piece of wood and whittles away at it with his knife:

> "So great and calm a master of the world
> Seemed Drake that as he whittled and the chips
> Fluttered into the blackness o'er the quay,
> Men said that in this hour of England's need
> Each tiny flake turned to a battle-ship."

3. Sanction and Persistence of Myth. — Were we able to explain just why a fashion, a catchword, or a phrase of slang becomes popular, we should likewise be able to account for the initial acceptance of a myth. All that we can say concerning such things is that they supply a need, or answer a craving, or

PLATE III

Dionysos and a Maenad

Dionysos is shown reclining on a very elaborate couch. In his right hand he holds a *kantharos* in a very fastidious manner, and in his left, a *thyrsos*. The long flowing ringlets of his hair, the curves of his arms and body, and the soft texture of his drapery combine to give the god a decidedly effeminate appearance. A Maenad is extending a tray of viands toward him from the right, and an Eros flies down from the left to crown him with a wreath of leaves. At the extreme left a *tympanon* and a *thyrsos*, in the hands of a second Maenad, are barely visible. From a red-figured *krater* of the late fifth century B.C., in Athens (*Catalogue des vases peints du musée national d'Athènes, Supplément par Georges Nicole*, Plate XX). See pp. 215 ff.

PLATE III

Dionysos and a Maenad

Dionysos is shown reclining on a very elaborate couch. In his right hand he holds a *kantharos* in a very fastidious manner, and in his left, a *thyrsos*. The long flowing ringlets of his hair, the curves of his arms and body, and the soft texture of his drapery combine to give the god a decidedly effeminate appearance. A Maenad is extending a tray of viands toward him from the right, and an Eros flies down from the left to crown him with a wreath of leaves. At the extreme left a *tympanon* and a *thyrsos*, in the hands of a second Maenad, are barely visible. From a red-figured *krater* of the late fifth century B.C., in Athens (*Catalogue des vases peints du musée national d'Athènes, Supplément par Georges Nicole*, Plate XX). See pp. 215 ff.

arouse the interest of the majority of a social group. But this really explains nothing. An established myth has all of these qualifications — and something more. That something is its religious appeal, and its strength lies in the fact that any religion embraces for the people who profess it the sum total of their highest interests. It is not hard, then, to conceive that certain circumstances should arise in which a story of powerful eternal beings suddenly engages the attention of a community and is received as though it were a confirmed truth. Once the acceptance of it has been granted, the path to the explanation of its persistence is clear and open.

In the first place, the mere fact that it has been accepted becomes to the social mind a reason why it should continue to be accepted. "Everybody believes it" is as valid a reason for the conformist in religion as "Everybody wears it" is for the devotee of a fashion. The social psychologist says the same thing in other words: the *mores* have the authority of facts.[1] In the next place, sheer habit and the difficulty of inventing new myths will often cause the retention of a legend long after it has lost its touch with the community's mode of life and thought — a phenomenon which is by no means confined to the ignorant stratum of a population. Again, conscious respect for the convictions and opinions of former generations plays an important part. In its ideal form this deference becomes a belief in a Golden Age in the past, a period not merely of ease and bliss, but one in which the wonders of legend were normal occurrences. Then man was close to the hearts and minds of the divinities and had thereby a special knowledge of their will and power. To deny the traditions which these enlightened souls have handed down is to brand them as liars. The spirit of the trite excuse of the orthodox, "My grandfather's religion was good enough for him, and is therefore good enough for me," has served as a valid reason for the perseverance of many ever since traditional faiths began to be. Finally, the *ipse dixit* of a priest, the pronouncement of an oracle, the words of a hymn or even of a secular poem, the allusion of a ceremonial formula, or the suggestion of a sacred symbol may give such an apparent confirmation of a myth in part or whole as to strengthen faith in its essential verity.

4. The Nature of the Greek Religion. — The Greek religion, so far as we can truthfully predicate anything at all of religious origins, had its roots in the pre-animistic stratum of thought. The primitive Greek, like the early Roman, as we shall see, worshipped natural objects and phenomena for their own sake, although his attitude toward them shifted according as they furthered or hindered his welfare. Proceeding a little further, he seems to have become convinced of the existence within them, yet inseparable from them, of a sort of potency or life-power (*anima*). He was now in the animistic stage. Finally, he observed that while in the main their powers manifested themselves in a uniform manner, yet they showed a remarkable tendency to vary, the only satisfactory explanation being that they must be due to agents as free in initiative as are human beings. Accepting this theory, he endowed the powers in his habits of thought with will, and, little by little, with the other attributes of personality. They had at last become gods.[2] The assignment of names to them and the localization of their cults strengthened the popular conviction in their personal nature. The history of one god in epitome may serve as an illustration. Zeus was first the sky; next the power within the sky; and, lastly, the divine person with whom the sky-power was identified.[3] We can now perceive the otherwise obscure truth of the statement that "The god himself [i. e. any Greek god], when conceived, was not the reality but only a symbol to help toward conceiving the reality." [4]

It is not to be inferred, however, that the several steps from potency to deity were as clearly marked as the necessity of gaining a compact view has forced us to represent them; nor must we think that when a god rose from one stage to the next he left behind him all traces of his lower estate. As a matter of fact, to practically every god at the very highest point of his spiritual career clung some disfiguring stains of the earth of the pit out of which he had been digged. This was due to the intense spirit of freedom of each community, its desire to worship the god as it saw fit and according to its own local needs. If the community was marked by a high degree of civilization, its gods were of the nobler type; if on a low stage of development, its gods were of a coarser grade; and further, if the community was open to influence from the outside, the traits of its gods were of a mixed character. This, together with a certain though sluggish tendency toward a change of the conceptions of the god within the independent community, will account in large part for the bewildering multiplicity of the Greek divinities and their attributes. The greatest difficulty that confronts the modern student is to determine which forms and which attributes of the developed god were the original ones; and it is almost humiliating to have to confess that the instances in which we can be even reasonably certain are very few.

The intimate relation of the gods to the life-interests of men gave the Greek religion its distinctive stamp; it brought the gods down to earth in the likeness and with the passions of men, so that in time of need the worshipper had but to reach out his hand to touch his divine helper. This constant sense of nearness lifted from his heart the leaden awe imposed by the worship of distant deities and filled it with a wholesome joy of life and a buoyant spirit of confidence. Yet the Greek cults were not individualistic nor marked by missionary zeal; the selfish interests of the clan, the tribe, and the state were altogether too imperious.

5. *The Unique Character of Greek Myth.* — It is probable that to the majority of readers the most striking feature of the Greek myths is the variety observable in all phases of their composition. The number of their themes falls little short of the sum total of the activities of Greek life, private and social,

intellectual and physical, religious and secular. The details with which they are embellished seem to represent all possible combinations of the circumstances of actual experience with the inventions of fancy. The technique of their presentation, like that of the greatest artists, is most sensitively adapted to the shifting subject-matter. In brief, they have in these respects the marks of the highest art, and this is the burden of Gruppe's pregnant statement, "Greek deity . . . is what nature lacks to become art," [5] interpreted in the light of the essential connexion between true myth and religion.

Another strong feature of the Greek myths is their sincerity. They have the ring of genuine chronicles of fact, and we feel no astonishment that for ages they should have been considered to be veritable history, although it is surprising that, charged as they were with such an authority, they never became dogmatic statements of inalterable truth. Belief in them did not constitute a measure of orthodoxy, and they could thus be freely employed for a variety of purposes — as vehicles of religious and moral instruction, as history, as themes for philosophical argument, as literature, or as a means of entertainment. The fact that they could be used to serve the purpose last mentioned without causing religious offence is remarkable testimony to the good comradeship existing between the Greek believer and his god.

6. Kinds of Myth. — The classification of myths must of necessity be arbitrary and must vary with the mood and object of the investigator. If, for instance, he seeks to discriminate between those which are the products of a sane and sober imagination and those whose elements are in the main absurd, grotesque, and monstrous, he would classify them as rational and irrational. If he were endeavouring to single out those which seem to have been invented as explanations, he would divide them into the two categories of aetiological and non-aetiological. The possibilities of classification are unlimited, and in every case the captions would consist of a positive and a

PLATE IV

1. Plouton

Plouton (Hades), with a lofty *kalathos* on his head, is seated on a throne, grasping a sceptre in his left hand and letting his right rest on one of the heads of Kerberos. On either side of him are Kastor and Polydeukes, each standing beside his horse. From a convex sardonyx (A. Furtwängler, *Antike Gemmen*, I, Plate XLIV, Fig. 4). See pp. 142–43, 233 ff.

2. Apollo and Marsyas

Apollo with a *plectron* in one hand and a lyre in the other is standing at his ease to the right. Seated beside him on the skin of a lion or a panther, and bound with his back to a bare tree, is Marsyas, bearing all the marks of his semi-bestial nature. A flute-case hangs from a branch on the tree. Kneeling at the feet of Apollo the boy Olympos (who does not figure in the myth as narrated in the text) seems to be pleading with the god to spare the Satyr's life. From a cut carnelian in Naples (A. Furtwängler, *Antike Gemmen*, I, Plate XLII, Fig. 28). See p. 181.

3. Head of Alexander

A diadem, knotted behind the head, can be seen binding the thick wavy hair. Just over the ear is the horn of Ammon. From a coin of Lysimachos, 355–280 B.C. (P. Gardiner, *The Types of Greek Coins*, Plate XII, No. 16). See pp. 223–24.

4. Persephone

The head of the goddess seems to be bound by a thin band of wheat-straw. The dolphins indicate not only that Syracuse is situated on the sea, but also that she is the mistress of it. From a coin of Syracuse, 385–280 B.C. (P. Gardiner, *The Types of Greek Coins*, Plate XI, No. 29). See pp. 327 ff.

5. Zeus and Dione

Zeus is here depicted with the earth goddess Dione, his wife at Dodona in Epeiros, the site of his oracular oak. From a coin of Epeiros, 280–146 B.C. (P. Gardiner, *The Types of Greek Coins*, Plate XII, No. 44). See p. 156.

6. Pan

Pan, in the guise of a young hunter, is seated on a rocky ledge of a mountain holding a *lagobolon* (hunting-club) in his right hand. At his feet lies his *syrinx*, the so-called pipes of Pan. From an Arkadian coin, 431–371 B.C. (P. Gardiner, *The Types of Greek Coins*, Plate VIII, No. 32). See pp. 167–68.

PLATE IV

1. Plouton

Plouton (Hades), with a lofty *kalathos* on his head, is seated on a throne, grasping a sceptre in his left hand, and letting his right rest on one of the heads of Kerberos. On either side of him are Kastor and Polydeukes, each standing beside his horse. From a convex sardonyx (A. Furtwängler, *Antike Gemmen*, i, Plate XLIV, Fig. 4). See pp. 142–43, 233 ff.

2. Apollo and Marsyas

Apollo with a *plektron* in one hand and a lyre in the other is standing at his ease to the right. Seated beside him on the skin of a lion or a panther, and bound with his back to a bare tree, is Marsyas, bearing all the marks of his semi-bestial nature. A flute-case hangs from a branch on the tree. Kneeling at the feet of Apollo the boy Olympos (who does not figure in the myth as narrated in the text) seems to be pleading with the god to spare the Satyr's life. From a cut carnelian in Naples (A. Furtwängler, *Antike Gemmen*, i, Plate XLII, Fig. 28). See p. 181.

3. Head of Alexander

A diadem, knotted behind the head, can be seen binding the thick wavy hair. Just over the ear is the horn of Ammon. From a coin of Lysimachos, 335–280 B.C. (P. Gardiner, *The Types of Greek Coins*, Plate XII, No. 16). See pp. 223–24.

4. Persephone

The head of the goddess seems to be bound by a thin band of wheat-straw. The dolphins indicate not only that Syracuse is situated on the sea, but also that she is the mistress of it. From a coin of Syracuse, 385–280 B.C. (P. Gardiner, *The Types of Greek Coins*, Plate XI, No. 29). See pp. 227 ff.

5. Zeus and Dione

Zeus is here depicted with the earth goddess Dione, his wife at Dodona in Epeiros, the site of his oracular oak. From a coin of Epeiros, 280–146 B.C. (P. Gardiner, *The Types of Greek Coins*, Plate XII, No. 44). See p. 156.

6. Pan

Pan, in the guise of a young hunter, is seated on a rocky ledge of a mountain holding a *lagobolon* (hunting-club) in his right hand. At his feet lies his *syrinx*, the so-called pipes of Pan. From an Arkadian coin, 431–371 B.C. (P. Gardiner, *The Types of Greek Coins*, Plate VIII, No. 32). See pp. 267–68.

1

2

3

4

5

6

negative term. The appended list is given merely by way of suggestion.

A. According to external elements.
  (1) Myths of the various periods of tribal or national development.
  (2) Myths of racial stocks.
  (3) Local myths (i. e. of shrines, towns, cities, states, districts, islands, etc.).
  (4) Popular and official myths.
  (5) Poetical and prose myths.

B. According to contents.
  (1) Myths of the gods.
  (2) Nature-myths.
  (3) Myths of origins (i. e. of the world, gods, men, arts, stars, political and social organizations, etc.).
  (4) Philosophical myths.
  (5) Allegorical myths.
  (6) Myths of the hereafter.

7. *What we may Learn from Myths.* — Naturally, most of the facts registered by a body of myths concern religion. Yet one must not expect to find in them more than a partial account of the particular religion to which they belong. Being concrete and pictorial in character, myths can set forth only those features which are susceptible of concrete and pictorial treatment. Sacred symbols and clear-cut attributes of the gods they can portray almost photographically; the figures of the gods they can sketch with fairly bold outlines; the histories of the gods and some of their subtle attributes they can suggest. On the other hand, they can tell us practically nothing about specific rituals and the exact attitude of the worshipper at the moment of worship; were they to become formal registers of such things, they would cease to be myths. One must, therefore, complement his knowledge of religion, as gleaned from myths, with the available records of cult.

If it is true, and we believe it is, that "religious expression moves along with the general progress of thought,"[6] then the myths ought to yield us certain facts of primitive life outside the domain of religion proper. For example, the Greek myths confirm our suspicions that the early Hellenes were addicted to magic. Again and again we are told of curses being invoked and of their terrible effects upon their victims; we need point merely to the curse of Alkmaion and the curse of Laios. The union of Demeter and Iasion in the thrice-ploughed field refers to a magic device to bring fertility to the soil, and the wild and noisy dance of the Kouretes undoubtedly represents a method of averting evil spirits by magic. Myths tell us, too, though by accident, the things of deepest interest to the people among whom the legends circulated. The frequent mention of flocks and herds, tillage, forest, and grazing land would be pointless to a nation of miners or manufacturers. The social organization of the Olympians would have no appeal were it not a replica of the society of men. The allusion to the bronze armour of Diomedes would not be understood if bronze were an unknown metal. From the stories of the winds one can gather in part the meteorological conditions of ancient Greece. By making deductions of this kind many facts of history may be recovered; they are detached, to be sure, but nevertheless of considerable value. Incidentally, some of them are useful in the determination of dates. Just as we can calculate the period before which Milton cannot have written *Paradise Lost* because of his attribution of the invention of cannon to Satan, so we can be reasonably sure that those myths which speak of an intimacy between Athens and Troizen cannot have been given the form in which we now know them prior to a certain historical alliance between Athens and a group of Argolid cities which included Troizen.

Here, as everywhere, the argument from silence is to be used with the utmost discretion. Greek myth is lacking in allusion to sidereal cults, and from this fact the inference is drawn that the Greeks were originally a northern people — a theory which is probably safe, since it conforms to the results of investigations among other peoples. In all such instances, however, one must demand an abundance of verified parallels before accepting conclusions.

8. Myth and Ethics. — Ever since the Greek myths began to be studied critically the conduct of their personages has been a serious ethical problem. Practically every evil deed forbidden by society and religion was committed by the gods and heroes, and generally with startling impunity. The common opinion of today that the myths are unsafe reading for the young was shared by Plato,[7] who, for this very reason, proposed to debar Homer as a text-book from his ideal state. In the *Hippolytos* of Euripides [8] the amours of Zeus and Semele and of Kephalos and Eos give the nurse a precedent for the illicit satisfaction of love which she suggests to Phaidra; thus the poet practically asserts that the acts of the gods, as narrated in myth, had a direct influence on the behaviour of the common people. In many passages in his treatise on ethics Aristotle castigates the moral standards of the legends in reference to certain acts. Certainly, a bad case is made out against the myths, and the question is, can any defence or mitigating explanation be offered in their behalf?

It might be well to learn, if we can, just why the myths contain such immoral elements. In the first place, one must remember that they are survivals of an earlier age when men were governed by inferior ethical ideals to which the gods and heroes were bound to conform, since the myth-maker knew no higher. Even had he fashioned higher motives for them out of his own mind, every act of god and hero would have been beyond the ordinary understanding, and the myth, no matter how beautiful to our thinking, would, like an undiscovered flower, have wasted its fragrance on the desert air. To the contemporaries of the myth-maker the behaviour of the divinities, however wrong it may appear now, was right, and an appreciation of this will render the immorality of the myths innocuous to the modern reader. Another fact — doubtless startling to many — must be emphasized here: that is, there is no obligatory connexion between every religion and morality. Christianity is almost unique in that it insists upon the inseparable union of the two, but we must not read this requirement into other faiths as a matter of fact. If, then, to the Greek religion was one function of man and morality another, there was no necessary conflict between the myth as a vehicle of religious thought and the ethical character of its details. Any positive moral elements discoverable in myth were largely accidental. They came in despite a certain contempt, common to most religions, for mere ethics. Moreover, the bard's task was not to preach; it was to present divine truths in an attractive and cogent form. Again, many primitive peoples allow for two ethical standards, one for themselves and the other for outsiders. It may be that the Greek tolerated the iniquity of his gods because, though like men, they were essentially a different folk. Lastly, we must be on our guard against counting as immoral or obscene what was in origin not of this character. For instance, it seems probable that the frequent attribution of the creation of certain things in the world to the sexual relations of divinities is due primarily to the inability of the Hellene to explain absolute beginnings in any other way.

But why did the later and more morally sensitive generations of Greeks not purge the myths of this evil? One reason is that it was conventional to accept the myths intact, and conventionality, like charity, covereth a multitude of sins. Instinctively we tolerate today the reading of certain passages of the Bible before mixed congregations because the Bible, like some secular thing, has come under the authority of conventionality. Doubtless the attitude of many high-minded Greeks was much the same toward the recital of their myths. Another reason lies in the nature of the Greek religion. It was not a revivalistic religion in any sense of the term, and especially

PLATE V

Zephyros

Zephyros, suggestively characterized as a winged youth of mild and kindly countenance and of soft bodily contours, is leisurely flying from the west bearing a generous burden of flowers in a fold of his garment. From a relief on the Tower of Andronikos (so-called Tower of the Winds) in Athens (Brunn-Bruckmann, *Denkmäler griechischer und römischer Sculptur*, No. 30). See p. 266.

not in the connotation which implies a conscious cutting away from the past. Changes there were in the myths, of course, but through acquisition and not through any spiritual refining. The new wine was put into the old bottles, and in the end the bottles burst and perished.

The evil of myths, like that of men, lives after them, but is that a warrant for interring the good that may be in them? Though their positive moral elements are, along with their general fabric, incidental survivals, they require due recognition. We must not forget the staunch moral character of Apollo, of the nobler Zeus, and of the Erinyes. In the punishment of certain sins they were relentless. Over against the frequent flouting of the law of conjugal fidelity by the gods and heroes we must hold the beautiful pictures of the faithful Penelope and of Prokris and Kephalos. There is a tone of censure running through the myths that tell of the adultery of Klytaimestra and Aigisthos. Diomedes' rejection of his wife on the discovery of her infidelity can mean nothing else than that the people among whom the myth was almost gospel truth insisted at least on a code of morals for wives. Alkinoös showed his respect for the social sanctity of marriage vows when he refused to part Iason and Medeia if they were already man and wife. Moreover, mere chastity had a value set upon it. Kallisto and Auge were certainly not held up in myths as models of what maidens should be, and Hippolytos, Bellerophon, and Peleus, though to some extent regarded as prigs, stood, nevertheless, as worthy examples of self-restraint. The enormity of taking human life, especially that of kindred and of friends, is emphasized in many myths. Orestes' fulfilment of a religious obligation by slaying his mother did not absolve him from the stain of shedding family blood. Herakles had to pay dearly for the murder of his children, and, later, for that of his trusting friend, Iphitos. Assaults upon the honour of women were recognized as distinctly immoral. For his attack upon Alkippe, Halirrhothios, though the son of a god, was haled before Areopagos. The story of Athene's wrath against the lesser Aias attests the inviolability of suppliants as an article in the primitive moral code. Lastly, but by no means the least important, is the fact that several cycles of myth recognize a moral taint that clings to certain families from generation to generation. The statement that curses rested on the houses of Tantalos and Laios was the mythic manner of recording the definite moral bent of these families and the inevitable consequences of their sins. To explain the phenomenon with our modern biologists as one of heredity, does not strip it of its moral significance.

9. *Myth and Art.* — Throughout the ages there has been a close affinity between religion and art — art in the broadest sense. The poet, the sculptor, and the painter have always been among the chief interpreters of the religion of their day and generation. Who can prove that they have not been more convincing and commanding than the priest? Certainly the products of their efforts have been more enduring, for when the faiths of which they were the exponents have long since ceased to stir the hearts of men they have still about them certain elements whose appeal is everlasting. Olympianism is dead, but the *Iliad* and *Odyssey* of Homer still live on. What is this vital spirit? It is seen in the difference between ritual and art. Ritual is religion in action, and as such it need not be reflective; indeed, it generally is not. Art, on the other hand, is the sincere endeavour of a human soul, momentarily detached from the activities of life and ritual and under the domination of a clarifying emotion, to find for itself and to reveal to others a vision of the highest social ideals of the time. Ritual appeals to the initiate, to the sect; art with its beauty and subtlety of suggestion appeals to a universal instinct. The measure of a work of art is the strength of its claim on all mankind. By this standard we can compare the worth of Hesiod and Homer, of an archaic Apollo and the Apollo Belvedere. Respective degrees of workmanship and finish are of value only so far

as they conform, or fail to conform, to the exactions of the ideal toward which the artist strives.

We have dwelt thus long on the nature and function of art in order the more clearly to reveal the relation of Greek myth to Greek religion. The religious material of most of the myths which have come down to us was simply crass superstition, but, taken over by devout and inspired bards, it was passed at the white heat of emotion through the refining pot of their spirits and came out transformed as poetry. Later Homer appeared.[9] With his superior gifts he fused this poetry and a number of crude superstitions into the noble epics that are attributed to his name. This gave the needed impulse to a long succession of lesser poets. The gods and heroes of Homer were common property and had a remoteness from the life-interests of the bards' own local communities which gave them, as it were, a licence for moulding them as they could not mould their local gods and heroes. The painter and the sculptor followed in their steps. Imitating, as they did, idealizing and relatively refined models, they could not themselves but represent the ideal and the refined. This is the reason why the gross elements of the myths and popular superstitions rarely thrust themselves into the higher sculpture, and with but little more frequency into vase-painting, the least noble of the Greek arts.

10. Methods of Interpreting Myth. — A citation of the most important methods of interpreting myths, with brief comment, is sufficient for the purposes of this volume.

1. The natural method. Followers of this system would trace practically every legend back to a primitive account of some natural phenomenon or group of phenomena. According to them myths are solar, lunar, or astral; or are to be referred to light, the winds, clouds, rain, vegetation, and so forth.

2. The philological method. The leading exponent of this school of interpretation was F. Max Müller. Its practice is to account for myths as the *sequelae* of "disease of language";

in other words, as confusions resulting from a misunderstanding of terms that have persisted in speech after their original meaning has been lost. The weakness of this method, now abandoned in its extreme form, is that it does not square with our present knowledge of the primitive mind; further, the etymologies on which it bases its conclusions are generally uncertain and often false.

3. The rationalizing (euhemeristic) method. The first to apply this method systematically was Euhemeros, a Greek of the third century B.C. The deification of the victorious Alexander forced many to the conclusion that the great gods of tradition were human beings who had been exalted to the sky for their benefactions to humanity. Euhemeros took over the idea and used it in his historical romance of Alexander. This school, therefore, regards myths as nothing more than perverted history.

4. The allegorical method. With the inability to accept the old legends attempts were made even long before our era to read higher meanings into them, and from them was evolved a science of allegory. Needless to say, the good doctrinal matter thus elicited from the myths was only in the rarest instances intended by their authors. Moreover, this method is too mechanical and leaves no room for the play of fancy.

5. The poetical method. A few scholars follow Ovid in candidly proclaiming their belief that myths are purely the figments of poetical imagination.

> "I prate of ancient poets' monstrous lies
> Ne'er seen or now or then by human eyes,"

sings Ovid. [10] His only faith in the legends was that which he had in any other work of art.

6. The ritual method. Many myths (but assuredly not all) can be classified as explanations of rituals whose original significance has been lost in the past. To this class belong the majority of the aetiological tales.

7. The anthropological or comparative method. This method is based on the hypothesis that peoples at the same levels of primitive development invent the same kind of stories. It leads the investigator, "when an apparently irrational and anomalous custom is found in any country to look for a country where a similar practice is found, and where the practice is no longer irrational and anomalous, but in harmony with the manners and ideas of the people among whom it prevails." [11] The results of this theory are often invalidated by the tacit assumption that its basic hypothesis is a fact. To be of service the method must be historical.

11. The Object and the Method of the Present Treatise.—The author's purpose in writing this volume is to present the myths of Greece and Rome as vehicles of religious thought. He forbears to call them records (though after a manner they are such), lest any reader be misled into believing that they bear the stamp of the deliberation and the finality which are generally ascribed to records. That they enable us to view only a part of the faiths of the Greeks and Romans, as from a single angle, is not merely admitted but insisted upon as fundamental to their interpretation. Inasmuch as art is psychologically posterior to religion, just as, economically, luxury is to wealth, the artistic worth and influence of the myths are here to be regarded as of secondary interest.

The system of interpretation to be followed is at base the comparative method. The entire stress, however, will not be laid upon the similarities of parallel instances; much emphasis will be placed upon differences. Moreover, the method will not be applied except to verify traces in the myths of their origin and meaning, or when all efforts to discover such signs have failed. In handling the legends singly the following features will be noted: the peculiar cast of the conception, the names and epithets of the gods and heroes and the several forms of their symbols, the variant versions of the myth, and the traditional interpretation of antiquity; but the utmost caution will be taken to avoid basing a conclusion on any one of these features in isolation from the others. Finally, it will constantly be borne in mind that a myth is, after all, a process and not a finished product.

12. The Sources of Myth. — It is to be regretted that there is no single work containing without comment a detailed compilation of the literary sources from which we draw our knowledge of Greek and Roman myths. The value of such a work to a student of religion and of literature and the advantage of being able to refer to it on the present occasion are obvious. So widely scattered, both among authors and in individual works, are the allusions to myths that we can here do no more than name the few outstanding classic writers to whom we are most indebted and the general departments of literature from which myths are most likely to be recovered.

SOURCES FOR THE GREEK MYTHS

Poetry: Homer, and the so-called *Homeric Hymns* to the gods; the fragments and summaries of the heroic epics — the *Kypria*, the *Aithiopis*, the *Little Iliad*, the *Nostoi*, the *Telegonia;* Hesiod; the lyric poets, especially Pindar; the extant plays and fragments of the great dramatists of Athens; the bucolic poets Theokritos, Bion, and Moschos; the fragments of the *Aitia* ("Causes") of Kallimachos; Apollonios of Rhodes; Quintos of Smyrna; Nonnos and Mousaios.

Much information concerning Greek myths is given us by certain Roman poets, notably the elegists Catullus, Propertius, and Tibullus; Vergil; Ovid; Horace; Valerius Flaccus; Seneca; Statius; Ausonius; and Claudian.

Prose: Herodotos; fragments of the logographers and historians; Plato; Apollodoros and the other mythographers; Pausanias; Lucian; the Christian apologists; the scholia (interpretative marginal notes) of Homer and the dramatists; the lexicographers. The Latin works attributed, probably wrongly,

PLATE VI

Silenoi and Maenads

Two nude and bearded Silenoi with horses' tails are each carrying a Maenad on their shoulders. One Maenad holds in her lap the fawn which is to be torn asunder in the ritual, while the other is beating a pair of rattles. The heads of both women are bound with garlands of ivy-leaves, which, together with the long sinuous stem dividing the two groups of figures, are among the emblems of Dionysos. From a black-figured *amphora* of about 475 B.C., found at Gela (*Monumenti Antichi*, xvii, Plate XXXVII). See pp. 267–70.

to Hyginus, may be included here, as well as the mythological treatises of Fulgentius and of the Vatican Mythographer.

SOURCES FOR THE ROMAN MYTHS

The existing sources of the Roman myths are of the same meagre proportions as the bulk of the legends themselves. The most important are Vergil; Livy; Dionysios of Halikarnassos in his *History of Early Rome;* Ovid; Varro; the antiquarian Verrius Flaccus; and Saint Augustine.

In the field of art outside of literature we can sometimes find new versions of mythic tales and can very often see the old forms from fresh points of view. It is the vase-paintings and sculpture which yield the most substantial results. The artisans who executed the former belonged to the ranks of the common people; consequently we may infer that those mythological themes which they pictured represent versions current in their own stratum of society and perhaps detached from literary traditions. For about two centuries, beginning approximately 700 B.C., it was the common practice to use such themes and to identify the personages portrayed by means of symbols or inscribed names. Through the combined effect of a number of hampering conditions — the limited space available for the picture on the vases, the artist's undeveloped skill, and the religious conceptions of his times and of his social class — it was impossible for the painter to impart to his figures the finer lineaments of individuality and character.

Sculptures in relief, especially those belonging to temple friezes, are more useful to us as sources of the details of myth than as interpretations, for a tendency to allegorize their themes obscures their primary, and even their contemporary, significance. It is to sculpture in the round that we must turn for the noblest and strongest interpretations of the god of myth and worship. The temple statue tells no story; that is not its function. On the contrary, it stands as a summary, sublimated to an ideal by the alchemy of the artist's genius, of all the highest attributes accorded the god in the thought of the majority of his worshippers. The trained and discerning eye can read the individual attributes in the summary. As compared with the temple image, the decorative statue does tell a story. The very purpose for which it is designed gives the artist an opportunity of choosing a situation, to use a term of dramatic criticism, in which to set his god; and situation implies narrative. Moreover, the sculptor has much more freedom in making his selection of attributes. The other forms of art to which the student of myth may refer are the wall-paintings of Pompeii, coins, metal-work, and cut gems. The wall-paintings generally deal with myths which are already known through literature; they are useful mainly as illustrations and verifications. Coin types not infrequently portray the leading cult statues of the state issuing the coin; like their models, then, they tell no story. The mythological scenes represented in relief or by means of incised lines on mirrors, bowls, and other objects of domestic use rank as sources in substantially the same class as the earlier vase-paintings. From cut gems we learn relatively little.

GREEK AND ROMAN MYTHOLOGY

PART I

MYTHS OF THE BEGINNING, THE HEROES, AND THE AFTERWORLD

IT may be thou hast follow'd
Through the islands some divine bard,
By age taught many things,
Age and the Muses;
And heard him delighting
The chiefs and people
In the banquet, and learn'd his songs,
Of Gods and Heroes,
Of war and arts,
And peopled cities,
Inland, or built
By the grey sea.—If so, then hail!
I honour and welcome thee.

MATTHEW ARNOLD, *The Strayed Reveller.*

PLATE VII

Hera

The regal decoration of the diadem, the fine and noble features, and the matronly bearing of the head, are convincing proofs that this is a portrait of the queen of Olympos and the divine patroness of wedlock. There does not exist in sculpture or in painting a revelation of her character superior to this. From an original marble, probably of the late fifth century B.C., in the Uffizi, Florence (Brunn-Bruckmann, *Denkmäler griechischer und römischer Sculptur*, No. 547). See pp. 7 ff., 163 ff.

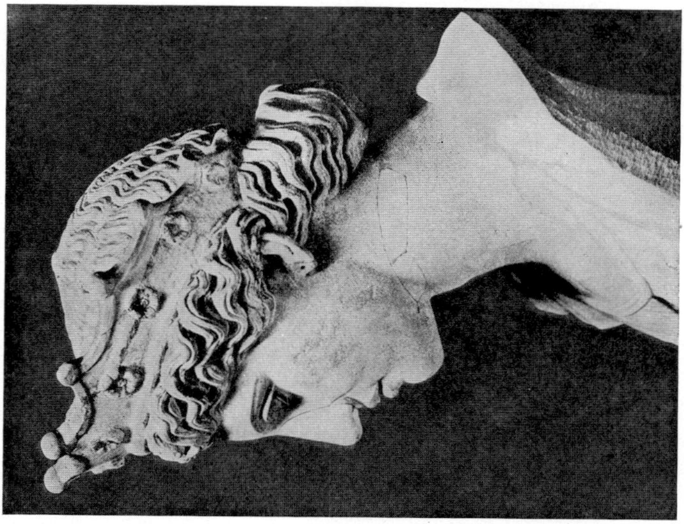

GREEK AND ROMAN MYTHOLOGY

CHAPTER I

MYTHS OF THE BEGINNING

THE early Greek looked out upon the world of men and things and asked himself the far from simple question, How and by whom was this great complex created? In answering the question he was bound, of course, to remain within the limits of his own personal experience — to explain the unknown in terms of the known or of what seemed to be known. Lacking the classified data of our modern sciences of geology, astronomy, and biology, he was as incapable of forming even a vague idea of the structure of the universe as he was of measuring the distance between the sun and the moon. Yet he possessed certain fundamental facts, and these composed his meagre body of science. Moreover, observation had taught him that the world was the theatre of the ceaseless operation of unseen powers that were certainly superior to man. Following his instincts, he personified these powers, called them gods, and did them worship; this constituted his religion. Since among most primitive peoples science and religion tend to be inextricably interwoven with each other, it was inevitable that the Greek should draw on these two sources of his funded experience in answering his question as to the beginning of things.

Broadly speaking, the fundamental facts known to the Greek are as follows. In all departments of her activity Nature steadily proceeds from disorder toward order. The great movements generally take place in regular cycles, such as days, months, seasons, and years; while the unforeseen and calamitous phenomena, like volcanic eruptions, whirlwind, and flood, are really less frequent and less potent than the normal operations. Like tends to beget like; life arises only from life. The great tree comes from a small seed, the bird from a fragile egg, and man grows to maturity from a helpless infant. What could be more natural for the Greek than to conclude, as he did, that the world and the races of men and of gods came into being in the same way? Once he could account for their creation, he could easily explain their subsequent growth and development through the ordinary visible processes of nature. For the supremacy of gods and men with their ideas of order and justice he could find an obvious reason in the superiority of the great regular forces over the irregular. In this method of thought he was unwittingly paying a great tribute to himself. The lower savage accredits some animal with the creation of the world; the more advanced savage might go as high in the scale as man himself in his search for the first maker; but to be able to point with conviction to personal creative forces immeasurably beyond man demands an extraordinary degree of intellectual advancement.

The Creation of the World. — Among the Greeks there was no single generally accepted account of the Creation, for the people were divided as to which of the several records was the most ancient and therefore likely to be the most authoritative. The view that prevailed in Athens during the fifth and fourth centuries B.C. was that the oldest was contained in a poem which passed as the composition of the inspired Orpheus. The many other so-called Orphic poems current at the time were frankly counted as forgeries, but, nevertheless, were believed to contain the same tradition of the Beginning as that found in the *Iliad*.

According to the Orphic story, uncreated Nyx ("Night") existed first, and was regarded as a great black-winged bird hovering over a vast darkness "without form and void."

Though unmated, she laid an egg whence golden-winged Eros ("Love") flew forth, while from the two parts of the shell Ouranos and Gaia ("Heaven" and "Earth") were created. They became the first pair of parents and brought into the world Okeanos ("Ocean") and Tethys ("Nurse"). These in their turn became a parental pair, begetting Kronos, Rhea, Phorkys, and the other Titans; and, similarly, Kronos and Rhea were united and begat Zeus and Hera. Now Kronos was warned that his reign would cease when Hera should bear a son to Zeus. To forestall such an evil he sought to kill her, but she was saved by her mother, who secretly brought her to the realm of Okeanos and Tethys, where, unknown to her father, she was wedded to Zeus. The Moirai ("Fates") led the bride to her husband, and Eros drew the bridal car, while in honour of the nuptials Gaia gave Okeanos permission to fashion the beautiful gardens of the Hesperides. The Orphic poet held this union of Zeus and Hera before the Greeks as the model of conjugal relations.

The Hesiodic story is different in many points and is much less satisfactory as a philosophical explanation of beginnings. First there was Chaos,

> ". . . the vast immeasurable abyss,
> Outrageous as a sea, dark, wasteful, wild." [1]

Then came Gaia, gloomy Tartaros (the dark "Underworld"), and Eros as the moving force within and about all things. Chaos brought into being Erebos ("Lower Darkness") and Nyx, and these in their turn begat Aither ("Heavenly Light") and Hemera ("Earthly Light," i. e. "Day"). Mother Earth bore Ouranos (star-sown "Heaven") to be a helpmeet to herself and at the same time a secure dwelling-place for the blessed gods. Now appeared the rugged mountains and the wild stretches of the sea. In their relation of husband and wife Ouranos and Gaia became the founders of what one might call the first royal house of the gods.

The Régime of Ouranos. — The children of Ouranos and Gaia were many. First, there were born the Titans,[2] such as Okeanos, Krios, Hyperion, Iapetos, Themis ("Justice"), Mnemosyne ("Memory"), and, last of all, Kronos. Besides these there were the Kyklopes, "the powers of the air" — Brontes ("Thunder-Roar"), Steropes ("Lightning"), Arges ("Thunderbolt") — each of whom had one huge eye in the middle of his forehead. In addition to these monsters were the giants Kottos, Briareos, and Gyes, each with fifty heads and a hundred hands springing from his shoulders. So terrible were they that Ouranos, their father, was afraid of them and thrust them back into the bosom whence they had come. At this Gaia was sorely offended, and calling her children together she laid before them a plan of putting an end to the violence of their sire. Only Kronos was fearless enough to carry it out. With a sickle given him by Gaia he attacked his father and terribly mutilated him, but Gaia caught the blood from the wound, and from it in the process of time were born the Erinyes ("Furies"), the armed Giants, and the Melian Nymphs, while the contact of the severed flesh with the sea produced Aphrodite, the goddess of love. With this attack the rule of Ouranos came to an end.

The Régime of Kronos. — By virtue of his strength and boldness Kronos assumed the kingship over the gods, whose number was now large, for during the rule of Ouranos, Nyx, Pontos (barren "Sea"), and the elder Titans had begotten many children, among these being Thanatos ("Death"), his brother Hypnos ("Sleep"), "the whole tribe of dreams," Nemesis, Friendship, Old Age, and Strife, who herself had brought forth "wars and rumours of war." Following the example of Gaia in wedding Ouranos, Rhea became the sister-spouse of Kronos, and the fruits of their wedlock were Hera, Aïdes ("Hades"), Poseidon, and Zeus, "the sire of gods and men." Kronos, remembering how he had displaced his father, became fearful that one of his children might overthrow him, and, accordingly, as soon as they were born he swallowed them as the easiest way of getting rid of them. Only Zeus escaped, and that because Rhea contrived and executed a plan that he should be born in Crete and hidden in a cave on Mount

FIG. 1. POSEIDON

Poseidon holding a dolphin in his right hand to indicate that the sea is his abode, and in his left hand a trident (originally a lightningbolt, but here a fish-spear) as a symbol of his sovereignty over the deep. From a red-figured *lekythos* of the fifth century B.C., found at Gela, Sicily (*Monumenti Antichi*, xvii, Plate XV).

Aigaion. Instead of a child she gave Kronos a stone which he swallowed in ignorance of the deception, whereupon Gaia caused him to disgorge what he had eaten and, naturally, the stone came first and the children last. On reaching manhood Zeus emerged from his hiding-place and after putting an end to the unjust rule of his father he wedded Hera and himself took the throne. Afterward he deposited the stone in Delphoi. Centuries later a certain meteor worshipped in Roman Africa was identified by mythologists as this same stone.[3]

Establishment of the Régime of Zeus; the Titans. — Many children were born to Zeus and Hera, and they were the first to be properly called gods. They established themselves on Mount Olympos, which stood directly opposite Mount Othrys, the seat of the Titans, who, being the older race (with the exception of Mnemosyne, Themis, and Prometheus), quite naturally regarded Zeus and his family as upstarts and usurpers. Bitter rivalry and strife arose between the two settlements, and for ten years they fought with no decisive results. A peace-parley held at the end of this period seemed only to add heat to the conflict, so that at length Zeus freed the three hundred-handed Giants whom Kronos had left bound deep down within the earth, and enlisted them in his ranks, deciding now to reveal his full strength and to bring the tedious strife to a sudden end. With their many hands the Giants hurled huge rocks at the foe until the sky was darkened, while Zeus cast thunderbolt after thunderbolt with their long tongues of flame:

> ". . . dire was the noise
> Of conflict; overhead the dismal hiss
> Of fiery darts in flaming volleys flew,
> And, flying, vaulted either host with fire."[4]

By this deadly assault the Titans were overwhelmed and driven into the depths of the earth. Down, down they went, a journey of nine days and nine nights, until they were as far from the plains of earth as the plains of earth are beneath the heaven. There a brazen wall with brazen gates was built about them, and the three Giants were placed on guard to prevent them from escaping.

Typhon (or Typhoeus); the Giants. — The sway of Zeus was not yet secure, for Gaia had borne to Tartaros a monstrous son

PLATE VIII

Gods and Giants

1. Ge rises from the earth as if to implore Poseidon to stay his hand as he thrusts his trident into the breast of her son, Polybotes.

2. In the centre of the picture Apollo, grasping his unstrung bow in his left hand, with his right hand drives his sword at Ephialtes, who defends himself with a spear. At the left, the armed Ares is pressing a spear-head into the breast of the falling Mimon, while at the right Hera endeavours to transfix Phoitos, who, though tottering backward, boldly continues fighting.

3. In the outer group at the right Athene is depicted trying to turn Enkelados to stone by holding before him the *gorgoneion* of her aegis, while at the same time she aims a lance at his breast. In the opposite group, Artemis appears in the act of burning Gaion with blazing torches, and in the centre, Zeus, marked by his sceptre, and Porphyrion are engaged in mutual combat, the one hurling a thunderbolt and the other a stone. From a red-figured *kylix* of the early fifth century B.C., in the Museum of Fine Arts, Boston (Furtwängler-Reichhold, *Griechische Vasenmalerei*, No. 127). See pp. 8–9.

named Typhon, the daemon of the whirlwind. Upon his shoulders he carried a hundred serpent-heads; his voice was like those of all formidable beasts in one; from his eyes there flashed out fire. In his might he assailed Zeus, and would have wrested the sovereignty from him had not the lord of the gods leaped down from on high and felled the monster with a thunderbolt. Upon Typhon Mount Aetna was set, and from its peak the smoke and fire of his laboured breathing rise to this very day.

Even yet the lordship of Zeus was challenged, this time by the Giants who had been born of Gaia by the blood of Ouranos, and whom some believed to be the forefathers of the human race. Among these mighty beings were Enkelados, Hyperbios, Ephialtes, and Polybotes. They were a haughty and warlike folk, and under their king, Eurymedon, they lived, some said, in the island of Kerkyra (Corfu), or as others preferred, in Spain or even in Chalkidike. For their insolence and hostility the gods, led by Zeus and Athene, overthrew them; in punishment volcanoes were piled on their prostrate bodies, and their groans and convulsions of pain can be perceived even today.

This myth is a restatement or a poetic imitation of the battle of the Titans, but it contains several features just as old as the body of the other story. It was a very popular theme in poetry and art throughout the Hellenic world. We find it employed in a vase-painting which dates at least as early as the sixth century B.C., in the eastern metopes of the Parthenon, and in the frieze of the great altar of Zeus at Pergamon.

Although the elements of these stories of the beginnings of things are varied and confused, their central meaning is clear. They reveal the belief of the early Greeks that their established social order never could have existed had not the cosmic forces previously been reduced to order by some power or powers. Moreover, they may be regarded as a gauge of the growing Hellenic faculty which apprehended these potencies at first as few and mutually overlapping in function, and later as many and distinct from one another. In the ascendancy of

Kronos over Ouranos and of Zeus over Kronos we see an increasing appreciation of the worth of intellect over mere brute strength and cunning. In short, the whole fabric of the stories sets forth in pattern the conviction that the world moves steadily toward better things.

The Creation of Man. — The Greeks, unlike the Hebrews and their religious successors, had no one orthodox account of the creation of man. On the contrary, there were almost as many traditions as there were city-states, and the multiplicity of both was due to the same cause, the isolating character of the Greek highlands. What more natural for the Greek local patriot than to believe that the first man was created in his own community? When one understands the spirit of the divisions in Greece, he cannot wonder that the attempts of Hesiod and the earlier logographers to construct a harmony of the conflicting local myths never proved to be eminently successful. In the legends that we are about to examine each act of the creation of man follows one of three processes: the man simply originates out of the elemental powers or objects of the earth; or he is begotten by one of the Olympians; or he is moulded out of lifeless matter by the hand of some divine or semi-divine artisan.

The first process is not as strange as it appears to be at first glance, for it is very easy to infer that that power which can produce the crops of the field and the mysterious second-growth of timber on the burnt lands, and can make sudden revelations of life in the wilderness, can also produce man. The Athenians believed that the first man was Kekrops, who sprang to life from the soil of Athens. Those Boiotians who lived near Lake Kopaïs held that the first man, Alalkomeneus, was born of the waters of the lake after the manner of fish. To the people of Arkadia the first man was their own earth-sprung Pelasgos. In Theban story men germinated from the dragon's teeth sown broadcast on the earth. Aiakos, the king of Aigina, had a country without a people until, at the command of Zeus, the ants on the island assumed human shape and became his subjects. Among those Hellenic stocks which inhabited districts of hill and forest the prevailing myths derived men from rocks and trees.

Zeus was accredited with being the great forefather of more families and stocks than was any other Olympian, and his title, "Father of gods and men," was therefore no idle appellation. He begat Hellen through his union with Pyrrha ("Ruddy Earth"), who was thus made the foremother of the Hellenes; by Dia ("Divine Earth"), he became the father of Peirithoös; Aiakos was his son by Aigina, the nymph of the island of the same name; Lakedaimon, the ancestor of the Lakedaimonians, was borne to him by Taÿgete, the nymph of the mountain of that region; Perseus was the issue of his approach to Danaë in the form of a shower of gold; and nearly all kings proudly traced their descent to Zeus. Yet the other gods were not wholly without such honours. Poseidon was represented as the great ancestor of the Aiolic stock, and Kronos became the father of Cheiron through his amour with Philyra ("Linden-Tree"). One meets but rarely with myths which attribute the origin of a race to the union of a goddess with a mortal man.

It is rather surprising that in most of their cosmogonic myths the Greeks succeeded merely in setting forth a plausible sequence of events, but failed to make really serious attempts at a real solution of the causes. The stories which we have just noted were not such as to satisfy a truly inquisitive mind. The Greeks themselves early came to a realization of this, and the simple conception rapidly gained ground that the first human being must have been, so to speak, a manufactured product. The maker (or makers, according to the variations of the story) was a god who formed man by a definite act of will, by means of a well-known process, and out of some tangible material. The method which is generally detailed is the very old and simple one of moulding the figure out of the dust of the earth, a concept which appeals to the imagination of the modern as well as of the ancient. In the myths of Prometheus and of Pandora we shall see it most attractively brought out.

Prometheus. — "Prometheus is . . . the type of the highest perfection of moral and intellectual nature, impelled by the purest and the truest motives, to the best and noblest ends." These words of the poet Shelley [5] give us a clear view of Prometheus in his relation to the thought and religion of the Greeks. He was a paradoxical character. In his one person he was both less than god and "more than god, being wise and kind." [6] His figure was clear where it represented the moral aspirations of the Hellenes, obscure where it touched their formal religion; it had just those lines which their imagination could not resist and which made it an inexhaustible literary theme.

Prometheus ("Forethinker") was generally held to be the son of the Titan Iapetos and Gaia (or Themis), and was the brother of Atlas and Epimetheus ("Afterthinker"). The legends are by no means in agreement as to the name of his wife, who is variously called Kelaino, Pandora, Pyrrha, Asia, and Hesione, all of which, it is worth noting, are epithets of the Earth Goddess. His marriage was fruitful, and among his children were sometimes counted Deukalion, Chimaireus, Aitnaios, Io, and Thebe. In many of the myths Prometheus and Hephaistos are curiously allied in their relations to human culture.

Although a Titan, Prometheus had espoused the cause of Zeus, thus manifesting his native sympathy for law and order; but as he was essentially a nobler type than Zeus himself, he could not long maintain the allegiance. When the chief Olympian found mankind hopelessly faulty and planned to create a new race in its place, Prometheus broke with him and defiantly became sponsor of the human cause. This generous devotion is the source of his power in myth.

In Hesiod's *Theogony* the story runs that a conference of gods and men was held at Sikyon to determine the homage owed by men to the gods. Acting as priest, Prometheus sacrificed an ox and divided it into two parts, one of which consisted of flesh and other edible portions enveloped in the skin of the animal, while the second was composed of bones and entrails alluringly garnished with strips of rich fat. It was the hope of Prometheus that Zeus would be misled by appearances and choose the poorer part, but to the Olympian the deceit was too plain, and, in order that he might have an excuse for punishing men, he deliberately took the bones and entrails, and withheld the gift of fire from men. Moved with pity, Prometheus stole some embers and brought them to mankind hidden in a hollow stalk.[7] In some myths it is said that he took the fire from the very hearth of Zeus; in others, from the workshop of Hephaistos and Athene on Lemnos; in still others, from the fiery chariot of the sun. Through this sublime theft men were enabled to lift the ban of Zeus, to begin life anew, and little by little to evolve the arts and crafts.

But Prometheus paid the penalty for his trespass on the divine rights of Zeus to the exclusive control of fire. Zeus had him chained to a crag (or pillar) in the range of Caucasus and appointed an eagle to gnaw at his vitals, consuming each day what had been restored during the night just past. Despite his many sufferings the spirit of Prometheus was unquenched, for he was comforted with the foreknowledge that some day he would be released and that Zeus would be overthrown even as Ouranos and Kronos had fallen. In due time his shackles were broken by Herakles and he was brought back to Olympos to serve his fellow-gods with his gift of prophecy. In one odd version of the story the rocks sank with Prometheus into the gloomy depths of Tartaros.

The notion that man was shaped from clay was relatively late. By the fifth century B.C. the belief in this process was general, and by the fourth it was the rule to identify Prometheus as the artist. From clay he fashioned both men and beasts and into them passed emanations of the divine fire which became their souls. The human-like boulders at Panopeus in Phokis were pointed out as material left over by him in the process of making men.

The myth of Prometheus teaches that the Greeks regarded all natural fire as originally divine, that it was at once the strongest and the subtlest of the forces of nature and the most potent factor in the advance of humanity. In the legend can be detected a plea for the dignity of perseverance and toil and

Fig. 2. Creation of Pandora

In the centre of the upper band the newly-created Pandora stands stiffly like a figure of wood or clay. To her right appear in order Athene (who holds a wreath toward her), Poseidon, Zeus, and Iris, while to her left are shown the armed Ares, Hermes, and Hera. The lower band represents a comic dance of Satyrs. From a red-figured *krater* found at Altemira and now in the British Museum (*JHS* xi, Plate XI).

the promise that they will bring their own reward in the form of increased efficiency. The picture of the noble suffering of Prometheus is testimony that very early the Greeks had a clear idea of self-sacrifice.

Pandora. — By accepting the stolen fire men were legally party to the offence, and to punish them Zeus condemned them to earn their daily bread by the sweat of their brow, besides doing them irreparable harm by bringing evil into their lives. At his bidding Hephaistos shaped an image of clay and endowed it with human faculties. In appearance the figure was like one of the Olympian goddesses — a beautiful maiden to whom all the Olympians contributed of their several qualities.

PLATE IX

Athene Parthenos

This statue of Athene, the maiden protectress of Athens, is one of a number of copies of the famous chryselephantine image made by Pheidias for the Parthenon, and many of its peculiar features betray its metallic original. In her right hand the goddess holds erect a long lance and allows her left hand to rest on a shield standing on edge at her side. On her head is a helmet on the top of which sits a sphinx, and over her shoulders and breast hangs the aegis. Her face is strong, dignified, just, and unemotional — in short, suggests all those ideal traits of character which the noblest myths have attributed to her. From a marble of the age of Hadrian, in the Prado, Madrid (Brunn-Bruckmann, *Denkmäler griechischer und römischer Sculptur*, No. 511). See pp. 169 ff.

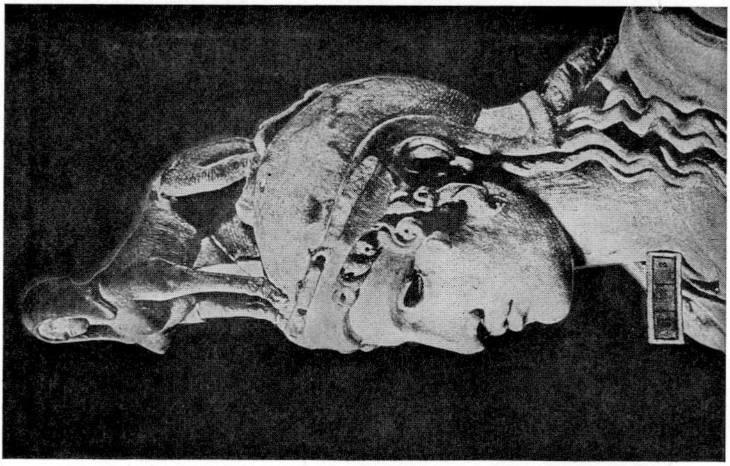

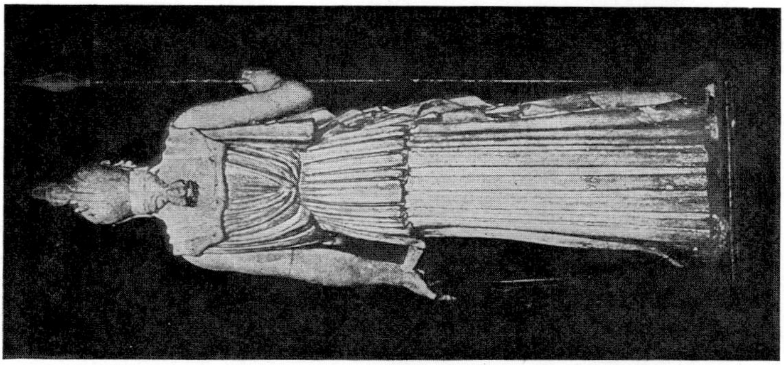

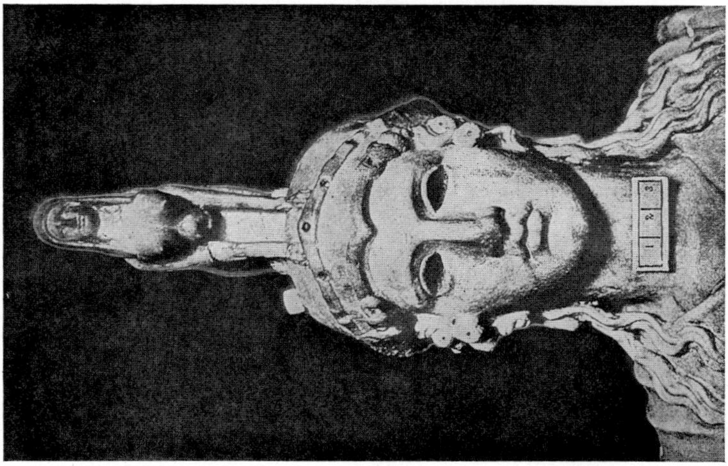

The Graces and the Hours decked her out in charming apparel and bright flowers so that desire awoke in the hearts of men, and as the gift of all the gods to the human race she was named Pandora.[8] Hermes brought her to Epimetheus, who received her in spite of Prometheus's warning to accept nothing from the gods, for, unhappily, it was the nature of Epimetheus to see no evil until it had come upon him. Pandora, curious to know what was stored in a large jar standing near her (fancy is free to conjecture the origin of the vessel), lifted the lid, and before she could replace it all sorts of evils and diseases flew out and covered land and sea. Only Hope was left, not buoyant, reassuring hope, but that kind which is

> ". . . to much mortal woe
> So sweet that none may turn from it nor go."[9]

Such, in the main, is the story of Hesiod. In the late poets the jar is said to have contained every good as well as every evil; the former flew away and were lost, while the latter were scattered among men.

The substance of this tale and that of the phrase *cherchez la femme* are the same — through woman came and still comes evil into the world. While the advent of the first man was explained in many ways, the first woman was always believed to be the handiwork of the gods.

Origins of Certain Animals and Plants. — We can here mention only a few of the many passages in the myths which describe the metamorphoses of human beings into animals and plants. When Keÿx, a son of Hesperos, perished by shipwreck, his broken-hearted wife, Alkyone, threw herself into the sea and was drowned. The gods changed them both into kingfishers, which were said by the ancients to make their nests on the surface of the sea in winter during a short period of calm which sailors called the alcyon (or halcyon) days. Asteria, the Titan's daughter who spurned an amour with Zeus, was transformed by him into a quail; at the death of Meleagros his lamenting sisters were changed into shrill-voiced guinea-fowl; in the Attic group of myths Tereus became the hoopoe, Philomele the nightingale, and Prokne the swallow, while Nisos of Megara was transformed into the sea-eagle.

Some instances are recorded in which human beings took the forms of quadrupeds. The impious Lykaon became a prowling wolf, Kallisto a bear, and Psamathe, a wife of Aiakos, a seal.

The origins of certain trees were sometimes traced back to a human or a divine personage. For instance, when Philyra first saw her monstrous son, the Centaur Cheiron, she was so filled with horror that she begged to be given a new form, and Zeus bestowed upon her that of the linden-tree. In pity for the innocently incestuous Smyrna, Aphrodite allowed her to become the myrrh-tree with its sweet aroma. The grieving sisters of Phaëthon were turned into tremulous poplars, and Daphne, as we shall see later, became the laurel.

Beginnings of Civilization. — By means of myth the Greeks endeavoured to explain the origins of the various features of civilization as they did other beginnings equally obscure. The Argives alleged that their Phoroneus was the first to teach men to abandon a solitary manner of life and to gather together into communities. It was he, and not Prometheus, according to their patriotic claim, who was the discoverer of fire. Among the Arkadians Pelasgos was believed to have been the first to contrive huts, to fashion garments from the skins of beasts, and to instruct men to cease eating leaves and grass like the brutes of the field and to adopt a more distinctively human diet. From Arkas, the Arkadians' eponymous ancestor, men learned how to make bread, spin thread, and weave garments. To the people of Eleusis Triptolemos was the pioneer in the cultivation of the staple grains, while the reading of the will of the gods in the flight of birds was first practised by Parnassos, and Deukalion was credited with having been the founder of religion.

The Ages of the World. — The Greeks and Romans, like most other peoples, believed that the world had passed through a series of ages, although the several theories as to the nature of these aeons are in many respects discrepant. The cyclic theory, the theories of both earlier and later mystics, and the theories of the Stoics and Cynics, while owing much of their fabric to mythology, belong more properly to philosophy, and hence, even though a great part of their teaching is presented in the form of myth, they can justly be ignored in this account.

Hesiod relates that in the beginning the Olympians under Kronos created the race of the Men of Gold. In those days men lived like gods in unalloyed happiness. They did not toil with their hands, for earth brought forth her fruits without their aid. They did not know the sorrows of old age, and death was to them like passing away in a calm sleep. After they had gone hence, their spirits were appointed to dwell above the earth, guarding and helping the living.

The gods next created the Men of Silver, but they could not be compared in virtue and happiness with the men of "the elder age of golden peace." For many years they remained mere children, and as soon as they came to the full strength and stature of manhood they refused to do homage to the gods and fell to slaying one another. After death they became the good spirits who live within the earth.

The Men of Bronze followed, springing from ash-trees and having hearts which were hard and jealous, so that with them "lust and strife began to gnaw the world." All the works of their hands were wrought in bronze. Through their own inventions they fell from their high estate and from the light they passed away to the dark realm of King Hades unhonoured and unremembered.

Zeus then placed upon earth the race of the Heroes who fought at Thebes and Troy, and when they came to the end of life the Olympian sent them to happy abodes at the very limits of the earth.

After the Heroes came the Men of Iron — "the race of these wild latter days." Our lot is labour and vexation of spirit by day and by night, nor will this cease until the race ends, which will be when the order of nature has been reversed and human affection turned to hatred.

It is only too plain that this version is marked by an inconsistent development, and the insertion of the Age of Heroes between the Age of Bronze and the Age of Iron is exceedingly clumsy. Ovid shows much more skill in the joinery of his material. In his narrative the four ages of the metals pass without interruption, and for their wickedness the men of the Iron Age are destroyed, the only survivors, Deukalion and Pyrrha, becoming the parents of a new race — the race to which we belong.

The basic idea of these two forms of the myth is that man was created pure and faultless and fell by degrees to his present unworthy condition, this being borne out by the descent of the metals. The legend points, perhaps accidentally, to an advance in human responsibility through the series of ages, although its transition from age to age is far from clear. From the point of view of modern ethics the story contradicts itself, but this must not be emphasized too strongly, since the original *motif* was apparently not ethical. The countless descriptions of the Golden Age in the literatures of Greece and Rome had a powerful influence over the early Christian delineations of Heaven.

The Great Flood. — The Greeks shared with almost all other peoples the belief in a great flood, but the event — if it actually occurred—was so enshrouded in the haze of a remote past that all the accounts of it which have come down to us are plainly the products of the fertile imagination of the Greeks. They even attempted to fix dates for it. The flood of Deukalion and Pyrrha was synchronized by some with the reigns of Kranaos of Athens and of Nyktimos of Arkadia. This particular deluge is the one of which the best myths treat, and in describing it we shall give in substance the account of Apollodoros, as being simpler and better proportioned than that of Ovid.

When Zeus would destroy the men of the Race of Bronze for their sin, Deukalion fashioned a great chest at the bidding of his father Prometheus. Into this he put all manner of food and drink, and himself entered it with his wife Pyrrha (daughter of Epimetheus and Pandora). Zeus then opened the sluices of heaven and caused a great rain to fall upon the earth, a rain which flooded well-nigh all Hellas and spared only a mere handful of men who had fled to the neighbouring hills. Deukalion and Pyrrha were borne in the chest across the waters for nine days and nine nights until they touched Mount Parnassos, on which, when at length the rain had ceased, Deukalion disembarked and offered sacrifice to Zeus Phyxios. Through Hermes Zeus bade him choose whatsoever he wished, and he chose that there be a human race. Picking up some stones from the ground at the command of Zeus, he threw them over his head and they became men, while the stones which Pyrrha cast in like manner became women. Hence from *λᾶας*, "a stone," men were called *λαοί*, "people."[10] In his version Nonnos localizes the flood in Thessaly.

Besides the foregoing, there are other flood-myths. Megaros, the founder of Megara, was said to have been rescued from a deluge by following the guiding cry of a flock of cranes; Dardanos escaped from a Samothracian flood by drifting to the Asiatic shore on a boat of skins; and the separation of Europe and Asia, it was related, was due to an unprecedented flow of water.

Most scholars of comparative mythology now agree that the flood stories of the various peoples are germinally of local origin, and in most instances consist of genuine tradition of a wide-reaching inundation mingled with pure myth.

CHAPTER II

MYTHS OF THE PELOPONNESOS

I. ARKADIA

PELASGOS. — The first man in Arkadia was Pelasgos, after whom the land was named Pelasgia, and a fragment of Asios says that "the black earth bore godlike Pelasgos on the wooded hills that there might be a race of men." Elsewhere he is called the son of Zeus and the Argive Niobe, and if Niobe was really an earth goddess, as we have reason to suspect, these two genealogies are in fact but one. Besides being the founder of human civilization, he was the first Arkadian king and temple builder. He was wedded to the sea-nymph Meliboia (or Kyllene, or Deianeira), by whom he begat a son Lykaon.

Lykaon. — Lykaon, too, was a founder who built the city of Lykosoura, established the worship of Zeus on Mount Lykaios, and erected the temple of Hermes of Kyllene. He married many wives, who bore him fifty sons, but they and their father manifested such impiety and arrogance before both gods and men that they became an offence in the eyes of Zeus. In order to make trial of them Zeus came to Lykaon's palace in the disguising garb of a poor day-labourer. The king received him kindly, but on the advice of one of his sons mingled the vitals of a boy with the meat of the sacrifices and set them on the table before the god. With divine intuition Zeus detected the trick. Rising in anger he overturned the table, destroyed the house of Lykaon with a thunderbolt, changed the king into a wolf, and proceeded to slay his sons. When one only, Nyktimos, was left, Ge (i. e. Gaia) stayed the hand of Zeus. This son suc-

PLATE X

1

Helen and Paris

Aphrodite rests her right hand and arm across the shoulders of Helen, a young woman of attractive but irresolute manner, and looks earnestly into her face as if she were entreating an answer to a question. Opposite to them stands Eros, who seems to be endeavouring to persuade Alexandros (Paris) to come to a decision in a matter which greatly perplexes him. From a marble relief in Naples (Brunn-Bruckmann, *Denkmäler griechischer und römischer Sculptur*, No. 439). See p. 125.

2

Asklepios

Since the myths failed to endow Asklepios with distinctive physical traits, artists, impressed by the nobility of his character and activities, habitually likened him to the sublime figure of Zeus, and certainly this representation of him cannot but remind one of the statuette of Zeus reproduced on Plate XXXVII. His face and outstretched left hand promise a gracious welcome to those who seek his aid. From a marble relief, perhaps copied from the temple-statue by Thrasymedes (fourth century B.C.), discovered at Epidauros and now in Athens (Brunn-Bruckmann, *Denkmäler griechischer und römischer Sculptur*, No. 3). See pp. 279 ff.

2

1

ceeded his father on the throne and during his reign came the great flood which Zeus sent to destroy mankind.

In this story Lykaon may represent an old Pelasgic god or king whom immigrating Greeks found established in the land. The resemblance between the Greek word λύκος, "wolf," and the initial syllable of the name Lykaon may perhaps in part have given rise to the myth of Lykaon's change into a wolf, while in the impious offering to Zeus one can see a record of human sacrifice[1] in an ancient Zeus-ritual.

Kallisto. — In addition to his fifty wicked sons Lykaon had another child, a daughter named Kallisto ("Fairest"), who was sometimes spoken of simply as a nymph, a circumstance which probably points to her original independence of Lykaon. She was a companion of Artemis, the "huntress-goddess chaste and fair," who exacted of her followers a purity equal to her own. But Zeus deceived Kallisto and took advantage of her. When she was about to bear a child to him, Hera discovered her condition, and, turning her into a bear, persuaded Artemis to kill her with an arrow as she would any other beast of the woodland. At the behest of Zeus, Hermes took her unborn child to his mother Maia on Mount Kyllene, where he was reared under the name of Arkas, but the slain Kallisto Zeus placed among the constellations as the Bear, which, never setting, ceaselessly revolves about the pole-star, for Tethys, obeying the command of Hera, will not allow the evil thing to bathe in the pure waters of Okeanos.

This myth, too, can be traced to a religious origin. In Arkadia the bear was an animal sacred to Artemis, one of whose cult-titles was Kalliste, a name which could readily be worked over into Kallisto. Kallisto, then, both maiden and bear, was none other than Artemis herself. Moreover, the similarity in sound between Arkas and Ἄρκτος ("bear") was a great aid to the development of the story without being its cause.

Arkas, Aleos, Auge. — Arkas, though generally considered to be the son of Kallisto and Zeus, was sometimes designated as the twin brother of Pan, the native god of Arkadia. One tale even makes him the child whose flesh Lykaon served to Zeus, but in this instance Zeus put the severed members together and breathed into them once more the breath of life. The child was then reared to manhood in Aitolia and later followed his uncle Nyktimos as king, the country being named Arkadia after him. Arkas wedded the nymph Erato, by whom he became the father of three sons who had many descendants, and even in our era his grave was pointed out to travellers near Mantineia.

The three sons of Arkas divided the rule among themselves, and one of his grandsons, Aleos, founded the city of Tegea, where he established the cult of Athene Alea. His daughter Auge ("Sunlight") had an intrigue with Herakles when he visited her city, and afterward secretly bore a son whom she concealed in the sacred precincts of Athene. About this time a dreadful plague came upon the land, and on consulting the oracle as to the cause of it, Aleos was warned that the house of the goddess was harbouring an impure thing. After a search he found the child and learned of his daughter's sin. Enclosing mother and son together in a chest, he cast them adrift upon the sea, and by the waves they were borne at length to the shores of Mysia, whence they were led to the court of King Teuthras who made Auge his queen and accepted her son, now called Telephos, as his own. In a variation of the tale we read that Aleos exposed Telephos on the mountain-side where he was suckled by a doe and afterward found by hunters or by herdsmen. Auge was given to Nauplios to be killed, but her life was spared, and she and her son ultimately found their way to Mysia. We shall meet with Telephos later on in the story of the Trojan war.

The Plague at Teuthis. — The people of the Arkadian village of Teuthis told an interesting myth which purported to account for a visitation of sterility on their soil. The villagers had sent a certain Teuthis (or Ornytos) to command a contingent of Arkadians in the war against Troy, but when the Greeks were held back at Aulis by head winds, Teuthis quarrelled with Agamemnon and threatened to lead his men back home. In the guise of a man Athene appeared to him and tried to dissuade him from his purpose, but in a fit of rage he pierced her in the thigh with his spear and withdrew to Greece. At Teuthis the goddess came before him with a wound in her thigh and a wasting disease fell upon him, while his country was stricken with a failure of the crops. The oracle of Zeus at Dodona instructed the people that if they desired to appease the goddess they must, among other things, make a statue of her with a wound in its thigh, and Pausanias[2] naïvely adds, "I saw this image myself, with a purple bandage wrapt round its thigh."

II. LAKONIA AND MESSENE

Lelex and his Descendants. — The first man and first king of Lakonia was Lelex, who, like Pelasgos, was autochthonous, i. e. the offspring of the soil. From him the country derived its name of Lelegia, and he had two sons, one of whom, Myles, succeeded him in the sovereignty, while the other, Polykaon, became the ruler of the kingdom of Messenia. At his death Myles' dominion passed into the hands of Eurotas, the largest river of the land, whose daughter, Sparta, became the bride of Lakedaimon; Amyklas, one of the issue of this union, begetting a famous son, Hyakinthos.

Hyakinthos. — This Hyakinthos was one of the chief personages in Lakonian worship and myth. A model of youthful beauty, he was much loved by Apollo, and Zephyros, the mild West Wind, also loved him, but since his devotion was unrequited, in an outburst of jealousy he permitted a discus thrown by Apollo in a friendly contest to swerve aside and kill Hyakinthos. From the youth's blood caught by the earth sprang up the deep-red hyacinth flower,[3] whose foliage is marked with the letters AI, which signified to the Greeks "lamentation." Long did Apollo grieve for his friend unhappily slain by his hand. The body was buried at Amyklai where in the temple of Apollo his grave was for long years visible to passers-by, and from the mourning of Apollo was developed the great Lakonian festival, the Hyakinthia, the first days of which were devoted to a demonstration of grief, while the last day was one long outburst of joy. These two kinds of celebration marked respectively the alternating dying and revival of vegetation as typified mainly by the hyacinth. The festival was probably pre-Dorian in origin.

The Family of Perieres. — According to one of the genealogies, Amyklas had a grandson Perieres (or Pieres) who held the throne of Messene. By his queen Gorgophone, the daughter of Perseus, he begat four sons, Tyndareos, Aphareus, Ikarios, and Leukippos, all of whom hold prominent places in myth through the fame of their children. Ikarios became the father of Penelope, the faithful wife of Odysseus; Aphareus, of Idas and Lynkeus; Tyndareos, of Helen, Klytaimestra (old spelling Klytemnestra), Kastor, Polydeukes, and others; and Leukippos, of Hilaeira and Phoebe.

Tyndareos, Helen, Kastor and Polydeukes. — Tyndareos was expelled from Sparta by his brothers, and, until restored to his kingdom by Herakles, he took refuge with Thestios, king of the Aitolians, whose daughter, Leda, he married.

The story of the birth of his daughter, Helen, is variously told. The version most widely known is that which depicts Leda as a human being approached by Zeus in the guise of a swan, Helen, the offspring of this union, being therefore Leda's own child. A late version, on the other hand, represents her as the daughter of Nemesis. It seems that Nemesis, after taking various other forms in order to elude the amorous pursuit of Zeus, finally assumed that of a swan, but by appearing in the same shape Zeus deceived her. After the manner of birds she laid an egg which was found by a peasant (or by

PLATE XI

The Contest for Marpessa

On the right the tall, athletic man drawing his bow is Idas, and before him stands Marpessa, a figure replete with feminine graces, who casts a look of quiet submission upon her lover. Balancing Idas in the composition is Apollo, a lithe and relatively immature young man, making ready to place an arrow on the string; and beside him is his huntress-sister, Artemis, carrying a quiver and wearing a fawn-skin on her shoulders. The man striding between the two groups as if to part them, must be Evenos, Marpessa's father, and not Zeus. From a red-figured vase, apparently of the school of Douris (about 500 B.C.), found at Girgenti, and now in Munich (Furtwängler-Reichhold, *Griechische Vasenmalerei*, No. 16). See pp. 27–28.

Tyndareos) and taken to Leda. In due time Helen emerged from the egg and was cherished by Leda as of her own flesh and blood. When she was nearing womanhood her parents sent her to Delphoi to inquire of the oracle concerning her marriage. One day, while the response was being awaited, she happened to be dancing in the temple of Artemis at Sparta, when Theseus of Athens and his friend Peirithoös suddenly appeared and seized her. The two drew lots for her possession, and she was given to Theseus, who carried her off to Attike and left her in charge of his mother Aithra in the mountain village of Aphidnai. Helen's brothers, Kastor and Polydeukes, thinking that she was at Athens, went thither and demanded her release, only to meet with refusal. Not long afterward, however, when Theseus departed for a distant country, the brothers learned of the place of Helen's concealment and by a sudden attack succeeded in carrying her home along with her custodian Aithra. The citizens of Athens, alarmed at the military demonstration of Kastor and Polydeukes, admitted them into their city and thereafter accorded them divine honours. This myth we can probably put down as a fiction to account both for an early clash between Athens and Sparta and for the introduction of the worship of Kastor and Polydeukes into the city first named.

On returning to her home after this, the earliest of her many adventures with men, Helen and her parents (particularly the latter, as we may readily surmise) were much perplexed by the importunity of a multitude of suitors for her hand. It was decided that the matter be settled by lot, but before the lots were cast Tyndareos, fearing trouble from those of the suitors who would be doomed to disappointment, shrewdly persuaded them to consent to swear that they would one and all defend Helen and the successful suitor in the event of her being wronged in the future. They took their oaths over the severed pieces of a horse, and the oaths were "bound," as magic terms it, by the burial of the pieces. By the lots Helen became the wife of Menelaos of Argos. Her later adventures belong to the story of the great Trojan War.

Helen's twin brothers, Kastor and Polydeukes, were known jointly as the Dioskouroi, "sons of Zeus," although it was popularly believed that only Polydeukes was in fact the son of the god, Tyndareos being the father of the other. These brothers were conspicuous figures in Spartan cult and myth, and were regarded by the ancient Greeks in general as the outstanding exponents of heroic virtue and valour. So faithful and deep was their affection for one another that their two personalities were blended as into one, and thus they stood as the divine guardians of friendship. They excelled in athletic sports and feats of arms, Kastor being the type of expert horseman and Polydeukes that of the skilful boxer, while to the accompaniment of Athene's flute they are said to have invented the Spartan military dance. Their altar stood at the entrance to the hippodrome at Olympia, and they appeared frequently on the heroic stage. They participated in the voyage of the Argonauts and in the great hunt at Kalydon, and at Sparta they fought against Enarsphoros, the son of Hippokoön, but their chief military exploit was their sanguinary encounter with their cousins Idas and Lynkeus, the sons of Aphareus.

This story is told in two distinct forms. In one, the two pairs of brothers were making raids on the cattle of Arkadia. Idas and Lynkeus were driving a captured herd into Messenia when they almost fell into an ambuscade laid for them by Kastor and Polydeukes. These latter had hidden themselves in a hollow oak, but they could not elude the keen eyes of Lynkeus, who was able to see through the hearts of trees and beneath the surface of the earth. Lynkeus attacked Kastor and killed him, but Polydeukes swiftly pursued his brother's slayer and struck him down as he was about to roll upon him the image of Hades which stood on Aphareus's tomb. Suddenly Zeus intervened and smote Idas with a thunderbolt which consumed the bodies of the slain brothers together, whereupon Polydeukes prayed Zeus to be reunited with Kastor, obtaining an answer in the divine permission ever afterward to live with him alternately on Olympos and in the underworld.

In its other form the story depicts the brothers of each family as rivals for the hands of their two cousins, the daughters of Leukippos. The sons of Tyndareos seized the maidens and carried them off, pursued by the sons of Aphareus who kept taunting them with having violated the custom of the country by withholding marriage presents from the brides' parents. In reprisal Kastor and Polydeukes appropriated their pursuers' cattle and gave them to Leukippos, the consequence being a double duel in which Kastor killed Lynkeus, and then Idas slew Kastor for his insults to the dead, and lastly Polydeukes killed Idas. After this the sons of Tyndareos were vouchsafed immortality, as in the first version of the myth. Their significance in cult, together with that of Helen, will be explained in our consideration of the divinities of light. Idas and Lynkeus are to be regarded as the Messenian doubles of the Dioskouroi.

Idas and Marpessa. — Evenos, the uncle of Leda, had a daughter Marpessa. Both Apollo and Idas, enamoured of her beauty, became her suitors, and the latter in his passionate love seized her and bore her away in a winged chariot, the gift of Poseidon. Eluding the pursuit of Evenos, he brought her to Messene, where Apollo attempted to wrest her from him and would have worked his will had not Zeus interrupted the quarrel and bidden the maiden choose between the rivals. Marpessa, fearing that the fickleness of Apollo in the past was a poor promise of fidelity in the future, chose the mortal suitor Idas.

"'If I live with Idas, then we two
On the low earth shall prosper hand in hand
In odours of the open field, and live
In peaceful noises of the farm, and watch
The pastoral fields burned by the setting sun.

And he shall give me passionate children, not
Some radiant god that will despise me quite,
But clambering limbs and little hearts that err.'

. . . .

When she had spoken, Idas with one cry
Held her, and there was silence; while the god
In anger disappeared. Then slowly they,
He looking downward, and she gazing up,
Into the evening green wandered away." [4]

III. ARGOS

The land of Argolis was so situated in relation to the main highways of navigation in the Mediterranean as to invite a great variety of foreign connexions. In this one may find an explanation of the motley fabric of Argive myth, and a careful study of its composition makes it possible to state with some degree of assurance the sources of its sundry elements. Naturally, it is outside the scope of this work to tag each constituent tale of the narrative with its national origin. Suffice it to say that we find a nucleus of native Argive myth overlaid in an irregular fashion with legends of Cretan, Euboian, Boiotian, Milesian, Corinthian, Megarian, and Aitolian provenance,[5] which, regardless of the question of their origin, are nearly all fraught with interest for the student of comparative religion and custom.

Inachos, Io. — The first figure in the purely Argive part of the complex of myths is that of Inachos, the principal river and river-god of the Argolid. In the developed genealogy he is the offspring of Okeanos and Tethys, and by a marriage with an Okeanid he begat two sons, Phoroneus and Aigialeus, the first of whom, also said to be an autochthon, we have already seen as one of the pioneers of human culture. Aigialeus, especially prominent among the people of Sikyon, was the personification of the southern shores of the Gulf of Corinth. Phoroneus had two children — Apis, after whom the Peloponnesos was called

PLATE XII

Io and Argos

Io, who can be identified by the mere point of a horn protruding from her hair, is seated on a stone and looks appealingly at her guardian. Argos stands with one foot on a stone and rests his right hand on a crag in the background, as he gazes straight in front of him with wide staring eyes. It is easily seen that the painter has entirely forgotten or ignored the original religious meaning of the myth. From a Pompeian wall-painting (Hermann-Bruckmann, *Denkmäler der Malerei des Altertums*, No. 53). See pp. 28–30.

Apia; and Niobe, by whom Zeus became the father of Pelasgos and Argos. One of the descendants of Argos of the third or fourth generation was Argos Panoptes ("All-Seeing"), a monster whose body was covered with eyes. He slew the bull which was ravaging Arkadia, flayed it, and used its skin as a garment, and he is also said to have killed Satyros as he was raiding the herds of the Arkadians, and to have trapped Echidna, the hideous issue of Tartaros and Gaia.

Io, the chief personage in this group of myths, was counted either as the daughter of Inachos (or of Peiren, perhaps a double of Inachos), or as a comparatively late descendant. An exact genealogy is not essential to her story. She was the priestess of the temple of Hera, the divine patroness of Argos, and her charms drew upon her the attentions of Zeus, who corrupted her, but who denied the deed when charged with it by his wife. Like a coward he changed into a white heifer the maiden whom he had wronged and surrendered her to Hera, who put her in care of the vigilant Argos Panoptes. By him she was tethered to an olive-tree in the grove of Mykenai, but at the command of Zeus, Hermes slew Argos, thereby earning for himself the title of Argeïphontes ("Argos-Slayer" [6]), and set Io free, whereupon, animated by a merciless spite, Hera sent a gad-fly to pursue her from land to land. She was driven first of all to the gulf whose name, Ionian, even today commemorates her visit, and thence across Illyrikon and Thrace, whence she made her way to Asia over the straits which from that day were called the Bosporos ("Ox-Ford" [7]). Through Caucasus, Skythia, and Kimmeria (Crimea), even across the Euxine, she was goaded by the fly until at length she reached Egypt, where she was given rest and restored by Zeus to her human form. On the banks of the Nile she bore a son Epaphos ("Touch") to the god, but the presence of the babe was offensive to the jealous spirit of Hera, and through her machinations Epaphos was taken from his mother and hidden in a far land. Again the distressed Io was compelled to wander on the face of the earth, until, after a long search, she found her son in Syria and brought him back to Egypt, where he became the forefather of several great peoples.

The suggestions put forth to account for the myth of Io are many and varied. Most of them try to identify both her and Argos with celestial phenomena. For instance, Io is the moon with its horned crescent wandering across the sky, and her guardian, Argos, is the starry heavens. Such suggestions as these, however, fail to satisfy the profounder student of folk-lore, since they do not even attempt to give a reason for the sentiment, almost akin to reverence, with which the Argives regarded the person of Io. The Heraion, the temple of Hera near Argos, was doubtless the source of the earliest form of the myth, and probably Io was none other than Hera herself, who elsewhere is said to have assumed the form of a cow. At all events, the cow was sacred in the cult of Hera. The tale of Io's wanderings is apparently a late addition brought in from outside when the original theme assumed new forms among the alien tribes and cities which had dealings with Argos.

The Families of Danaos and Aigyptos. — Belos, a grandson of Epaphos, ruled over Egypt, and by a daughter of the Nile had four sons, in only two of whom, Danaos and Aigyptos, we are interested at present. The latter was appointed king of Arabia by his father, but by conquest he added to his realm the country of the Melampodes ("Black Feet") which he named Aigyptos[8] ("Egypt") after himself. He had a family of fifty sons, and his brother Danaos, the sovereign of Libya, the same number of daughters. The two brothers became involved in a political quarrel, and Danaos with his daughters fled by ship to Argos, whose king, Gelanor, yielded the crown to him, thus restoring it to the line of Io. As it happened, the land had been without sufficient water since the time when Poseidon had dried up the springs and streams to punish Inachos for his award of the divine supremacy of Argos to Hera, but one of Danaos's daughters, Amymone, gained the love of Poseidon and through him received knowledge of the abundant springs of Lerne, which thenceforth were a perpetual blessing to the land and to the people. Presently the fifty sons of Aigyptos appeared in Argos and demanded their fifty cousins in marriage. Though distrusting them, Danaos acquiesced in their demand, but secretly he gave to each daughter a weapon with which she was to slay her husband at the earliest opportunity, and on their wedding-night all except Hypermnestra stabbed their bridegrooms to death in bed. For her disobedience Danaos imprisoned Hypermnestra, but later, relenting, allowed her to live with her husband, Lynkeus, while her sisters buried their husbands' heads in the spring of Lerne and interred the bodies before the city. In compliance with the behest of Zeus, Athene and Hermes cleansed them of the guilt of bloodshed, after which Danaos held a series of athletic contests, to the winners of which he gave his widowed daughters in marriage. In an older form of the myth than that which we have just outlined, Lynkeus immediately avenged the murder of his brothers by killing not only the guilty daughters, but Danaos as well. In Hades these women were condemned to the endless task of filling a bottomless jar with water drawn in leaky vessels.

This myth is a strange conglomerate of primitive magic and cult. It seems to be, in part, of an aetiological character, and to purport to reveal the origin of the ritual of a rain-charm which had somehow become associated with the cult of the dead. In this ritual a bottomless jar would be placed over the grave of one who had died young or unmarried, and the liquids poured into the vessel passed forthwith into the ground and to the souls of the dead, the *δαναοί*, "thirsty ones," who would put an end to the drought as soon as their own thirst should be satisfied. In all probability Hypermnestra was a priestess of Hera in her capacity of goddess of wedlock, and thus constitutes a link binding this myth with those emanating at an earlier period, and more directly, from the Heraion.[9]

The connexion of Amymone and the springs of Lerne with the myth of the Danaïds cannot be original.

Proitos and his Daughters. — On the death of Danaos his son-in-law Lynkeus became king. He had two grandsons, Akrisios and Proitos, who were said to have fought with one another even before birth, so early did a quarrel over the succession arise between them. When they became men, Akrisios got the upper hand and exiled his brother who went to Lykia, in Asia Minor, where he was hospitably received by King Iobates and was given the princess Anteia (or Stheneboia) in marriage. With the aid of a Lykian army he returned to the Peloponnesos, captured Tiryns in spite of its strong fortifications, and there established his rule. His wife bore him three daughters, who in young womanhood were stricken with madness, either for refusing the rites of Dionysos, or for treating an image of Hera with contempt. Raving wildly, they roamed throughout the land until Melampous ("Black Foot," i. e. Egyptian) of Pylos, a seer skilled in the use of healing drugs, promised to cure them on condition that Proitos surrender to him one third of the kingdom. This Proitos refused to do, but meanwhile the evil grew, for the other women of the country were becoming infected with the madness. The seer renewed his promise of healing, this time with the added condition that a second third of the kingdom go to his brother Bias. At last Proitos yielded, and his daughters were made whole by means of Bacchic rites. Bias wedded one of the two younger maidens, and Melampous the other, by whom he became the founder of a family of seers.

The instructive feature of this myth is its revelation of two strata of cults in primitive Argos, the earlier that of Hera, the later that of Dionysos. The alleged impious acts of the daughters of Proitos seem to serve as explanation for certain wanton words and rites in the worship of these two gods in historical times.[10] With this story we may compare a Boiotian legend which records the madness of the daughters of Minyas.

PLATE XIII

PERSEUS

Although unaccompanied by an inscription this figure can be definitely identified as Perseus. In his right hand he holds the *harpe*, or sickle-sword, the gift of Hermes, on his shoulders hangs the pouch which he received from the Nymphs, and on his feet are the winged sandals which bear him swiftly through the air. His head-gear seems to be not the dog-skin cap of Hades, but a special form of the *petasos*, or travelling hat. From a red-figured *amphora* of about 500 B.C., in Munich (Furtwängler-Reichhold, *Griechische Vasenmalerei*, No. 134). See pp. 32 ff.

Akrisios, Danaë, and Perseus. — Akrisios, who continued to hold sway over Argos, was told by an oracle that his daughter's son would kill him. To circumvent the prophecy he enclosed his daughter Danaë in a brazen chamber, thinking thereby to cut her off from all human intercourse; but he failed in his purpose; for, as some say, the maiden was corrupted by her uncle Proitos, or, as others claim, by Zeus, who won his way to her in the form of a shower of gold falling through an aperture in the roof of her prison. When she had given birth to a son whom she called Perseus, Akrisios put them both in a chest and sent them adrift on the waters of the Aegean. By wind and wave the chest was carried to Seriphos, where it was dragged ashore by Diktys, the brother of Polydektes, the king of the island, who released Danaë and her child and gave them a home. After a number of years Polydektes made love to Danaë but was rejected. Fearing to take her by force, since Perseus was by this time quite capable of defending his mother, he devised a plan to get her son out of the way. To all his friends he sent invitations to a wedding-feast, and Perseus, with the extravagant asseveration of youth, replied that he would not fail to be present even if he had to bring the Gorgon's head. When the guests had assembled and it was discovered that all of them except Perseus had brought horses as presents, Polydektes dismissed him until he should have fulfilled his promise to the letter, warning him, moreover, that in event of failure his mother would be wedded by force. Sadly Perseus withdrew to a lonely spot; but in the midst of his perplexity Hermes and Athene appeared and led him to the Graiai, the ancient daughters of Phorkys and Keto. These had been grey from birth and had amongst them only one eye and one tooth, which they used in turns. By getting possession of these indispensable members and by threatening to keep them, Perseus compelled the Graiai to tell him the way to the dwelling-place of the nymphs who guarded the dog-skin cap of Hades, the winged sandals, and the magic pouch. Following the directions given him, he made his way to the nymphs and secured the objects which he so much desired. With the sandals he flew through the air to the land of the Gorgons near distant Okeanos, where he found the three monstrous sisters asleep. Their heads were covered with the horny scales of reptiles, their teeth were like the tusks of swine, and they had hands of brass and wings of gold. Their most formidable endowment, however, was their power to turn to stone those who looked upon them. Aware of this, Perseus with averted face approached Medousa, the only one of the three who was mortal, and, guiding himself by the reflection of her image in his shield, he struck off her head with a single blow of the scimitar which Hermes had given him, dropping the precious trophy in his pouch. From Medousa's severed neck leaped forth Pegasos, the winged horse, which flew aloft to the house of Zeus to become the bearer of the thunderbolt and lightning; and from the wound also sprang Chrysaor who was to be the father of the three-bodied Geryoneus. It is said that Athene was witness of the Gorgon's death and on the spot invented the flute on which she imitated the dying monster's shrieks and groans. As Perseus flew across Libya after his successful exploit drops of blood dripped from the pouch upon the land and became the germs of a breed of poisonous serpents, this being the reason why there are so many of these reptiles in this part of Africa. Medousa's sisters on waking were unable to pursue Perseus since the cap of Hades rendered him invisible.

On his return flight Perseus found the land of Aithiopia suffering from the ravages of a great monster sent by Poseidon to punish the boast of Queen Kassiepeia that she was more beautiful than the sea-nymphs. In an endeavour to appease the monster in a manner counselled by an oracle, Kepheus, the king, bound his daughter Andromeda to a rock beside the sea, and just as Perseus came the monster was about to devour her. Moved to pity and love at the sight of her as she cowered before the great creature, Perseus without delay forced from her father the promise that she should become his bride if he could succeed in releasing her. Approaching the monster, Perseus drew from his pouch the Gorgon's head [11] and turned him to stone, and later, when his claim to the freed Andromeda was disputed by her uncle Phineus, to whom she had been betrothed, he treated him, too, in the same fashion. After his marriage he lingered many months in Aithiopia and begat by Andromeda a son Perses who was destined to become the parent of the Persian people. On coming back to Seriphos, Perseus found Polydektes on the point of offering violence to his mother, whereupon, summoning him and his courtiers to his presence, he turned them to stone and made Diktys king in place of his brother. The winged sandals, the pouch, and the cap he restored to their original guardians and gave Medousa's head to Athene, who attached it to her shield.

After an absence of many years Perseus returned to his native Argos with his mother and his wife. Akrisios, apprehending that the oracle might yet be fulfilled, fled to Thessaly, and while there chanced to be present at certain funeral games in which Perseus was a contestant. Purely by accident the young man threw a discus so that it struck and killed his grandfather, whereupon, through remorse for his deed, he refused to go back to Argos and took the kingdom of Tiryns in exchange. From Tiryns he founded the cities of Mideia and Mykenai, and in the latter place Andromeda bore to him many illustrious sons and one daughter, Gorgophone, whose name commemorated her father's most famous exploit.

Another story is told of Perseus which has all the marks of great age. Dionysos came to Argos and when bidden to depart refused to go. Thereupon Hera, in the form of Melampous, prompted Perseus and the Argives to give battle to him and his host of Maenads and satyrs. Grasping his scimitar in one hand and the Gorgon's head in the other, Perseus flew aloft with the winged sandals and tried to attack the god from above, but Dionysos foiled him by increasing his stature until he touched heaven. At the sight of Medousa's head Ariadne, the wife of Dionysos, became an image of stone, and this so filled her husband's heart with rage that he would have destroyed Perseus and all the cities of his realm, with Hera as well, had not Hermes checked him by force. On becoming calm the god recognized that the attack had been inspired by Hera, and he accordingly absolved Perseus from all blame, whereupon the Argives instituted rites in honour of both Dionysos and Perseus. Later generations, it was said, were able to locate the graves of the Maenads who fell in the struggle, as well as the hiding-place of Medousa's head.

It has been suggested by one school of scholars, who have the foible of tracing almost every deity back to a Cretan or Philistine origin, that Perseus sprang from a Cretan offshoot of the sun-worship of Gaza, and that the story was borne from Crete to Thronion of the Lokrians, where Perseus was identified with Hermes and assimilated many of his attributes. A much more plausible theory holds, however, that Perseus was a pre-Dorian hero of the Peloponnesos whose cult was so wide-spread as to make it necessary for the Dorian conquerors to connect themselves with him genealogically in order to maintain their supremacy among the people. The story of Perseus impresses one as being an ancient folk-tale.[12]

Historically, the account of the birth of Herakles should be included among the Argive myths, but we shall prefix it to the narrative of the hero's career to which it logically belongs.

IV. CORINTH

The Divine Patrons of Corinth. — The great patron deity of Corinth was Poseidon who gave prosperity to her mariners and traders. Yet he did not have this high place from the beginning, for when he made his claim, Helios, the sun, disputed it. Both disputants submitted their respective cases to Briareos of the

PLATE XIV

1

Endymion

Endymion has fallen asleep on a ledge of rock on the steep face of Mount Latmos. Across his left shoulder rests the spear with which he defends his flocks against the wild beasts. Just above him his dog, tied by a leash, is looking upward and baying, perhaps at the Moon, his master's lover. From a marble relief in the Capitoline Museum, Rome (Brunn-Bruckmann, *Denkmäler griechischer und römischer Sculptur*, No. 440). See p. 245.

2

Perseus and Andromeda

This relief seems to represent a moment just after the death of the monster. Perseus, wearing the winged sandals, extends his right hand to Andromeda to help her descend from the rocks to which she has been bound, while he holds his left hand behind his back as if to hide the Gorgon's head, one glance at which would turn Andromeda into stone. The sea-monster's head, apparently severed from the body, or, perhaps, as the symbol of the entire body, is lying at the foot of the rocks. From a marble relief in the Capitoline Museum, Rome (Brunn-Bruckmann, *Denkmäler griechischer und römischer Sculptur*, No. 440). See pp. 34–35.

hundred arms, and he awarded the Isthmus to Poseidon, and Akrokorinthos, the citadel, to Helios.

Sisyphos. — The eldest son of Deukalion and Pyrrha was Hellen whose destiny it was to have his name perpetuated in that of the Hellenic race. One of his sons, Aiolos, the ruler of certain districts in Thessaly, had a large family of sons and daughters, the most important of whom, in the opinion of the people of Corinth, was Sisyphos, reputed to be the "craftiest of men" in so real a sense that he was even "as wise as a god." His gift of wisdom was at once his profit and his bane. He is said to have founded Corinth, then called Ephyra, "in a corner of horse-breeding Argos," and to have seized the citadel as a base of operations for piracy and brigandage; although, on the other hand, the statement is also made that he was merely the royal successor of Korinthos, or of Medeia after her flight to Athens. His skill and astuteness are reflected in the person of Odysseus, whose father he became, if we are to believe one legend, through his violence to Antikleia before her marriage to Laërtes, Odysseus's traditional father. Sisyphos was credited by some with having established the Isthmian games in honour of Melikertes, his nephew, whose drowned body had been cast by the waves on the shore of the Isthmus.

The account of his punishment in the underworld is twofold. In the less known form it is alleged that it was inflicted on him for an unnatural act against the daughter of his brother Salmoneus. The better known form has more of the characteristics of a genuine folk-tale. Zeus, conceiving an illicit passion for Aigina, the daughter of Asopos, had seized her and hidden her from her father. Knowing the great wisdom of Sisyphos, Asopos came to him and promised that he would provide the lofty hill of Akrokorinthos with a spring of pure water, if he would tell him where Aigina was to be found. Sisyphos promptly disclosed her hiding-place as the island of Oinone (thereafter known as Aigina), but Zeus, learning of this deed of Sisyphos, in a rage consigned him to Hades and bound Death about his neck. The wily Corinthian, however, turned the tables on Death and shackled him so effectively that no mortal on earth could die. In the meantime Merope, the wife of Sisyphos, was withholding from the dead the libations customarily offered to them, and thus finally forced Hades to release her husband and to permit him to ascend to the upper world. It was Hades' hope that the husband and wife would confer concerning the renewal of the libations; but he was destined to be sadly disappointed, for Sisyphos forgot to return below and remained in Corinth pursuing his former round of toils and pleasures. Hades did not gain possession of him until he was carried off by sheer old age, and to prevent a recurrence of his trickery Hades imposed on him the task at which Odysseus saw him toiling. "Yea, and I beheld Sisyphos in strong torment," said Odysseus to the Phaiakians, "grasping a monstrous stone with both his hands. He was pressing thereat with hands and feet and trying to roll the stone upward toward the brow of the hill. But oft as he was about to hurl it over the top, the weight would drive him back, so once again to the plain rolled the stone, the shameless thing. And he once more kept heaving and straining, and the sweat the while was pouring down his limbs, and the dust rose upward from his head." [13]

Many explanations of the derivation of the name Sisyphos have been offered, but none has any claim to reliability, the most popular being one that makes it a reduplication of the base of *σοφός* ("wise").[14] The significance of the personality of Sisyphos is just as obscure; he has been shown to be now the restless tide, now a god of light, now a personification of craftiness; while the stone is allegorically interpreted as a symbol of the futility of human endeavour.

Glaukos. — Glaukos of Potniai, a town of southern Boiotia, was said to be the son of Sisyphos or of Poseidon. He became king of Corinth and was famous for the swiftness of his horses in the chariot-races. In one type of the legend which concerns him it is related that his steeds, becoming mad as he was driving them in the funeral games of Pelias, turned on him and tore him to pieces. Causes of their madness are variously given — the deliberate act of Aphrodite, their drinking from a sacred spring, or their eating of a magic herb or of human flesh. In later years when horses became frightened while racing during the Isthmian games, people said it was because of the spirit of Glaukos which haunted the course. Another type of the legend says that he met his death in a collision of chariots at Olympia. Doubtless this Glaukos is a transplantation of the Glaukos of Anthedon in Boiotia.

Bellerophon. — By his wife, Eurymede (or Eurynome), Glaukos begat a son Bellerophon, who, having shed the blood of a kinsman, though unintentionally, fled from his homeland to the court of Proitos in Argos. There Queen Stheneboia was taken with a shameful passion and made advances to him, but Bellerophon utterly spurned her, whereupon, full of resentment, she slandered him before her husband, representing that she was the one sinned against rather than the sinner.[15] Proitos believed her story and sent Bellerophon away to the land of Lykia across the Aegean Sea, giving him a letter to King Iobates, the father of Stheneboia, requesting the monarch to devise some means of putting Bellerophon out of the way. Accordingly Iobates commissioned him to go forth and kill the Chimaira, the issue of Typhon and Echidna, a dire creature part lion, part dragon, and part goat, which was devastating the land and with her breath of fire was consuming all those who ventured to attack her. Undaunted by the danger, Bellerophon mounted Pegasos, the winged horse, flew high above the monster, and shooting down upon her laid her low, after which he returned unhurt to Iobates. Still determined to carry out his plan, the king sent him out again, first against the Solymoi, and later against the Amazons, but once more Bellerophon came back unharmed, having not only accomplished his tasks but also having slain a band of young Lykians who had laid in wait for him. Disarmed by admiration, Iobates now ceased his plotting against Bellerophon's life, and, revealing to him the contents of Proitos's letter, asked him to take up his abode in Lykia, which he gladly did. Later he wedded the princess Philonoë, and on Iobates' death came to the throne. Elated by his successes, it is said, he essayed to ride Pegasos to heaven, but fell from his mount at a great height and was killed.

The Chimaira seems to have been a storm-divinity who acquired her development in the primitive belief that wind-storms originate about volcanic heights.

Of the birth of Pegasos we have already spoken. The credulous Hesiod tells us that he derived his name from having been born near the springs (πηγαί[16]) of Okeanos. It was through a miracle that he came into the hands of Bellerophon, for in a dream Athene appeared to the young man and gave him a bridle which he found at his side when he awoke. In gratitude he erected an altar to the goddess and then approached Pegasos, over whom the bridle seemed to cast such a spell that the horse was easily subdued. Another story describes Bellerophon as finding Pegasos drinking at the spring of Peirene on the Akrokorinthos, and as catching and mounting him by main strength. After the death of his rider, the horse, being of divine descent, flew upward to the ancient stables of Zeus where he was harnessed to the thunder-car. Once he returned to earth, the poets say, and on Helikon, the Boiotian mountain of the Muses, created the spring of Hippoukrene ("Horse's Fount") with a blow of his hoof. Since then he has been associated with the Muses and their arts.

The development of Pegasos as a mythological figure is one of the most interesting, and is comparatively easy to trace. In the Homeric epic Bellerophon achieved his exploits without him, but by the time of Hesiod the two were inseparably linked, Pegasos having by that time a general and not merely a local import in myth. Not until Pindar do we find any demonstrable evidence of his being endowed with wings. A theory has been advanced to the effect that his mythological growth was due to the influences of the winged horses of Assyrian art which reached the Hellenes through the medium of the Phoinikians, in which event the rule that art types tend to take their forms from myths would be reversed. Perhaps Pegasos originally stood for the rain-bearing clouds which rise to heaven and bring the lightning and the thunder.

The Corinthians had other tales to explain the genesis of their famous springs. Peirene was at first a woman who was changed into the spring through the tears which she shed for her son accidentally slain by the arrows of Artemis; and the spring into which Glauke threw herself to quench the flames caused by Medeia's drugs was afterward known by her name.

CHAPTER III

MYTHS OF THE NORTHERN MAINLAND

I. BOIOTIA AND EUBOIA

NEXT to Argolis Boiotia supplied the largest body of locally developed myths; and when we say Boiotia we must understand the inclusion of Euboia, for mythologically the two are not severed by the Strait of Euripos. It must be borne in mind, however, that the legends of the island never attained to that degree of literary organization which has immortalized the stories centring, for instance, about Thebes. The oldest cults and myths of both Euboia and Boiotia can be traced back to Crete, principally through the formation of doubles of the personages of Cretan legend, so that, for instance, the Euboian Arethousa was a copy of a Cretan model; Europe appears in Boiotia as Io, and Glaukos of Anthedon duplicates the son of Minos. The extent to which these Cretan importations were changed by Phoinikian and other allied Oriental influences is one of the many unsettled points of Greek mythology, but the decline of the old Boiotian states and the rise of Argos were admittedly responsible for a large measure of modification.

The First Inhabitants of Boiotia. — After the flood of Deukalion, Zeus, uniting with Iodama ("Healer of the People"), a form of Europe, became the father of Thebe, a spring-nymph of Boiotia, whom he gave in marriage to Ogygos, the autochthonous king of the Ektenes, said to be the first inhabitants of the land. When the entire people of the Ektenes perished by a plague, their country was occupied by the Hyantes and the Aonians, who called it Aonia. Later, however, the name was changed to Boiotia after Boiotos, the son of Poseidon, or,

PLATE XV

Dirke Bound to the Bull

The artists of this group (popularly known as the Farnese Bull) have followed the text of the myth in laying the scene of the episode on Mount Kithairon, which they have not merely indicated by the depiction of rocks and crags, but also personified in the small human figure in the right foreground. Amphion (identified by his lyre) is striving with all his strength to subdue a powerful bull so that his brother Zethos can pass a rope, attached to the struggling creature's horns, around the body of Dirke. Their mother, Antiope, a complacent spectator, stands lance in hand in the right background. From a Greco-Roman marble group by Apollonios and Tauriskos (end of second century B.C.), in Naples (Brunn-Bruckmann, *Denkmäler griechischer und römischer Sculptur*, No. 367). See pp. 43–44.

as some allege, after the cow (βοῦς) which Kadmos followed to the site of Thebes. With certain allowances, the latter derivation is probably nearer the truth than the other.

Amphion and Zethos. — The story of Amphion and Zethos, though woven into that of Kadmos, is in origin independent of it and is therefore better told separately. Antiope, the mother of these heroes, was reputed to be the daughter of Asopos, the river-god, or of Nykteus ("Night"). Charmed by the attentions of Zeus, she yielded herself to him, but when her father became aware of her condition she fled to Sikyon, where she became the wife of a certain Epopeus. Nykteus, overwhelmed with the disgrace which his daughter had brought upon him, took his own life after first requesting his brother Lykos ("Light") to punish Antiope and her husband. When some time had elapsed Lykos proceeded to Sikyon, slew Epopeus, and brought his niece a captive to Thebes. On the homeward journey, however, she gave birth to twin sons, whom she exposed on the mountain-side where they were afterward found by a shepherd who reared them to manhood, one of them, Zethos, becoming a herdsman and hunter, and the other, Amphion, a skilled player on the lyre. In the meantime Lykos and his wife Dirke cruelly maltreated Antiope, but by a desperate effort she succeeded in escaping from Thebes and made her way to the fastnesses of Mount Kithairon, where she was hospitably received by her own sons, who, of course, failed to recognize her. By chance Dirke, coming to the mountain to perform some rites to Dionysos, discovered Antiope and in vindictive fury commanded the shepherds to tie her to a mad bull which, when loosed, would carry her to a horrible death. Just in time Amphion and Zethos learned that the unhappy woman was their mother. Catching the bull, they released Antiope and bound Dirke by the hair in her place, afterward picking up the mangled body and casting it into a spring which has borne Dirke's name ever since. The young men then went to Thebes, killed Lykos, took the chief authority, and built the walls of the city, Amphion charming the stones into their places by means of the sweet strains of his lyre, the gift of the Muses.

According to one account, Zethos married Thebe, from whom the city got its name; but according to another, his wife was Aëdon, who bore him a son Itylos, whom, by a mere chance, she killed. Overcome by grief, Zethos pined away and died, while Aëdon was given the form of the nightingale and endowed with those plaintive notes with which she may yet be heard mourning for her son's untimely death. Amphion became the husband of Niobe, the daughter of Tantalos, and a family of many sons and daughters blessed their union. In her maternal pride Niobe boasted that she, a mortal, had brought into the world more children than Leto, and this so incensed Leto's children, Apollo and Artemis, that Apollo slew the sons of Niobe as they were hunting on Kithairon, while Artemis killed the daughters beneath their mother's roof. Niobe fled from Thebes to her father in Asia Minor, and there

> ". . . for her sons' death wept out life and breath
> And, dry with grief, was turned into a stone." [1]

What is said to be her form is still to be seen on the cliffs of Mount Sipylos.

Kadmos. — Agenor, a great-grandson of Io, established himself in Phoinikia, where he had a daughter named Europe, whom Zeus one day carried away to Crete by force. On her disappearance Agenor sent his wife and sons throughout the neighbouring lands in quest of her and ordered them not to return without her, but all failed in their errand, and, fearful of Agenor's anger, they resolved never to go back home, Phoinix settling in a district of Phoinikia, Kilix in Kilikia, and Thasos, Kadmos, and their mother Telephassa in Thrace. After the death of Telephassa, Kadmos felt free to continue his search for Europe, and going to Delphoi he inquired of the oracle concerning her. The god commanded him to cease worrying over his sister and to turn his thoughts into another channel, bidding him to follow a heifer which he would find outside the shrine and to establish a city on the spot where she would first lie down to rest. In obedience to the divine command Kadmos journeyed after the animal across Phokis until at length she sought repose beside a hill in the heart of Boiotia, and there he founded Thebes.

Desiring to sacrifice the cow to Athene, Kadmos dispatched a number of his men to draw water for the rites from the spring Areia, but most of them were killed by the dragon, the issue of Ares, which guarded the water, whereupon Kadmos himself slew the beast and at the suggestion of Athene scattered the teeth broadcast over the earth as a farmer strews his grain. From the teeth sprang a host of armed men who were called Spartoi ("Scattered") from the strange manner of their birth. At the sight of these warriors suddenly gathering about him, Kadmos was stricken with fear and began to hurl stones at them; and they, thinking that the missiles were thrown by their fellows, murderously set upon one another until only five of them were left alive. For his part in this tragedy Kadmos was bound in servitude to Ares for eight years, but at the end of this period Athene bestowed the kingship upon him and with the surviving Spartoi he began to build up the city of Thebes. Zeus gave him in marriage Harmonia, the daughter of Ares and Aphrodite, and all the gods came down from Olympos to attend the nuptials and brought with them rare and costly gifts, Kadmos's own presents to his bride being a robe and the necklace, wrought originally by Hephaistos, which Zeus had formerly given to Europe. To Kadmos and Harmonia were born a son, Polydoros, and four daughters, Semele, Ino, Agave, and Autonoë.

The Daughters of Kadmos; Semele. — Having won the favour and love of Zeus, Semele secured from him a promise that he would grant her whatever she might ask, and prompted by Hera who appeared before her in the guise of her nurse, she requested that her lover would show himself to her in the form in which he had paid court to Hera. Bound by his promise, the Olympian entered her chamber in a chariot amid the flashing of lightning and the roaring of thunder, but, being a mortal, Semele could not endure this terrible wooing and died. From her body Zeus took their unborn child and sewed it in his thigh, where it remained for three months, at the end of which time he loosed the stitches and brought it forth to the light. The child, who was none other than the god Dionysos, was entrusted to Ino and her husband Athamas, a son of Aiolos, to be reared. For their care of him the vindictive Hera visited on them a plague of madness, but Zeus saved Dionysos by changing him into a kid and secretly conveying him to the nymphs of Mount Nysa in Asia, who in after years were rewarded with a place among the constellations under the name of the Hyades.

Ino. — When the madness came upon Athamas he imagined that his elder son Learchos was a deer and killed him, while Ino, with their younger son Melikertes in her arms, leaped from the Molourian rocks into the waters of the Gulf of Megara. The body of the child was washed ashore at the Isthmus, and the Isthmian games were instituted in his honour by Sisyphos. After their death both mother and son used to give aid to those endangered by storms at sea, and sailors knew the one as Leukothea, the "White Sea-Spirit," and the other as Palaimon, the "Storm-Lord."

Autonoë. — Autonoë was married to Aristaios and bore him a son Aktaion ("Gleaming One") who, under the training of Cheiron, the Centaur, became an ardent huntsman. One day when engaged in the chase on Kithairon he chanced to see the goddess Artemis bathing in the spring Parthenios ("Maidenhood"), but as soon as the goddess discovered his presence she changed him into a stag and instilling madness into his fifty hounds sent them in hot pursuit of him. They caught him and rent him in pieces. Then, not knowing what they had done, they wandered over hill and dale searching for their master and found satisfaction only when they saw his portrait before the cave of Cheiron.

Agave. — The remaining daughter of Kadmos, Agave, became the wife of Echion, one of the Spartoi, and bore to him a son Pentheus, who in the course of time received the kingship of Thebes. During his reign Dionysos returned to Thebes after a long period of wandering in many lands of the east whither he had been driven by a frenzy which Hera had inflicted on him for his discovery of the vine, and so great a power over the women of Thebes did the god come to possess that they all left their homes and betook themselves to Kithairon to celebrate his rites. Pentheus treated this "barbarous dissonance of Bacchus and his revellers" with the utmost contempt, until, rashly approaching the women votaries, he got a glimpse of his mother performing some secret ceremony, whereupon, with vision distorted by a sort of divine frenzy, she mistook him for a deer, and, rushing upon him, tore him asunder.

Sorrowing over the evils which had befallen their family, Kadmos and Harmonia abdicated the throne and withdrew to the land of the Illyrians. By force of arms they ruled among these people for a time and were then sent by Zeus to live forever in the Elysian Fields, while their son Polydoros remained at Thebes wielding his father's sceptre.

The chief import of the legend of Amphion and Zethos is that it affords evidence of the great antiquity of Thebes. Even at the remotely early time of the legend's creation men had utterly forgotten the circumstances of the building of the city's defences, else this would never have been explained by the miraculous power of a lyre. That the story of Kadmos contains anything of genuine historical value is far from receiving general assent. Some read in it the substantially true account of the actual settlement of Thebes by Phoinikians who came thither direct from Phoinikia. Others maintain that, on the contrary, no sea-faring folk would have founded a city situated as far inland as was Thebes; moreover, they point out that the Phoinikian theory was unknown in Greek literature before the fifth century B.C. Those who occupy a middle ground are probably closer to the actual facts; they believe that at some very early date Thebes had extensive connexions with Phoinikians, but they cannot accept them as primitive.[2] The legend of Melikertes seems to have grown up about the cult of the drowned, but the interpretation of others of this group of myths will be more appropriately discussed elsewhere.[3]

The Sorrows of the House of Labdakos; Oidipous. — When Polydoros died, he left a son Labdakos who was killed shortly after he became king, some people believing him to have been slain by a god for much the same kind of sin as that of which Pentheus had been guilty. His son Laios was banished from the realm by Amphion, but on Amphion's death he returned to assume his inherited rights. Dreadful calamities awaited him and his descendants, for he was under a curse — and to the ancients curses were as inevitable as the decrees of Fate. During his exile he had carried off Chrysippos, the son of Pelops, and Pelops had solemnly cursed him with childlessness, or, should he have a child, with death at the child's hand. As ruler of Thebes he married Iokaste (Epikaste), the daughter of Menoikeus, who brought him a son, thus foiling the first alternative of Pelops's curse. In order to avert the second the parents pierced the babe's ankles and gave him to a herdsman to be exposed in the wilds of Kithairon, but it happened that he was found by a shepherd of King Polybos of Corinth who took him to the queen, Periboia.

The child, who was called Oidipous ("Swollen Foot") from the swollen condition of his ankles, grew to manhood in the court of Corinth, where he was the strongest and most athletic of the youths of his circle and aroused the envy of many, who thus found occasion to taunt him with his uncertain birth. The innuendoes perplexed him, and being unable to induce Periboia to throw any light on the matter of his parentage,

PLATE XVI

The Death of Pentheus

The artist has been true to the Theban myth in making the rocky summit of Kithairon the theatre of this tragedy. Pentheus, nude and defenceless, is being beaten to the ground by the onslaught of three wild votaries of Dionysos, evidently the surviving daughters of Kadmos — Agave, Ino, and Autonoë. The fiercest of the three who attacks Pentheus with a *thyrsos* and tears out his hair, is probably Agave, his unnatural mother, but the other two cannot be definitely distinguished by name. In the upper corners of the background are two Maenads brandishing whips and torches. From a wall-painting in the House of the Vettii, Pompeii (Hermann-Bruckmann, *Denkmäler der Malerei des Altertums*, No. 42). See p. 47.

he repaired to Delphoi and made inquiry of the oracle, which warned him never to enter his native country, else he would kill his father and marry his mother. Instead, therefore, of returning to Corinth and to his supposed parents, Oidipous harnessed his car and drove eastward through Phokis. On a narrow road he met Laios, his real father, to whom the royal herald bade him yield place. For his refusal one of his horses was cut down, and in retaliation Oidipous killed Laios and the herald, after which he proceeded on his way to Thebes.

When the news of the death of Laios came to the city, Kreon, the brother of Iokaste, was appointed king. During his reign a great disaster came upon Thebes, for Hera sent the Sphinx, another of the horrible issue of Typhon and Echidna, to destroy the citizens. This monster had the face of a woman, the body and feet and tail of a lion, and the wings of a bird; and her strange weapon of destruction was a riddle which she would put to passers-by, devouring those who failed to give the right answer. The riddle was this: "What is it which, having but one voice, is first four-footed, then two-footed, and is at the last three-footed?" After many had perished in their unfortunate attempts to solve the riddle, Kreon proclaimed that the wife and the kingdom of Laios would be given to the one who should succeed. To the question of the Sphinx Oidipous replied: "The creature is man, for in infancy he crawls on all fours, in mature years he walks upright on two feet, and in old age goes as it were on three by the aid of a cane." When she heard these words, the Sphinx cast herself down from the cliffs, and Oidipous received the promised rewards. At last he had fulfilled the two conditions of the oracle.

For many years the life and reign of Oidipous were happy, and through his marriage with Iokaste he had two sons, Polyneikes and Eteokles, and two daughters, Antigone and Ismene. At length, however, pestilence and famine wasted both land and people, and when the oracles were consulted, their answers revealed his blood relationship to his queen. Though their sin had been committed in ignorance, Iokaste hanged herself, in the anguish of remorse, and Oidipous put out his own eyes. The Thebans banished him from their city, and as he departed his sons made no effort either to help him or to defend him. For this base ingratitude he called down bitter curses on their heads from which they were thenceforward to suffer; for the curses of parents on children were the direst of all. With the faithful Antigone he went to Kolonos in Attike, where he became a suppliant at the shrine of the Eumenides, the avenging spirits of the dead. Theseus of Athens welcomed him and afforded him a home in which to end his days in peace. After a number of days Ismene joined the two exiles. When Oidipous knew that his end was near, he called his daughters to his side to perform for him the last rites for the dying, and, taking them tenderly in his arms, he said:

"My children, on this day ye cease to have
A father. All my days are spent and gone,
And ye no more shall lead your wretched life,
Caring for me. Hard was it, that I know,
My children! Yet one word is strong to loose,
Although alone, the burden of these toils,
For *love* in larger store ye could not have
From any than from him who standeth here,
Of whom bereaved ye now shall live your life." [4]

After uttering these words he passed away, another victim of the far-reaching curse of Pelops.

The friends of Oidipous desired to bury his body in Thebes, but the Thebans, remembering the sufferings brought upon them by the much-cursed dynasty of Laios, forbade them to do so. They interred it, however, in another place in Boiotia, but when this, too, became afflicted with calamities, its citizens ordered the removal of the corpse. Taking it to Eteonos, the friends ignorantly laid it in a shrine of Demeter. When the people of the locality discovered this, they inquired of the goddess what they should do, and received the reply: "Remove not the suppliant of the god." So they left the bones of Oidipous where they were and gave the shrine the new name of Oidipodeion, a name which distinguished it for centuries.

The Sons of Oidipous, and the Seven against Thebes. — After the banishment of Oidipous Kreon became regent for the youthful princes, Polyneikes and Eteokles. As soon as they took the power into their own hands, they determined on an arrangement by which they would rule singly in alternate years, but this agreement, like all of its kind, was not proof against the great weakness of the human heart, the lust for autocratic dominion. Eteokles, it is said, refused to relinquish his authority at the end of a term, and a bitter feud resulted, the consequence being that Polyneikes was exiled and went to Argos, taking with him the wedding-robe and necklace of Harmonia, which had apparently become the symbols of the kingship in Thebes. In Argos he met Tydeus of Aitolia, also an exile from his native land, and, impelled by the combative spirit which marked the family of Laios, engaged him in a duel. Adrastos, the king of Argos, hearing the noise of the conflict came out of his palace to learn what it might mean, and seeing that the shield of one of the combatants bore the device of a boar's head while that of the other was marked with a lion, he recognized the fulfilment of a prophecy which had said that he would marry his two daughters to a boar and a lion. So he made Polyneikes and Tydeus his sons-in-law and pledged them his aid in restoring them to their kingdoms. One form of the story relates that Polyneikes had left Thebes of his own free will in order to avoid the consequences of his father's curses, and that he returned later at Eteokles' request when word of the death of Oidipous reached Thebes. It was then, this version states, that the quarrel began which resulted in the expulsion of Polyneikes and in his affiliation with Adrastos.

Adrastos, planning first of all to restore Polyneikes to his rights, called the chieftains and warriors of the land to his colours. Among those summoned was Amphiaraos ("Doubly Holy"), but, inasmuch as he was a seer, he foresaw the ultimate failure of the expedition and the death of all its leaders, and refused to go. Polyneikes, however, had learned of a pact between him and Adrastos to decide all their mutual differences by an appeal to Eriphyle, the wife of Amphiaraos, and taking advantage of the feminine love of personal adornment he gave her the necklace of Harmonia and beguiled her to decide in favour of her husband's adherence to the cause of Adrastos. Full of resentment at being thus forced to join the expedition, Amphiaraos before his departure enjoined his sons to slay their mother and avenge his inevitable death.

The army set out under Adrastos and seven generals, one of whom was Polyneikes. On their way they halted at Nemea to obtain water, and there Hypsipyle, a slave woman of King Lykourgos, left the ruler's infant son whom she was tending and led them to a spring. While she was gone a serpent killed the child, and Amphiaraos declared that this portended how the army would fare. Burying the infant's body, the Argives instituted the Nemean games at his grave, and ever afterward "the solemn funereal origin of the games was kept before the mind by the dun-colored raiment worn by the umpires and emphasized by the cypress grove which in antiquity surrounded the temple." [5]

Marching to the walls of Thebes, Adrastos sent a herald to demand that Eteokles hand over the kingdom to his brother according to their agreement. Meeting with refusal, he divided his host into seven parts under the seven leaders and stationed each before one of the seven great gates of the city, within which the Theban army was similarly arranged. Before giving battle Eteokles inquired of the blind seer, Teiresias, what the fortunes of war would be, and when the answer was given that if Kreon's son, Menoikeus, were to sacrifice himself to Ares, the Theban arms would be victorious, the young man, with noble devotion, killed himself before the city. Nevertheless, victory did not come immediately to the Thebans, since they were compelled to retire before the enemy within the fortifications. One of the Argive leaders, Kapaneus, in the ardour of pursuit attempted to scale the walls by means of a ladder, but for his temerity Zeus struck him down with a thunderbolt. This was the beginning of the Argive rout and slaughter. When many had been slain, both sides agreed that the fate of the city should be determined by a duel between Polyneikes and Eteokles. They fought, but since they killed one another, they left the city's future still uncertain. After this the fighting became irregular and promiscuous, fortune steadily going against the Argives until, at last, of all their commanders Adrastos alone survived, he owing his escape not to his skill but to the speed of his divinely born horse Areion. Amphiaraos had been pursued by one of the enemy, but before a missile could strike him he had been swallowed up in the earth, chariot, horses, driver, and all, and was granted immortality, while on the spot where he disappeared the city of Harma ("Chariot") was founded.

With the death of Eteokles Kreon assumed the powers of king, and from his palace he sent out a decree that the bodies of the fallen foes of Thebes should be left without due funeral rites. This placed Antigone, the sister of Polyneikes, in a grievous dilemma. To forego the rites would mean that her brother's soul would forever suffer in unrest and would haunt the places and persons it had known in life; on the other hand, to perform these ceremonies would be disloyalty to the state. Guided by the law of the gods, she defied the law of the king, and gave rest to her brother's soul. Kreon had her seized and sealed alive in a cavern, despite the pleadings of her betrothed lover, his own son Haimon. Under the denunciations of Teiresias, the king repented of his deed, but it was too late! When the cavern was opened, Antigone was already dead, and at the entrance lay the body of Haimon, slain by his own hand. At the news of the tragedy Eurydike, the queen, hanged herself, and Kreon was left alone in life, a victim partly of his own obstinacy and partly of the curse of Pelops.

Adrastos, too, felt the same burden of duty to his dead that weighed upon Antigone. Unable to secure the bodies of the Argives owing to Kreon's mandate, he called Theseus of Athens to his aid, and an Athenian army, capturing Thebes, secured the Argive dead. As the body of Kapaneus lay on the pyre, his wife Evadne threw herself into the flames and was consumed with her husband.

The Epigonoi. — After ten years the sons of the seven Argive generals marshalled another host against Thebes to avenge the death of their fathers. They were known in story as the Epigonoi, or "Later-Born," and the oracle of Apollo foretold that victory would rest with them if they could obtain Alkmaion, the son of Amphiaraos, as leader. Thersandros, the son of Polyneikes, repeated his father's strategy, and by means of Harmonia's robe bribed Eriphyle to enlist her son's aid. Under Alkmaion the army marched to Thebes, sacked the surrounding villages, and drove the city's defenders back behind their walls. Counselled by Teiresias that defence was fruitless, the Thebans evacuated the city with their wives and children, and founded the new city of Hestiaia, while the conquering Argives entered the gates, razed the walls, and collecting the booty gave the best portion of it to the Delphian Apollo, the patron of their victory.

Alkmaion. — Alkmaion was now free to carry out his father's last request, but hesitating to do so horrible a deed he sought the advice of Apollo, who bade him not to stay his hand. Feeling that he had right on his side, he slew Eriphyle, his mother, perhaps with the aid of his brother Amphilochos, but forthwith an avenging Erinys, or Fury, began to hound him and soon drove him mad, so that he wandered from place to place until at last he came to the home of Phegeus in Psophis, by whom he was purified of the guilt of shedding kindred blood. Later on he received Phegeus's daughter Arsinoë in marriage, giving her the fatal robe and necklace of Harmonia, but it turned out that his purification was not complete, for his

PLATE XVII

The Departure of Amphiaraos

Amphiaraos, fully armed, is reluctantly mounting his chariot beside his driver, Baton, who stands reins in hand ready to urge his four horses forward. Around the chariot and the horses the kinsfolk and friends of the seer are gathered to bid him farewell. By the outside column of the palace façade to the left stands Eriphyle holding the fatal necklace. The boy seated on the shoulders of the woman in front of her and the other boy close to Amphiaraos are probably Alkmaion and Amphilochos, who later avenged their father's untimely death. From a Corinthian *krater* of about 600 B.C., in Berlin (Furtwängler-Reichhold, *Griechische Vasenmalerei*, No. 121). See pp. 51–52.

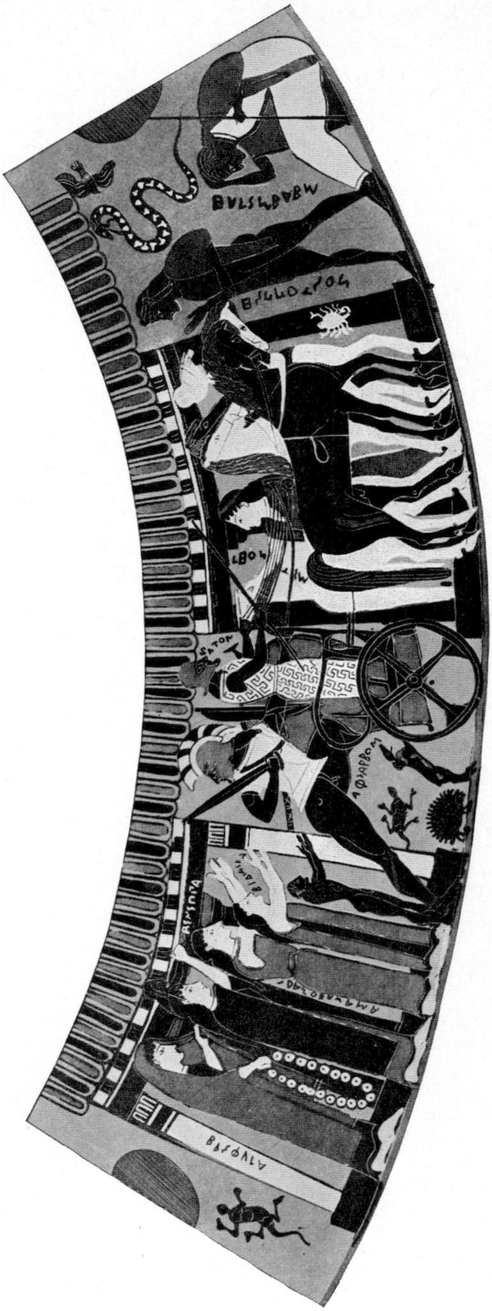

presence brought sterility to the soil of Psophis. Banished from there, he roamed about until he reached the sources of the river Acheloös, where he was cleansed once and for all and wedded to Kalliroë, the daughter of Acheloös. After some years of marriage his wife refused to live longer with him unless he would get for her the famous robe and necklace, and to gratify her whim he set out to secure them by craft from his former wife, but was waylaid and killed by her brothers. His death was soon avenged, for his and Kalliroës' sons, Amphoteros and Akarnan, came to Psophis, slew Phegeus and his family, and after depositing the wedding-gifts with the god of Delphoi, proceeded westward and founded the country to be known after one of them as Akarnania.

The collective substance of this series of myths concerning the house of Labdakos apparently points to a historic fact that the early period of Thebes' existence was marked by a number of disturbances and calamities in the ruling families. The interpretations of the sundry details are so numerous and conflicting that one cannot treat of them adequately here. Suffice it to say that the most modern school tends more and more to explain them as based on fact. For instance, this school would say that the Sphinx stands for a league of pirates and brigands who harassed Thebes and threatened its very existence until crushed by some Theban leader; and it would also take Pausanias at his word when he says that he saw all seven of the ancient gates, although he describes only three of them.[6]

II. AITOLIA

The Founding of Aitolia. — Endymion, the grandson of Aiolos, led the Aiolians from Thessaly and established them in the land of Elis on the western side of the Peloponnesos. Wedding a nymph Iphianassa, he had a son Aitolos who killed Apis, the Argive, and fled across the Gulf of Corinth to the mountainous country of the Kouretes, where he continued his murderous career, and, killing his hosts, took possession of their land and named it Aitolia. In the course of time he had two sons, Pleuron and Kalydon, who gave their names to the two chief cities of Aitolia, and their children and their children's children intermarried until finally two cousins, Oineus and Thestios, were supreme in the country's councils.

Meleagros and Atalante. — Oineus ruled over Kalydon and took Althaia, the daughter of Thestios, as his wife. Their union was blessed by a son Meleagros, and although some said that his true father was Ares, they probably judged his parentage from his exploits with the spear. When Meleagros was only seven days old, the Moirai prophesied that he would meet his death as soon as the brand on the hearth should be consumed. Thereupon, to prevent her child's untimely end, Althaia took the faggot then blazing on the hearth, extinguished it, and hid it away in a chest. Many years afterward at harvest-time Oineus, while offering sacrifices of the first-fruits, in some way overlooked Artemis, who, embittered at the slight, sent a huge boar to ravage the tilled land and to destroy the men and herds of Aitolia. Of themselves the Aitolians were unable to kill the beast, and Oineus accordingly summoned the mightiest spearmen of the Greeks to engage in a great hunt, promising the skin of the boar as a reward to the one who should succeed in slaying it. From all parts of Hellas the warriors came — Kastor and Polydeukes, Idas and Lynkeus from Lakonia and Messenia; Theseus from Athens; Admetos, Iason, and Peleus from Thessaly; Meleagros and the four sons of Thestios from Aitolia; and, most conspicuous of all, the huntress Atalante of Arkadia.

This Atalante was of doubtful parentage, if the conflicting statements of the myths mean anything, but she was generally said to be the daughter of Iasos and Klymene. So great had been her father's disappointment that she was not a boy that he exposed her in the forest shortly after her birth, and there she was nursed by a bear until she was discovered by some huntsmen who brought her up and trained her in the chase. When she became a woman she spent her time hunting amid the hills and valleys of Arkadia, and kept her life as chaste as that of Artemis herself. With her bow she had slain two Centaurs who had made a lustful attack on her, and at the funeral games of Pelias she had shown her skill and strength by throwing Peleus in wrestling. Made confident by these exploits, she appeared among the heroes as a contestant for the great boar's skin.

For nine days Oineus entertained the assembled huntsmen in Kalydon, and on the tenth the hunt began. In a short time the boar had mangled and killed a number of his pursuers. The first blow he had received was from the spear of Atalante, but it did little more than graze him, and the mortal thrust was reserved for the weapon of Meleagros. When at last the beast had fallen, Meleagros flayed it and took the skin as his prize; but his uncles, the sons of Thestios, who in the contest represented the Kouretes, or old Aitolian stock living in Pleuron, grudged him his lawful gain and stirred up a quarrel with him, which resulted in pitched war between the people of Kalydon and the people of Pleuron. Meleagros showed himself to be as great a warrior as he was a hunter, and among his many enemies whom he killed was one of his uncles. Appalled at the act, Althaia imprecated curses on his head, and sullenly Meleagros retired from the strife to his wife Kleopatra, allowing his people to fight their battle alone. In the appeal of Phoinix to the angry Achilles in the *Iliad* this part of the story is forcefully told.

"Now was the din of foemen about their gates quickly risen, and a noise of battering of towers; and the elders of the Aitolians sent the best of the gods' priests and besought him [i. e. Meleagros] to come forth and save them, with promise of a mighty gift; to wit, they bade him, where the plain of lovely Kalydon was fattest, to choose him out a fair demesne of fifty plough-gates, the half thereof vine-land and the half open plough-land, to be cut from out the plain. And old knightly Oineus prayed him instantly, and stood upon the threshold of his high-roofed chamber, and shook the morticed doors to beseech his son; him too his sisters and his lady mother prayed instantly — but he denied them yet more — instantly too his comrades prayed, that were nearest him and dearest of all men. Yet even so persuaded they not his heart within his breast, until his chamber was now hotly battered and the Kouretes were climbing upon the towers and firing the great city. Then did his fair-girdled wife pray Meleagros with lamentation, and told him all the woes that come on men whose city is taken; the warriors are slain, and the city is wasted of fire, and the children and the deep-girdled women are led captive of strangers. And his soul was stirred to hear the grievous tale, and he went his way and donned his glittering armour. So he saved the Aitolians from the evil day, obeying his own will; but they paid him not now the gifts many and gracious; yet nevertheless he drave away destruction."[7] In this fray he slew the remaining three sons of Thestios and then himself was killed. At his death his mother and his wife hanged themselves, and his sisters as they mourned over his body were changed into guinea-fowl.

There is another and later version of the sequel of the boar-hunt. In this, Meleagros, fascinated by the charms of Atalante, gave the skin to her, though his uncles openly resented its bestowal on a woman, especially on one outside the pale of their own family. Finally they seized Atalante and wrested her prize from her, but in chivalrous anger Meleagros set upon them and made them pay the penalty with their lives. Grieving for the loss of her brothers, Althaia took the charred brand from the chest and burned it, and Meleagros died immediately after.

The Kalydonian hunt was not the last of the exploits of Atalante. According to one story, she joined the heroes in the voyage of the Argo, and in one of their battles she was wounded, but was healed by Medeia. Another legend relates that she desired to go on the voyage, but was restrained by Iason. After a number of years Atalante found her father, but when he rather abruptly tried to exercise a parent's prerogative in marrying her to a suitor, she fled from him to a refuge of her own choosing. This place afforded a straight level stretch of ground of about the same length as a stadium, and thither she invited her wooers to repair. One by one she challenged them to a race, stipulating that the man whom she should overtake would be killed and that the one overtaking her should wed her. All those who ventured to match their speed with hers lost their lives, until a certain Melanion came to the course. Very astutely he had brought with him golden apples of Aphrodite, and as he ran he cast them behind him. In stooping to pick them up Atalante lost so much time that Melanion won the race and a bride. Once they were wedded they went away toward Boiotia to share the joys and freedom of the hunt together, but their happiness was short-lived, for in the flush of success Melanion had forgotten to thank Aphrodite for her help. So, as they rested in a grotto near a temple of Kybele, the goddess threw a spell upon them both by which they became lions and were forbidden to know the joys of mutual love.

All the outstanding characteristics of Atalante, her skill with the bow and in the chase, her chastity, and her swiftness of foot, together with her early association with the bear, go to reveal her as Artemis in human form.

CHAPTER IV

MYTHS OF CRETE AND ATTIKE

I. CRETE

EUROPE. — Europe, as we have already seen in the first part of the legend of Kadmos, was the daughter of Agenor (or, by some accounts, of Phoinix). One day, when she was plucking flowers with her friends in a beautiful meadow of Phoinikia, Zeus spied her from afar and became so enamoured of her that, in order to deceive the watchful Hera, he took the form of a grazing bull and approached the happy group of maidens. Drawing close to Europe, he cast a charm over her by his gentle manner, so that she fearlessly stroked and petted him and led her comrades in playing merry pranks with him. Further emboldened, she climbed upon his back, endeavouring to lure some of her companions after her, but before they could come near, the bull with a bound leaped into the sea and swam away with her. In answer to her tearful pleadings Zeus at length revealed himself and his love. Continuing westward across the deep, he brought her to the island of Crete, where he wedded her and begat the heroes Minos, Rhadamanthys, and Sarpedon, while in the meantime the vain search for Europe prosecuted by her mother and brothers resulted in the final dispersal of the family of Agenor into various parts of the Mediterranean and Aegean.

In the course of a few years the love of Zeus waned and he abandoned Europe to Asterios, king of the Cretans, who reared her children as his own. After the sons had reached adult years, they quarrelled amongst themselves over a beautiful youth named Miletos, and when Minos triumphed over Sarpedon,

PLATE XVIII

Europe and the Bull

The painter has as it were photographed Europe and her companions caressing the bull at the moment just before the creature leaped into the sea. The group of figures is shown against a rocky and partly wooded hillside, and not in a meadow, as the myth would lead one to expect. The round column in the centre is apparently sacred in character, while the square pillar and the water-jar at the right may mark a fountain at which the maidens have been drawing water. A narrow strip of pale blue along the lower edge of the picture symbolizes the proximity of the sea. From a Pompeian wall-painting (Hermann-Bruckmann, *Denkmäler der Malerei des Altertums*, No. 68). See p. 60.

they all fled from the kingdom. Miletos took up a permanent abode in Asia Minor and founded the city which bore his name; Sarpedon attacked Lykia and won its throne, and Zeus gave him the boon of a life three generations long; Rhadamanthys, who had enjoyed sovereignty over the islands of the sea, left his dominions and took refuge in Boiotia, where he became the husband of Alkmene; Minos remained in Crete and drew up a code of laws by which he was to gain immortal renown. The commonly accepted story relates that he married Pasiphaë, the daughter of Helios, although another states that his wife was Crete, the daughter of his step-father Asterios. A large family was born to him, the most famous of his sons being Androgeos, Glaukos, and Katreus, and of his daughters, Ariadne and Phaidra.

Myths of Minos and his Sons; Minos. — When Asterios died, Minos claimed the crown, but was thwarted in his efforts to secure it, until, as a last resort, he asserted that it was his by divine right and promised to demonstrate this by eliciting the open approval of the gods. Offering a sacrifice to Poseidon, he prayed that the god would send up from the depths of the sea a bull as a sign of his sovereignty, adding the promise that he would forthwith make the bull a victim on the altar of Poseidon as a thank-offering. The deity hearkened to the petition, but so beautiful was the beast which he thrust upward from the waters that Minos became greedy for it, and thinking to deceive the god sacrificed another in its place. He gained the kingdom which he so much coveted, and, besides, the undisputed command of the Great Sea and its islands, but punishment was in store for him. Poseidon, remembering the attempted deception, sowed in the heart of Pasiphaë an unnatural love for the bull, and drove her to consummate her desire with the help of the skilled craftsman Daidalos; but her sin became known when she brought into the world a hideous monster with the body of a man and the head of a bull — the Minotaur.[1] Advised by an oracle, Minos shut the creature in the labyrinth which Daidalos had constructed for him, this building consisting of so intricate a tangle of passages that it was impossible for one to find his way out of it. There the Minotaur remained feeding on the prey brought to him from all parts of Crete until the day when he was killed by Theseus of Athens. This story, however, is best told in connexion with the career of Theseus.

Androgeos. — The experiences of the sons of Minos were a medley of tragedy and miracle. Androgeos heard that the sea-born bull which Herakles had taken to Argolis had escaped from that territory and was ravaging the lands about Marathon. Apparently thinking that a Cretan arm was more skilled to do battle with a Cretan beast, he took ship and sailed to Attike in the hope of killing the bull. As it happened the animal killed him, but from this incident developed the circumstances which led, later on, to Theseus's voyage to Crete.

Glaukos. — The legend of Glaukos relates that, when a small child, he was once pursuing a mouse and fell into a jar of honey in which he was smothered to death. Minos sought for the child everywhere, but without success, and at last he appealed to the soothsayers, who answered him in the form of a riddle: "In thy fields grazeth a calf whose body changeth hue thrice in the space of each day. It is first white, then red, and at the last black. He who can unravel the meaning of this riddle will restore thy child to thee alive." After Polyidos the seer had divined that the enigma alluded to the mulberry, he found the body of Glaukos in the honey-jar, and Minos enclosed him in a chamber with the corpse, bidding him bring it back to life. While wondering what to do, Polyidos chanced to see a snake crawl across the floor to the child's body, and he killed it with a stone. Soon afterward he observed a second serpent come near to the body of the first, and, covering it with grass, revive it. Inspired by this example, the seer did the same thing to the body of Glaukos, and to his unbounded delight beheld it slowly come to life. Minos gladly received his son back from the dead, but, in the hope of learning the method of the restoration, he ungratefully refused to allow Polyidos to return to his home in Argos until he should reveal the secret to Glaukos. Under compulsion the seer yielded, but when about to sail away he spat suddenly in the boy's mouth and all remembrance of the manner of his recall to life was erased from his mind.

Katreus. — The story of Katreus, like that of Oidipous, clearly reveals the conviction of the ancient Greeks that it was impossible to escape from the mandates of Fate. Katreus had one son Althaimenes, who, an oracle declared, was destined to kill his father. To avoid so monstrous a deed he fled to Rhodes, but as the years went by Katreus felt the disabilities of age creeping upon him and longed for his son that he might entrust to him the responsibilities of the government. Despairing of the young man's voluntary return, he went himself to Rhodes in search of him, but when disembarking on the shore, he was met by Althaimenes, who, mistaking him for a robber, killed him. On discovering that he had fulfilled the oracle in spite of himself, the son prayed for the ground to open and swallow him up. His entreaty was heard, and the earth suddenly took him away from his companions.

Deukalion. — Deukalion, a fourth son of Minos, became king on his father's death, and his son Idomeneus led a contingent of Cretans against Troy.

The Character and Achievements of Minos. — It remains to say more of Minos himself, on the interpretation of whose life and person much thought and ingenuity have been expended. He has been explained as a pre-Hellenic god of Crete, a double of Zeus, as a sun-god in conjunction with the moon-goddess Europe, as a human representative of the Phoinikian Ba'al Melqart, or as of the same primitive origin as the Indian Manu. Yet the farther the Cretan excavations are carried, the stronger grows the conviction of scholarship that in the single person of Minos mythology has compounded the chief characteristics of the powerful race of sea-kings who ruled over Crete in the days which preceded the dominion of the Argives. In a certain sense, then, the tradition is correct which places him three generations before the Trojan war; he is not far from being a historical character.

Minos is chiefly known as a ruler of powerful initiative in many fields. He founded numerous cities in Crete, the most notable being his capital, Knossos; to facilitate the administration of government he divided the island into three districts with Knossos, Phaistos, and Kydonia as head cities; and he extended his sway far out over the islands and the coasts of the mainland, and many settlements were named after him. He divided the Cretan burghers into two main classes, farmers and soldiers — producers and defenders; with the assistance of the people of Karia he is said to have cleared the sea of pirates; and to enable his citizens to develop their maritime commerce he invented a type of small coasting vessel. The code of laws which he established among the Cretans he received in the first place from Zeus, and, in order to obtain advice with reference to such modifications of it as should be necessary from time to time, he went to Mount Ida every ninth year and conferred with Zeus. In his administration of the law his brother Rhadamanthys assisted him in the cities, and Talos, the man of bronze, in the country, but Rhadamanthys succeeded only too well, so that he incurred the jealousy of Minos and was banished to a remote part of the island. As a warrior Minos showed himself cruel and harsh and in conflict with his character as a just and mild ruler, although this side of his portrait is, no doubt, coloured by Athenian prejudice. His career in arms will be narrated in the myths of Attike.

Daidalos. — Though a native of Athens, Daidalos is more closely connected with the legends of Crete than with those of Attike. At Athens he killed his nephew in a fit of jealousy and fled to Crete, where Minos received him in his court and encouraged his inventive genius. Among the many wonderful things which he created for the king was the labyrinth of Knossos which we have already described; but he prostituted his ability by aiding Pasiphaë in her intrigue with the bull of Poseidon, and with his son Ikaros he was thrown into prison by Minos. By means of cleverly contrived wings the two managed to escape from their confinement, the father enjoining Ikaros not to fly too low, lest the wings dip in the sea and the glue which held them together be softened, nor too high, lest the heat of the sun have the same effect. Ikaros disobeyed, sought too lofty a flight, and fell headlong into that part of the Mediterranean which since that day has been known as the Ikarian Sea, whereas the more cautious Daidalos flew safely to the Sicilian city of Kamikos, whose king, Kokalos, secretly gave him protection. Thither Minos followed by ship, and resorted to a shrewd device to find out if Daidalos were really there. Showing Kokalos a snail-shell, he told him that a great reward would be bestowed upon the man who could put a linen thread through its coils, whereupon Kokalos gave the shell to Daidalos, who pierced it, tied a thread to an ant, and sent it through the hole drawing the thread behind it. Minos, knowing that only Daidalos could have done this, demanded that Kokalos surrender him, but this the Sicilian king would not do, though he consented to entertain Minos in his palace. One day when the Cretan ruler was bathing, the daughters of Kokalos suddenly appeared and killed him by pouring boiling pitch over him. His followers buried his body and erected a monument over the grave, founding the city of Minoa in the vicinity.

Daidalos is probably to be regarded as the representative of the artists and artisans of the later Minoan or Mykenaian age. One of the highly prized relics preserved in the temple of Athene Polias on the Athenian Acropolis was a folding chair said to have been fashioned by his hands. Of images attributed to him Pausanias says that they "are somewhat uncouth to the eye, but there is a touch of the divine in them for all that." [2]

II. ATTIKE

The body of Attic myths is a relatively late creation. Careful study of it shows that its component parts were drawn from many different local Hellenic sources and that the process of weaving them together was long; but just what this process (or processes, it may be) was, will probably never be more than the object of conjecture. It is enough to say that the evidences point to an abundance of both conscious and unconscious imitation of other bodies of myth at various periods, to a deliberate fabrication of genealogies, and to the naïve issuance of stories to account for rituals whose meanings had been lost in a dark past; but it is difficult to cite with certainty even a few instances of these, for there is a great gulf, as yet only precariously bridged, between the historical cults of Attike and the earliest period of which we have any religious remains.

Kekrops. — The early genealogies were, even to the ancients, a weird tangle, containing as they did many acknowledged double appearances, not a few dummy personages, and patent inversions of time relationships. Kekrops, who was commonly accepted as the great original ancestor of the Athenians, was reputed to have been born of the soil, and was regarded as being part man and part serpent. The most recent scholarship regards him as a form of Poseidon, the sea-god, imported from the east and later identified with the native agricultural divinity Erichthonios. Kekrops became the first ruler of Attike and changed its name from Akte ("Seaboard") to Kekropia. During his reign Poseidon came to Athens and with his trident struck a spot on the summit of the Acropolis whence gushed forth a spring of salt water afterward sacred to Poseidon and known as the "Sea." Poseidon was now the supreme divinity of the kingdom, but Athene soon came and wrested the supremacy from him. To bear legal witness to her conquest she summoned Kekrops, or, as some say, the citizenry of Athens, or the circle of the Olympians; and as material evidence of her

PLATE XIX

The Birth of Erichthonios

Ge, emerging from the ground, entrusts the infant Erichthonios to Athene, this being a mythological way of saying that Athene herself is an earth goddess. The tall manly figure, who looks paternally on the scene before him, is Hephaistos. On both sides of this group are the Erotes ("Loves") who presided over the union of the god and goddess. From a red-figured *stamnos* of about 500 B.C., in Munich (Furtwängler-Reichhold, *Griechische Vasenmalerei*, No. 137). See p. 67.

contention she planted on the Acropolis near the salt spring the long-lived olive which was to be the mother-tree of the Attic orchards. The witnesses awarded the dominion to Athene, whereupon Poseidon, angry at being dispossessed, covered the fertile plain of Attike with a flood. Kekrops now wedded Agraulos, the daughter of Aktaios, to whom some mythographers assigned the first kingship; and they had three daughters, Agraulos (Aglauros), Herse ("Dew," or "Offspring"), and Pandrosos ("All-Bedewing"), and a son Erysichthon, "a shadowy personality" who died childless.

Erichthonios. — On the death of Kekrops, Kranaos, another son of the soil and the most powerful of the native chieftains, became king, and when Atthis, one of his daughters, died, he attached the name of Attike to the country as a memorial to her. In his reign the flood of Deukalion occurred, and then came a series of dynastic changes. Kranaos was driven from the throne by Amphiktyon, also a son of the soil, and Amphiktyon was expelled in his turn by Erichthonios, whose father was Hephaistos and whose mother was either Athene, Earth, or Atthis. The legend which makes him the son of Athene relates that without the knowledge of the other gods she placed him as an infant in a chest, which she entrusted to Pandrosos with the injunction that on no account was it to be opened. Feminine curiosity, however, got the better of the sisters of Pandrosos and they opened the chest, out of which sprang a serpent that killed them, or, as some said, drove them mad so that they leaped to their death from the cliffs of the Acropolis.[3] Athene then took the child into her own care and reared him in her shrine; and when he had grown up, he expelled Amphiktyon, erected a wooden statue of his mother on the sacred hill, and established the Panathenaïc festival. After his death his body was buried in the precinct of Athene, and his kingdom was left to his son Pandion.

Boutes and Erechtheus. — Pandion is simply a link in a chain of genealogy. He was the father of the unhappy women,

Prokne and Philomele, and of two sons, Boutes and Erechtheus, who divided the royal duties between them on their father's death, the first taking the joint priesthood of Athene and Poseidon, the second the administration of the government. Boutes became the founder of a priestly family which continued down to historical times. Erechtheus was really a double of Erichthonios, as is indicated by his name, which is only an abbreviated form of Erichthonios, and thus, after a fashion, Erechtheus also was a ward of Athene. It was said that he had snake-like feet and that to hide them as he went about among his people he invented the chariot and thus avoided walking, although in some sources he is described as entirely of human form. As secular leader of the Athenians he conducted an expedition against the people of Eleusis, and in accordance with the behest of an oracle he sacrificed his youngest daughter to bring victory to the Athenian arms. His success was indeed tragic, for though he slew Eumolpos, the commander of the Eleusinians, his other daughters took their own lives on learning of the offering of their sister, and he himself was killed by Poseidon, the father of Eumolpos. Of his daughters Kreousa, Prokris, and Oreithyia became famous names in Attic myth. He was followed in order by a son and a grandson, Kekrops and Pandion, the second of whom was dispossessed of his throne by his usurping cousins, the sons of Metion. Taking refuge in Megara, he there brought up a family of four valiant sons, Aigeus, Pallas, Nisos, and Lykos. These, to avenge their father's wrong, invaded Attike, evicted the usurpers, and partitioned the realm amongst themselves, allowing Aigeus, however, the chief authority. The legends of the marriages and the early reign of Aigeus belong more properly to the account of the life of his son Theseus.

The Sons of Pandion; The War with Minos. — After returning from a sojourn in Troizen, Aigeus celebrated the Panathenaïc festival. It happened that Androgeos, the son of Minos of Crete, was the victor in all the athletic contests, and as a supreme test of the young man's skill and swiftness of foot Aigeus sent him against the bull of Marathon, but Androgeos lost his life in the undertaking. On the other hand, the authors of certain accounts state that on his way to the funeral games of Pelias he was killed by jealous rivals who had lost to him in Athens. In either event Minos held Athens as blameworthy for his son's death and to punish her led a great army and fleet against her, taking Megara by storm and making Nisos prisoner. Now Nisos had growing in his head a purple hair, and an oracle had declared that as long as he retained it his kingdom would stand; but his daughter Skylla, falling in love with Minos, plucked the hair in order to win favour, and brought about her father's fall. When Minos sailed away she asked to be taken with him, but meeting with a refusal on account of her treachery, she threw herself into the sea and became a fish, while Nisos, in pursuit of her, was changed into a sea-eagle. Lykos, a third son of Pandion, was credited by some Athenians with having founded the famous Lykeion in Athens.

Athens herself held out against all the assaults of Minos, until, finally, he appealed to Zeus to visit vengeance upon the city, and the god sent famine and pestilence to do what human efforts could not avail. The Athenians sacrificed four maidens over the grave of Geraistios, but still their troubles did not abate, and at last they yielded and accepted the terms of Minos, who cruelly exacted that each year Athens was to send to Crete seven unarmed youths and maidens to be the prey of the Minotaur. From this dreadful tribute the Athenians suffered until released years afterward by Theseus.

The Daughters of Kekrops. — Agraulos, one of the three daughters of Kekrops, became the wife of Ares and by him the mother of a daughter, Alkippe, who, while still a mere girl, was shamefully attacked by Halirrhothios, a son of Poseidon. Ares promptly killed the offender, and, on the appeal of Poseidon, was tried before a tribunal of the gods on a rocky eminence at the foot of the Acropolis, being acquitted, as it were, on the strength of the "unwritten law." After this the Athenians, essaying to follow the divine example, established a criminal court on the same spot and designated it Areopagos, "Hill of Ares."[4] The two sisters of Agraulos, Herse and Pandrosos, were both united in wedlock to Hermes, by whom the one became the mother of the beautiful Kephalos and the other bore Keryx, the forefather of a great Athenian family.

The Daughters of Pandion. — When war broke out between Athens and Thebes over the question of the marchlands, Pandion asked Tereus, son of Ares, to come from Thrace to help him. By means of his assistance he won the war and as a reward gave him his daughter Prokne, but after a few years of married life the love of Tereus cooled and a passion for his wife's sister, Philomele, mastered him. He told his sister-in-law that Prokne was dead and professed so warm a love for her that she consented to become his wife. But it was not long before she discovered his trickery, wherefore, lest she tell her story to the world, Tereus cut out her tongue and confined her in a solitary place. Notwithstanding his precautions, she wove a message into a garment and sent it to her sister. After a long search Prokne found Philomele, and together they devised a revolting revenge on Tereus, in pursuance of which Prokne, inviting him to a banquet, set before him the flesh of their own son Itys. The sisters then made haste to fly from the land, but Tereus overtook them in Phokis, and as they piteously prayed the gods for escape from their ruthless pursuer, they were all changed into birds, Prokne becoming a nightingale, Philomele, a swallow, and Tereus a hoopoe. The ancient Athenians, accordingly, used to say that the sweet plaintive song of the nightingale was the wail of Prokne for her unhappy Itys. The resemblance between this story and that of the Boiotian Aëdon and Itylos needs no pointing out. In reference to a similar story Pausanias[5] remarks, with the *naïveté* of a child: "That a man should be turned into a bird is to me incredible."

The Daughters of Erechtheus; Kreousa.—Kreousa found favour in the eyes of Apollo and bore him a son named Ion, but, keeping her secret to herself, she abandoned the child and married Xouthos, an Athenian soldier of fortune. As it happened, Ion was found and was placed in the temple of Apollo at Delphoi as an attendant. Together Kreousa and her husband went to Delphoi to seek the advice of the oracle in reference to offspring, and received a response which Xouthos interpreted to mean that Ion, whom they met in the temple, was their child. In a fit of jealousy at the readiness of her husband to adopt one whom she secretly felt could not be his offspring, she made an attempt to poison Ion, who was saved by a mere accident. Roused to revenge he formed a plan to murder her, but his intention was happily frustrated by the Pythian priestess, who, in the nick of time, produced the trinkets and clothing that had been found with him, and Kreousa, recognizing by these that he was the son whom she had borne to Apollo, took him into her home. Afterward she and Xouthos were blessed with a son, Achaios. If we are to accept a different account from the foregoing, Ion, and not Kekrops, succeeded Erechtheus as king of Attike and became the founder of the Ionian stock, Achaios and his descendants being later overshadowed by the family of Ion because Achaios was not of divine blood.

Prokris. — At the time when Prokris and Kephalos became husband and wife they pledged themselves to conjugal fidelity with more than ordinary solemnity. Now Kephalos was a hunter by occupation, and of comely countenance and form. Early one morning, when he was scouring the Attic hills for game, Eos ("Dawn") spied him, and, drawn by his charms, asked of him that he would give her his love. Bound by the ties of affection and of his oath, Kephalos refused her, but the passion of the divinity was not to be denied. Slyly insinuating that under like circumstances Prokris would be less scrupulous than he, she gave him the appearance of a stranger, and then, bestowing on him lovely gifts such as please the heart of woman, suggested that he make trial of his wife's fidelity. To his surprise Prokris weakened at the sight of the gifts, but when he resumed his real form she became ashamed and fled away to Crete. There she wished to follow Artemis in the hunt, but the goddess would have none of her in her chaste company. Breaking into tears, Prokris told Artemis of the wicked deceit practised on her, and in pity the divinity gave her a never-erring hunting-spear, and a dog, Lailaps, which never missed its quarry. Disguising herself as a youth, Prokris returned to Attike, and, winning the attention of Kephalos through her prowess with the gifts of Artemis, promised him that she would give them to him in return for his affection, saying that neither gold nor silver could buy them from her, but only love. At that he granted her desire, and forthwith she became her own old self and their former relations were resumed. Prokris was still fearful of the wiles of Eos, however, and one day she hid in a thicket near her husband as he was hunting in order to spy on her beautiful rival. Kephalos, seeing a movement of twigs and thinking that it was caused by some beast, hurled his javelin, which, according to its nature, flew straight to its mark, but, to his dismay, he discovered that the quarry he had slain was his own dear wife.

A second form of the story differs from this in several details. Bribed by the glitter of a golden crown, Prokris surrendered herself to one Pteleon, and, when detected by her husband in her sin, took refuge at the court of Minos. Minos, too, made love to her, for Pasiphaë had so bewitched him with a certain drug that he could not escape a passion for every woman whom he met, a passion which was bound to work evil for both lovers alike. By the use of a magic antidote Prokris freed him from this spell, and in gratitude Minos gave her the spear and the dog. Nevertheless, apprehensive of some evil design on the part of Pasiphaë, she made her way to Attike and patched up her former alliance with Kephalos. One day,

PLATE XX

Eos and Kephalos

Eos, suddenly approaching Kephalos from behind, has laid her left arm across his shoulders, and with her right hand has grasped him firmly by the wrist, thus endeavouring to check his flight as he starts away in fear; at the same time she spreads her wings, and with an upward glance indicates whither she wishes to convey him. From a red-figured *kylix* signed by Hieron (early fifth century B.C.), in the Museum of Fine Arts, Boston (*photograph*). See pp. 71–73.

as they were hunting together, he slew her by mistake with her own javelin, whereupon, appearing before the court of Areopagos, he was adjudged guilty and banished for life from the bounds of Attike. His exile coincided in time with his receipt of a request from Amphitryon that he go to Thebes with his unerring hound, and rid the country of the she-fox that was ravaging the crops and people. This animal's life seemed to have been protected by a charm so that none could take her, and each month the Thebans used to send a youth to her for her to devour. Kephalos, bribed by the offer of a portion of Taphian booty, went to Thebes and put his dog on the trail of the ravenous beast; but the dog never overtook her, for in the midst of the pursuit Zeus changed them both to stone. Kephalos was given his reward, however, and withdrew to a western island thenceforth to be known as Kephallenia, where, brooding over his unhappy love, he committed suicide by throwing himself from the white cliffs of the island. The chief figure in the original story seems to have been only Kephalos, Prokris being a later addition. The legend arose from the very ancient expiatory ritual in which a human being bore the burden of sin to be expiated, and, leaping into the sea, was drowned.

Oreithyia. — Oreithyia, the remaining daughter of Erechtheus, was once playing with her companions on the bank of the Ilisos, or, as one source of the myth states, was on her way to the Acropolis to sacrifice to Athene, when Boreas, the north wind, suddenly seized her and carried her off to his home in Thrace. There he forced her to wed him, and she bore to him two winged sons, Zetes and Kalaïs, who afterward sailed on the Argo and were killed in the pursuit of the Harpies. The substance of this legend was not originally a product of the Attic fancy; rather, it is an embellishment of a widespread belief that in the turmoil of the storm the passionate wind-god seeks his bride. Perhaps to the Athenians Oreithyia represented the morning mist of the valley-lands driven away by the strong clear winds of day.

Boreas and Oreithyia also had two daughters, Kleopatra and Chione ("Snow-White"). The former married Phineus, to whom she bore two sons, but her husband grew tired of her and formed an alliance with Idaia of Troy, by whose heartless wiles he was persuaded to put out his children's eyes. This crime was never forgotten throughout Hellas, and with the help of Boreas the Argonauts visited on Phineus a dreadful punishment. Chione became closely associated with Attike through her descendants. After a clandestine amour with Poseidon she gave birth to a son Eumolpos ("Sweet Singer"), whom she cast into the sea in fear of her father; but Poseidon rescued him and had him cared for in Aithiopia until he had attained manhood. For a foul crime against hospitality Eumolpos was forced to leave this country and with his son, Ismaros, was received into the home of a Thracian king, where, too, he showed himself ungrateful for kindness, and plotted against his host. Leaving Thrace, he came at last to Eleusis, and in the war against Athens he led the Eleusinian army and fell by the sword of Erechtheus. This latter myth contains several features which incline one to believe that Eumolpos was a figure deliberately created by the Eumolpidai, the priestly order of Eleusis, for the purpose of winning the respect which would readily come to religious orders of admittedly ancient descent. The Thracian connexion of Eumolpos linked him geographically with Dionysos and increased his prestige at Eleusis.

CHAPTER V

HERAKLES

HERAKLES is a bewildering compound of god and hero. While he may properly be called the most heroic of the Grecian gods, he cannot with equal propriety be termed the most divine of the heroes. Indeed, so far is he from possessing that dignity which becomes a god that some writers have argued his claim to divinity to be merely an inference from his exploits. But whether god or hero, or both god and hero, Herakles represents the Greek idealization of mere bigness. Everything about him is big — his person, his weapon, his journeys, his enemies, his philanthropy, his sins, and his sense of humour. To explain him as a degenerate Zeus, as some do, may account for his origin, but it will not give the reason for more than his initial popularity. His hold on the people through many centuries was due to his colossal humanity; in him men could see their ideal for every moment of the day and the consummation of every aspiration, whether good or bad. Now and again Zeus or Apollo would stoop to the level of a weak humanity, but an apology, open or tacit, generally followed. For Herakles, on the contrary, no apology was forthcoming. Men took him as he was, and ignored his flouting of moral laws as a necessary accompaniment to the achievement of big things. He was "big business" personified, and the petty restrictions that hampered lesser beings were impertinent as regarding him. Thus he represented a phase of Greek idealism which rebelled against the cold and soaring idealism of the thinkers, and embodied the frank confession of all classes of the Hellenic populace that the more spiritual elements of their advanced civilization were not as yet perfect instruments for securing and maintaining the welfare of human society. The story of Herakles' rejection of Aphrodite and his choice of Athene at the parting of the ways makes a very pretty apologue, but it does not reveal to us the Herakles whom the Greeks knew; rather he is here put on exhibition as a sort of reformed "character" by those who know and fear the effects of his moral example.

At the earliest point to which he can be traced Herakles seems to have been a hero of Tiryns in Argolis, but his exploits were narrated in Rhodian sagas and carried by the ubiquitous Rhodian sailors to many ports of the Mediterranean. In various places the sagas were modified and enlarged by foisting stories of purely local origin on Herakles, until, as his fame spread, some poet was inspired to assemble the many sagas under one title and to give to the world the first version of the Labours. Herakles was apparently not at first the possession of all the Dorians, but became their hero *par excellence* through the influence of the Delphic oracle, perhaps not later than 700 B.C.[1]

The Birth of Herakles. — When Perseus died, he left behind him in Mykenai four sons, Alkaios, Sthenelos, Mestor, and Elektryon, the descendants of all of whom enter in some way or other into the story of Herakles. Alkaios had a son Amphitryon; Elektryon, a daughter Alkmene, and, besides lawful sons, a natural son Likymnios; Sthenelos, a son Eurystheus; and Mestor, a daughter who bore to Poseidon a son, Taphios, the colonizer of the island of Taphos. During the reign of Elektryon in Mykenai, Pterelaos, a son of Taphios, came thither with his people and demanded a share of Mestor's kingdom, but, failing ignominiously in their errand, they attacked the sons of Elektryon and slaughtered all except Likymnios. When the battle was over their fellow Taphians sailed away to Elis with Elektryon's cattle, although not long afterward Amphitryon redeemed them and brought them back to My-

PLATE XXI

Herakles and the Lion of Nemea

Herakles is leaning forward, his knees almost touching the ground, and is throwing the weight of his body on the lion's head and shoulders; at the same time with his right hand he seizes the beast by a hind quarter and powerfully draws it toward himself, while his left arm, passing under the lion's throat, is choking him to death. The hero's quiver and sheathed sword are suspended in the background. Athene, partly armed, stands at the left eagerly watching the fray. From a black-figured *amphora* of about 500 B.C., found at Gela (*Monumenti Antichi*, xvii, Plate XL). See pp. 80–81.

kenai. Elektryon, bound on exacting vengeance for the outrage, assigned the affairs of state to Amphitryon and betrothed his daughter Alkmene to him on the condition that the marriage be deferred until the outcome of the expedition should be known; but after making these arrangements, and when about to take back his cattle, a missile from the hand of Amphitryon, probably wholly by accident, struck him and killed him. With the stain of family blood upon him, Amphitryon fled with his betrothed to Thebes and allowed the power to fall into the hands of Sthenelos, but in their new home Alkmene promised him she would ignore the strict letter of the terms of their betrothal and would wed him should he avenge the murder of her brothers at the hands of their Taphian kinsmen. He met the promise by leading a well-equipped army of Thebans and their allies against Taphos. Although he was successful in his numerous raids, he was unable to secure a decisive victory as long as Pterelaos was alive, for this man, not unlike Nisos of Megara, had growing in his head a golden hair, on the continued possession of which hung the fate of himself and of his kingdom. Crazed with love for Amphitryon, Pterelaos's daughter plucked the hair from her father's head and by that act surrendered her country to its enemies, but, filled with contempt for her treason, the victor killed her and took to Thebes the booty of Taphos.

Now in Amphitryon's absence Alkmene had been visited by Zeus in the guise of her husband and by him had become with child, so that when the real Amphitryon returned, he and his wife were confronted with a perplexing domestic riddle which was not satisfactorily solved till more than a year had passed. Just before Alkmene gave birth to her child, a scene was enacted on Olympos which had a profound influence on the child's career. The event is well described in the words of Agamemnon in the *Iliad*.[2]

"Yea even Zeus was blinded upon a time, he who they say is greatest among gods and men; yet even him Hera with female wile deceived, on the day when Alkmene in fair-crowned Thebes was to bring forth the strength of Herakles. For then proclaimed he solemnly among all the gods: 'Hear me ye all, both gods and goddesses, while I utter the counsel of my soul within my heart. This day shall Eileithyia, the help of travailing women, bring to the light a man who shall be lord over all that dwell round about, among the race of men who are sprung of me by blood.' And to him in subtlety queen Hera spake: 'Thou wilt play the cheat and not accomplish thy word. Come now, Olympian, swear me a firm oath that verily and indeed shall that man be lord over all that dwell round about, who this day shall fall between a woman's feet, even he among all men who are of the lineage of thy blood.' So spake she, and Zeus no wise perceived her subtlety, but sware a mighty oath, and therewith was he sore blinded. For Hera darted from Olympos' peak, and came swiftly to Achaian Argos, where she knew was the stately wife of Sthenelos the son of Perseus, who also was great with child, and her seventh month was come. Her son Hera brought to the light, though his tale of months was untold, but she stayed Alkmene's bearing and kept the Eileithyiai from her aid. Then she brought the tidings herself and to Kronos' son Zeus she spake: 'Father Zeus of the bright lightning, a word will I speak to thee for thy heed. To-day is born a man of valour who shall rule among the Argives, Eurystheus, son of Sthenelos the son of Perseus, of thy lineage; not unmeet is it that he be lord among Argives.' She said, but sharp pain smote him in the depths of his soul, and straightway he seized Ate by her bright-haired head in the anger of his soul, and sware a mighty oath that never again to Olympos and the starry heaven should Ate come who blindeth all alike. He said, and whirling her in his hand flung her from the starry heaven, and quickly came she down among the works of men. Yet ever he groaned against her when he beheld his beloved son in cruel travail at Eurystheus' hest." When at length Alkmene's full time had come, she gave birth to Herakles and Iphikles, the one the son of the deceiving Zeus and the other born of Amphitryon.

Childhood and Youth of Herakles. — When Herakles was only eight months old, Hera sent two great serpents to his bed to destroy him; but a measure of the strength of mature years had come to him and he rose and strangled them unaided. There is a version of this story to the effect that Amphitryon, in order to determine which of the two boys was really his son, put the serpents into the bed containing the children, the flight of Iphikles proving him to be the offspring of a mortal.

Under the instruction of a number of the famous heroes, Herakles was taught the accomplishments becoming a man, chariot-driving, wrestling, archery, fighting in armour, and music. His teacher on the zither was Linos, the brother of Orpheus, but in this branch he was less apt than in the others, so that once, when Linos had occasion to punish him for his lack of diligence, Herakles hurled his zither at him and killed him. After trial for murder, he was acquitted through his clever quotation of a law of Rhadamanthys, but his father, fearing another outburst of violence, sent him to the glades as a herder and there he grew in strength and stature and in skill with the lance and the bow. His height was now four cubits, and his eye flashed fire like that of a true son of Zeus.

Early Manhood of Herakles. — About the time when Herakles was on the verge of manhood, he determined to kill a lion which was ravaging his flocks and herds on the slopes of Kithairon. By using Thespiai as a base of operations, he at length achieved his task, and flaying the beast he took its skin as a cloak. As he was on his homeward journey, he met heralds of Erginos, king of the Minyans, going to Thebes to get the annual tribute of the city. Herakles seized them, lopped off their ears and noses, bound their hands to their necks, and sent them back thus to their own land. Erginos dispatched an army against Thebes, but in the battle which ensued he was killed by Herakles, and the Minyans had from that day to pay to Thebes double the tribute which Thebes had formerly rendered to them. As a compensation for his efforts in arms Herakles was given Megara, Kreon's daughter, as his wife, who in the course of time bore him three children.

The Madness of Herakles. — Herakles' successes heated the jealous wrath of Hera and she visited a terrible madness upon the hero, who, not knowing what he did, killed his own children and those of his brother Iphikles, some with his bow, some by fire, and some with his sword. When he came to himself, overwhelmed with remorse he left Thebes and went to Thespiai, where he was ceremonially purified of his sin. He departed thence for Delphoi, where, in Apollo's shrine, the priestess uttered this prophecy: "From this day forth thy name shall no more be Alkeides but Herakles. In Tiryns thou shalt make thine abode, and there, serving Eurystheus, shalt thou accomplish thy labours. When this shall be, thou shalt become one of the immortals." With the words ringing in his ears, Herakles set out for Tiryns wearing a robe, the gift of Athene, and carrying the arms which the gods had given him — the sword of Hermes, the bow of Apollo, the bronze breastplate of Hephaistos, and a great club which he had himself cut in Nemea.

The Twelve Labours of Herakles;[3] *First Labour.* — The first labour which Eurystheus enjoined on Herakles was to kill the lion of Nemea, the seed of Typhon, and to bring its skin to Tiryns, although no man had been able as yet even to wound the beast. Going to Nemea, Herakles found its trail, which he followed until it led him to a cavern with two mouths, one of which he blocked up, and, entering by the other, grappled with the lion and choked him to death. From Nemea to Mykenai he carried the body on his shoulders. Eurystheus stood aghast at the sight of the monstrous creature and at these proofs of Herakles' superhuman strength, and in his fear he prepared a storage-jar in which to hide, forbidding Herakles ever to enter his gates again, and henceforth issuing his orders through heralds. As for Herakles, he turned this his first labour to good account, for from that day he wore the lion's skin, which no weapon could penetrate, at once as a cloak and a shield.

Second Labour. — In the springs and swamps of Lerne dwelt a huge hydra which used to lay waste the lands round about, and to ensure his death Herakles was sent against this creature, from whose enormous body grew nine heads, the middle one being immortal. The monster had defied all attempts to capture or to kill it, and had brought many strong men low; but finding the creature crouching sullenly in its lair, the hero forced it out by means of flaming missiles and grasped it at the same instant that it seized him. Stoutly swinging his club, he knocked off the hydra's heads one by one, but to his alarm two heads grew in the place of each one that he destroyed, while a huge crab came to the aid of the hydra and gripped its assailant by the foot. This crab Herakles easily killed and then, with the assistance of his nephew Iolaos, burned away the hydra's newly sprouting heads. At last he cut off the deathless head and placed it under a heavy stone, lest it rise to life again, and in the monster's gall he dipped all his arrowheads. The achievement of killing the hydra Eurystheus quibblingly disallowed on the ground that Herakles had not performed it alone.

Third Labour. — Herakles was next ordered to proceed to a mountain range in the north of the Peloponnesos and to carry away alive the Keryneian doe, which had golden horns and was sacred to Artemis. So swift of foot was it that it led the hero a weary chase for a whole year, but finally its strength flagged and it fled across the mountain of Artemision to the banks of the river Ladon, where Herakles took it alive. Apollo and Artemis, however, disputed his rights to his prize, and Artemis even accused him of trying to kill her sacred animal, but by adroitly laying the blame on another, Herakles was at length allowed to bear the doe on his broad shoulders to Mykenai.

Fourth Labour. — Still another beast of the wild was he commanded to capture alive — the fierce boar that came forth from the ridges of Erymanthos and wasted the town of Psophis. Herakles went to the mountain and was entertained by Pholos, a Centaur, who, yielding to his guest's importunate request for wine to give zest to their repast of meats, opened a jar taken from the Centaurs' common store. The other Centaurs of the neighbourhood sniffed the aroma of the wine and in a belligerent mood gathered about the dwelling of Pholos, whereupon Herakles attacked them, killing some and routing the others, so that they took refuge with the wise Centaur, Cheiron. Unfortunately, an arrow shot at them chanced to hit Cheiron, inflicting a wound which Herakles would have healed, had not the pain of it driven the Centaur to exchange his immortality for the mortality of Prometheus and thus voluntarily to die. After this, by another unhappy accident, Pholos was killed by dropping one of Herakles' poisoned arrows on his foot. When the hero had buried his friend, he pursued the boar high up the slopes of Erymanthos to the deep snow and snared it; and on his arrival at Mykenai with the huge creature Eurystheus hid in the great jar.

Fifth Labour. — Augeias, King of Elis, had so many herds of cows and goats that the offal from them had accumulated until all tillage was stopped. Eurystheus ordered Herakles to clean away the nuisance, and, going to Augeias, the hero offered to perform the task on the stipulation that he should receive one tenth of the flocks and herds, to which the king hesitatingly agreed. Without delay Herakles broke down a large part of the foundations of the stables and through the breach thus made diverted the united waters of the rivers Alpheios and Peneios, thus flushing the filth entirely away. Augeias, with the scrupulosity of an Eurystheus, now withheld the promised reward on the ground that Herakles was acting at the command of another and not of his own free will. "But," he added, "I will submit the question to arbitration." His sincer-

PLATE XXII

HERAKLES AND THE HYDRA

Herakles, wearing the protecting lion-skin, in his left hand grasps one of the hydra's many heads and is about to cut it off with the sword held in his right hand. On the opposite side of the monster the helmeted Iolaos is imitating his master's manner of attack. With its free heads the hydra is biting fiercely at its assailants. Behind Herakles stand Athene, identified by the branch of olive in her hand, and Hermes. The identity of the three women next Iolaos is unknown. From a black-figured Eretrian *amphora* of the sixth century B.C., in Athens (*Catalogue des vases peints du musée national d'Athènes, Supplément par Georges Nicole*, Plate IX). See p. 81.

FIG. 3A. THE ERYMANTHIAN BOAR AT MYKENAI

Herakles, lifting the struggling boar by the hind quarters, forces the creature forward on his fore legs only. The hero's lion-skin, quiver, and sheathed sword are shown suspended in the background, while his great club leans obliquely in the lower left-hand corner.

FIG. 3B. THE FLIGHT OF EURYSTHEUS

Eurystheus with garments flying in the wind hastens to hide himself in the great *pithos*, or storage-jar. The female figure facing him may be Hera. From a black-figured *amphora* of the sixth century B.C., found at Gela (*Monumenti Antichi*, xvii, Plate IX).

ity was soon put to the test, for when his own son reproved him for his ingratitude, he turned both son and benefactor out of the country. This labour, too, Eurystheus refused to place to the credit of Herakles for the technical reason that he had bargained for a reward. The story seems to be an old folk-tale.

Sixth Labour. — Herakles' next errand was to clear the marshes of Arkadian Stymphalos of the man-eating birds which used to congregate there, and which, owing to the dense growth of underbrush and trees bordering on the marshes, were difficult of access. But Athene came to the help of Herakles and gave him some brazen cymbals by the clashing of which he compelled the birds to take to the air; and as they circled above his head, he shot them down one by one with his unerring arrows. It is probable that these birds typified a pestilence that arose from the areas of stagnant water.

Seventh Labour. — With this labour Herakles began his activities outside the Peloponnesos, being sent by his task-master to Crete to lead thence to the mainland the beautiful bull which Poseidon had caused to be born from the sea for the sacrifice of Minos. Mastering the powerful creature, he rode it through the sea to Tiryns and from there drove it overland to Mykenai, where it was loosed; but instead of remaining here, it roamed all over the land, mangling men and women as it went, until it was slain in Marathon by Theseus.

Eighth Labour. — It was to the northern land of Thrace that Herakles was next dispatched, his task being to subdue and catch the man-eating horses of Diomedes, the son of Ares and the king of the Bistonians. By main strength he seized them and dragged them to the sea, but at this point the Bistonians harassed him to such a degree that he gave the steeds to his companion Abderos to guard. While he was engaged in routing the foe, the horses killed Abderos, who was buried by Herakles with the customary rites, and beside whose tomb the city of Abdera was founded by the hero. On receiving the horses, Eurystheus immediately loosed them as he had the bull, and they, rushing off to the highlands, were harried to death by the wild beasts.

Ninth Labour. — Prior to this labour the strength of Herakles had been pitted against beasts and men only, but now Eurystheus directed him to match it against the warrior-women, the Amazons, who lived in a remote district of Asia Minor near the shores of the Euxine. Their chief interest was war and only indirectly that of motherhood, and of all the children to whom they gave birth they reared the females only, whose right breasts they cut off so as not to interfere with proper handling of the bow. Their queen was Hippolyte, a favourite of Ares, who had given her a beautiful girdle as a token of her prowess in arms, and to win this cincture was the errand of Herakles.

Sailing from Greece with a group of companions, the hero touched at Paros and warred on the sons of Minos. Thence he proceeded to King Lykos of Mysia, whose territories he increased by the conquest of neighbouring tribes, and at last he reached the port of Themiskyra, where Hippolyte visited him to learn the object of his mission. To his surprise she promised to surrender her girdle without a struggle, but Hera, in the guise of an Amazon, stirred up the women against him and Herakles, suspecting a plot in the ready promise, summarily slew their queen and sailed homeward with the prize.

His route led him past Troy, and, landing there, he found the city in the throes of a dreadful calamity. Years before Apollo and Poseidon had jointly built the walls of the town for its king Laomedon on condition of receiving a certain recompense. This, however, had never been given to them, wherefore, in anger, Apollo afflicted Troy with a plague and Poseidon sent a monster to devour the people as they went about the plain. Just before the hero's arrival, Laomedon, in order to spare his citizens, had bound his daughter Hesione to the sea-rocks as a prey for the monster, and Herakles pledged himself to slay it and save Hesione should the horses which Zeus had given Laomedon for the theft of Ganymedes be surrendered to him. He performed his part of the contract by leaping down into the monster's throat and cutting his way out through its belly, but the Trojans failed to fulfil theirs, whereupon, breathing out threats of a later punishment, Herakles embarked in his ship and sailed to Mykenai with his prize. Many scholars are now inclined to think that the original models of the Amazons were the Hittites, whose strange customs and apparel seemed to the Hellenes to be strikingly feminine.[4]

Tenth Labour. — Near the distant river of Okeanos was an island called Erytheia, where lived Geryoneus, son of Chrysaor and the nymph Kalliroë. He was a human monster with three bodies instead of one, and he was known all over the world for his herd of red cattle which were guarded by Eurytion and the two-headed dog Orthos, a brother of the hell-hound Kerberos. Herakles was assigned the task of driving this herd to Mykenai. Crossing Europe, he came to the straits between that continent and Africa and set up two pillars as memorials of his journey. Here Helios beat so hotly upon his head that he shot an arrow at him, and in admiration for his attempt of the impossible Helios gave him a golden cup in which he crossed Okeanos and reached Erytheia. With his club he easily put the warders of the herd out of the way, but it was only after a long struggle that he killed Geryoneus himself with an arrow. Gathering the cattle into the cup of Helios, he transported them to Europe and drove them eastward overland in successive stages. At Rhegion a bull broke loose, and, swimming the straits to Sicily, mingled with the herds of King Eryx, and when Eryx resisted an attempt to regain the animal, Herakles wrestled with him and threw him to his death. From the toe of Italy to the extremity of the Adriatic the cattle were driven, and thence to the Hellespont, but many of them, maddened by a gad-fly sent by Hera, wandered away from the main herd and were lost in the wild lands of Thrace. When Herakles arrived at Mykenai, he sacrificed the rest of the herd to Hera.

Eleventh Labour. — The ten labours had consumed eight years and one month, but the end was not yet, for, owing to the quibbling of Eurystheus, the ten counted as only eight. To complete the prescribed number Eurystheus enjoined two more, in the first of which Herakles was required to bring back the Golden Apples of the Hesperides ("Daughters of the Evening-Land"). These apples were very precious, having once been the wedding-gift of Zeus to Hera, and to obtain them was perhaps the most difficult of all the labours of Herakles, for they were guarded not only by the Hesperides but also by a deathless dragon of one hundred heads, besides all which the hero did not yet know in just what part of the world they were to be found. Setting out at random in the hope of chancing upon his goal, Herakles came to the river Echedoros where, in a contest of strength, he would have slain Ares' son Kyknos had Zeus not separated them by a thunderbolt. Happening to find Nereus, the Ancient of the Sea, asleep on the banks of the Eridanos, the great river of the north, he seized him, and, in spite of his power to change into many forms, did not release him until he told where the Golden Apples were to be found. On learning this, he turned south to Libya, in which ruled Poseidon's son Antaios, who used to compel all strangers passing that way to wrestle with him. They were invariably killed in the struggle, but in Herakles he met more than his equal, for the hero lifted him aloft as though he had been nothing and dashed him to pieces on the ground. From Libya Herakles passed on to Egypt, the kingdom of Bousiris, another son of Poseidon, who, too, was unkind to strangers, making a practice of sacrificing them to Zeus, alleging that he was thus obeying an oracle. His attendants bound Herakles to the altar, but with a single effort the hero burst the bonds and stained the shrine with the king's own blood. From Egypt he went on through Asia to the island of Rhodes, where he is said to have stolen a team of oxen and to have sacrificed them, notwithstanding the imprecations of their owner. From that time onward it was customary to utter imprecations when sacrificing to Herakles. Wandering across Arabia and Lydia, he chanced to come to the place where the unhappy Prometheus was chained. Moved with pity, he shot the bird that was tormenting him, unbound his fetters, and with the permission of Zeus gave him Cheiron's eternal immunity from death. At last he reached the end of his weary journey, the land of the Hyperboreians where Atlas stood bearing the heavens on his shoulders. With little more ado Herakles killed the dragon, plucked the apples, and conveyed them to Eurystheus, but as they were too divine for mortal keeping, they were later restored to the Hesperides. Another version of this legend, in which Atlas is beguiled to accomplish the theft, is inconsistent with the character of the traditional Herakles.

Twelfth Labour. — One realm of nature was as yet unconquered by Herakles — the underworld — and thither he was sent on his last mission to fetch Kerberos, the hell-hound with three heads and the tail of a serpent, and out of whose body grew a writhing tangle of snakes. On his way to Tainaron in Lakonia, the most spacious entry to the lower world, Herakles halted at Eleusis, and, as soon as Eumolpos had purified him of the blood of the Centaurs, he was initiated into the mysteries. Once at the cave of Tainaron, he descended and found among the shades those of many whom he had known in the world above. Though the place was entirely strange to him, he could not be daunted from continuing his deeds of chivalry. He released Theseus from the bonds which Hades had thrown upon him, overpowered Menoites, the herdsman of Hades' kine, until Persephone had to beg for him to be spared, and, killing one of the cattle, he shed its blood to gratify the gibbering shades. Kerberos he found on guard at the entrance to Acheron. Protected by his breastplate and impenetrable lion's skin, he cautiously approached the beast, and, suddenly grasping him

PLATE XXIII

1. Herakles and Nereus

Just to the right of the centre of the composition Herakles may be distinguished by the lion-skin which he wears on his head and the front of his body; above his shoulders can be seen the rim of a quiver and the end of an unstrung bow. He stands with his feet wide apart so as to brace himself against the struggles of Nereus, whom he holds tightly in his arms. The sea-god is shown with human head and shoulders, while his body, which he lashes wildly about in his endeavours to escape, is that of a fish. At the left of the picture Hermes, with the *caduceus* (herald's wand), sandals, *chlamys* (a sort of cape), and *petasos* (travelling hat), draws near to the combat. The two frightened women on either side may be Nereids. From a black-figured *lekythos* of the late sixth century B.C., found at Gela (*Monumenti Antichi*, xvii, Plate XXV). See p. 87.

2. Herakles and the Cretan Bull

Herakles, a sinewy and beardless young man, is running beside the bull and endeavouring to retard its speed by pulling back on its right horn. In his right hand he is swinging his knotted club preparatory to dealing the creature a heavy blow. He is lightly clad for his strenuous task, wearing only a short, sleeveless *chiton*. On his head is a peculiar cap, with a conical crown and a projecting peak, such as is often worn by Hermes and Perseus. At his left side appears the hilt of a sword. From a black-figured *lekythos* with a white ground, found at Gela and apparently of the early fifth century B.C. (*Monumenti Antichi*, xvii, Plate XXVIII). See p. 84.

3. Herakles and Apollo

Herakles can be very easily identified by his club, lion-skin (the legs of which are knotted across his chest), and the quiver, out of which five shafts are protruding. In his left hand he grasps one of the legs of the Delphic tripod which he is trying to wrest from Apollo, a lithe, boyish figure bearing a laden quiver on his back. Directly in the path of Herakles and with her face toward him stands Athene, fully armed, and, behind her, Hermes with his characteristic attributes. The women who witness the contest cannot be identified. From a black-figured *lekythos* of the early fifth century B.C., found at Gela (*Monumenti Antichi*, xvii, Plate XXIII). See pp. 89–90.

I

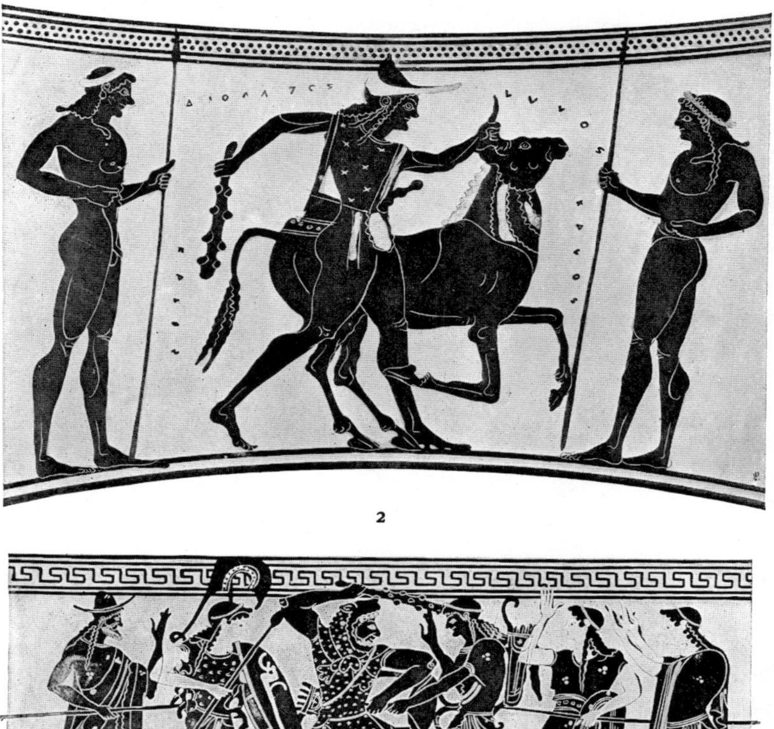

2

3

by the head and neck, forced him to submit to being led away. He made his ascent by way of the grotto at Troizen, and when he had shown the dog to Eurystheus as indisputable proof of his success, he took him back to Hades.

The Later Adventures of Herakles; In Euboia. — On his release from his servitude to Eurystheus, Herakles returned to his home city of Thebes, where his first act was to get rid of his wife without proper cause by heartlessly handing her over to Iolaos like a mere chattel. In casting about him for another spouse, he learned that Eurytos, lord of the Euboian city of Oichalia, had offered his daughter Iole to the man who should excel himself and his sons in archery. Herakles took up this very general challenge and won, but his fair prize was withheld from him on the ground that his madness might return and drive him to repeat the murderous deeds of his earlier years. Not long after this episode the wily Autolykos stole some of Eurytos's cattle, but their owner attributed the theft to Herakles as an act of revenge. It chanced that Iphitos, one of Eurytos's sons, when searching for the lost animals, fell in with Herakles, whom he engaged to join him in his errand; but suddenly, in the midst of their peaceful intercourse at Tiryns, a fit of madness came over Herakles, and, grasping his friend in his powerful arms, he dashed him to destruction from the summit of the city walls. Now in the eyes of the Greeks an act of violence against a friend was one of the most reprehensible of sins, so that a dreadful disease which came upon Herakles was regarded by all as a just retribution for his evil-doing. He sought purification at the hands of Nereus (Neleus), but was ignominiously turned away as an offender for whom there was no pardon. Later, at Amyklai, he received it from the more tender-hearted Deïphobos, but this removed only his pollution, and in order to find a cure for his disease he went to Delphoi, where the priestess refused to dispense to him the healing wisdom of the oracle. Overmastered by rage, Herakles proceeded to sack the shrine, scattering its furnishings about as would an angry child, and, laying hold of the sacred tripod, he was on the point of setting up his own independent oracle when Apollo resisted him with force. In the midst of their struggle they were unexpectedly separated by a thunderbolt of Zeus, whereupon the oracle revealed to Herakles that he would obtain relief from his malady and would make proper amends for his crime only when he had been sold into slavery and had served three years in bondage.

In Lydia. — Hermes sold Herakles to Omphale, the widow of Tmolos, a former king of Lydia, and Eurytos, to whom the money realized from the sale was offered, refused it with a much more genuine scrupulousness than that which marks the actions of most characters of myth. This period in Herakles' life was relieved by many episodes which had a mirthful as well as a serious side. During a part of his servitude Omphale, possessed of a saving sense of humour, made this most masculine of all the heroes wear woman's garb and engage in the narrow round of domestic duties, while she herself went about wearing the lion's skin and wielding the huge club. Yet Herakles was given enough freedom to allow him to go from land to land accomplishing great exploits. Near Ephesos there were two men called Kerkopes who made a practice of waylaying travellers, and one day, when Herakles waked from a nap by the roadside, he saw them standing over him wearing his armour and brandishing his weapons. Relying on his strength alone, he seized them, tied their feet together, and, hanging them head downward, one on each end of a great stick of timber, he proceeded to carry them off, but soon, won over by their irrepressible pleasantries, let them go. In Aulis lived a certain Syleus who used to force passers-by to till his vineyards; but Herakles was not to be thus treated. Uprooting all the vines in the vineyard and piling them into a heap, he placed Syleus and his daughter on the top and kindled it; although in one form of the tale he gorged himself at Syleus's larder and then washed away the entire plantation by diverting the waters of a river across it. During his slavery he was of service to Lydia in crushing her enemies, and he also made a second expedition against the Amazons and with the other heroes sailed on the Argo in the quest of the Golden Fleece. One of his many thoughtful acts was to bury the body of the bold but unfortunate Ikaros, which he found cast by the waves on the seashore, and in gratitude Daidalos erected a statue of him at Olympia.

At Troy. — On attaining his liberty, Herakles promptly carried out his threat against Troy for her perfidy. Accompanied by many of the nobles from all parts of Greece, he went against the city with a fleet and an army, and having effected a landing and repulsed an attack of the Trojans he drove them back and besieged them. Through a breach made in the walls the Greeks finally entered the city, but at the expense of an altercation between Herakles and Telamon, one of his generals, who, Herakles pettily urged, had inconsiderately deprived his leader of the honour of being the first to set foot in the conquered city. Their quarrel was patched up, however, and Telamon was given the princess Hesione as a prize of war. Herakles slew the ungrateful Laomedon, but granted life to his son Podarkes ("Swift Foot"), who was afterward to be called Priamos. As the victors were sailing away to the west, Hera caught Zeus napping and sent violent storms upon them, but the Olympian punished her for her deceit by suspending her from heaven. Touching at Kos, Herakles engaged in a battle with Eurypylos, king of the island, slew him, and, when himself wounded, was mysteriously removed to safety by his divine father Zeus. On reaching home he was summoned to support the cause of the gods against the rebellious Titans.

In the Peloponnesos. — As Herakles had repaid Laomedon for his failure to keep a pledge, so was he to have revenge on Augeias. Assembling a host of volunteers, he invaded Elis and met with a powerful resistance. Falling ill, he succeeded in making a truce with the enemy, but they, on learning the reason of it and thinking to take him off his guard, attacked him treacherously. Herakles, however, was a master of retaliation, for when he subsequently caught them in an ambuscade, he put Augeias and his sons to death, captured the city of Elis, and gave the kingdom to another. "Then the valiant son of Zeus assembled in Pisa all his hosts and all the spoils of war, and measured off the boundaries of a precinct which he made sacred to his mighty sire. In the midst of the plain did he set aside a level space, the Altis, and fenced it round about. The land without this space did he ordain to be a place for feasting and for rest. Then to Alpheios' stream he sacrificed and to the twelve sovereign gods." [5] In the space which he had consecrated Herakles celebrated the first Olympian games.

From Pisa he went against the city of Pylos, which fell before his arms, and here he encountered Periklymenos, one of the sons of Nereus, who tried to escape his fate by resorting to the powers of transformation which Poseidon had given him. He could change himself into a lion, a snake, a bee, or even so small an insect as a gnat, but when he had taken the form of this last and was about to escape, Herakles' vision was miraculously cleared so that he detected and caught him, and slew him along with all the rest of his family except his brother Nestor. In this struggle Hades fought on the side of the Pylians and was grievously wounded by Herakles.

Among the allies of Nereus had been the sons of Hippokoön of Sparta, against whom Herakles organized an expedition for their opposition to him and for their wanton murder of one of his kinsmen, as well as for a grudge against the Spartans who had withheld cleansing from him after the death of Iphitos. After much persuasion he enlisted on his side King Kepheus of Tegea, and to save Tegea from capture during the absence of its defenders he left with Kepheus's daughter a lock of the Gorgon's hair enclosed in a bronze water-jar. In the war that ensued Iphikles and the men of Tegea were killed, but in spite of this loss Herakles was able in the end to overcome his foes

PLATE XXIV

Amazons in Battle

To the left of the centre of the picture an Amazon, wearing a turban-like helmet and mounted on a horse, thrusts with a lance at a fallen Greek warrior, behind whom one of his fellows battles with another Amazon attacking with an axe. Both of the warrior-women are clad in tight-fitting garments conspicuous by reason of their peculiar chequered and zigzag patterns. From a red-figured volute *krater* of the latter half of the fifth century B.C., in the Metropolitan Museum of Art, New York (*photograph*). See pp. 85, 103–04.

and gain their city, which he restored to its rightful king, Tyndareos (or, perhaps, to his sons), who had been driven out by the sons of Hippokoön. It was just after this occasion that Herakles met Auge in Tegea.

In Aitolia and the Mountains. — Herakles crossed the Gulf of Corinth to Aitolia and became a suitor for the hand of Deianeira, the daughter of Oineus of Kalydon, although in so doing he became a rival of the powerful river-god Acheloös. While wrestling with the divinity, who had taken the form of a bull, the hero broke and retained one of his horns, which was so precious to its owner that for its restoration he allowed Herakles to possess Deianeira, and, besides, to take the wonderful Horn of Plenty, which would give to him who held it as much food or drink as he should wish for. For many days Herakles was entertained by Oineus, and even helped him in a war of conquest along the coast of the Adriatic, but, as usual, his bulk and strength got him into trouble in spite of himself. One day he chanced to kill a lad who was related to the king, and though forgiven by the lad's father, he went into voluntary exile, as the custom of the country required, and set out with Deianeira to take up his abode with Keÿx of Trachis, a city on the other side of the mountains. Arriving at the river Evenos, over which Nessos the Centaur used to ferry on his back those who travelled afoot, Herakles crossed alone, leaving his wife in the care of Nessos. As soon as the husband was a little distance away, the Centaur made a vicious attack upon the woman, but at her outcry Herakles turned and with a well-aimed shaft pierced her assailant through the heart. When Nessos had crawled out on the river's bank to die, he called Deianeira to his side and gave her a mixture of his blood which, he promised, would serve as a love-philtre to revive her husband's affection for her should it wane at any time.

As Herakles passed through the country of the Dryopians, he found himself in need of food. He had apparently forgotten the boundless capacity of his magic Horn of Plenty, so that, when none would give him food, he seized an ox and prepared a meal from it. The inhospitality of the Dryopians he never forgot, and later he punished them with a devastating war, killing their king as he was impiously feasting in a shrine of Apollo. Not long afterward he went to the aid of Aigimios, king of the Dorians, who was being beleaguered by the Lapithai, and drove the besiegers away. In this district there was a place well adapted for an ambuscade which the votaries of Apollo had to pass on their southward journey to Delphoi, and there Kyknos, a son of Ares, used to lie in wait and attack them as they went by; but when he met with Herakles he was overpowered and slain, and thenceforth the pilgrims were unmolested.

At last the moment arrived for Herakles to punish the faithlessness of Eurytos. Going against Oichalia, he slew the king and his sons and many of their allies, and then sacked the city and took Iole captive. When the news of this seizure reached the ears of Deianeira, her heart was aflame with jealousy, and she prepared to make use of the gift of Nessos. It happened that Herakles sent a messenger to her from Oichalia to bring back to him a ceremonial vestment for a solemn sacrifice. Choosing a robe, she poured over it some of the magic liquid, but her trust in Nessos turned out to have been too hasty, for it was no philtre that he had given her, but a fiery liquid which wrapped the body of Herakles in deadly flames as soon as he donned the garment. Recognizing that his end was near, the hero ascended Mount Oita above Trachis and had a great pyre of wood built. Upon this he lay down and ordered those about him to kindle it, but none had the boldness of heart to take their master's life. At length a passer-by, Poias (or perhaps Poias's son, Philoktetes) was induced to do the deed by the gift of Herakles' bow and arrows. As the flames rose and consumed the hero, a cloud from which thunder proceeded was seen to gather over him and to take him into its bosom, and in heaven he was given the boon of immortality and wedded Hebe, the daughter of Hera. With Hera herself he was at last reconciled, while Deianeira, when she contemplated the result of her awful deed, hanged herself.

The Descendants of Herakles.—The sons of Herakles, the issue of his many amours at home and abroad, were in number as the sands of the sea. Of them all Herakles' favourite was Hyllos, a son of Deianeira, and to him the hero gave the kingship of the Dorians, thus establishing the traditional bond between his line and the Dorian stock. On his father's death Hyllos married Iole. The children of Herakles, now fearing Eurystheus, fled to Trachis, and thence, still menaced, to various parts of Hellas. In the course of their wanderings they came to Athens, begging for protection, and the Athenians, by giving them an army, did better for them than the fugitives had dared to hope, for the united forces routed the foe, and Hyllos, pursuing Eurystheus as far as the Skironian rocks, slew him. The Heraklids then overran the Peloponnesos, but on the advent of a plague they obeyed the injunction of an oracle and withdrew to Marathon, where they established a colony. Some time later Hyllos again sought the advice of an oracle and received the response that he and his brothers would come into their own "at the end of the third harvest." Interpreting this literally, as was natural, they made several unsuccessful attempts against the Peloponnesos, in an early one of which Hyllos lost his life in a duel with Echemos of Tegea. Finally the god made known to the remaining brothers that the "three harvests" referred to three human generations, and thus, patiently awaiting the end of this period, they achieved their desire and divided the Peloponnesos into three parts, Argos, Lakedaimon, and Messene, each part being assigned to a branch of the family.

CHAPTER VI

THESEUS

IN the story of his life as it now stands Theseus is frankly an imitation of Herakles, although this does not mean that his figure owes its entire existence to its model. Apparently, legends of a certain Theseus were very early brought from Crete to the coasts of the Argolid about Troizen, and through long years of repetition they became so familiar to the people as to be regarded as of local origin and thus as fit themes for local poets. By means of poetry and cult the name of Theseus was spread throughout Greece, but in Athens it won especial recognition because of friendly relations between Athens and Troizen and her neighbour cities, thus supplying a foundation for the conscious manufacture of new myths and the compounding of old ones. When the Athenians reached the stage of possessing a political consciousness, they found themselves very different from their older neighbours in that they were without an organized body of myth extolling their descent and detailing the glorious exploits of a great hero-forefather. Just like upstart wealth in a modern democracy concocting its aristocratic coat of arms, the Athenians resolved to set up a national hero and to drape his figure in the narrative of his alleged exploits. Theseus was ready at hand, partly Athenian, partly outsider. As an Athenian he could easily win local affection; as an outsider he was in a position to square with the people's political aspirations by breaking with the aristocracy and introducing a new order of things. The Athenians, therefore, took him as he was, and, for the sake of fixing him still more definitely in their locality, added a number of stories of

PLATE XXV

Theseus and Amphitrite

Theseus, a slender youth with long fair hair, stands on the upturned hands of Triton before Amphitrite, enthroned in her palace in the depths of the sea. With her right hand the Queen of the Waters extends a greeting to the lad, while in her left she holds against her breast the crown which she will place on his head as a sign that he is the son of Poseidon. Between her and Theseus stands the noble and unusually human figure of Athene. From a red-figured *kylix* by Euphronios (early fifth century B.C.), in the Louvre (Furtwängler-Reichhold, *Griechische Vasenmalerei*, No. 5). See p. 101.

long-established local currency to the stock of tales already gathered about him. So keenly aware were they of the calculated deliberation of the process that to them Theseus, of all the heroes, was in a class by himself, a personage almost across the threshold of history.

Birth and Childhood. — King Aigeus of Athens, though twice married, was not blessed with children, and in his disappointment he sought the counsel of the oracle, receiving a riddling answer which only served to perplex him the more. Going to Troizen, he made known his trouble and the answer of the oracle to King Pittheus, who quickly perceived the drift of the response and just as quickly devised a scheme by which to fulfil it. Plying Aigeus with wine until his wits deserted him, Pittheus left him overnight in the company of his daughter Aithra, and when morning dawned and Aigeus came to himself, he bade Aithra to rear the son she was destined to bear, and not to disclose his paternity to him until the proper time should come, which would be, he said, when their boy should be able to roll away a certain stone under which Aigeus had hidden a set of armour and weapons, and a pair of sandals. In due time the child was born, and was immediately, as most agree, given the name of Theseus. His grandfather Pittheus diligently circulated the story that he was the son of Poseidon, the tutelary deity of Troizen, but his mother held her peace. Even as a mere child Theseus showed himself fearless, for once, when Herakles, his kinsman, visited Troizen, he gazed without flinching at the dreadful lion-skin. At sixteen years of age he was fully grown, and as was the custom of young men went to Delphoi and presented to the god a clipped lock of his hair as a token of surrender of his life to the divine will. Then his mother took him to the stone, and when he had lifted it and donned the armour revealed to him the mystery of his birth and sent him to his father in Athens.

The young man, confident in his strength and impelled by the desire to rival Herakles, decided to take the long and dangerous land-route instead of the short and easy voyage across the gulf. Nothing could dissuade him from his purpose, not even the stories which Pittheus told him of the cruel robbers infesting the highway; indeed, these only whetted his appetite for adventure. With the intention merely of defending himself should need arise and of wantonly harming none, he set out from Troizen on a journey that was fated to involve him in six great labours.

The Labours of Theseus; First Labour. — As Theseus passed through Epidauros going northward, he was confronted by the robber Periphetes, a son of Hephaistos and Antikleia, who, inheriting his father's lameness, used an enormous club as an aid in walking. Standing across Theseus's path, he forbade him to proceed, but the hero, too quick and strong for him, pounced on him, killed him, and took his club both as a memento of the exploit and as an invincible weapon for the future.

Second Labour. — At the Isthmus of Corinth lived Sinis, a giant son of Poseidon, who made a practice of seizing travellers on the Isthmian highway and of binding them to one or more resilient saplings that had been bent to the ground, the release of the trees allowing them to spring back to an upright position and in so doing to tear asunder the bodies of the victims. This heartless wretch Theseus hoisted with his own petard, even forcing him to lend a hand in bending down the tree to which he was to be tied. On the death of Sinis his daughter fled to a bed of tall asparagus and implored the plants to hide her, but when reassured by Theseus that no harm would befall her, she came out of her hiding-place and consorted with him, afterward bearing a son Melanippos whose descendants worshipped the asparagus plant. This story may be a mythical version of a ritual of a Poseidon-cult in the Isthmian groves.

Third Labour. — To the right of the road, just as one left the Isthmus, was the town of Krommyon. About this place roamed an unusually ferocious wild sow to which the terrified neighbourhood had given the name of Phaia. Though personally unprovoked by the beast, Theseus turned aside from his path, and, to show his valour and fearlessness, attacked and slew her single-handed. Some of the ancient writers, rationalizing this myth, suggested that Phaia was really a licentious murderess who was called a sow from her evil habits. This and the preceding theme seem to be of Isthmian origin.

Fourth Labour. — A little distance to the west of the city of Megara were some lofty limestone cliffs on the edge of which ran the road from the Isthmus. Here was the station of the robber Skiron, who would compel passers-by to stop and wash his feet, and, as they stooped before him, would kick them over the precipice at the foot of which a huge turtle devoured their mangled bodies. Turning the tables, Theseus threw him over. Some of the Megarians, in an endeavour to avoid speaking evil of a fellow-countryman, claimed that, in reality, Skiron was a suppressor of brigandage on this important highway. Be that as it may, it now seems probable that the story arose from a misunderstanding of a primitive ritual in which a human victim was thrown over the cliffs to remove pollution from the land and thus to ensure good crops.

Fifth Labour. — At Eleusis Theseus engaged Kerkyon of Arkadia in a wrestling bout and killed him with a violent throw.

Sixth Labour. — The road between Eleusis and Athens was beset by a cruel brigand known as Damastes ("Subduer"), or Prokroustes ("Stretcher"), who took travellers captive and fitted them perforce to his bed. If they were too tall, he would mercilessly lop off their extremities, and, if too short, he would stretch them to his own length, invariably killing them by either process; but at Theseus's hands he met death by the treatment which he gave to others. Probably in Damastes we are to see the god of death, and in the bed the democratic seven feet of sod to which we must all come sooner or later.

Theseus in Athens. — Theseus had now reached the borders of Athens, but he did not cross them until he had been purified of the blood of Sinis, who was a kinsman of his own through their joint relationship with Poseidon. As he went across the city clad in a long flowing robe, he passed a temple on the roof of which the builders were still at work. These, noticing his peculiar garb, began to make sport of him and asked him why a proper young lady like himself was out walking unescorted, whereupon, without a word, Theseus unyoked a team of oxen standing by and tossed them higher than the peak of the building.

The household of Aigeus he found to be in a desperate state, for the king had become old and the people had grown restless under his feeble sceptre, but as there was no heir he still clung tenaciously to the throne. Medeia, who was now his wife, with the vision of a witch recognized Theseus as soon as he appeared, but she kept her discovery to herself and plotted to take his life by poisoning him at a feast. Theseus, however, detected her design and at a timely moment revealed himself to his father by drawing his sword as if to cut the meat on the table. Aigeus and the populace received him with great joy and acknowledged him as the prince of the realm.

But the cousins of Theseus, the sons of Pallas, were very angry, for his arrival had spoiled their chances of succeeding jointly to the throne. Declaring that Aigeus was only an adopted brother of Pallas, and that Theseus was an unknown outlander, they proclaimed war against him and plotted to entrap him, but a traitor revealed their plans, and Theseus retained the supremacy.

Theseus in Crete. — It was not long before Theseus had the opportunity of doing his greatest deed for Athens, for the time arrived when the Athenians must make their third payment of tribute of Attic youths to Minos, and the populace began to find fault with Aigeus on the ground that he had taken no steps to rid them of this periodic calamity. To still their chiding Theseus offered himself as one of the victims of the Minotaur, while all the others were chosen by lot, although one

PLATE XXVI

Lapiths and Centaurs

In this scene three separate combats are being enacted. In that on the right, a Centaur is wielding a tall tripod against a Lapith and parrying the blow of a dagger. The Centaur of the central group is with one hand forcibly drawing his antagonist toward himself and with the other hand clenched is beating him in the face. At the left a Lapith and a Centaur are battling, the one with a double-axe, and the other with the neck of a broken jar. From a red-figured *kylix* by Aristophanes (late fifth century B.C.), in the Museum of Fine Arts, Boston (Furtwängler-Reichhold, *Griechische Vasenmalerei*, No. 129). See pp. 104–05.

account of the legend states that Minos selected them all, naming Theseus first. Before going on board the ship Theseus secretly assured his father that he would succeed in killing the Minotaur and thus free his people from their bondage; and since the tribute-boat ordinarily carried a black sail to betoken the hopelessness of its passengers, Aigeus gave the helmsman a white one to be hoisted far out at sea on the voyage home if Theseus were returning safe and sound.

It was probably after the arrival of the Attic youths in Crete that Minos expressed his doubts that Poseidon was the father of Theseus, and to make a test of his parentage he threw a ring into the sea. Theseus plunged in after it and was borne by a dolphin or a Triton to the thrones of Poseidon and Amphitrite. There Poseidon granted him the fulfilment of three wishes that he might make in the future, while Amphitrite gave him a garland, and then, bearing the latter as an emblem of his divine birth, he emerged from the water bringing the ring to Minos.

Before the captives were enclosed in the labyrinth, Ariadne, a daughter of Minos, fell in love with Theseus and promised to help him find his way out of the prison, if he would bind himself to take her to Athens and make her his wife. Theseus promptly gave this easy pledge, and at the suggestion of Daidalos Ariadne then presented him with a skein of linen thread which he was to unwind as he advanced to the innermost recess of the labyrinth. Once there he easily slew the Minotaur with his fists, and by following the thread made his way back to the light. Embarking on his ship with Ariadne, he fled from Crete and touched at the island of Naxos, but as to just what happened here the sources are not agreed. One has it that Theseus, tiring of his bride, deserted her, and that she in despair hanged herself; another, that Dionysos, enamoured of her, conveyed her to Lemnos and forced her to wed him; and still another, that, driven by a storm on the shores of Cyprus, Ariadne died from exposure and Theseus instituted regular sacrifices at her tomb. At all events, Theseus reached home without her, but as the ship drew near to Athens, the helmsman in his great joy forgot to hoist the white sail, and Aigeus, seeing the black one, threw himself over the cliffs on which he stood and was dashed to pieces. On landing Theseus buried his father's remains and paid his vows to Apollo.

Fig. 4. Theseus and the Minotaur

Theseus, an athletic young man, with his left hand seizes the Minotaur by a horn, while with his right hand he is about to thrust at the monster with a short sword. Compare this manner of killing with that mentioned in the text. The two spectators of the struggle may be Minos and Ariadne. From a red-figured *krater* of the fifth century B.C., found at Gela (*Monumenti Antichi*, xvii, Plate XXX).

Theseus and the Bull of Marathon. — The story of Theseus and the bull of Marathon is really a continuation of that of his Cretan adventures. It will be remembered that the beast had killed Androgeos, the son of Minos, and after this it continued, unchecked, its ravages among both men and crops. Assigning himself the task of subduing it, Theseus went to Marathon, grappled with the bull, and by sheer strength of muscle forced it to submit to his will, after which he drove it across country and through the streets of Athens, at last sacrificing it on the altar of Apollo.

Theseus as King and Statesman. — When, on the death of his father, Theseus became the head of the state, he soon perceived that the lack of proper political association among the scattered townships of Attike was a great source of weakness for his country, and in order to secure co-operation among them in the works of peace and war alike he persuaded the various communities to unite in the formation of a commonwealth. He then appointed central places for meeting and conference, instituted a national festival, drew up laws, and issued a state currency; he divided the populace into three classes, nobles, farmers, and artisans, giving each class its special political function; he invited outsiders to settle in Athens and enjoy the rights of citizenship; he annexed Megara, and in emulation of Herakles founded games on the Isthmus in honour of Poseidon. In order to appear democratic he proposed to the people that he be known, not as king, but as commander-in-chief of the army and defender of the laws, yet, despite all this, he was always regarded as king.

The Later Adventures of Theseus; the Amazons. — Like Herakles, Theseus had what we may call his supernumerary adventures, the first of which is generally accounted to have been his expedition against the Amazons. Whether this was purely his own venture, or whether he was merely the comrade of Herakles, is by no means clearly determined, but in either instance, he won Antiope as the prize of his efforts and took her back to Athens. For her seizure the Amazons declared war against Athens and besieged the Acropolis, encamping on an eminence at its foot, and since they were the daughters of Ares, this height was from that time known as Areopagos (for another legendary explanation of the name, see above, p. 70). The siege lasted four months and was broken only through the intercession of Theseus's Amazon wife, although some authorities, on the contrary, assert that she fought against her own race and died at her husband's side, pierced by a javelin. Many of the slain Amazons were buried in the vicinity of Athens, and their graves were objects of interest to travellers for many centuries. This mythical conflict foreshadowed the later wars of history in which Athens was to be the leader of the Greeks against invading barbarians.

Theseus and Hippolytos. — If we are to discredit the story of Antiope's noble death, we must accept another in which she was set aside by the fickle Theseus in favour of Phaidra, a sister of the deserted Ariadne. According to this version, her rejection gave her a pretext for leading the Amazons to prosecute a war against Athens, but by Theseus she left a son Hippolytos who turned out to be "a somewhat intractable compound of a Jehu and a Joseph." As a youth he was devoted to the hunt and was a diligent worshipper of the chaste Artemis, while Aphrodite and all her works he hated with a holy hatred. For this Aphrodite punished him, causing his step-mother Phaidra to burn with love for him and to make evil advances, but when he haughtily rejected these, she slandered him before his father, who banished him and besought Poseidon to visit destruction upon him as the fulfilment of one of the three wishes he was to grant. Poseidon heard the prayer and raised up from the sea an enormous bull which so frightened the horses of Hippolytos that they ran away and killed him. When it was too late, the truth of the matter was revealed to the remorseful Theseus, while the guilty Phaidra took her own life by hanging.

Friendship with Peirithoös. — Peirithoös had heard of the great strength of Theseus, and, in order to test it, drove some of Theseus's cattle from the plain of Marathon. Theseus pursued the raider, but, when they came face to face, they found themselves unexpectedly attracted to one another. Peirithoös promptly offered to pay whatever damages Theseus might claim, but all that the latter would accept was a pledge of friendship, and thenceforth they were inseparable. Theseus was present at the wedding of Peirithoös to Deïdameia in the country of the Lapithai, when some Thessalian Centaurs, who were also guests, became heated with wine and attacked the Lapith women; but, led by Theseus, the men fought them off, slew some, and drove others from the land.

When Theseus was about fifty years old, the two friends kidnapped Helen of Sparta and held her for a while in Attic territory, this constituting an adventure with whose details we have already become acquainted. During her detention Theseus accompanied Peirithoös to the home of Hades to seize Persephone and make her the bride of Peirithoös, but the task was not like that of capturing the partly mortal Helen, for Hades had the two abductors overpowered and bound with serpents to the Seat of Lethe ("Forgetfulness"). Herakles later set Theseus free, but even his great strength was insufficient to enable him to loose Peirithoös.

Death of Theseus. — On returning to Athens Theseus learned that Helen's brothers had stormed the fortress where she had been held captive and had taken her back to Sparta, and, along with her, his own mother Aithra, while, to increase his troubles, another political party was in the ascendancy and was instigating the people against him. Finding the opposition too great, he solemnly cursed the Athenians and with his family withdrew to the rocky island of Skyros, where, it is said, at the command of the king of the island he was pushed over the sea-cliffs and killed. After the fall of Troy his children returned to Athens and reigned. Nevertheless, the spirit of Theseus was not dead, for at Marathon he fought on the side of the Athenians and turned the tide of battle in their favour. At the close of the Persian wars his bones were brought to Athens from Skyros in obedience to an oracle, and buried with great pomp in a tomb in the heart of the city.

CHAPTER VII

THE VOYAGE OF THE ARGO

THE voyage of the Argo is the great culminating episode in the vicissitudes of certain branches of the family of Aiolos, and it will, therefore, be necessary to review the lives of the most important personages of this family.

The Descendants of Aiolos; Salmoneus, Pelias. — Salmoneus, a son of Aiolos who had settled in Elis, drew upon himself the divine anger for having attempted to usurp some of the prerogatives of Zeus, for he made a practice of imitating the thunder and the lightning of a rain-storm and was killed by a real bolt from the hand of Zeus. From this description of him we are to infer that he was of the class of rain-making magicians still to be found in some primitive communities. His daughter Tyro was forced to yield to the embraces of Poseidon and bore twin sons, Nereus (Neleus) and Pelias, who were exposed in infancy, but were found and reared in another family than their own. Nereus and his children were slain by Herakles at Pylos, but Pelias took up his abode somewhere in Thessaly, married, and had, among other children, a son Akastos and a daughter Alkestis who was destined to become one of the most famous of women. For an impious act of his youth Hera visited on Pelias a curse which was to follow him through life. Tyro, after the abandonment of her children, was legally wedded to Kretheus, her father's brother, and became the mother of three more children, Amythaon, Aison, and Pheres, who lived together in the Thessalian city of Iolkos which Kretheus had founded, until Pheres, with laudable enterprise, built the new city of Pherai, on an inland site

PLATE XXVII

The Argonauts

The interpretation of this scene is by no means certain. It has been explained as depicting a band of Athenian warriors about to give battle to the Persians in the presence of the gods and heroes of old. Generally, however, it is thought to represent a group of the Argonauts, without reference to any particular episode. If this interpretation is correct, one can easily perceive the appropriate appearance of Athene, the divine patroness of the Argo, of Herakles, with club and lion-skin, and of one of the Dioskouroi, with his horse. Any attempt to identify the other figures would be purely fanciful. From a red-figured *krater* of the end of the fifth century B.C., in the Louvre (Furtwängler-Reichhold, *Griechische Vasenmalerei*, No. 108).

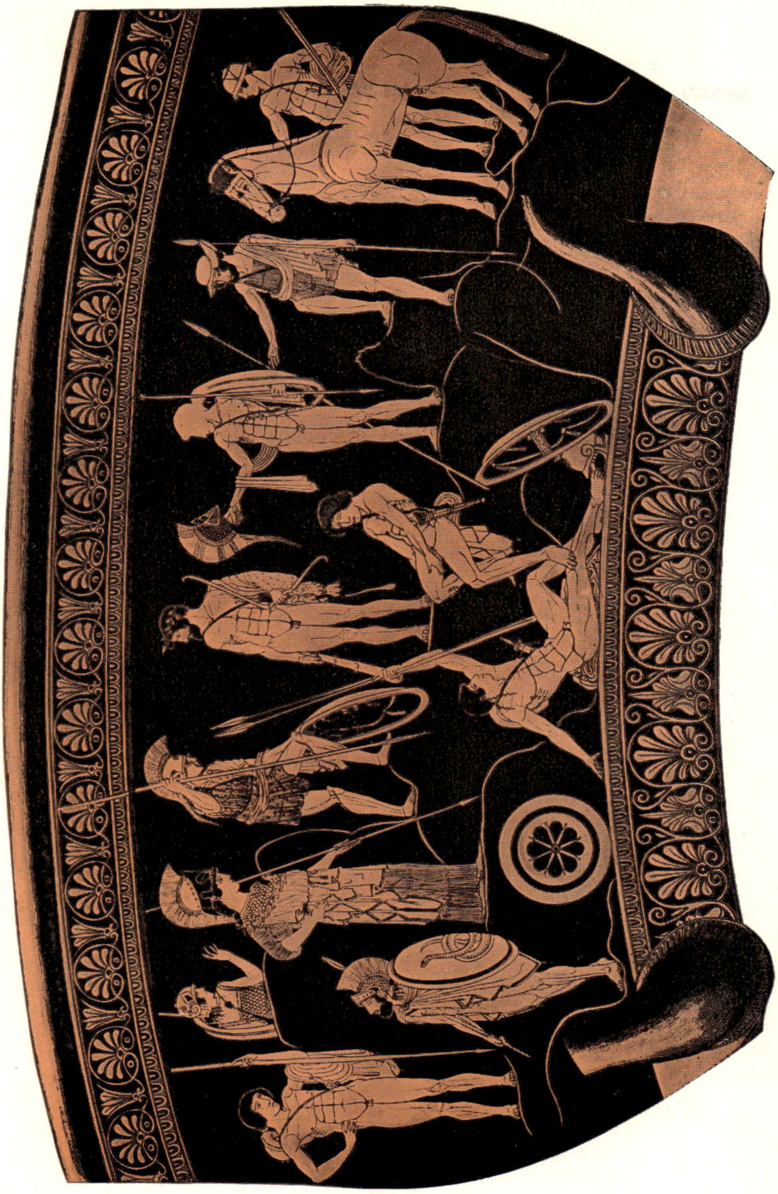

not many leagues away, and became its king. In his old age Pheres gave up the throne to his son Admetos.

Admetos and Alkestis. — The story of the courtship and wedded life of Admetos is the theme of the *Alkestis* of Euripides. The beginning of the story goes back to Apollo's slaying of the Kyklopes in revenge for the death of his son Asklepios, and for this murder he was punished by Zeus, being sent to serve as a slave to a mortal man. That man chanced to be Admetos, who treated the god with the kindest hospitality and was rewarded by a great increase in his flocks and herds. Seeking in marriage Alkestis, the daughter of his kinsman Pelias, he went to Iolkos and paid her court, but her father had promised that he would give her only to the man who should succeed in yoking to a car a lion and a wild boar. When it seemed to Admetos as if this impossible condition would compel him to forego his love, Apollo yoked the animals, and helped him win his bride. At the wedding-sacrifice, however, Admetos forgot to give victims to Artemis, who, to requite him, filled his bridal chamber with serpents, but Apollo bade him offer suitable propitiation and obtained for him from the Fates the boon that, when about to pass away, he should be spared the actual terrors of dissolution through the death of a voluntary substitute. At last Admetos's fated day came, and of all his friends and kin none but his dear wife Alkestis was willing to die for him. He became well again while she sickened and died and was buried; but by chance Herakles passed through Pherai bound for Thrace, and learning the cause of the mourning in the house he entered the tomb, defeated Death, and amid general rejoicing brought Alkestis back to her husband.

Athamas, Phrixos, and Helle. — Athamas, another son of Aiolos, had two children, a son Phrixos and a daughter Helle, by an earlier marriage than that with Ino, who was very jealous of them and plotted to destroy them. Secretly advising the women of the country to roast the corn before sowing, she brought about a failure of the crops, and when Athamas sent messengers to the oracle to inquire how to remove this condition, Ino suborned them, and they brought back a false report, announcing that the land would again bear fruit if Phrixos were sacrificed to Zeus. As the lad stood by the altar to be slain, his mother Nephele suddenly led out a ram with a golden fleece, the offspring of Poseidon and Theophane, and placing Phrixos and Helle on the animal she drove it away. Swiftly it went eastward overland to the straits between Europe and Asia, but as it was swimming these Helle fell off its back into the water and was drowned, whence, ever afterward, the Greeks knew the straits as the Hellespont ("Helle's Sea"). Phrixos, on the other hand, was borne by the ram to the farther end of the Euxine, where was the land of Kolchis, over which King Aietes ruled. There, as one story says, he grew to manhood and afterward returned to his old home in the west; although, according to a variant legend, he was killed by Aietes, and the ram was sacrificed to Zeus, while its golden fleece was hung on a mighty oak in the grove of Ares and guarded by a dragon.

The Return of Iason. — The narrative now returns to Iolkos. When Kretheus died, his son Aison was dispossessed of his kingdom by his half-brother Pelias, but he still lived on in Iolkos and offered no resistance to the usurper. To prepare, however, for a day of vengeance he craftily announced that his son Iason was dead, whereas, in reality, he had sent him away to Cheiron to be educated, while to Pelias he made the prophecy that some day he, Pelias, would die at the hands of an Aiolid or by an incurable poison. Years after this Iason returned to Iolkos, and with many others was invited by Pelias to a feast of Poseidon, but in crossing a swollen stream on the way he chanced to lose his left sandal in the mire. As he approached with only his right foot shod, Pelias observed him, and when he learned who he was called to mind with a great shock that this was the mark of the man by whom he was doomed to die.

After a conference of several days with his father and other kinsfolk, Iason, appearing before Pelias, boldly asked him to surrender the throne and sceptre, and the usurper weakly assented, but begged him to have pity on his old age. Would he not first of all, he asked, recover the Golden Fleece, and by thus appeasing the soul of Phrixos bring peace to the line of Aiolos? On this condition Pelias was willing to step down from the throne without a struggle. Iason accepted the task, but, suspecting a ruse against his life, engaged Akastos, Pelias's son, to share the dangers of the adventure with him.

The Voyage of the Argo. — Summoning Argos, a son of Phrixos, Iason bade him build a fifty-oared ship, and with the help of Athene Argos fashioned "the most excellent of all ships that have made trial of the sea with oars,"[1] and named it the Argo. Into its prow Athene fitted a piece of the talking oak of Zeus at Dodona, and when it was completed Iason sent heralds throughout Greece announcing his expedition. From all parts men hastened to enroll themselves as his companions. Their number was too great for us to catalogue them here, but we may say that all of them were real "heroes, the crown of men, like gods in fight," many of whom we have met in the myths already recorded. Bidding farewell to the people of Iolkos, the company withdrew to the seashore, and beside the ship held a council in which with one accord they elected Iason their leader. After a sacrifice to Apollo in which they found the omens favourable, they launched the Argo and sailed away through the Gulf of Pagasai to the open Aegean, "and their arms shone in the sun like flames as the ship sped on."[2] Skirting the coast, they held first a northward and later an eastward course, until they came to Lemnos, where lived a race of women, ruled by Hypsipyle, who out of jealousy had killed off all their husbands, but who, by this time weary of single existence, joyfully welcomed the Argo's crew and tempted them to delay among them for a season. With the weakness of true sailors the men yielded to their beguilements and lingered many days; and perhaps they would utterly have forgotten their goal had not Herakles vigorously brought them to their senses. Embarking once more, they sailed north to Samothrace, where they accepted initiation into the sacred mysteries in order to ensure themselves a safe return, and thence they passed through the Hellespont, "dark-gleaming with eddies," to the island of Kyzikos, the land of the Doliones. Here they obtained stores and information, and had to ward off an attack of the six-armed Earth-born men, many of whom fell before the bow of Herakles. After proceeding only a short distance eastward, they were buffeted by head winds and driven back to another part of the island. The same Doliones who had given them food saw them land but were unable to recognize them owing to the distance, and taking them for pirates they set upon them, only to bring destruction upon themselves. For twelve days and twelve nights the Argonauts were detained here by reason of storms, which abated, however, after a sacrifice to Hera. When they had rowed to a point on the coast of Mysia, Herakles and Hylas, his favourite youth, went ashore and made their way into the forest, the one to get wood and the other to draw water; but as Hylas stooped over a spring, the water-nymphs, won by his beauty, reached up and drew him under. One who heard him cry out ran and told Herakles, thinking that a beast had slain him, and in vain the hero wandered back and forth through the forest searching for the lad, being away so long that his friends on the Argo forgot him and put to sea without him.

Coming next to the country of the Bebrykians, the Argonauts were challenged by King Amykos to choose one of their number to contend with him in boxing, and Polydeukes, brother of Kastor, offered himself. Fighting, each with his boxing gauntlets on, they smote one another with such blows "as when shipwrights with their hammers smite ships' timbers," [3] until at last Polydeukes placed a blow squarely on Amykos's head, and he fell to the ground with his skull crushed

PLATE XXVIII

Medeia at Corinth

(Lowest panel.) Beginning at the left the sculptor has depicted serially the last scenes in Medeia's life at Corinth. In the first, she dismisses her two children with the fatal gifts for Glauke. In the second, the princess, wrapped in the burning robe and with her hair aflame, is writhing in agony, while Kreon, her father, stands near her, visibly tortured by the thought that he is unable to help her. Meanwhile the children, terrified at the havoc which they have wrought, hasten to find their mother. In the last scene Medeia is stepping into the chariot, drawn by winged dragons, opportunely sent to her by her grandsire, Helios. From a sarcophagus in Berlin (Brunn-Bruckmann, *Denkmäler griechischer und römischer Sculptur*, No. 490). See p. 115.

in. At that moment the Bebrykian people assailed the slayer of their king, but his companions repelled them and overran the land, taking much booty.

On the following day they passed through the Bosporos and touched at the home of the blind old seer Phineus, whom the gods had not only punished with blindness, but had doomed never to taste of food from his own board. Whenever viands were placed before him, the Harpies would pounce upon them and carry them off, leaving an overpowering stench. Phineus asked the Argonauts, Zetes and Kalaïs, to fulfil a certain prophecy and free him from these pests, and, accordingly, when the Harpies came to seize the next meal, the winged heroes fled aloft and pursued them so far out to sea that Iris took pity on them and pledged that their depredations would cease. The Argo's crew then spread a bountiful feast for Phineus to celebrate the breaking of his long fast, and heard from his lips a prophecy outlining their journey and foretelling their success as far as Kolchis. The rest of their future he veiled in silence.

Leaving the Bosporos, they were safely guided by Athene through the dangerous Symplegades, two great moving rocks which cleaved the waves more swiftly than the tempest, and coming to the open Euxine they turned their prow to the east and pressed on to the island of Thynias, and thence to the mouth of the river Acheron, where several of them were killed. Though discouraged, they sailed to Sinope, past the mouth of the river Halys and the country of the Amazons, to the Chalybes (the nation of iron-workers) and to the Mossynoikoi (the people of topsy-turvy morals), and halted at the Isle of Ares, where the sea-birds dropped sharp, feathered shafts upon them. Here they found four sons of Phrixos who had been shipwrecked in sailing away from Kolchis, and who endeavoured to dissuade Iason from pursuing his errand further, but to no purpose, for Iason all the more eagerly urged his companions on. At last they came to the river Phasis, on one bank of which stood the city and palace of Aietes, while on the other was the grove sheltering the Golden Fleece.

The gods now began to intrigue in favour of the Argonauts. Hera and Athene beguiled Aphrodite to instil a passion for Iason in the heart of Medeia, one of the daughters of Aietes. This was of supreme moment for the Argonaut leader, since without her assistance he would have been helpless before the task which Aietes demanded that he accomplish as the price of the fleece, this requirement being to plough a field with a yoke of bulls with brazen feet and flaming breath, to sow it with dragon's teeth, and then to slay the armed men that should spring up from this strange seed. Now, since Medeia was a sorceress and a priestess of Hekate, she compounded a drug which would render one anointed with it immune from fire and iron for one day, and secretly meeting Iason she gave it to him. After telling one another of their love, they parted, and at dawn Iason, with his body and armour anointed with Medeia's charm, faced the ferocious bulls. Throwing them with ease, he forced them to submit to the yoke and to plough the field, and when the warriors had sprung up from the dragon's teeth scattered broadcast, he hurled a stone into their midst, as Kadmos had done at Thebes, and set them to killing one another. He had now completed his task unharmed, and Aietes was filled with dismay.

As soon as Medeia realized the full meaning of what she had done, she fled secretly to Iason and promised to help him win the Golden Fleece if he would pledge his word to take her with him to Hellas and make her his bride. Accepting this condition, Iason was led by her to the oak on which the fleece was hung, and while she cast a spell on the dragon, he snatched the prize and fled with her to the Argo. They were soon well out to sea, hotly pursued by Aietes, but when Medeia saw her father drawing nearer, she resorted to a cruel device to check him. Killing her brother Apsyrtos, whom she had taken with her, she scattered his severed members over the water, thus forcing Aietes, through his sense of piety, to collect them and to go ashore and give them proper burial. In the meantime the Argo had out-distanced him and safely reached the delta of the Danube, and although a few Kolchians came up a little later, they were beaten off.

Somehow (in defiance of the geography of the region as it is known today) the Argonauts made their way by water to the head of the Adriatic Sea, and thence went southward to the island of Kerkyra (Corfu). With human voice the Argo now spoke to them solemn words of warning, declaring that for the murder of Apsyrtos their home-coming would be delayed by Zeus until they should reach Ausonia and be purged of their sin by Kirke. In search of this strange land they sailed to the river Eridanos and to the Rhodanos (Rhone), but, warned by Hera, avoided the Rhine. At length they found their goal, and, being purified, with joyful hearts turned their prow toward Hellas under the safe guidance of the Nereïds.

The Argonauts' route led them past Anthemoëssa, the island of the Sirens, whose blandishments, however, did not overcome them, for the song of their companion Orpheus drowned the alluring voices. They fared past Skylla and Charybdis and the island of Thrinakia, with its herds of the cattle of the Sun, and came to the land of the Phaiakians. In this place they were met by a band of Kolchians who demanded the restoration of Medeia, but the Phaiakian king intervened as arbiter, and said that she would be surrendered only on condition that she were yet unwedded to Iason, whereupon the pair made haste to become man and wife and foiled the Kolchians' plans. After a sojourn of many days among the hospitable Phaiakians, the men of the Argo resumed their journey, but when they were just in sight of the Peloponnesos they were driven by a northerly gale across the sea to Libya, and were held by the shoals of the Syrtes. As Iason was wondering how to extricate his ship from these dangerous waters, he had a fortunate dream, being told in vision that he would see a horse emerge from the deep and that the Argonauts, taking their vessel on their shoulders, were to follow the steed whithersoever it might lead. The prediction came true, and for twelve days and twelve nights they were guided overland by a horse to the Tritonian Lake, near which they found the Hesperides, who informed them that Herakles had been there only the day before in quest of the Golden Apples. Desirous of seeing their former comrade, they searched the wild country roundabout, but with no more result than to discover that they were hopelessly lost in a strange land, until, in their despair, Triton appeared to them and showed them the way to the Sea of Minos.

Reaching the sea, they sailed to Crete, but when they attempted to land they were beaten off by the Cretan coast-patrol, Talos.[4] Now this man was one of the Race of Bronze, and from his neck to each of his ankles ran a great vein, the lower end of which was stopped by a bronze stud, which was his vulnerable spot. Putting Talos under a spell, Medeia drew out a stud and let him bleed to death. After a delay in Crete of only one day the heroes hastened past Aigina and Euboia and soon entered their home port of Pagasai from which they had set out four months before.

The Death of Pelias. — The end of the voyage is not the end of the story. So far was the perfidious Pelias from yielding his kingdom now that his conditions had been fulfilled that he even plotted against Iason and his family. Aison and his wife were driven to take their own lives, and Iason, for safety's sake, withdrew to Corinth, where he dedicated the Argo to Poseidon and from where he never ceased sending messages to Medeia, encouraging her to devise some means of removing Pelias. According to another form of the story, Medeia by her magic arts restored both Iason and his father to youth, thus arousing in the hearts of the daughters of Pelias so keen a desire that their father, too, should be rejuvenated that the sorceress professed to give them a recipe for this transformation and a demonstration of its working. Cutting up the body of an old goat, she boiled the pieces with some herbs in a cauldron, and at the conclusion of the process a kid emerged from the magic stew. Just as the wily Medeia had calculated, the loving daughters of Pelias submitted their father to a similar process and brought about his death. For her part in this murder Medeia was exiled from Iolkos along with Iason.

Iason and Medeia in Corinth. — The exiles took refuge in Corinth. For about ten years they lived happily together, but at length the differences between the Greek and the barbarian temperaments became painfully apparent, and a domestic clash ensued, so that finally Iason set Medeia and her two children aside, and took the Corinthian princess, Glauke, as his wife. Iason ought to have known his revengeful Medeia too well to have followed such a course, for through her children she sent a poisoned robe and garland to Glauke, who, when she put them on, was burned to death. After her children had returned from their errand, Medeia pierced them with a sword and fled to Athens in a chariot drawn by winged dragons which had been sent to her by her grandsire, Helios.

Medeia in Athens. — In Athens Medeia became the wife of Aigeus and bore him a son Medos, but when she plotted to take the life of Theseus, she and her son were banished from the kingdom. Medos conquered the barbarians of the east and called the country Media, while his mother returned in disguise to her native land, expelled her uncle Perses, who had usurped the throne, and restored her father Aietes to his rights.

Some students of myth interpret the incidents gathering about the life and death of Pelias as originating in a nature-myth, but it seems much more in harmony with the known processes of the growth of myth to infer that the story is an epic development of an early historical incident, or of a group of related incidents. Pelias appears to have been the hero of an agricultural people of southern Thessaly who were led with great reluctance to abandon agriculture as their chief means of subsistence and to take to sea-faring instead. The adventures of the Argonauts are, therefore, wild exaggerations of the yarns of sailors, who in very early times penetrated the strange lands of the Mediterranean basin, interwoven with many genuine folk-tales.

PLATE XXIX

1

Priam before Achilles

Achilles, a beardless young man, half-reclining on a couch beside a table laden with viands, holds in his left hand a piece of meat while with his right hand he raises a dagger or a knife to his lips. He seems to be giving orders to a slave in utter disregard of the presence of Priam, who stands before him at the head of a group of slaves bearing a variety of gifts. The body of Hektor lies limply at full length beneath the couch. In the background can be seen Achilles' shield with its *gorgoneion*, Corinthian helmet, quiver, and some garments. From a red-figured *skyphos*, apparently by Brygos (early fifth century B.C.), in Vienna (Furtwängler-Reichhold, *Griechische Vasenmalerei*, No. 84). See p. 130.

2

Peleus and Thetis

This scene, in which the artist has boldly violated the law of the unity of time, depicts the attempts of Thetis to escape from the embraces of Peleus. In the background the goddess appears in human shape, while her assumption of the form of a dolphin is suggested by the dolphin which she holds in her right hand. The lion-fish between her and Peleus, the flame on the altar, and the serpent above it, similarly suggest other of her transformations. The woman hurrying away to the right may be a sea-nymph. From a black-figured *lekythos* (fifth century B.C.) with a white ground, found at Gela (*Monumenti Antichi*, xvii, Plate XIII). See p. 122.

1

2

CHAPTER VIII

THE TALE OF TROY

THE tale of Troy, like that of the Argonauts, is in its complete form a tissue of many stories woven at sundry times about a single great incident. Some of the legends deal with secular facts directly pertinent to the incident, the war for Troy and the command of the Dardanelles. Some are plainly folk-tales of a variety of origins, dragged in, so to speak, as embellishments to an interesting theme. Some, not wholly to be differentiated from the preceding class, are myths drawn from certain cults and rituals, and others must be purely conscious inventions. The tale of Troy is not a drama, but rather a great treasury of dramas, and most of its personages, both human and divine, have been made known to us in scenes already portrayed. We must now marshal the human personages by families and sketch those parts of their histories which, in combination, led up to the great war.

The House of Dardanos. — Dardanos, a son of Zeus, lived in the island of Samothrace with his brother Iasion, who was struck dead by a thunderbolt for a shameful crime, while Dardanos, in grief, left his home and established a new one on the Asiatic mainland near the mouth of the Hellespont. Finding favour with Teukros, the king of the land, he was given a tract in which he built a city called after himself, and later he inherited the sovereignty and changed the name of the entire country to Dardania. After him the throne was occupied successively by a son Erichthonios, and by a grandson Tros, who saw fit to call the country Troia. This Tros had three sons, Ganymedes, Assarakos, and Ilos. The first, while still a youth, was loved by Zeus for his beauty and was carried away by an eagle to Olympos, where he became the cup-bearer of the king of the gods. Assarakos is known chiefly through his descendants; a grandson, Anchises, became by Aphrodite the father of the great Aineias. In a wrestling contest in Phrygia Ilos won as a prize fifty youths and fifty maidens, and received from the king of the country a spotted heifer which he was directed to follow until it should lie down; on that spot he was to establish a city. In accordance with these directions he founded Ilion, and after praying for a sign of the approval of Zeus, he discovered standing before his tent the palladion, an image of Pallas Athene of almost human size. Building a shrine, he placed the statue within it as a symbol of his city's life, and at his death the chief authority was left in the hands of his son Laomedon, whom Herakles afterward killed for his failure to keep his word.

With Ilos's son Podarkes, later known as Priamos (Priam), begins the important part of the history of Ilion or Troy. Priam first wedded Arisbe, and afterward Hekabe (in Latin, Hecuba), the daughter of Kisseus (or Dymas, or Sangarios). The first child that Hekabe gave him was the mighty Hektor, but when she was about to bring another infant into the world, she dreamed that she had given birth to a flaming torch which fired and consumed Ilion, and this vision a reader of dreams interpreted to mean that the babe would destroy his native city. Priam, in fear of the sign, had him exposed immediately after birth on the slopes of Mount Ida, but, as the Fates would have it, he was first nourished by a she-bear, and was then found by a herdsman, who reared him till he had attained the years of manhood. The name first given to him was Paris, but for his success in warding off robbers from the folds and for his beauty it was changed to Alexandros ("Defender of Men"). It happened that a favourite bullock of his herd was sent to Priam as a victim for a sacrifice which the king was to offer for the very son whom he had exposed, but Paris followed the beast to Ilion and in a series of contests overcame a number of his brothers. Just as Deïphobos, one of them, was about to thrust him through with a sword, Kassandra, his sister, with her divine vision recognized him and led him to Priam, who gave him a place in his rightful home. Later on he married the prophetess Oinone.

The House of Tantalos. — Tantalos, who was a son of Zeus and the nymph Plouto, and lived on Mount Sipylos near the Lydian city of Sardeis, was so wise that Zeus confided to him his secret thoughts and even admitted him to the banquets of the gods. At one of these feasts he placed before the gods the severed members of his son Pelops, but only Demeter took a portion, whereas the others, observing that the flesh was human, united in restoring the boy to life. Instead of the shoulder which she had eaten Demeter inserted a piece of ivory which remained with him all his days and became so much a natural part of him that each of his descendants inherited an ivory shoulder. For his sin against the gods Tantalos received special punishments in the underworld.

The restored Pelops was endowed with such beauty that Poseidon gave him a chariot which would fly over land and sea, and confident in his charms he presented himself as a suitor of Hippodameia, the daughter of Oinomaos, king of Pisa in Elis. The maiden reciprocated his love, but he was unable to wed her because of the strange conditions imposed by her father, who had been told by an oracle that he would be murdered by the man who should wed his daughter. Resolved to defeat the oracle by having no son-in-law, he challenged each of his daughter's suitors to a chariot-race, stipulating that if the suitor won he was to receive Hippodameia, but that if he lost he was to be killed. Carried by his horses, which were swifter than the north wind, Oinomaos had always overtaken the suitors, as a row of heads before his palace eloquently testified, but Pelops knew all this and bribed Myrtilos, the king's charioteer, to draw the linchpins of his master's car, so that in the race with Pelops Oinomaos was thrown, and, caught in the reins, was dragged to his death. With Hippodameia Pelops sailed to his home in Argos, where there were afterward born to them, among other sons, Atreus and Thyestes.

For the sins of Tantalos an inevitable curse of family strife and bloodshed followed all the generations of his house. Unknown to Atreus, his wife yielded herself and her affections to Thyestes. Now Atreus had promised to sacrifice to Artemis the most beautiful animal that should be found among his flocks, but when one of his ewes gave birth to a golden lamb,[1] he greedily coveted the precious creature, and strangling it hid its body in a chest that the goddess might not see it. Besides himself, only his wife knew of this lamb, which he seemed to regard as the emblem of the kingship at Mykenai, and she privily gave it to Thyestes, who thereby secured the throne. Prompted by Zeus, Atreus made a pact with his brother that if the sun should be seen to reverse its usual course, the kingship was to revert to himself. One morning the sun chanced to be in total eclipse. Interpreting this as the setting of the sun in the east, Thyestes yielded to Atreus, and then, when all his iniquity was revealed, was expelled from the country. Some time afterward, under the guise of a reconciliation, Atreus recalled him, but actually it was in order to wreak a most revolting revenge, for he killed Thyestes' children and served their cooked flesh to their parent, and in the midst of the meal, with ghoulish satisfaction, made known to the father the nature of the food. Thyestes fled, plotting revenge in his turn, and an oracle declared to him that his desire would be realized through a son whom he should beget by his own daughter. His spirit rebelling at the thought, he endeavoured by all possible means to avoid bringing the oracle to fulfilment, even though he should lose his kingdom. Destiny was against him, however, for Aigisthos, a son of unwitting incest, restored him to Mykenai, where he ruled until driven

PLATE XXX

The Sacrifice of Iphigeneia

Diomedes and Odysseus, a strongly built, bearded man, are carrying Iphigeneia to the altar faintly visible at the right of the scene. The maiden raises her hands toward her father, Agamemnon, the veiled personage to the left, in a last appeal for help. Between her and the altar towers the foreboding figure of Kalchas, clad in his ceremonial robes and meditatively holding the sacrificial knife in his raised right hand. High in a background of cloud a nymph is leading a deer to Artemis, whose image, flanked by hunting-dogs, stands on the column beside Agamemnon. From a Pompeian wall-painting (Hermann-Bruckmann, *Denkmäler der Malerei des Altertums*, No. 15). See pp. 125–26.

out by Atreus's sons, Agamemnon and Menelaos, aided by Tyndareos of Sparta. These two sons married daughters of Tyndareos; the former took Klytaimestra and ruled at Mykenai, and the latter wedded Helen and succeeded his father-in-law on the throne of Sparta.

The House of Aiakos. — After her removal to the island of Oinone, as we have read in the tales of Corinth, the nymph Aigina bore to Zeus a son named Aiakos. Noticing that he was without companions, his father, turning the ants of the island into human beings, made Aiakos their king, and by a play on the Greek word for ant (*μύρμηξ*) these ant-men were known as Myrmidons. By a first marriage Aiakos had two sons, Peleus and Telamon, and by a second, another son, Phokos. Of all men of that age Aiakos was the most devoted to the worship of the gods, and so dear was he to them on that account that when a famine came upon Hellas, they removed it in answer to his supplication alone, while after death he was accorded a high place in the kingdom of Hades.

Spurred on by jealousy, Peleus and Telamon killed their brother Phokos and for their crime were sent into exile. Telamon took refuge in the island of Salamis, where later he became king and married into the line of Pelops, the fruit of this union being the hero Aias (Ajax). Afterward Telamon accompanied Herakles on his expedition against Troy, and as a reward for his services received Hesione, by whom he became the father of Teukros.

Peleus made his way to Phthia in Thessaly and there won the king's daughter and a portion of land. Accidentally killing his father-in-law, he hastened to Iolkos, where Akastos purged him of his pollution, and where, too, Akastos's wife made the same charge against him that Proitos's wife had alleged against Bellerophon. Akastos believed the tale, as was only too natural, but fearing to take Peleus's life openly resorted to many underhanded plots, although in the end Peleus was saved by the Centaur Cheiron, and from that day these two were fast friends. Becoming enamoured of the sea-nymph Thetis, the daughter of Nereus, and finding himself baffled by her power to assume any shape she wished, he was counselled by the wise Cheiron to seize her and defy her elusiveness. This he did, and though she became now fire, now water, and now beast, he clung to her until, resuming her normal form, she consented to marriage, and they were wedded on Mount Pelion in the presence of all the gods, who gave them many priceless gifts.

In due time a son was born to Peleus and Thetis, and to cleanse him of his inheritance of mortality his mother would bathe him in ambrosia by day and pass him through fire by night, but Peleus protested at the harshness of the treatment, and Thetis, offended, retired to her home in the sea. Peleus placed the infant in the care of Cheiron, who fed him on the flesh and marrow of wild beasts, and gave him the name of Achilles because his lips had not touched a mother's breast (by a false etymology with ἀ-, "not," and χεῖλος, "lip"), training him, too, in the hunt and in those sports that develop the peculiar strength and beauty of a man. When the boy was nine years old, Kalchas, the prophet, foretold that, if he went with the Greeks against Troy, he should surely die there; and yet, he said, the Hellenes could not conquer the city without him. Through a strange infatuation Thetis hoped to evade the prophecy and sent Achilles, dressed as a girl, to the court of Lykomedes, king of Skyros, where he remained for six years. At the end of this time Odysseus was deputed by the Greeks to go to Skyros and bring Achilles to Troy, but the young man's disguise safely concealed him for a while. At length the wily Odysseus had his men blow a loud alarm of trumpets, when out into the main hall of the palace rushed Achilles, who thinking an enemy was upon them threw off his feminine garb and donned his armour. Now that his identity was established, he was easily persuaded by Odysseus to espouse the cause of the Greeks, and with his bosom friend Patroklos he joined the host at Aulis.

Diomedes and Odysseus. — Of all the other heroes who fought about Troy the most conspicuous are Diomedes and Odysseus, the first of whom was the son of that Tydeus who fell before Thebes. A warrior from his youth, he took part in the capture of Thebes by the Epigonoi and led to Troy eighty ships from the Argolid and outlying islands. He was valiant in battle, resourceful in plotting, and wise in the councils of his peers. Frequently associated with him, especially when trickery was to be employed, was Odysseus. This man generally passed as the son of Antikleia, a daughter of Autolykos, and of Laërtes, though some gossipy myths will have it that he was in reality the son of Sisyphos, his craftiness and versatility being thus explained as inheritances from both sides of the house. Once during his youth, when on a visit to his grandfather Autolykos near Mount Parnassos, he was wounded on the knee by a boar, and in healing, the wound left a scar by which he was recognized years afterward by his old nurse. Another time, when Laërtes sent him to the mainland to demand restitution from certain Messenians who had carried off some of their sheep from Ithake, he met Iphitos and received from him the bow which only Odysseus could draw. He won as his bride Penelope, the daughter of Ikarios of Lakedaimon, one of whose acts, soon after their marriage, foreshadowed the unswerving fidelity of her later years. It is said that when Odysseus refused to make his home in Lakedaimon, Ikarios, like a fond parent, persistently besought his daughter to remain behind her husband, until at last Odysseus, losing patience, bade her choose between himself and her father, whereupon, without a word, she drew down her veil and followed her husband. In Ithake she bore him a son Telemachos, but while the child was still in arms, Menelaos came with Palamedes to Odysseus to entreat his aid against Troy. Being averse to war, he feigned madness, but Palamedes saw through the ruse, and taking Telemachos from his mother made as if to run him through with a sword. At this Odysseus admitted his pretence, but though he consented to their request he ever after bore a grudge against Palamedes.

The Kypria; Traditional Causes of the War. — "There was a time when thousands upon thousands of men cumbered the broad bosom of earth. Having pity on them, Zeus in his great wisdom resolved to lighten earth's burden. So he caused the strife at Ilion to the end that through death he might make a void in the race of men; and the heroes perished, thus bringing to pass the will of Zeus." In these words the late epic known as the *Kypria*,[2] with an almost modern political casuistry, traces the cause of the war back to overpopulation. Instead of solving the problem by thunderbolt and flood, Zeus decided to use a much less direct method. First of all he brought about the marriage of Thetis with the mortal Peleus, and then he begat a daughter Helen, who was so beautiful that it could be said of her:

> "She snareth strong men's eyes; she snareth tall
> Cities; and fire from out her eateth up
> Houses. Such magic hath she, as a cup
> Of death." [3]

In brief, she was a trouble-maker by birth. Into the midst of the gods, gathered at the wedding of Peleus, Zeus sent Eris, who stirred up a quarrelsome debate among Hera, Athene, and Aphrodite, as to which of them was the most beautiful; and Zeus, knowing that, woman-like, they could never settle the question of themselves, had them appear on Mount Ida before Paris as arbiter.

> ". . . And this Paris judged beneath the trees
> Three Crowns of Life, three diverse Goddesses.
> The gift of Pallas was of War, to lead
> His East in conquering battles, and make bleed
> The hearths of Hellas. Hera held a Throne —
> If majesties he craved — to reign alone
> From Phrygia to the last realm of the West.
> And Cypris, if he deemed her loveliest,

PLATE XXXI

Hektor Taking Leave of Andromache

Owing to its lack of feeling this scene is an inadequate illustration of the famous episode in the sixth book of the *Iliad*. The central figures are, of course, Hektor and Andromache. Behind the former his driver Kebriones is mounted on one of the two chariot horses, while behind the latter stand Paris and Helen. The figures approaching from the sides are not named. From a Chalkidian *krater* of about 550 B.C., in Würzburg (Furtwängler-Reichhold, *Griechische Vasenmalerei*, No. 101). See p. 120.

Beyond all heaven, made dreams about my face
And for her grace gave me [i. e. Helen]. And, lo! her grace
Was judged the fairest, and she stood above
Those twain." [4]

Paris then awarded Aphrodite the apple inscribed with the legend, "To the most beautiful."

At the suggestion of the goddess whom he had honoured Paris built a ship and with fair omens went to Sparta, where he was courteously entertained. During an absence of Menelaos, however, he threw the laws of hospitality to the winds, made love to Helen, and at last, with her full consent, carried her away in his ship along with her jewels and handmaidens, landing her in Troy after a devious and stormy voyage. When Menelaos demanded her return and was refused, he remembered the oath sworn by his fellow-suitors and resolved to invoke their aid in a war of punishment; wherefore, with his brother Agamemnon of Mykenai, he gathered together the chieftains of the Greeks and set sail from Aulis. They landed first on the coast of Teuthrania, which they attacked under the impression that it was Troy, and here it was that Telephos, the son of Auge and Herakles, was sorely wounded by the spear of Achilles. When the Greeks endeavoured to sail thence to their proper destination, they were caught by a storm and driven back to their home coasts. Again Menelaos marshalled them at Aulis, but this time he took the precaution of securing some one to guide them straight to their goal, and such a leader was present in the person of Telephos, who, out of gratitude for having his wound healed by the same spear with which it had been caused, consented to serve the Greeks. At Aulis Agamemnon killed a sacred hind of Artemis and the goddess in anger sent "on that great host storms and despair of sailing," [5] whereupon Kalchas consulted the omens and made known to Agamemnon that he could not obtain fair winds until his daughter Iphigeneia should be sacrificed on the altar of Artemis. Shrinking from the task of taking the maiden from her mother, Agamemnon deputed it to Odysseus, who, shamelessly representing that she was to become the bride of Achilles, led her away from Mykenai. Just as her blood was about to be spilt on the altar, however, Artemis put a deer in her place and bore her away unseen to the land of the barbarous Tauri, where she became a priestess in her service. Then the seas became calm, and the fleet set sail.

On their way the Greeks touched at Tenedos, where Philoktetes, the possessor of the bow of Herakles, received on the foot a serpent's bite which developed into so loathsome a sore that he had to be removed from Lemnos. At length the army came to the shores of Troy and found their landing disputed by the Trojans. Desirous to acquire the fame of being the first to land, although it meant certain death, Protesilaos, one of the younger heroes, leaped ashore and fell then and there before the spear of Hektor. When the tidings of his untimely death reached his young bride Laodameia, she besought the gods that for three hours her husband be restored to her. They heard her prayer, but so great was her grief at the hour of his final departure to Hades that in despair she made an image of him, and finding no comfort in it took her own life. Unable to assail Troy directly with any chances of success, the Greeks sacked many of the Trojans' supply cities and captured much booty. After one of these raids Achilles received as his prize a maiden, Briseïs, and Agamemnon another maiden, Chryseïs, a daughter of Chryses, a priest of Apollo; and it was through the presence of these maidens in the camp that the great wrath of Achilles was kindled with such momentous consequences for the Greeks.

The Iliad. — The poet of the *Kypria* gathered up the legends describing the events of the war prior to the action of the *Iliad* of Homer. The theme of the *Iliad*, on the contrary, is one episode alone, the Wrath of Achilles, though it has been so treated that by skilful allusions it gives glimpses of earlier happenings of the war; and in this way the recital of the poem is devoid of the monotony that would otherwise result from its failure to touch on raids on the outlying territories of Troy during the twenty-eight days allotted to the action of the epic.

Books I–VI. — A plague fell upon the Greek host, smiting man and beast so grievously that "the pyres of the dead burnt continually in multitude," [6] and when Kalchas explained this as the visitation of Apollo's anger for the seizure of Chryseïs, Agamemnon, with bitter reluctance, restored her to her father, and the plague was stayed. In his thoughtless selfishness, however, Agamemnon took Achilles' Briseïs in her place, whereupon, maddened with anger, Achilles swore that from that day he would withhold his strength and skill from the Greeks even though many of them should fall by the hand of Hektor; and in her sea-home Thetis heard her son's complaint and won from Zeus the promise that victory would be denied the Greeks until they should do honour to Achilles. Prompted by Zeus in a dream, Agamemnon mustered the army for an assault on Troy, but at the sight of the Trojans' preparations for resistance he weakened in his purpose and like a craven suggested to the Greeks that they abandon the war as hopeless. The stubborn Odysseus opposed him, however, and forced him to change his will and do battle with the foe. Long the tide of strife swung uncertainly this way and that, until at length Hektor, impatient for a decision, and weary of the shameless Helen, proposed that Paris and Menelaos fight a duel and that to the victor Helen and her wealth be finally surrendered. By an oath and a sacrifice the opposing leaders ratified their willingness to stand by the outcome of the duel, and Paris and Menelaos then came forth and fought. At one moment, when Menelaos had Paris at his mercy and the end of the war seemed to be in sight, to the unspeakable despair of the Greeks Aphrodite veiled Paris in a cloud and hurried him away to safety behind the walls. The gods, taking sides, willed that the strife continue uncertain, and inspired the combatants to mingled deeds of bravery and recklessness. Pandaros the Trojan lightly wounded Menelaos, and later the valiant Diomedes as he stormed across the plain, and Diomedes, in his turn, stung to rage by his pain, struck both Aphrodite and Ares until their divine blood flowed from gaping wounds, while Apollo, resentful at the insolence of a mortal, roused the Trojans to still greater resistance. This climax of human ferocity, however, was relieved by scenes of tenderness and affection more characteristic of peace than of war, for when Glaukos and Diomedes were about to join in combat they discovered that their fathers had been associated in friendship years before. Forthwith they exchanged armour and vowed to avoid one another thenceforth in the field of battle, and though Glaukos gave gold armour for bronze, for friendship's sake he kept hidden within his heart any regret he might have felt. Hektor, returning to the battle, took a brave soldier's farewell of his wife Andromache and of his child Astyanax in words that none can ever forget: "Dear one, I pray thee be not of over-sorrowful heart; no man against my fate shall hurl me to Hades; only destiny, I ween, no man hath escaped, be he coward or be he valiant, when once he hath been born." [7]

Books VII–XII. — Even the gods grew weary of this fruitless *mêlée* and seeking to end it they caused Hektor and Aias to fight in single combat until a truce was established for the two armies. During the armistice the Trojans urged Paris to give Helen up, but he would consent only to a compromise, the surrender of her wealth with the addition of some of his own. An offer to this effect the Greeks scornfully rejected and prepared to carry the war to the bitter end, so that on the next day the battle began afresh, and so threatening were the assaults of the Trojans that Agamemnon, fearful of his cause, sent an embassy to Achilles bearing a confession of wrong and promises of amends. But neither confessions nor promises moved the wrathful man, who even hardened his heart the more. The hopes of the Greeks fell, only to be revived that

PLATE XXXII

ACHILLES AND THERSITES

The most conspicuous features of this rather detailed composition depict a scene from the *Aithiopis*. Achilles, taunted by Thersites for being touched with pity for the fallen Penthesilea, has drawn his sword and beheaded his annoyer, whose mutilated body is seen lying in the lower foreground. The elderly Phoinix, perplexed at the occurrence, stands near Achilles in the façade. Above their heads hang various accoutrements of war, and before them on the ground near Thersites' body are several overturned utensils, emblematic of a scene of violence. From a large South Italian *amphora* of the fourth century B.C., in the Museum of Fine Arts, Boston (*photograph*). See p. 130.

very night by a successful raid of Diomedes and Odysseus within the Trojan lines. On the morrow, however, fortune went once more against them, for Agamemnon, Diomedes, and Odysseus were all wounded, and the Greeks without their aid were forced to retreat to the line of their ships.

Books XIII–XVIII. — When Agamemnon was on the point of ordering his followers to launch the ships and withdraw home, Poseidon came to his help and breathed strength and valour into the hearts of Aias, the son of Telamon, and Aias, the son of Oileus. At the head of the Greeks these two wounded Hektor and routed his fellow-warriors; but their glory was brief, for Hektor was revived by Apollo and led his men in a counter-attack which brought them once more to the ships. Thereupon Patroklos tried to persuade Achilles to forego his anger and rally the Greeks, and failing in this he borrowed Achilles' armour and impetuously rushed into the battle himself, scattering the foe before him until he fell a victim to the weapons of Hektor and the guile of Apollo. Hektor despoiled him of his famous armour, but the Greeks after a long struggle obtained possession of his body. Achilles' grief kindled within him a hatred of the Trojans great enough to quench his wrath at Agamemnon, and unburdening his heart to Thetis she brought him a marvellous set of armour newly made for him in the forges of Hephaistos, at the sight of which the spirit of vengeance came upon him.

Books XIX–XXIV. — The next morning Achilles appeared before the Greeks, saying: "I will now stay my anger. It beseems me not ever implacably to be wroth: but come rouse speedily to the fight the flowing-haired Achaians, that I may go forth against the men of Troy and put them again to the proof." [8] With these words he sallied out to battle, slaying many of the Trojan heroes and pursuing many others into the waters of the river Skamandros, which, when it turned on him, he quelled with the fires of Hephaistos. The Trojan cause seemed lost, and to save it, Hektor, despite Priam's entreaties, stepped forth from the city gates face to face with the victorious Achilles. Struck suddenly with fear, however, the Trojan hero turned and fled, while Achilles pursued him, once, twice, and thrice around the walls, and then brought him to the ground, dead, after which he mutilated the body, and binding it to his chariot dragged it in the dust while Priam and Andromache looked down from the walls of Troy. On his return to the camp he duly burned the body of Patroklos and held funeral games, and moved by the tender appeal of Thetis, he yielded the body of Hektor to Priam, besides allowing the Trojans a truce of twelve days in which to perform the burial rites of their noble defender.

The Aithiopis; [9] *The Death of Achilles.* — Arktinos of Miletos, the oldest Greek epic poet definitely known, wrote the *Aithiopis* as a chronicle of the events of the war from the death of Hektor to the death of Achilles. Achilles himself, broadly treated, and not one of his moods, was the theme of the poem, and consequently the scenes were rather mechanically strung together without essential unity.

At the beginning of the epic the Amazon, Penthesilea, was represented as coming to the support of the Trojans. Achilles battled with her as though she had been a man and killed her, but the sight of her beauty as she lay fallen before him awakened his remorse. Thersites observed it and mocked him for his weakness, but with a thrust of his sword Achilles smote him dead, while the Greeks, divided among themselves as to the justice of the deed, became involved in a dissension that was not healed until Achilles was ritually washed of his sin in Lesbos. Another ally now joined the defenders of Troy — Memnon, a nephew of Priam and the son of Eos and Tithonos, who came from Aithiopia. Like Achilles, he wore armour curiously fashioned by Hephaistos, but he was inferior to the Greek in head and hand and fell before him, although, at the supplication of Eos, Zeus granted him immortality. Achilles, just as he was about to follow up his victory with the rout of the foe, was slain by an arrow guided by Apollo from the bow of Paris, but in the *mêlée* which ensued Aias, the son of Telamon, carried the body away to the Greek ships, and over it Thetis, her sister nymphs, and the Muses made piteous lamentation. When at last it lay burning on the pyre, Thetis, unseen, snatched it from the flames and bore it away to the White Isle in the friendless waters of the Euxine Sea, where Achilles was restored to life and lived with Helen as his wife, although some said that the Greeks mingled his ashes with those of his friend Patroklos, and that after death he consorted with Medeia in the Islands of the Blest.

Fig. 5. The Death of Penthesilea

The Amazon, mortally wounded by Achilles, has fallen to the ground, and Odysseus (right) and Diomedes (left) are trying to help her to stand; but their efforts are in vain, for her head droops helplessly forward and her arms hang limply in the hands that support them. From the design incised on the back of an Etruscan mirror (Gerhard and Körte, *Etruskische Spiegel*, v, Tafel CXIII).

The Little Iliad and the Ilioupersis;[10] *The Fall of Troy.* — In the *Little Iliad* Lesches of Lesbos recounted the events of the siege from the death of Achilles to the entrance of the wooden horse into Troy, these events being so set forth as to centre about the person of Odysseus. As its name implies, the *Ilioupersis* ("Sack of Ilion") of Arktinos deals with the overthrow of the city.

Aias, the son of Telamon, demanded that as a kinsman of Achilles he should be given the dead warrior's arms, but since Odysseus made a counter-claim, the sons of Atreus instituted a contest to decide the future ownership of the weapons. With the help of Athene Odysseus won them, and so sore a wound was this to the pride of Aias that he became a raving madman and slew himself. By means of an ambuscade Odysseus captured Helenos, a son of Priam who was gifted with prophecy, and obliged him to forecast the outcome of the war. When his answer was that Troy would fall before the bow of Herakles, Diomedes went to Lemnos and by blandishments and wiles brought back with him Philoktetes, who had the bow, and after Philoktetes' wound had been healed by Machaon, he strode out to the battle. With an arrow from the great bow Paris fell mortally wounded. Only Oinone, his former wife, was in a position to aid him, but she took advantage of this opportunity for revenge and let him die; and after Menelaos had spitefully abused the body, the Trojans gave it burial. Neoptolemos (or Pyrrhos), the son of Achilles, was now brought from his home in Skyros to buttress the Greek cause, and through his valour the enemy were sealed within their walls. Craftily Odysseus made his way within the city and after slaying several Trojans returned safely with the sacred palladion on which the Trojans' fortunes hung. Now Epeios, instructed by Athene, had made a huge hollow horse of wood, in which were hidden fifty of the most valiant of the Greek warriors, while the rest were ordered to withdraw to Tenedos, leaving the horse before the gates of Troy. When they were gone, the citizens, thinking that their troubles were ended, emerged from their gates and gathered about the horse, but were much puzzled by the inscription which it bore: "A thank-offering from the Hellenes to Athene for their home-return." Was this true, or was it only a ruse? Those who believed it to be a trick spoke for destroying the horse. Laokoön, a priest, thrust a spear into its side, and at the hollow sound given back pronounced it Greek guile, but shortly afterward two serpents came out of the sea and crushed him and his two sons to death. Helen walked about the horse imitating the voices

PLATE XXXIII

The Death of Aigisthos

The personages of this tragic episode are identified by the names inscribed beside them. Orestes, the young man in the centre, thrusts his sword into the body of Aigisthos and looks back half-fearfully, half-defiantly at his mother Klytaimestra, who (in a panel on the opposite side of the vase) endeavours to wrest from Talthybios a double-axe with which to defend her paramour. The terrified maiden is Chrysothemis, a sister of Orestes, who is but little known in legend. From a red-figured *pelike* of the style of Euthymides (early fifth century B.C.), in Vienna (Furtwängler-Reichhold, *Griechische Vasenmalerei*, No. 72). See p. 135.

of the Greek leaders' wives, and Antikles, one of the men within it, would have answered had not Odysseus stopped his mouth. Nevertheless, those who accepted the inscription as innocent prevailed, and the horse was drawn into the city through a breach in the walls, after which the citizens gave themselves over to revelry until they were overcome by the heavy sleep of exhaustion. Creeping out from their lair, and led by Sinon, a Trojan traitor, the Greeks now took the citadel by surprise, and afterward proceeded to ravage the city, butchering the sleeping populace like helpless cattle. In their fury they disregarded all the restraints of religion. Neoptolemos slew Priam, though a suppliant at the altar of Zeus; Aias, the son of Oileus, dragged Kassandra from the altar of Athene; Odysseus threw Hektor's son Astyanax from the walls "for fear this babe some day might raise again his fallen land."[11] Together the Greeks set fire to the city and in the sight of its flame and smoke sacrificed Polyxena, Priam's youngest daughter, at the tomb of Achilles. Neoptolemos carried off Andromache, and Odysseus Hekabe, as prizes of war; Menelaos slew Helen's new husband, Deïphobos, and conveyed Helen herself to his ships. Now that the object of the war was attained, the Greeks with the utmost joy prepared to sail away to their distant homes. But alas! They had not counted on the wrath of Athene, who, roused by the offence of the son of Oileus at her shrine, almost implacably condemned them to "an homecoming that striveth ever more and cometh to no home."[12]

The Nostoi ("*Returns*"[13]). — In addition to Homer's *Odyssey*, which describes the devious return of Odysseus, there were five epic books of "Returns" written by Agias of Troizen, and dealing with the wanderings of the other heroes, especially those of the two sons of Atreus. These books are now lost, our knowledge of their contents being derived from a single brief summary, from a few casual references, and from some of the dramas of the fifth century.

Menelaos and Helen. — Naturally one's first interest is to learn the fate of Menelaos and Helen. As the fleet was about to depart for Hellas, Athene provoked a quarrel between the sons of Atreus, and to appease the goddess Agamemnon remained at Troy for a space, while Menelaos sailed away with his newly-recovered wife, the first point of Greek soil on which they set foot being Sounion, the extremity of the Attic peninsula. After a delay caused by the death of the pilot they set forth again, but ere they could round the point of the Peloponnesos the vessels were scattered by a storm. With only five sail left Menelaos made the island of Crete, whence, vainly attempting to steer homeward, he was driven to Cyprus, Phoinikia, Aithiopia, Libya, and, last of all, Egypt. Again head winds long detained him, but these ceased when, heeding the advice of Proteus, he sacrificed to the gods of the Nile, after which he and Helen were carried swiftly to Sparta, where they lived together for many years, until, the time coming at last for them to end this life, they were given immortality in the Islands of the Blest, by virtue of their divine descent. Many centuries later the tomb which held the body of Helen was shown to visitors in Sparta as one of the important sights of the city.

Agamemnon.—While Agamemnon was pressing toward Hellas with Kassandra the shade of Achilles appeared to him, and warning him of an unhappy home-coming endeavoured to turn him aside from his course. During his absence Aigisthos, by reason of the old family feud, had fomented trouble in his kingdom and had induced Klytaimestra, who was very unlike the faithful Penelope, to live with him in adultery. On Agamemnon's return to Mykenai (or to Argos) [14] Aigisthos, with the connivance of Klytaimestra, killed Kassandra, and then, inviting Agamemnon to a feast, treacherously murdered him too, although in another form of the narrative, it was Agamemnon who fell first, slain in the bath by the hand of his wife, ostensibly to punish him for the sacrifice of Iphigeneia ten years before. Aigisthos and Klytaimestra now reigned as king and queen.

A sure, though slow, vengeance was advancing upon the wrongdoers. Orestes, the youngest son of the murdered king, was secretly conveyed by his sister Elektra to the home of Strophios, a friend, who brought him up with his own son Pylades, and through long years of companionship the two boys became devoted friends, whom nothing but death could part. Knowing his mother's unspeakable crime, Orestes harboured revenge in his heart, and urged on by the Delphic oracle he went to Mykenai, where, by representing himself as a stranger bearing tidings of the death of Orestes, he was accorded the hospitality of the palace. Later Pylades, carrying an urn which he alleged to contain the bones of Orestes, was also received, and having thus insinuated themselves into the privacy of the royal home, at a favourable opportunity they killed both Klytaimestra and Aigisthos.

From the moment in which Orestes stained his hand in his mother's blood he was "hunted by shapes of pain" and through Hellas was "lashed like a burning wheel,"[15] for the avenging Furies of his mother were upon him. Pursued by them to Athens, he was tried on Areopagos and acquitted, after which, appealing to the oracle, he was told that to remove his blood-guiltiness he must first carry away from the land of the Tauroi the sacred image of Artemis which had fallen from heaven. Going thither with Pylades, he found that the priestess of the goddess was his own sister Iphigeneia, and after succeeding, by means of a cunning plot, in evading the watchful Taurians, he sailed away with the image and his sister, some say, to Rhodes, where he was at last given rest from the Furies.

The Other Heroes (*except Odysseus*). — On leaving Troy, Neoptolemos went across Thrace and conquered the country of the Molossians, but later he seized Hermione, the wife of Orestes, and for this act was killed by her husband at Delphoi. The lesser Aias, for his impiety against Athene, was cast up on the coast of Euboia and would have been saved had he not boasted of his ability to rescue himself without the aid of the gods. After escaping many dangers, Diomedes reached his home in Argos, but, finding that his wife was living in adultery, he immediately departed for Aitolia. When making an attempt, some time afterward, to return to his home, he was shipwrecked on the shores of Italy, and, being saved, lived there until his death. Demophon, the son of Theseus, on his way back to Athens visited the Bisaltian Thracians and married Phyllis, a princess of the land. When he expressed to his wife a wish to return to his native country, she gave him a chest which he was not to open until he should despair of seeing her again, but once out of her sight he sailed to Cyprus instead of Athens, and there took up his permanent abode. Phyllis at last, utterly weary of waiting longer, invoked a curse on him and killed herself. At about the same time Demophon opened the chest, but something he saw within it inspired him with fear, and hastily mounting to ride away he was thrown on the point of his sword by the fall of his horse and instantly killed.

The Odyssey. — In order to recount the adventures of the homeward journey of Odysseus in their proper sequence one must begin with the hero's own narrative in the middle of the *Odyssey* and later return to the first and succeeding parts.

Books IX–XII. — A fair wind bore Odysseus from Ilion to Ismaros, which he sacked, and then held his course for Cape Malea, although, before he could round it, Zeus swept him southward past Kythera to the land of the Lotos-Eaters, where men ate of the spicy bloom of the lotus and became forever oblivious of their old home. Apprehensive lest his companions, too, be minded

> "In the hollow Lotos-land to live and lie reclined
> On the hills like gods together, careless of mankind," [16]

Odysseus led them to the ships against their will and sailed to the country of the Kyklopes, a race of giants each with a single eye in the middle of his forehead. One of them, Poly-

PLATE XXXIV

Odysseus Slaying the Suitors

The groups on either side of the central ornament constitute a single scene. Odysseus, standing with drawn bow in front of two frightened maid-servants, is about to shoot at the suitors opposite him. One of them, already pierced by an arrow, is attempting to escape by climbing over a couch on which a companion is frantically defending himself against the missiles by means of a garment hung over his arm; a third suitor, crouching on the floor, holds a table before him as though it were a shield. From a red-figured *skyphos* of the first part of the fifth century B.C., in Berlin (Furtwängler-Reichhold, *Griechische Vasenmalerei*, No. 138). See p. 139.

phemos by name, entrapped Odysseus in his cave, but the cunning man of Ithake put out his eye and escaped with a remnant of his men. He now made for the island of Aiolos, the master of the winds, and as he set sail thence after a sojourn of many days, his host gave him a bag in which were enclosed all the winds except that one which would speed him on his way to Ithake. His companions, however, suspecting that some treasures were concealed in the bag, opened it while their leader slept, and the winds, rushing forth, beat the vessel back to the island which they had just left, but where Aiolos refused them further hospitality and sent them away from his coasts. They came next to the land of the cruel Laistrygonians, who destroyed all of their ships but one, on which they had the good fortune to reach the island of the sorceress-goddess Kirke, a daughter of Helios. By means of a charm she changed Odysseus's men into swine, but the hero himself she took as her lover into her home. Nevertheless, the call of home was upon him, and he could endure the sweet bondage for no longer than a year, so that at length he persuaded Kirke to aid him in an attempt to return to Ithake. As a first step she counselled him to make the descent to Hades, where he saw the shades of his mother and of many of the heroes, and learned from Teiresias, the Theban seer, the route which he should pursue to reach his home. Launching his ship once more, he sailed safely past the Sirens, having his men bind him tightly to the mast and himself stopping their ears with wax. On he pressed through the Clashing Rocks, and past Skylla and Charybdis, to the island of Thrinakia, where further disaster befell him, for his men, unable to be restrained, slew some of the sacred cattle of the Sun and caused a storm to break upon their ship so that all were lost save Odysseus himself. During ten days he was tossed about on a raft and then left by the waves on the shore of the island of the goddess Kalypso, with whom he lived for the space of eight years.

Books I–VIII. — At the end of this time Zeus hearkened to

the request of Athene and gave permission for Odysseus to be restored to his native soil. In the meantime, Athene, in the guise of Mentor, had visited Telemachos, Odysseus's son, in Ithake, and had bidden him send his mother's many wooers to their homes and to go in search of his father; but the suitors would not listen to the youth's words, even though they were accompanied by a prophetic warning of a dreadful doom that awaited them should they persist in their course. Unknown to them, Telemachos went to Nestor in Pylos, and thence to the court of Menelaos and Helen in Sparta, and although the only tidings which he could glean of his father were vague and far from recent, nevertheless, they encouraged him to hope.

Through Hermes Zeus commanded Kalypso to release Odysseus. Reluctantly she helped him build a raft and after twelve days of labour on it saw him depart from her island. Twenty days later he was washed up on the shore of Scheria, the island-country of the Phaiakians, whose king was Alkinoös. The princess Nausikaa chanced to find him in his distress and led him to the palace, where he told the long story of his still longer wanderings, and received from the king the promise of a safe convoy to Ithake.

Books XIII–XXIV. — The next day a magic ship of the Phaiakians bore Odysseus away and left him on the shore of his home-land in a deep sleep, but when he awoke, he was unable to recognize the place until Athene cleared his bewildered vision. Disguising himself as a beggar in obedience to her word, he made his way to the hut of the swineherd Eumaios who had remained loyal to his long absent master, and without revealing his identity, he learned from his old servant many things concerning the suitors. Just at this time Telemachos chanced to return from Sparta, safely eluding an ambuscade prepared for him by his enemies, and on landing he went to the hut of Eumaios and sent the swineherd to the palace with a message for his mother. In the interval he and Odysseus were left alone together, and at this supreme moment

Athene brought about a recognition of father and son, who jointly plotted the destruction of the importunate wooers.

On the following day Odysseus entered the palace. Though still disguised, he was recognized by his old dog Argos, which died of sheer delight; yet of all the people in the palace, including even Penelope, only Eurykleia, his nurse, knew him. As it happened, it was on that very day that Penelope announced to her suitors that when the next sun had risen she would definitely settle the question which had brought them all to Ithake. During all the months of their wooing she had put them off with the promise that as soon as she should complete a fabric then on her loom she would make her selection from among them; but the day of the choice never came, for each night, it was said, she unravelled what she had woven the day before. At last, however, she now declared that she would accept that man who with Odysseus's bow could send an arrow through the holes of twelve axe-blades arranged in a row, but when the trial of strength and skill came, not one of the suitors was able even to bend the bow. Though much derided, Odysseus then stepped forward and to the consternation of all sent the arrow through the appointed mark, after which, turning quickly on the suitors, he shot them one by one. Yet so changed was he through the many hardships which he had suffered as well as through the mere lapse of years that it was long before Penelope could believe he was really her own Odysseus. At length convinced, she welcomed him back to the home and to the place which she had kept sacred for him in her affection, and thenceforward they lived together at Ithake, as they had lived before, happy in their mutual love, and save for an unsuccessful attack of the dead suitors' friends at peace with all mankind.

The Telegonia.[17] — The later adventures of Odysseus and his sons are detailed in the sixth century epic, the *Telegonia*, the work of Eugammon of Kyrene, which completed the Trojan cycle of myths.

After the burial of the suitors by their kinsmen, Odysseus sailed across to Elis to inspect his herds. Returning to Ithake for a brief time only, he went to the land of the Thesprotians and wedded their queen Kallidike, for, some allege, he had dismissed Penelope on account of her wavering affections. On the death of Kallidike their son took the crown of Thesprotia, and Odysseus went back to Ithake about the same time that Telegonos, the son whom Kirke had borne to him, set out to find his father. Chancing to land on Ithake, he proceeded to plunder the country, and, defying a band of Ithakans whom Odysseus led against him, he killed his father in the conflict, in utter ignorance of what he was doing, but when the import of his act was made known to him, accompanied by Penelope and Telemachos, he bore the body of Odysseus back to Kirke.

CHAPTER IX

THE AFTERWORLD

THE *Greek View of the Soul and of Death.* — To comprehend, even in part, the Greek stories of the afterworld one must keep before him the fact that they are all based on the conception that the soul has a life apart from the body. This the Greeks held to be as certain as anything could be in the realm of the inscrutable, and all the phenomena of life seemed to point to its truth. When, however, they came to state their belief as to what the soul really was, they frankly argued from probability. The soul could not well be very unlike the living man; therefore, it was his shade, or airy double. This shade either comprised or was identical with all that was characteristic of the man — his personality, we say — for this is what vanished at death, while the inert body remained. Moreover, like the man himself, the shade was able to think, feel the drive of desire, and move about from place to place. On the other hand, the soul could not be very like the man, for the conditions of concrete existence could not surround it, and, moreover, it must be of a very tenuous substance, for it seemed to leave the body through a wound or with the passing of the invisible breath, and untrammelled by the body it was free to go about, as on wings, whithersoever it would, like the birds of heaven. Yet all its thoughts and desires were faint and futile, for it utterly lacked the material means of gratifying them, so that the existence of the disembodied soul was joyless and the end of all that men esteem worth while. The words of Hekabe to Andromache well sum up the attitude of the Greek toward death:

> "Death cannot be what life is, Child, the cup
> Of Death is empty, and Life hath always hope." [1]

But the Greeks strangely contradicted themselves. Though affirming the immateriality of souls, they were unable to conceive of their conscious existence without at least some of the accessories of the material. After death a man's shade pursued the same occupations which it had followed in life and cherished the same characteristic passions. Orion still hunted the wild beasts of the woodland; Aias still harboured his anger against Achilles; Aiakos and Rhadamanthys still sat on the tribunals of judgement; Teiresias still dispensed his prophecies. This bondage to the material extended even to the punishments of the arch-criminals: Ixion was bound to a real wheel, and Sisyphos struggled with a real stone.

When the Greeks came to localize the abode of the assembled shades, they not unnaturally, like many other peoples, believed it to be under the earth, an idea which probably sprang from the primitive custom of burial; and after the belief had once been established, it was easy to think of those souls that had been banished from their bodies by cremation as going to the same place. In this underworld were gathered the souls of all except a special few, souls that were thenceforth like to

> ". . . pale flocks fallen as leaves,
> Folds of dead people, and alien from the sun." [2]

It was a spacious democratic realm in which they abode, a realm in which there was no fear of overcrowding. Its boundaries were impassable, and rarely did a soul return from it to the upper light, even for a brief season. It was a kingdom organized like a kingdom of earth; Hades and Persephone sat on its two thrones as king and queen; and it had its several benches of judges. Hermes mustered the immigrants bound for its shores, and Charon, the grim, grey ferryman, transported them at the established tariff of an obol a head,[3] while Kerberos,[4] the three-headed hound, stood guard at its main

PLATE XXXV

Charon

This design is sketched with coarse yellowish lines of glaze on a white background. Charon, a tall and rather ungainly bearded man of a not unkindly countenance, stands at the stern of his boat and looks straight before him at a tiny winged soul descending toward him from the right. He is clad in a short, belted *chiton* without sleeves, and has his *petasos* hanging by a cord at the back of his head. He leans with his left hand on a long pole, the lower end of which rests in the water, while with his right hand he steadies himself on the up-curving stern of his boat, behind which a clump of reeds is growing. From a white *lekythos* of the fifth century B.C., in Karlsruhe (A. Fairbanks, *Athenian White Lekythoi*, ii, Plate XIV, Fig. 4). See pp. 89–90.

entrance. Its area was delimited into various precincts determined by natural boundaries, and its population was divided into classes, the ordinary rank and file of the departed on the one hand, and the sinners extraordinary on the other. The lower realm was indeed a world in itself.

Entrances to, and Rivers of, the Underworld.—Although some were sceptical enough to say that "no roads lead underground,"[5] yet the average Greek entertained no other opinion than that such paths did exist. In a number of places the inhabitants pointed to local caves whence the ways ran downward; for instance, at Tainaron in Lakonia, at Troizen in Argolis, at Ephyra in Thesprotia, and at Herakleia in Pontos, while Hermione in Argolis offered so short a route that those who travelled along it were exempted from the payment of the usual obol. Often white rocks by the banks of streams were held to mark the proximity of the lower world, or, again, the channels through which springs or streams disappeared beneath the ground passed as entrances to Hades. Indeed, it seems probable that the Styx and the Acheron, the oldest of the rivers of Hades, were originally just such streams. In time the imagination of the Greeks gave them almost wholly an infernal existence and developed from them three others — Kokytos, Pyriphlegethon, and Lethe. The relations of all these to one another, that is, whether they were main streams or tributaries, were by no means uniform; nevertheless, each had its own distinct significance in literature: the Styx was the river of hate; Acheron, with its chill, stagnant water, the river of mourning; Kokytos, the river of lamentation; Lethe, the river of forgetfulness; and Pyriphlegethon, the river of flame.

The Judges. — The better and earlier tradition recognizes three judges in Hades — Aiakos, king of Aigina, and Rhadamanthys and Minos, the sons of Zeus and Europe; the later and Attic tradition adds Triptolemos as a fourth. The first three were endowed with distinct individualities. Aiakos, by virtue of his being the "wisest in deed and in counsel" among mortals, was given the principal place among the judges, and to his care, moreover, were entrusted the keys of Hades' house. To him the souls from Europe came to be judged, while his brother Rhadamanthys, seated at the crossways where one road led to the Happy Isles and the other to Tartaros, judged the souls from Asia. Souls whose origin was in doubt appeared before Minos, who, wielding a golden sceptre, exercised both civil and judicial power, as he had done on earth.

The Punishments of Hades. — Only that class of the inhabitants of Hades whom we have called the sinners extraordinary suffered special punishments. Their sins had been against the gods. For disclosing to men the counsel of Zeus and for his horrible banquet Tantalos was condemned to stand in a pool that ever receded from his thirsty lips, while near him hung branches laden with fruit that always sprang away from his hungry grasp, and over his head was poised a stone that continually threatened to fall but never did. Tityos had in his lifetime attempted violence on Leto, and for this, his huge body was stretched out supine on the soil of Hades and two vultures never ceased gnawing at his vitals. Ixion forgot his debt of gratitude to Zeus and made a foul attack on Hera, so that in Hades he was lashed to a wheel and whirled around forever, his fate being a perpetual warning to ingrates. For their sacrilegious attempt to scale heaven by piling up mountains into a grand staircase Otos and Ephialtes were bound by serpents to two great columns. Of the punishments of Sisyphos and of the daughters of Danaos enough has already been said.

Visits of the Living to Hades. — Consistent with the belief in roads leading to the lower world is the tradition that certain human beings of almost divinely rare endowments, or through some interposition of the gods, had been able to follow these paths to their end and again to see the light of day. Protesilaos returned to life for a few short hours only, but Alkestis and Glaukos, the son of Minos, for many years.

Herakles descended by Tainaron and came back by Troizen, bringing Kerberos with him, and Theseus accompanied Peirithoös below in his foolhardy mission to rob Hades of Persephone, although his safe return was due only to the superior strength of Herakles. The most famous descents were those of Odysseus and Orpheus, that of the former furnishing inspiration to Vergil and Dante in their treatment of similar themes, and to those modern poets who have depicted Christ in Hades.

At the word of Kirke Odysseus approached the underworld by way of the land of the Kimmerians, a people who dwelt amid clouds and gloom and never looked upon the face of the sun. Here he dug a trench and poured into it the blood of black victims, and soon the gibbering ghosts began to gather about the trench, clamouring for the blood, which, for a time, Odysseus would not permit them to touch. First there appeared to him the restless shade of his former shipmate Elpenor, begging him to accomplish the due rites over his unburied body, and at length there came the ghost of Teiresias, the blind seer of Thebes. When Odysseus allowed him and the other shades to taste of the blood, memories of the upper world and the power of speech returned to them, and from Teiresias he learned the vicissitudes that were to mark the remainder of his life down to the day of his death. Then he saw his mother Antikleia, who, though now merely a phantom, had not lost the tenderness of a mother for him, recounting to him what had happened in Ithake during his long absence, just those things that only a mother thinks of telling, the little happenings about the home that make or mar the life within it. After her he saw a host of the famous wives and mothers of the gods and heroes, both the chaste and the unchaste, and when the shades of the women folk were scattered by Persephone, the ghosts of the men crowded about, and drinking of the blood told Odysseus, one by one, the sorry tales of their last days, and with grief or delight listened to the tidings which he had brought them of the kinsfolk whom they had left behind. First came Agamemnon, surrounded by the shades of those who had died with him at Aigisthos's fatal banquet; and then Achilles, proud to learn of the glory of Neoptolemos among the living; Aias, still brooding over his imagined dishonour; Minos, wielding his golden sceptre and dealing out dooms to the dead; and Orion, hunting across the asphodel meadows the ghosts of the animals which he had slain in life. Last of all Odysseus beheld the great sufferers of Hades,—Tantalos, Tityos, Sisyphos, Ixion,[6] and the rest, and would have seen more of the renowned heroes had not the increasing throng and clamour of the shades filled his breast with fear and caused him to fly to his ship and sail away down the stream of Okeanos. From the account of this visit of Odysseus to Hades, as it stands in the *Odyssey* itself, more can be learned of the prevailing Greek conception of the state of the dead than from any other single source.

Fig. 6. The Death of Aias (Ajax)

This design depicts an unusual variant of the story that tells of the death of Aias, the son of Telamon. Aias, brooding over his defeat by Odysseus in the contest for the arms of Achilles, has tried in vain to kill himself. Athene now appears before him and points out to him a vulnerable spot in which to plunge his sword. From an incised design on an Etruscan bronze mirror of the third century B.C., now in the Museum of Fine Arts, Boston.

The story of the descent of Orpheus is of a very different character. Eurydike, the young wife of Orpheus, the sweet singer of Thrace,[7] was bitten by a serpent, and, dying, her soul passed within the pale of Hades' realm. Orpheus resolved to win her back, and as he entered the abode of the shades with

PLATE XXXVI

Ixion on the Wheel

Ixion is bound by several thongs to an eight-spoked wheel. His "running" attitude and the wings on the wheel, after the manner of archaic art denote rapid revolution. The flower beside Ixion's right foot serves only to fill up the space between the spokes. From an Etruscan bronze mirror of the fourth or third century B.C., in the British Museum (A. B. Cook, *Zeus*, i, Plate XVII). See p. 144.

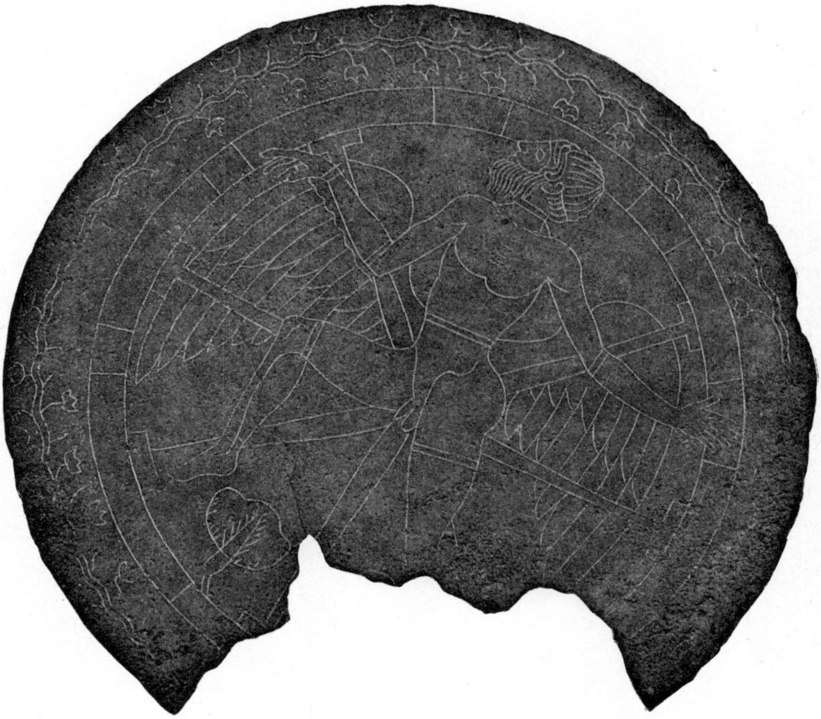

a song on his lips, "the pallid souls burst into weeping, Tantalos ceased to pursue the retreating water, Ixion and his wheel stood still, the vultures abandoned their torment of Tityos, the daughters of Danaos deserted their jars, and Sisyphos sat down upon the rock. Down the cheeks of the Erinyes flowed moist tears, and the king and queen of Tartaros yielded to his plea" [8] that they set his dear wife free. One condition, however, was imposed, that as Eurydike followed her husband on the way out, he was on no account to turn around and look upon her; but, in the ecstasy of his joy at his recovery of her, he violated the condition, and Eurydike was recalled to Hades, never more to return to earth.

Elysion, The Islands of the Blest. — The domain of Hades was not, however, the only abode of those who had come to the end of this life, for there was, besides this, a land of eternal happiness with broad flowery fields known now as Elysion, and now as the Islands of the Blest. The Greeks naturally thought of this land as lying in the distant west, some even identifying it with the island of the Phaiakians, or again with Leuke ("White Isle") at the western end of the Euxine. According to Pindar, only those mortals were translated thither who had come through a triple test in life and had remained good and brave and true, although from other literary sources one gathers that the common belief was that the land was reserved for those in whose veins flowed the blood of the gods. It was indeed for this reason alone, and not for any special piety, that Menelaos and Helen were admitted into its bliss, though Peleus, Achilles, Kadmos, and many others of the heroes were there who by virtue of passing either test could have entered this land, whose charm can be best conveyed by the words of Proteus to Menelaos: "But thou, Menelaus, son of Zeus, art not ordained to die and meet thy fate in Argos, the pasture-land of horses, but the deathless gods will convey thee to the Elysian plain and the world's end, where is Rhadamanthys of the fair hair, where life is easiest for men. No snow is there, nor yet great storm, nor any rain; but always Ocean sendeth forth the breeze of the shrill west to blow cool on men: yea, for thou hast Helen to wife, and thereby they deem thee to be the son of Zeus." [9]

PART II

THE GREEK GODS

CHAPTER I

THE GREATER GODS — ZEUS AND HERA

ALMOST all the gods who are considered in this and the next few chapters are universally regarded as the greater personages of the Greek pantheon, although a few who are confessedly not of this rank have been given a place here because of the difficulty and impropriety of dealing with them apart from their more distinguished fellows with whom they are inseparably associated. For instance, Hekate is the natural companion of Artemis, Eros of Aphrodite, and Persephone and Hades of Demeter. We have obtained our list of greater gods by combining the Homeric, Athenian, and Olympian systems, though from the last named we have omitted Kronos, Rhea, Alpheios, and the Charites.

ZEUS

Between the Zeus of the historical period and the Zeus of the primitive Greeks there is a great gulf fixed.[1] It is not, however, entirely unspanned, for the diligent research of many years has succeeded in throwing over it bridges of inference and deduction, which, while slender, afford the hope that they may serve as the foundations for stronger structures in the future. Any statements that we may make, therefore, in reference to this void we give with reserve, even though we may not preface each individual statement with a specific word of caution. It must be remembered that our present endeavour is to trace the transformation of the Zeus, not of a single locality, but of all Hellenic localities, to sketch the lineaments, as it were, of a great composite Zeus who would be recognized at first glance by all Hellenes as the chief god of their cults and myths.

The Original Significance of Zeus. — Zeus was the great aboriginal god not only of all the Hellenic stocks, but of the so-called Indo-European race, nor does the predominating importance of his celestial functions in ritual, myth, and epithet permit of any other inference than that he was a personification of the bright sky.[2] The coincidence of these activities with those of the great sky-god of cognate name of other Indo-European peoples points in the same direction, and, moreover, his name alone is a proof of his origin, for it is a development of the base *deyā*, "to shine," probably passing through the stages of pronunciation — if not of orthography — *Διήϝς, *Διηύς, *Διεύς, Ζεύς, while in the invocation Ζεῦ πάτερ ("Father Zeus") we can readily perceive a parallel to the Latin Iuppiter (Diespiter), and in the Indian Rig Veda the phrase *dyau pitar* ("Father Sky") occurs in several passages. In most instances the non-celestial functions of Zeus can be shown to be more or less natural efflorescences, so to speak, of his celestial activities, although sometimes they may be suspected of being the results of contamination with the worship of other divinities.[3]

In dealing with the personality of Zeus one must avoid being misled by his mere name, which was occasionally applied to other beings than the chief Olympian. Thus Hades, or Plouton, was sometimes spoken of as Zeus, but it was through metaphor, for was not Hades the Zeus of the underworld? Rain-making fetishes in various districts were at times addressed as Zeus by local votaries; and through haste and ignorance Hellenic travellers would often designate as Zeus the leading male divinity of a strange community, this identity being presumed most frequently of all when they were journeying in distinctly barbarian countries. It is the genuine Zeus, the sky-god, with whom we are concerned.

PLATE XXXVII

Zeus

This beautiful statuette (only 4 1/8 inches high) of the seated Zeus, although of Roman execution, is remarkable for its fidelity to the Greek type. In his right hand, which rests on his knee, the god grasps a thunderbolt, while his left hand, raised to the height of his head, is supported by, rather than supports, a sceptre. The treatment of the face, beard, and hair is similar to that of the Zeus of Otricoli. The slight forward thrust of the head, and the much less formal grasp of the sceptre, together with certain other features, differentiate this type from that of the Olympian Zeus of Pheidias. From a Roman bronze copy of a fourth century Greek type, in the Metropolitan Museum of Art, New York (*photograph*).

The Zeus of Homer. — In the *Iliad* and the *Odyssey* Zeus no longer appears as the sole divine arbiter of the sky and the supreme lord of the weather, for both Hera and Poseidon stir up wind and wave against those who have incurred their anger, apparently with only little less freedom of initiative than has Zeus himself.[4] Yet when the Greeks set sail homeward from Troy, we learn in the *Odyssey*, it was Zeus who scattered the ships; and after Odysseus's companions perfidiously slew the Cattle of the Sun in Thrinakia, it was Zeus who brought the disaster of shipwreck upon them. Despite the encroachments upon his power, he still remained the undisputed master of the thunder and the lightning, so that when, on the morning before the slaughter of the suitors, Odysseus heard the roar of thunder, he knew it to be a sign from Zeus that he would not thwart his plans. This sort of omen could, however, be interpreted as unfavourable or even as doubtful, as when, on one occasion, thunder which lasted all night long set both the Greek and Trojan armies to wondering what Zeus had in store for them, and made all the warriors turn pale with fear.

Although in Homer the original character of Zeus had become dim, whether in reality or by contrast, one side of his nature was very clearly illumined: he was potentially the ruler of the universe. The other gods had their departmental functions in nature, but Zeus could usurp them if only he chose to do so, and in the last analysis his will was supreme, being limited by nothing, for it was itself Fate. He was not merely an Olympian; he was *the* Olympian; [5] nor was he the petty god of a tribe or nation, for all the peoples of whom Homer had cognizance acknowledged his supremacy as "Father of gods and men," although the title "Father" conveyed not so much the idea that he was of necessity a physical father or the creator of men and things (on the contrary, Okeanos was the great creative source of all things in Homer) as that he exercised over the great family of beings, human and divine, that kind of rule which we call paternalistic. To men he dispensed joys or ills, as he pleased; he determined for them the issues of their battles in arms until they became mere puppets; and according to his whim he warned or deluded by omens. Unlike the other gods, he observed a strict neutrality in the Trojan War, save when it suited his purposes to lean toward this side or toward that, and he became gravely ethical on occasion, as when he rebuked Ares as a lover of contention, or when he ordered concord among the Ithakans; though at other times, open-eyed, he flung ethics to the winds, as he did when he devised means for breaking the solemn truce between the Trojans and the Achaians. He wielded, Roman-like, a *patria potestas* over the universe, for he weighed the Fates of Hektor and Achilles in the scales and assented to Hektor's death. This paternalistic attitude showed most clearly in the circle of the gods, whom he convened in the dictatorial manner of a feudal chieftain, and who espoused one or the other cause before Troy simply because he said they might. His *ipse dixit*, conveyed by Hermes, forced Kalypso to release Odysseus against her heart and will; he bestowed boons upon the other gods, but only as he was convinced of the real need for them in each instance, or as he was forced through guile. At times he stepped down from his throne to mingle with his fellows on the common floor of Olympos, but he never lost consciousness of his superiority. In all this we are to see not the absolute political ideal of the Homeric period, but, rather, the refined portrayal of the conditions of state to which the Greeks of that time had advanced.

The Birth and Death of Zeus. — When Pausanias frankly admits that he found it hard to enumerate all the Greek localities which claimed to be the birthplace of Zeus, the difficulty and folly of our attempting at this late date to draw up anything like a complete catalogue of them is very apparent. In Messenia and Arkadia alone he records no less than five such places, among them Mount Ithome, the acropolis of the city of Messene. The account makes no mention of the parentage of Zeus, which leads one to think that the traditional legend of the Hesiodic story is to be assumed. Born, then, of Kronos and Rhea, Zeus was hurried away by the Kouretes, an order of priests, to Mount Ithome for fear of the evil designs of his father, and there was placed in the care of two local nymphs, Neda and Ithome, who washed him in the waters of a spring on the slopes of the mountain, Neda giving her name to the near-by river and Ithome hers to the mountain, while in a most childish fashion the theft of the child and his bath in the water of the fountain were combined to attach to the spring the name Klepsydra, "Stolen Water." The god was also said to have been born on Mount Aigaion in Arkadia, where he was suckled by a goat, although Mount Lykaion of the same district and a mountain near Lydian Sardeis were likewise claimed for this honour. The most famous of all the birthplaces, however, was the island of Crete, the legends variously pointing to Mounts Dikte, Ida, and Lyktos as the exact locality of the birth. In the most widely prevailing version Rhea succeeded in escaping from Kronos just in time to bear Zeus in a cave in one of these mountains, and in answer to the rapacious demands of the new father gave him a wrapped stone to swallow instead of the child. The infant was cared for by Amaltheia, a goat, or by local nymphs, who, one story runs, hung him in a cradle on a tree to elude the keen searches of Kronos, while, in order to add to the deception, the Kouretes were appointed to take up their post close by and to make a great din by clashing their arms and brazen shields together, thus drowning the child's cries. Other legends say that it was a cow or a sow which nursed the infant. On the death of Kronos Zeus assumed the dominion over the world.

While the fully developed pan-Hellenic Zeus was truly one of the immortal gods who feasted on ambrosia and nectar, yet several local forms of Zeus were said to die, and an epigram attributed to Pythagoras[6] marked a spot in Crete where reposed the remains of Zeus: "Here lieth in death Zan, whom men call Zeus." This conflict between immortality and death is easily explained if the fact is borne in mind that in some districts of Crete he was, like Hyakinthos in Lakonia, a god of vegetation who alternately lived and died; while in Phrygia his descriptive title of "Summer-God" carried substantially the same significance.

The Marriages of Zeus. — Zeus is represented as the most uxorious of all the gods. Of his almost countless unions with goddesses and women many were accepted by the Greeks with that absence of comment which, as a rule, is the sanction of legitimacy, but they looked askance at a number of others in a way which made them, to say the least, the objects of social suspicion.[7]

In the Hesiodic tradition the first marriage of Zeus was with Metis and his last with Hera, while in that of the older epic Hera was his first and only legitimate wife. At all events, Hera became his canonical wife in Greek, and later, as Iuno, in Roman myth; but the portrayal of their conjugal relationship we shall postpone to our discussion of the personality of Hera. His marriages with Metis, Themis, Mnemosyne, and Eurynome were probably simply poetical, and through the influence of suggestion added to the conception of his dignity and power. The symbolism is evident in itself. On receiving a warning that a son of Metis ("Constructive Thought") would be more powerful than his father Zeus, he swallowed her and assimilated her into his own being; Themis ("Justice") he married after the defeat of the Titans and incorporated her personality into his *régime;* Mnemosyne ("Memory") he made his wife as a constant reminder (to others, of course) of his great might; and his affiliation with Eurynome ("Wide Rule") emphasized the extent of his dominions. Besides the foregoing, the most important goddesses with whom he was united were Dione, who may have been his spouse in Pelasgic times; Demeter, the mother of Persephone; Leto, the mother of Apollo and Artemis; and Maia, the mother of Hermes; while Pyrrha and Dia, who also became his wives, are probably two aspects of the earth goddess. The chief nymphs with whom he was associated were Taÿgete of the Lakedaimonian mountain; Aigina, of the island which bears her name; and Plouto of Lydia. Of his wives among women of purely human or of partly divine descent we can mention only Io, Leda, Danaë, Europe, Iodama, Antiope, Semele, and Alkmene.

The Offspring of Zeus. — No children of any other god but Zeus ever attained to places in the divine circle. Poseidon, Hera, and Hades were of the same Titanic parentage as Zeus himself, but Athene, Apollo, Artemis, Ares, Aphrodite, Hephaistos, Hermes, Dionysos, Herakles, Persephone, and the Dioskouroi were all his children. Of the race of the heroes many claimed him as father, notably Hellen, the founder of the Hellenic stock; Minos, and his brothers Sarpedon and Rhadamanthys; Dardanos, Tantalos, and Aiakos, heads of the families chiefly concerned in the war of Troy; Lakedaimon, the first of the Lakedaimonian strain; Perseus, the demi-god of the Argolid; and Amphion, Zethos, and Thebe, who were concerned with the beginnings of Thebes.

The Functions of Zeus; As Supreme God. — In Zeus's sphere of action as the supreme god we must distinguish the Zeus of pure myth from the Zeus of serious religious import. In the former his supremacy is very often encroached upon by the caprices of other divinities, with the result that it is logically annulled; it is the same thing as limiting the absolute. In serious cult, on the contrary, Zeus was the *one* god; not the only god, but the one god among many subservient gods. This is henotheism as opposed to monotheism, but since much of this aspect has invaded the field of myth, it is precisely this which we must endeavour to note. From Homer to the dramatic poets the unqualified use of Θεός, "god," invariably refers to Zeus, who was the "Father of gods and men," chiefly in a spiritual and moral sense, in which last capacity it is natural to see in him the ultimate court of appeal for offences against the gods and the higher law, and the final arbiter of punishments. With the Great Flood he punished mankind for their impiety; to Lykaon's sons he meted out death for their wickedness, and Lykaon himself he changed into a wolf for having essayed to hoodwink a deity. After he had condemned men to earn their bread by the sweat of their brow, none else could alter the decree. Because Tantalos and Sisyphos abused their endowment of knowledge almost divine he imposed on them terrible penalties in Hades, while Prometheus suffered untold agonies for trespassing on the divine prerogative to fire and for his gratuitous enlightenment of the race of men. For brazen insolence in attempting to scale the walls of Thebes, which his son Amphion had built, Zeus laid Kapaneus low with a bolt, and he smote Salmoneus in a like manner for invading the divine right of rain-making. He retarded the home-coming of the Argonauts for their part in the murder of Apsyrtos, the brother of Medeia, and, finally, so comprehensive was his power, he lessened the population of the earth by making men slaughter one another in the great War of Troy. On the other hand, as the spiritual head of the universe, what better judge could there be than Zeus of the right of heroes or of men to immortality and allied blessings? So it was he who bestowed a special form of immortality on Polydeukes, who sent Kadmos and Harmonia to Elysion, and who uttered the word permitting Prometheus and Cheiron to exchange mortality and immortality as Glaukos and Diomedes exchanged bronze and golden armour; and it was he, too, who granted Sarpedon a lifetime three generations long. In his power to confer various forms upon men, as he did, for instance, in making Lykaon a wolf, Philyra a linden, and Io a heifer, and in giving the protection of invisibility to his favourites, as he did to the wounded Herakles in Kos, he is not especially differentiated from the other Olympians; such acts predicate no moral or spiritual power.

PLATE XXXVIII

Zeus and the Kouretes

The chief significance of this scene in low relief is that it is the earliest certain representation of Zeus, and scarcely less important is the transparent Euphratean style of its composition and execution. Flanked by winged, male figures the god stands like an Assyrian divinity on a bull, and, after the manner of the Babylonian epic hero Gilgamesh, as depicted on the seal cylinders, with both hands swings a lion over his head. This conception of Zeus as a man in the prime of life rather than as an infant is true to an ancient Cretan myth recently recovered. The winged figures, each beating a pair of *tympana*, are evidently Kouretes. From a design on a Kouretic bronze *tympanon* of the ninth or eighth century B.C., discovered in the sacred cave of Zeus on Mount Ida in Crete (A. B. Cook, *Zeus*, i, Plate XXXV). See pp. 154–55.

Zeus as God of the Heavens. — Although the name Zeus perhaps originally denoted "sky," it is only very rarely, notably in a few local cults in Crete, that we find this god brought into connexion with any of the celestial luminaries. At first he was probably regarded as the source of all light, that of the heavenly bodies included, and in this circumstance we can find the reason why there was no well-developed native cult of the sun, the moon, and the stars among the Greeks. It is quite possible that those rare Cretan cults in which Zeus seems to be a sun-god are distant offshoots of a Mesopotamian sun-cult.

It is in his meteorological functions that Zeus is pre-eminent in the sky. The rain descends from the sky; therefore, it is Zeus the "cloud-gatherer" who dispenses it, and Theokritos mentions[8] "the rain of Zeus," while Ζεὺς ὕει ("Zeus rains") was a popular saying. It was quite natural, then, for the demon of the magic rain-stones of primitive communities to be confused and even identified with Zeus, and the story of the stone which Rhea gave Kronos to swallow was doubtless derived from some magic rain-making ritual, while if Zeus was thus the supreme rain-maker, the essential nature of the sin of Salmoneus is manifest. Now in order to influence the great weather spirit with an immediate directness one must get as close to him as possible; and what could be nearer to him than the highlands? Hence, the frequency with which we find the cults of Zeus on mountain-peaks — on Dikte and Ida in Crete, on Olympos in Thessaly, on Lykaios in Arkadia, or on Kithairon in Boiotia, while such general epithets as Ὕπατος ("Highest"), Κορυφαῖος ("of the peaks"), and Ἀκραῖος ("of the summits") point to his association with great elevations in general. Yet he is god of the thunder and lightning as well as of the rain. At Mantineia and Olympia he was the lightning itself and not the directing agent, and with the poets he is the "Mighty Thunderer" and the "Hurler of Lightning." The lightning and the thunderbolts forged by his smiths, the

Kyklopes, were the weapons with which he overthrew the Titans, while Pegasos drew the thunder-car for him from the ancient stables of heaven, and with the lightning he separated the battling Herakles and Apollo, and visited sudden death on those who incurred his displeasure. Zeus was also held to be the sender of the dew, which in times of drought was so essential to the welfare of the crops and pasturage.

Zeus as God of Fertility. — It was but an easy step for the god of the rain and the dew to become the god of the fertility produced by these forms of moisture. It seemed to the Greek that with these some fertilizing substance or vital principle fell upon the receptive soil, and who but Zeus was the giver of it? It entered into plants from the soil and into animals and men from plants, so that the whole cycle of life was dependent on Zeus, who was the great "Begetter." [9] The native Zeus of Attike was originally a deity of agriculture, as is clearly seen in the ritual of the Bouphonia, while such epithets as "Increaser of Fruits," "Giver of Fruitage," and "Husbandman" reveal him as a god of harvest.

Zeus in his Political and Ethical Aspects. — From the Aristotelian point of view these two aspects cannot be scanned separately, for ethical standards are nothing else than the crystallized experience of organized society. In both myth and cult Zeus was the ideal statesman of the Greeks, having had that serenity of judgment which awakens the confidence of the governed. His lordship over himself inspired self-control in those who looked up to him, and the very stains upon his dignity which the myths often revealed gave the legends an air of convincing reality. Yet in spite of his generally accepted high political estate, we rarely meet with the cult of Zeus Panhellenios — the Zeus of the United States of Greece, so to speak — for the Greeks' keen sense of local independence never allowed them to realize this ideal in politics. He frequently appeared, however, as the guardian of the family property, of boundaries, of wealth, of the domestic and state hearths severally, and of tribal and family kin; and he was also the patron of the higher social interests collectively and separately, of freedom, of the centralized union of tribes and brotherhoods, and of concord among the people. While he was sometimes qualified by epithets like "War-Lord" and "Bearer of Victory," yet he was seldom known purely as a god of war — a testimony to the advanced character of the Greek religion.

To such an extent was Zeus the most ethical of all the gods of the pantheon that he almost shrank the Greek polytheism into monotheism, and it was this fact which enabled the Greeks to withstand the inroads of Christianity for so long a time, even though it was the very feature which in the end facilitated the acceptance of the new faith. While Zeus was the bringer of evil as well as of good into the life of men, occasionally the Greeks rose to the noble idea that he was above all that was evil. He was Ὕψιστος ("Most High"), and doubtless later generations erroneously read this same ethical meaning into Ὕπατος. Being such a god, he was logically at enmity with iniquity, and was driven by an inevitable necessity to chastise it, whence his punishments were not the results of caprice, although their suddenness might often lead one to think that they were. Herakles murdered a friend; his slavery to Omphale was a natural retribution visited on him by the god of friendship. Tantalos took the life of his own son Pelops; his punishment in Hades was a measure of his crime against the guardian of blood kinship. To violations of pledges and of oaths taken in his name Zeus could give only short shrift. Before the eyes of the spectators at Olympia stood a row of bronze images of Zeus called, in the dialect of Elis, Zanes ("Zeuses"), which had been made with the fines imposed on those who had broken the rules governing the great games, and which, in their conspicuous position, were national reminders that Zeus was ever watchful of the fidelity of men in the works of organized society.

Zeus as Prophet, Fate, Healer, and Helper. — At Dodona in Epeiros stood the talking oak of Zeus, which delivered to men messages concerning the future, and a piece of which, we recall, was built into the prow of the Argo and with human voice spoke to the heroes. It was believed that the tree gave utterance to the thought of Zeus through the whisperings of its foliage, and these were interpreted by skilled priests who made the meanings known to consultants by inscribing them on small plaques of lead. Just why the oak of all the trees was chosen as the vehicle of Zeus's communication we may never know; but perhaps Sir J. G. Frazer is as near to the truth as is any one when he claims the oak as the special tree of Zeus because it is more often struck by lightning than any other tree of the forest. The power of Zeus to foretell at least the immediate future by means of the thunder and the lightning we have already pointed out in our consideration of the Zeus of Homer, but he could also reveal his will through the flight of birds across the sky, especially through that of the eagle, which was pre-eminently his bird.

In a certain sense Zeus as Fate exercised a prophetic function; he could foretell because he predestined. In Homer it was he alone who foreordained, and Moira ("Fate") was, as it were, an impersonal decree issuing from him; but in the fifth century the idea rapidly gained currency that there was a power preforming the future to which Zeus himself must bow. In Aischylos, accordingly, it is the three Fates who limit his dominion, but in spite of this the Homeric belief never wholly died out.

One need not seek far for the source of the strength of Zeus as a healer and helper of a weak and feeble humanity, for a god of his broad general powers could do anything in particular, so that we are not surprised to find attached to his name such epithets as "Defender from Ill," "Bestower of Immunity," "Healer," "Saviour," and even "Averter of Flies," one of his titles at Olympia. Some scholars claim that the stories of the birth of Dionysos from the thigh of Zeus and of the springing of Athene from his head hark back to an early function of his as a god of child-birth.

Zeus as a Chthonic Divinity. — The few instances where Zeus appears as a chthonic divinity, or deity of the underworld, were probably the result of a mistaken identification, or of an extension of function. The Zeus Chthonios of Corinth was a counterpart of Hades, while Zeus Meilichios of Attike became a chthonic god through the character of Zeus as a deity of agriculture, and Aiakos of Aigina, a son of Zeus in the legend, seems to have been in origin a local Aiginetan chthonic Zeus.

Zeus in Art. — The maturer periods of Greek art represented Zeus as a fully developed man standing or seated in an attitude suggestive of serene dignity and undisputed power. As a rule he holds the thunderbolt in his hand, but sometimes a ruler's staff or an image of Victory, and occasionally an eagle can be observed at his side.

HERA

The Origin and the Name of Hera. — The original significance of the person and of the name of Hera is lost in the obscurity of a remote past, but inasmuch as at all periods she manifested surprisingly few traces of Oriental influences, we are probably not to look to the East for her introduction into Greece. She was certainly very early a pan-Hellenic divinity, though none can say whether she came to the land with the invaders from the north or was a native goddess already established. Her acknowledged antiquity in Argos has led some to suspect that she was there a Pelasgic earth goddess whom the invaders adopted as their own under the new name of Hera;[10] yet this explanation is puzzling in the light of the paucity of Hera's earth-functions, for in the historical period she was certainly not of the earth, earthy. Moreover, why was she so implacable a foe of Dionysos? Why did she dispense no oracles? Why, too, had her children, Ares and Hephaistos, no chthonic functions? The hypothesis that she was originally a moon-goddess may be summarily dismissed on the ground that it deals with an admittedly late conception. The name Hera seems to have had some connexion with that of Herakles and perhaps with ἥρως ("hero"), but the statement that it signifies "the strong one" is based without warrant on assumed relations of Hera with a goddess of Phoinikia.

Hera in Homer. — As in the *Theogony* of Hesiod, Hera is the daughter of Kronos and Rhea, and sister-spouse of Zeus. Indeed, she and Zeus are the only married pair on Olympos, but their conjugal life is anything but smooth, for Hera is far from being a model wife like Andromache or Penelope; rather, she is a sort of divine Xanthippe. She often nags her husband until his Olympian patience is exhausted, and fear of such nagging many a time deters him from pursuing courses which his judgement has decided are right and proper; and she has the bad habit of taking the off side of any question which he may favour. She envelops the Trojans in a mist to detain them when Zeus has willed that they advance; against the wish of Zeus she hastens the sun westward; and by her guile the birth of Herakles is retarded so that her favourite Eurystheus may gain the upper hand. So persistent is her interference with the actions of Zeus that, humanly speaking, there is no reason for surprise when he cruelly punishes her by hanging her head down from the heights of heaven.

Yet, despite all this, she is "the noblest of the goddesses," and when she moves on her throne, tremors are felt throughout Olympos, while sometimes she even wields the thunderbolt, and like her husband sends storm and cloud. She is the beautiful divinity of the white arms (λευκώλενος) and lives in a "great luxurious calm," and she is, too, a helpful goddess of child-birth, under whose direction her daughters, the Eileithyiai, control the births of Herakles and Eurystheus.

PLATE XXXIX

Hera

This statuesque and majestic figure represents Hera as the queen of the immortals. On her head she wears a chastely ornamented golden diadem, from beneath which her hair falls over her breast and shoulders in long full tresses. Her *chiton*, of a delicately patterned, gauzy linen, drops to her ankles which are faintly visible through it, and over this hangs a cloak of some heavy, closely woven fabric with a middle band and borders of purple. Her right hand is concealed, but in her exposed left she holds upright a long sceptre studded with gold from top to bottom. From a *kylix* with a white ground (about 475 B.C.), in Munich (Furtwängler-Reichhold, *Griechische Vasenmalerei*, No. 65).

HPA

Hera as the Wife of Zeus. — The ἱερὸς γάμος, or holy union, of Zeus and Hera, which we have described in our chapter on Beginnings, was to all the Greeks the ideal of married existence, and although the Homeric character of Hera as wife persisted in mythology down to a late period, yet her marriage was always popularly held to have been a happy one. This savours, however, more of courtesy than of truth, inasmuch as the Greeks must have felt that with a faulty model before them the stability of their social life was imperilled. The union itself is variously explained. Some are tempted to see in it an affiliation of natural forces, so that where meteorological elements are concerned, the domestic strife of Zeus and Hera would be interpreted as an allegorical representation of the conflicts of air-currents. Yet this cannot hold if Hera derived her few celestial functions from her long and intimate contact with Zeus. One extremely ingenious theory [11] outlines a very different origin of the union. It points out that as the ἱερὸς γάμος was most celebrated in the chief Pelasgic centres like Euboia, Boiotia, Argolis, and Samos, it was probably generally accepted in Pelasgic times. In Dodona, however, the oldest Pelasgic centre of the cult of Zeus, the wife of Zeus was not Hera but Dione, whence his marriage with Hera must have originated in the same Pelasgic period. But how was it brought about without a fatal wrench of religious sentiment? The myth-makers had a way. If, by means of a myth, Dionysos could be foisted on Zeus as a son, it was surely just as easy to explain away one wife and give him another. The necessity for so doing arose, this theory holds, with the intermingling of two racial stocks one of which was matrilinear and worshipped Hera as its chief divinity, and the other of which was patrilinear and followed the cult of Zeus. To unite the two divinities in a sacred wedlock would be to secure a religious sanction for the connubial and political fusion of the two strains of blood, and, accordingly, Hera was torn from the embrace of her lawful husband, Herakles, and thrown into the arms of a divorced Zeus, the separation being so carefully hushed up, however, that only scanty traces of it are left.

The children of Hera and Zeus were Hephaistos, Ares, Hebe, and the Eileithyiai, but they exhibit few traits which reveal their maternity. Hephaistos takes his mother's part when Zeus punishes her for her interference, and Zeus himself apologizes for Ares' warlike disposition in that he inherits it from his mother. Hebe is a sort of personification of the well-preserved beauty of her mother, and in one legend she has no relationship at all with Zeus, Hera bearing her after a most mysterious impregnation by a leaf of lettuce. The Eileithyiai reflect their mother's care for women in childbed.

The Functions of Hera. — Whether or not Hera was originally a goddess of the weather and fertility, she occasionally appears as such in the myths, and, less often, in her cults. The gale which bore Agamemnon to his home shores after the fall of Ilion was of Hera's making, and she it was, too, who caused the mist to enshroud the Trojans. The cuckoo, often regarded as a rain-bird, was sacred to her, and Polykleitos represented it perched on her sceptre, while in one brief legend Zeus assumed the form of the cuckoo to win her love. In times of drought processions of her worshippers would march to the mountain-tops and there invoke her aid, and the luxuriant growth of bloom which appeared after a dry period had been broken sprang, people said, from Hera's bridal bed. She was, moreover, protectress of such staple plants as the pomegranate and the vine, the full development of which depends so directly upon the volume of rainfall.

Hera's power to cause insanity was notorious. Herakles and Athamas and Ino she impelled in their madness to take the lives of their own offspring; Io she drove mad with a gadfly; and she made the daughters of Proitos roam wildly over the Peloponnesos. Nor did the gods entirely escape, for she cast a spell of frenzy on Dionysos for his introduction of the vine, and under its influence he wandered hither and thither in both the nearer and the farther east. There is a wide-spread primitive belief that lightning brings madness, and perhaps this, in conjunction with Hera's association with the phenomena of the weather, may have given rise to her special power over lunacy.

Throughout the Hellenic peoples Hera was the chief protectress of women, having surveillance over their part of the conjugal relationships and acting as their helper in the hour of travail, while, by a logical projection of these functions, she was thought to have especial care for the well-being of children. She encouraged matrimony and discouraged celibacy. The great crime of the forty-nine daughters of Danaos lay not in the murder of their husbands but in their stubborn will to remain single, and the punishment meted out to them in Hades was that imposed on celibates after death, according to certain of the mysteries. Hypermnestra, who spared her husband, seems to have been in origin a priestess of the Argive Heraion.

Hera's contact with the higher interests of corporate society was slight. Nowhere outside of Argos, and perhaps Samos, were her political functions conspicuous, and nowhere, except in Argos, did she have much to do with the arts of civilized existence. Hephaistos, the artisan-god, was her son, to be sure, but his gifts defied the laws of heredity. Though the queen of all Olympian goddesses, she possessed much less ethical force than Athene, and contrary to our expectation it was not she but the Erinyes who punished violations of the marriage vow. All this tends to convince one that her personality was not the ideal of the Greek wife, but was a reflection of the restricted conditions of life surrounding the Hellenic matron.

Herodotos's story of the death of Kleobis and Biton is not only effectively told, but shows the Argive faith in Hera as the final judge of what constitutes the *summum bonum*, that is, as an ethical deity. The "father of history" tells how a certain woman of the city of Argos planned to ride in her oxcart to the Heraion, some forty furlongs distant, and when the oxen did not appear, her sons Kleobis and Biton put the yoke across their necks and drew her to the temple. Filled with pride at the many felicitations which she received on having such sons, the mother stood before the image of Hera and prayed that she would bestow upon Kleobis and Biton the greatest boon that men could have. After sacrificing and feasting, the young men lay down and slept in the precinct of the goddess, and never woke.

It is not a pleasantry based on her matrimonial quarrels when we state that there are some evidences that Hera was regarded as a goddess of war. Traditions to that effect seem to underlie some of the cults, although the only tangible hint of this in myth is found in the story of Herakles, since Alkmene's name indicates that she was primitively a divinity of war, and her close association with Hera through her son may mean that she was actually Hera herself.

Hera in Art. — The Hera of art lacks the clear-cut attributes of personality belonging to the Hera of myth and cult. She has no sure tag of identification about her representations, such as Artemis has in her bow and Athene in her aegis, although at a late period she occasionally had a peacock beside her. In her great statue in the Argive Heraion, the work of Polykleitos, she was shown holding a pomegranate in one hand, and on the top of her staff, held in the other hand, perched a cuckoo. She generally appeared as a beautiful mature woman, with or without a veil, seated on a throne.

CHAPTER II

THE GREATER GODS — ATHENE

THE Origin and the Name of Athene. — The most that one can say of the origin of Athene is that she belonged to the so-called Achaian period and was worshipped by Dorian and Ionian alike, while her cult was diffused uniformly over the entire Greek world. No observable traces of a Pelasgic descent cling to her person, although she may have been Pelasgic. Equally lacking are marks of her importation from the Orient; this we confidently assert in the face of apparently well-supported statements that she, along with Hera, was an offshoot of the Philistine goddess ʿAṣṣah of Gaza; and her identification at Corinth with the Syro-Arabian goddess Allāt was a mere accident. The main lines of her character and the forms of her worship observed, for instance, in Tegea, Sparta, Kyrene, Rhodes, and Athens were all developed primarily in Argos, but of all these places Athens alone added new traits and stimulated the logical unfolding of old ones, so that, for this reason, it is in Athens that we can study Athene to the greatest advantage. As for the meaning of her name, here again we must confess to ignorance, although one suggested etymology is at least worth consideration. This derives her appellation from *ἀ-θήνιον* ("without mother's milk") and interprets it either passively or actively, the reference in the former sense being to Athene's unmothered birth from Zeus and in the latter to her sexless character, which is much like that of the Amazons.[1]

Athene in Homer. — Homer constantly depicts Athene as the beloved daughter of Zeus, but nowhere does he allude to her birth from his head. She is more like the chief Olympian than is any one of the other divinities, male or female, not only resembling him in the wide range and directness of her activities as well as in the high type of her mentality, but also possessing a large measure of her father's spontaneous resourcefulness in crises. By reason of her ready wit she has a natural affinity for Odysseus, and, on the principle that "God helps those who help themselves," stands ready at all times to assist him. She is the patroness and model worker of all those arts of life which demand ingenuity and dexterity; she is skilled in the smithing of gold, in weaving and other domestic accomplishments. She endowed Penelope and the daughters of Pandareos with their skill in all handiwork, and she it was, too, who gave deftness to the thought and hand of Epeios in fashioning the wooden horse, the instrument of Troy's fall. While she frequently takes sides in the actual strife before Troy, she does so rather as a great strategist than as one who delights in carnage and havoc.

The Birth of Athene. — In the *Theogony* of Hesiod we are told that Ouranos and Gaia warned Zeus that his wife, Metis, then pregnant with Pallas, would bear a son who would become the king of gods and men. Keeping his counsel to himself, Zeus approached Metis and craftily persuaded her to assume the form of some very small animal (a late legend says that she became a fly), whereupon he promptly swallowed her, and, after a time, Pallas Athene leaped forth from his head in a panoply of gold. "And mighty Olympos shook dreadfully beneath the fearful bright-eyed goddess, and round about earth loudly re-echoed; the sea was moved, being stirred with purple waves; suddenly the spray was thrown aloft and the glorious son of Hyperion halted his swift steeds till such time as the maiden Pallas Athene had removed her divine armour from her immortal shoulders. And all-counselling Zeus rejoiced."[2] In a variant form of this myth Brontes, one of the Kyklopes, begat Athene by Metis, who was swallowed by Zeus before she could bring her offspring into the world; and

PLATE XL

ATHENE

To understand this statue fully one must restore to the right of it the remainder of the group to which it seems to have belonged; i. e. Marsyas drawing back from a pair of flutes lying on the ground before him. The goddess, a self-possessed and thoroughly maidenly figure, glancing indifferently toward the instruments, is about to turn away to the left as though instinctively aware of her native superiority to the half-bestial creature near her. The Corinthian helmet, the crest of which is lost, here serves only as a means of identification. This statue is apparently a replica of the first century B.C. or A.D. of a bronze original by Myron (latter part of the fifth century B.C.), and is now in Frankfort (*JHAI* xii, Plate II).

in other stories she is the daughter of Pallas, or of a sea-nymph, Koryphe, by either Zeus or Poseidon. The canonical myth of her birth seems to have been invented very early to account for her already established traits of wisdom and moral sense, while the legend in which Koryphe mothers her is apparently an outgrowth of a cult-title, such as Κορυφαία, which commemorated her birth from the head of Zeus. It is not impossible that in the first place Metis was Athene herself.

The Functions of Athene. — The Athene of myth and worship alike was a goddess of practical and not of speculative life. None but a utilitarian philosophy could spring from contemplation of her being, and there was very little symbolism in her rites. She neither personified nor controlled any special department of nature, although, as occasion required, she could work in a number of them. In her mature development she was the social deity *par excellence*, unmarred by many of the primitive crudities which still clung to the distinctively nature-gods.

Athene was the inventress and craftswoman among the Olympians, and in that capacity was associated with Hephaistos and Prometheus. It was she who contributed the soul to the fashioning of Pandora, and she invented the plough, and first contrived spinning, weaving, and working in metal. To artisans she gave special thought. Phereklos, the builder of the ships of Paris, she loved above all men, and she herself assisted in the building of the Argo. It was said that she invented the flute and with it imitated the wails of the two surviving Gorgons as they lamented over the body of their sister Medousa; and although this story seems to be a fiction to account for only a certain *motif* on the flute, yet elsewhere Athene was credited with the invention of flute music in general. The honours of having contrived the Pyrrhic dance were indefinitely divided between Athene and the Kouretes; some claimed that she originated it to celebrate the victory over the Titans. She was the first to subdue horses to human use, and for their control devised the bit and bridle, while from her hands Bellerophon received the bridle with which he guided Pegasos. It was as a divinity of skill rather than of the sea that she exercised a patronage over seamanship and gave success to the Athenian marine, and she it was who safely steered the Argo past the perilous Symplegades.

In Attike, Athene was active in another practical field — that of agriculture. She was especially associated with the olive, and it was in Salamis

> ". . . where first from the earth
> The grey-gleaming fruit of the maiden
> Athena had birth." [3]

After creating the olive, she revealed its uses to mankind. She and Poseidon contested the ownership of Attike, and a decision was promised by arbiters to that one of the two who would confer the greatest benefit upon the citizens, whereupon Poseidon, with a stroke of his trident, produced the salt spring and Athene planted the olive-tree, both on the Acropolis. The land was awarded to Athene, and from her gift were grown the olive orchards of the Attic plain. Her associations with agriculture, in general, seem not to have been original, but, as it were, a legacy of an earlier agricultural divinity whom she displaced. The serpent in the Erechtheion and the obscene fertility rites hinted at in the story of Erichthonios's birth from Athene apparently go back to such a divinity.

As a war-goddess Athene was much the same outside of Homer as within, and her attitude was that of a defender rather than that of a provoker of war. She took her part in the just defence of Zeus from the attack of the Titans, her special antagonist in this conflict being Enkelados; and she directed particular attention to the development of efficiency in the cavalry and to difficult siege operations. A branch of her olive was an emblem of peace won by arms.

Although Athene provoked the storm that scattered the

Achaians departing from Ilion, although she shattered the ship of Aias with a lightning-bolt and aided Odysseus time and again with favourable changes of wind and weather, she cannot be regarded as decidedly a weather-goddess, her activities in this sphere doubtless coming from her intimate relationship to Zeus.

Most of Athene's social aspects have been brought out incidentally in the foregoing discussion of her attributes. Occasionally, however, she appeared as the patroness of the deliberative and executive branches of the state, and as Athene Polias in Athens she was the divine mainstay of the entire body politic. Her outstanding moral characteristic is her unimpeachable chastity, so that on Tegea she brought a plague because Auge's babe, born out of wedlock, had been concealed in her precinct, while her anger against the son of Oileus was aroused more by his offence against a general moral law protecting suppliants than by the desecration of her shrine in particular.

Athene in Art. — There are two outstanding types of representations of Athene. In the first, which is the more common, she is shown standing with lance and shield, wearing a helmet, and carrying the aegis with the Gorgoneion, or Gorgon's head; in the other type she is seated and unarmed; in both the owl and the snake sometimes appear as distinctive attributes.

CHAPTER III

THE GREATER GODS — LETO, APOLLO, ARTEMIS, HEKATE

LETO

LETO (Latin Latona) was the daughter of the Titans Koios and Phoibe. In Homer she was already held to be the mother of Apollo and Artemis, and, in more than a transient sense, the spouse of Zeus. When Aineias was wounded, she assisted in caring for him, but her act is not to be regarded as significant of a religious function, for her chief importance lies in her motherhood of Apollo and Artemis.

The Birth of Apollo and Artemis. — The story of the birth of Apollo and Artemis can be made complete by piecing together a portion of a *Homeric Hymn* to Apollo [1] and several supplementary myths. The statement in one of the latter that Artemis was born the day before Apollo must be held in mind as an explanation of her presence at her brother's birth.

Being great with child by Zeus, Leto wandered from land to land about the Aegean searching for a place in which to bring her son to the light; but everywhere the people feared his predestined power, and she was turned cruelly away. At last she reached the island of Rheneia, and at her own request was taken from there to Delos, which she earnestly begged to afford her the refuge that she so much needed. After long hesitation the island consented to receive her on condition that she would swear a solemn oath that her son's first shrine would be erected there, and that he would abundantly honour and not despise this unproductive tract of rock. Leto swore by the Styx (the most awful of all oaths), and was forthwith received. Then her birth-pangs began, enduring for nine days and nine nights, but with no result, although she was helped by Artemis, Themis, Amphitrite, and other divinities, until finally these sent for Eileithyia, who, hastening to Delos, soon consummated the birth. The attending goddesses cared for the infant Apollo, wrapping him in fine linen, and Themis gave him nectar and ambrosia. As soon as the divine food put strength into him, up he leaped, burst his bands, suddenly attained the stature of a man, and taking the zither and the bow and arrows into his hands strode to the summit of Mount Kynthos, while the whole island gleamed with a golden light.

The union of Leto and Apollo as thus set forth seems to have been founded on some local cult-association of the two divinities; and that between Leto and Artemis probably developed from a similarity in function as helpers of women in travail and as protectresses of children, the wandering of Leto being symbolic of this so far as it depicts her as retarding or as advancing birth at will.

Leto and Tityos; Leto and Niobe. — Travellers on their way to Apollo's shrine at Delphoi were often waylaid by a brutal giant named Tityos, and when Leto was once bound thither, he attempted lustful violence upon her. Both to avenge his mother and to aid peaceful pilgrims Apollo slew Tityos, who was condemned in the underworld to pay a horrible penalty for his crimes. For her insolence in boasting that her mortal children were superior to the immortal offspring of Leto, Niobe was changed into a figure of stone, and her children were slain by the arrows of Apollo and Artemis.

APOLLO

The Origin and the Name of Apollo. — Apollo, the brightest and the most complex creation of polytheism, seems to have been originally the leading god of a people who migrated into Greece from the north in prehistoric times, his northern origin being apparently reflected in the fixed routes followed by the sacred processions to his two chief shrines. The one way, which, we may note, Apollo himself followed, according to the longer *Homeric Hymn* in his honour, ran southward from Tempe through Iolkos and Thebes to Delphoi; and the other led the pilgrims bearing the Hyperboreian fruits overland

FIG. 7. APOLLO AND TITYOS

Apollo, shown as an effeminate youth with long hair, is striding forward with a double axe in his right hand. The backward look, the bent knees, and the swinging arms of Tityos together indicate the giant's great fear and rapid flight. From a red-figured Attic *amphora* of the Nolan type found at Gela (*Monumenti Antichi*, xviii, Plate X).

along the coast of the Adriatic to Dodona, thence eastward to the Gulf of Euboia, and from that point by ship to Delos. Apollo's initial function is by no means certain, nor has any satisfactory explanation of the source and meaning of his name yet been offered.

Apollo in Homer. — In Homer Apollo is already the son of Zeus and the brother of Artemis, but, although his chief physical traits and the leading features of his character are fixed,

PLATE XLI

The Apollo Belvedere

The position of the god, standing as he is with his feet well apart and extending one hand forward while the other drops almost to his side, suggests that he has just shot an arrow from his bow and with his eye is following its distant flight. This interpretation is certainly in harmony with other representations of him, although here he seems to be playing the *rôle* of archer before a throng of admirers rather than to be engaged in the serious business of hitting a living mark, and although, too, almost all of his individual characteristics have been idealized away. From a marble (a copy of a Hellenistic bronze) in the Belvedere of the Vatican (Brunn-Bruckmann, *Denkmäler griechischer und römischer Sculptur*, No. 419).

he has yet to evolve the complex personality by which he is to be known to the Greeks after the fifth century B.C. He has to do with light, but is not convincingly identified with Helios. He is *a* god of healing, but not yet *the* god of healing, so that he revives Hektor after he has been wounded in conflict. With the power of healing must be assumed its opposite, the ability to inflict harm, whence it was Apollo who, in consequence of a slight, sent the pestilence upon the men and beasts of the Achaian camp. He is himself the expert archer of the Olympians and confers on Pandaros and Teukros skill in the use of the bow, but, though he wields the bow and occasionally takes part in the strife as a violent partisan of the Trojans, he is only accidentally a god of war. He is associated with prophecy in that seers, like Kalchas, draw their inspiration from him. Descriptions of him always represent him as in the prime of young manhood, with flowing locks of golden hair.

Apollo in Delphoi. — Python, the huge dragon-offspring of Earth, learned that he was doomed to die at the hands of a son whom Leto should bear, and to forestall the future he sought to kill her, but was frustrated by Zeus, who removed her to a place of safety until her children were born. Soon after his birth Apollo took from Hephaistos a quiver of arrows and with them slew his mother's foe at Delphoi, thereby earning for himself the title Pythios, and, burying the body of the Python in the temple, he instituted over it funeral games which were thereafter known as the Pythian Games. Closely allied with this legend is the account which, in the *Homeric Hymn* dedicated to the god, tells of his founding of his own shrine. Leaving Olympos, Apollo pressed southward, passing through Iolkos, Euboia, and Thebes, and at last came to Delphoi, on the slopes of Mount Parnassos overlooking the Gulf of Corinth, where he built a beautiful temple from which to deliver oracles, he himself laying the foundation but entrusting the rest of the work to human hands. Hard by the fane was a spring where lurked Typhon, a destructive monster, unlike both gods and men, which Hera begot without Zeus in answer to her prayer that Earth grant her a son who would overthrow her husband. With one of his sharp shafts Apollo laid Typhon low, and because he left the carcass upon the ground to rot, the deity was called Pythios,[2] if a play upon words can convince any one. In these two narratives we may perceive indications that the Earth Goddess had a mantic seat at Delphoi before the cult and oracle of Apollo were established there, this being partially verified by the story that Earth, jealous of Apollo's usurpation, sent dream-oracles to visitors at the fane to thwart the Apolline method of revealing the future, whereupon the god appealed to Zeus, who ordered that no more prophecies of this type be dispensed in the shrine. When Apollo had completed his temple, the *Homeric Hymn* continues, he cast about for suitable priests to serve him, and, spying a company of Cretans in a ship bound for Pylos, he leaped into the sea in the form of a dolphin and thence into the hollow of the vessel. None durst touch or disturb him, and, as long as he lay there, the sailors lost all control of their helm, so that, in spite of themselves, they were carried past their goal and eastward up the Gulf of Corinth until they came to Krisa, the port of Delphoi. There Apollo, in the form of a beautiful youth, revealed himself to them, and, appointing them the holy servitors of his temple, bade them worship him thenceforth under the title Delphinios ("Dolphin-Like"), the site of the shrine, formerly called Pytho, being now given the name of Delphoi. This legend apparently records a historical fact that the Delphinian Apollo, who was widely regarded as a saviour from shipwreck, was of Cretan provenance.[3]

The Functions of Apollo. — Undoubtedly the best known power of Apollo was that of prophecy. As has already been clearly intimated, his chief prophetic shrine was Delphoi, although other centres, probably offshoots of Delphoi, like Branchidai, were found in various places. His foreknowledge was consulted in all sorts of matters. Aigeus and later Kreousa and Xouthos sought it in reference to offspring; Herakles, regarding a cure for the dreadful malady which afflicted him; Kadmos, in order to find the lost Europe. The Epigonoi were assured through it of the ultimate victory of their cause against Thebes, and Alkmaion used it as a sanction for the murder of his mother Eriphyle. In historical times the oracle was consulted time and again,[4] and although many of the more enlightened Greeks, Thoukydides for instance, frankly held the popular confidence in the oracle to be pure superstition, they did not question the value of Delphoi as essential to the maintenance of Greek political and moral unity. The story of Kassandra reflects the oracular powers of Apollo. It seems that Apollo desired her to yield him her love, but she refused, although he promised to endow her in return with the gift of foreseeing the future, whereupon, to punish the obstinate maiden, he gave her the promised boon, but added to it the penalty that her prophecies would never be believed.

Inasmuch as the oracle was most commonly consulted concerning the healing of disease, it was easy for Apollo to become a god of healing. If he was aboriginally a divinity of light, this function becomes more readily understood, for the ancients were well aware of the purifying nature of light, and moreover the physician has always been regarded as a sort of compound of seer and healer. As healer, Apollo was known under many names, notably that of Paian, and it is probable that the purpose of the Paian hymn sung before battle and after victory was to invoke healing for the wounds of conflict.

Apollo was the divine guardian of navigation, a function which seems to have had its root, not in any special lordship over the sea, but in the wide diffusion of his cult in all Hellenic settlements. He exercised control not so much over the sea as over those elements and physiographical features which make for the convenience and safety of voyages — tradewinds, harbours, estuaries, and the like. From the highways of the ocean his supervision was naturally extended to the highways of the land, and he became the protector of wayfarers, whence the presence of his images in the streets before housedoors.

The *rôle* of Apollo as the divine founder of colonies is doubtless as early as the period of the immigration which brought him into the Hellenic world. As the years went by, this part was greatly enlarged through the frequency with which prospective colonists appealed to his oracle to throw light on the destiny of their settlements abroad, and epithets like "Founder" point to this. He was even said to guide emigrants to their new homes in the form of some bird, especially of a sea-bird, such as the diver or the gull, and he came himself, in one account, to Delphoi from the land of the Hyperboreians in a chariot drawn by swans. In just such a car he conveyed Kyrene to Africa, and we have already noted how, as a dolphin, he led his ministers to his shrine in Delphoi. Owing to this intimate connexion with the establishing of new states his name easily became woven into the genealogies of their human founders, so that, for instance, as Patroös he was literally known in Athens as the flesh-and-blood father of Ion by the Athenian maiden Kreousa. Now it was logical to expect the founder to continue his favour past the initial stages of settlement and to ensure the well-being of the established community, whence we find Apollo as the protector and ideal of youth, i. e. of the citizens to be, in which connexion it will be remembered that Herakles dedicated to him a lock of his hair on attaining to manhood. We see him, too, protecting all useful plants as well as herds. As Smintheus, he saves the crops from the ravages of mice; the Karneian Apollo of Lakedaimon was a god of horned cattle; and Apollo himself herded the flocks of Admetos for a season. Of the trees the laurel, apple, and tamarisk were sacred to him. His relation to the laurel is dimly pictured in the story that Apollo loved Daphne, the daughter of the river Peneios and Earth, but, evading his embrace, the maiden besought her mother to save her. Earth, hearkening to the prayer, allowed her to sink partly from sight and changed her into the laurel-tree, whereupon, breaking off a branch, Apollo crowned his head with it.

Although Hermes was credited with the invention of the lyre, Apollo was the skilled performer upon it. In myth he is but rarely represented as employing the flute, a pictorial manner of saying that the wailing notes of this instrument were not in harmony with the Apolline ritual, and the superiority of the lyre is the substance of the story of the contest between Apollo and Marsyas. Athene, it is said, invented the flute out of a deer's horn and played before the gods, but her grimaces created such ridicule that in disgust she threw the instrument away and cursed with torture whosoever would pick it up. Marsyas the satyr found it and having, by dint of much practice, attained great proficiency, he boastfully challenged Apollo to a contest in which the muses, as judges, awarded the palm to the god, who, in fulfilment of Athene's curse, proceeded to flay his defeated adversary alive. Besides being a performer on the lyre and the flute, Apollo was a singer, and, in short, he was the god of all music and of the allied art of poetry. Bards drew their inspiration from him, and it was he who impelled the priests and priestesses of the oracles to cast their utterances into measured language having the form, if not always the spirit, of poetry. Before the assemblies of the gods he led the chorus of the Muses, and in certain late philosophical beliefs the harmony not only of the movements of the sun but also of the universe was attributed to him. No straining of the fancy is required to follow him as he advances from this exalted position of abstract thought to the lordship of all social harmony.

The recognition of Apollo as Helios was early but not original, and may have arisen from Oriental influences; [5] and from this, perhaps, came the conception of his long fair hair, while either here or in his affiliation with Artemis lies the origin of his arrows.

In spite of his dexterity with the bow, he was never technically a god of war, being, on the contrary, consistently just as he was represented on the western pediment of the temple of Zeus at Olympia, the exponent of peace and civilization as opposed to the ceaseless strife of barbarism.

Apollo in Art. — In representing Apollo archaic art borrowed from the epic the feature of the unshorn hair, and added it to the rough fetishistic images of the god in order to produce bodily reality. From this was easily evolved the type of the best period, a type which we must forbear from reading into the epic. Here Apollo was depicted as a young man in his prime, nude or lightly clad, standing or striding. Sometimes he wears a long flowing cloak or a tunic, and the bow, the zither, and the twig of laurel in the hair are almost constant attributes, singly or jointly.

ARTEMIS

The Origin and the Name of Artemis. — Artemis may have originated among the Greeks, or, on the other hand, among Phrygians or other barbarians, and later have received a Greek name. Conjectures as to her primeval functions are sharply divided, the two aspects selected by opposing schools as the oldest being, first, that in which she interests herself in the life of the wild, and, secondly, that in which she appears as a destroyer of life. Her cult-title Meleagros ("Hunter of Members") is thought to describe her as the demon of a disease, perhaps of leprosy, which slowly devours the members of the body. By a very natural converse manner of reasoning the one who could destroy could also arrest the process of destruction and could heal. Yet for Artemis to acquire from these functions her dominion over the wild, we must admit, taxes the fancy and reason, so that it seems much more probable that a divinity who has oversight, among other things, of wild plants with medicinal properties, would become a divinity of healing, and that, once the capacity of curing disease was established, the converse process of argument would explain

PLATE XLII

Artemis

No inscription is needed to mark this statue as that of the "Lady of the Beasts." On her head rests an elaborate crown on the top of which is a perforated border of animal figures, while the band passing obliquely over her breast is ornamented with a somewhat similar design in relief. As the goddess steps slowly forward she allows a playful fawn to suck the fingers of her right hand. From a Roman copy of a Greek type of the fifth century B.C., in Munich (Brunn-Bruckmann, *Denkmäler griechischer und römischer Sculptur*, No. 562).

a capacity for destruction. At any rate, her cult must be very old, exhibiting, as it does, remnants of totemism in the ritual eating of the goddess in the flesh of a quail or of a bear, as well as traces of human sacrifice in the slaughter of strangers in the land of the Taurians. Although Artemis enjoyed a pan-Hellenic cult, the oldest Hellenic conception of her was Boiotian; yet her matured personality is not purely Hellenic, for her alien characteristics are many. The Artemis of Ephesos, for instance, is a hybrid of the Great Mother, the maternal principle of nature, and the original Greek goddess; and she not only acquired traits from the Cretan Rhea, but was identified with the barbarian Diktynna, Britomartis, Bendis, Anaitis, Astarte, and Atargatis. The source of her association with Apollo is unknown, though some accidental local contact may be suspected. Her appellation appears to be connected with the root of the name Arkadia, but we are in the dark as to its meaning.

Artemis in Homer. — Artemis takes next to no part in the action of the Homeric poems, most mentions of her being merely allusions to her activities in the various localities in Hellas prior to the Trojan War. Her personality is marked by three outstanding features: she is a huntress and the mistress of wild life, a bringer of sudden death, and the virgin sister of Apollo. Through instruction received from her the Trojan Skamandros learned to hunt the beasts of hill and woodland, and she herself was said to roam the ranges of Taÿgetos and Erymanthos "delighting in the wild boars and swift hinds." She was the slayer of Orion, of a daughter of Bellerophon, and of the daughters of Niobe; and when women died a sudden but peaceful death, people said that they were the victims of her swift arrows.

The Functions of Artemis. — The traits which have just been mentioned, with others added, still cling to Artemis in the field of myth beyond Homer, while her relation to the vast tracts beyond the settlements of men can be observed in her almost certain identity with Kallisto, Atalante, the mountain-nymph Taÿgete, and Kyrene, under whose name she became the mother of Aristaios by Apollo. The Keryneian doe, which Herakles captured alive, was sacred to her, and for killing another of her sacred hinds Agamemnon was sorely punished and his fleet was detained at Aulis by head winds, while it was she who placed a hind on the Aulid altar in lieu of the innocent Iphigeneia. Kallisto in the form of a bear fell before her bow, and the unerring spear and dog were given to Prokris through her good will, if we follow a particular version of the legend. One of her shrines, we are told, was surrounded by a veritable zoological garden, and in her capacity as protectress of such collections may perhaps be found the origin of her common epithet "Lady of the Beasts." Of the birds the quail, the partridge, the guinea-fowl, and the swallow were intimately related to her cult, but only rarely did domestic animals, like the horse, the ox, and the sheep, come within the scope of her supervision, although in this connexion we may call to mind the failure of Atreus to keep his promise to sacrifice to her the golden lamb. With all beasts her protecting functions come first and the destroying second. As a huntress and in her general oversight of wild nature she contracted affiliations with Dionysos and the Maenads and was thought to be the same as the Cretan Diktynna, while in the old Boiotian culture she was held to be the hunting partner of Orion, together with whom she shot her sharp arrows at man and beast alike. Not unnaturally she was a goddess of plant life, primarily that of the untilled lands, the trees of the forest, for instance, being sacred to her; yet she must also have had an interest in the plants of tillage, else the stories of her pique at the harvest-home sacrifices of Oineus and Admetos have no point.

As the goddess-physician, Artemis had broad functions, and no hard and fast line can be drawn about the kinds of ailments under her control. Malarial chills, leprosy, rabies, gout, epilepsy, phthisis, and mental diseases are all mentioned as coming within the range of her activities, and she even undertook to heal snake bites. Her methods of treatment savour strangely of magic, particularly of that branch known as homoeopathic, a circumstance which may be counted as good proof of her antiquity as a healer. The quail, partridge, guinea-fowl, goat, swine, and the fabulous hippocamp were included in her *materia medica;* and, among plants, the juniper, and the white and the black hellebore, the healing property in all these being Artemis herself, who, counteracting the power of Artemis the cause of the disease, effected a cure by virtue of the famous principle (here to be interpreted, of course, in a magical sense) of *similia similibus curantur* ("like is cured by like"). Bathing in certain lakes and streams near her shrines, as in the Alpheios of Elis, was supposed to remove some diseases, the process to be understood obviously being that of magical ablution. It was apparently through her contact with magic that she entered into connexion with Hekate.

One of the oldest powers of Artemis was that of expediting the delivery of women in child-birth, and by a contradictory manner of reasoning no longer strange to us, she was also regarded as both bringing and healing puerperal fever. In her exercise of these functions one can see why she was so closely bound to Leto.

The icy chastity of Artemis has long been proverbial, yet it is a fact that only in myth was she endowed with this trait, for no traces of it are to be found in her public cults. The myths which record her puritanical rejection of the almost innocently unchaste Prokris, her inordinate punishment of the peeping Aktaion, and her well-nigh Pharisaic patronage of the precocious Hippolytos have the air of being comparatively late attempts to cloak an originally unmoral character with moral attributes — to make a virtue out of an accident; but her chastity is inconsistent with her great interest in maternity and with her impersonation by Atalante and others.

Artemis had a number of miscellaneous attributes which we can only mention here. On rare occasions she appears as a water-goddess, being invoked, for instance, in the search for springs, while as a protectress of travellers and emigrants she seems to have absorbed some of the duties of Apollo. In the story of Iphigeneia at Aulis she exercised control over the conditions of the weather, and although she was not equated with the moon until a comparatively late period, this identification has become one of her ineradicable marks in poetry. The links binding her to the higher intellectual and social life are slender, yet they exist.[6]

Artemis in Art. — One of the two oldest types of Artemis delineates her with spreading wings and as holding a lion in her hand, while the other shows her between two lions, both of these forms exhibiting Asiatic influence. The fully developed Artemis of art is a huntress, just emerging from maidenhood into womanhood, equipped with bow and quiver, and followed by one or more dogs.

HEKATE

The greater prevalence of the cults of Hekate in the northern districts of Greece, her resemblance to the goddess Bendis of Thrace, and certain other features point convergently toward some northern land as her first home. If she were actually of Hellenic origin, her cult must have died out and after a long period have been revived at the very threshold of the historical era. Her name may be a Greek equivalent of some title borne by her in her native habitat; it appears to be connected with ἑκάς ("far") and may be a short form of ἑκατηβόλος, designating her as the "Far-Shooter" or as "the one who comes from afar."

Hekate was grudged free entry into the domain of myth and was denied an established pedigree — facts which cast suspicion on her alleged Greek nativity. In Hesiod she was the daughter of the Titan Perses and Asteria, and in Mousaios, the daughter of Zeus and Asteria. A Thessalian myth speaks of Admetos and a woman of Pherai as her parents, although elsewhere her mother was said to be Night or Leto. Strangely, no stock looks back to her as its divine foremother, and Homer seems to have been ignorant of her, for otherwise her strong connexion with the underworld would have necessitated a mention of her in the description of the descent of Odysseus to Hades. In one account of the war of the gods and giants, however, Hekate kills the giant Klytios with burning brands.

In the *Theogony* of Hesiod Hekate is already a fully formed and fully endowed divinity exercising control equally over heaven, earth, and sea; but the very extravagance of the attributions brands the passage as almost certainly an interpolation, composed by a defender of her cult when it was yet new in Boiotia. Her most conspicuous, and, perhaps, her original, function was chthonic. Among the goddesses she stands in substantially the same relation to sorcery and necromancy as does Hermes among the gods, and in myth Medeia is one of her priestesses.[7]

To modern readers Hekate is best known as the original "Diana of the Crossways," and she was supposed to drive evil influences away from crossways, doors, and gates. To retain her favour, or to placate her anger and that of the hordes of *revenants* which trooped after her, people used to make offerings to her (commonly known as "Hekate's suppers") at the forks of roads, her special haunts, these being given at night under a new moon, and consisting of foods prepared according to a ritual bill of fare.

Not until the middle of the fifth century B.C. was Hekate established as the moon-goddess, an identity which she doubtless acquired and maintained through the insecure position of Selene (the lunar divinity proper) in popular belief. This feature and her connexion with child-birth she held in common with Artemis.

The most widely disseminated type of Hekate in art is one that goes back to the image made for her shrine at the entrance to the Athenian Acropolis, over which she had surveillance. This portrays her as having three bodies, all back to back, one facing forward and the other two to the left and right respectively. In the outer hands of the side figures are held a pitcher and a deep sacrificial saucer, while each of the remaining four hands grasps a torch. It was probably in this form, capable of looking three ways at once, that she was popularly conceived as the divine protectress of cross-roads.

PLATE XLIII

An Attic Hekataion

The central feature of this attractive group is the tall plain column, a primitive symbol of Artemis-Hekate. With their backs to this as at the three points of an equilateral triangle stand three similar figures, stiffly architectural in character, of Hekate Phosphoros. Each is crowned with a lofty *polos* and holds two torches bolt upright at her sides. Around this group, in marked contrast in style as well as in stature, is a ring of three Charites, all alike, dancing lightly and gracefully hand in hand. From a small marble of the late fifth or early fourth century B.C., in the collection of Heinrich Graf Lemberg of Austria-Hungary (*JHAI* xiii, Plate IV).

CHAPTER IV

THE GREATER GODS — ARES

THE Origin and the Name of Ares. — So obscure is the origin of Ares that we are scarcely in a position even to entertain a suspicion as to whether he came from within or from without Hellas. Certainly his cult was most deeply rooted in Boiotia and farther north, yet this cannot be taken as an indication of origin, since we cannot prove that he had been established here longer than elsewhere. His name has a Hellenic cast, but it cannot be satisfactorily derived, although it appeals strongly to the imagination to connect it with ἀρά, "a curse." By that token war, the province of Ares, would be the curse *par excellence.*

Ares in Homer. — Throughout Homer Ares is the only god whose one thought and task it is to wage war, yet it is not the strategic element for which he stands, but rather, as one writer aptly puts it, the blind berserker-rage of battle. Beating wildly about him with his blade, he achieves but little glory before Troy, although, unlike any other god, he does succeed in slaying some mortals with his own hand. He is sorely wounded by the hero Diomedes, and in his great pain bellows like an army ten thousand strong, while Homer says that Otos and Ephialtes, the stalwart sons of Aloeus, once bound him in a bronze vessel for thirteen months,[1] and in a conflict among the gods he is overthrown by Athene. He is as fickle as he is blustering, one moment favouring the Greeks and the next instant lending aid to the Trojans. He is the son of Zeus and Hera, and his father takes pains, perhaps facetiously, to let it be known that his love of brawling is purely a maternal inheritance. His brother is Eris ("Strife"), and Deimos

("Panic") and Phobos ("Fear") are his steeds. Soldiers are known as his servants and the bolder heroes as his sons; and by metonymy his name often stands for war or the spirit of strife in arms. Homer records that he was detected in an intrigue with Aphrodite.

Ares outside of Homer. — Although Ares generally passed as the son of Zeus and Hera, one account, apparently of ancient origin, made him the unfathered offspring of Hera alone after she had become impregnated by plucking a certain flower (the parallel instance of the conception of Hebe will naturally occur to us here). We have already seen how, in the Attic cycle of myths, Ares became associated with Areopagos through Alkippe, his daughter by Aglauros, and through the group of his professionally belligerent daughters, the Amazons. All of his children reflect his character in some way: Enyeus, the king of Skyros, was his son by Ariadne; Lykourgos, who drove the votaries of Dionysos into the sea, Kyknos the wrestler, and the Bistonian Diomedes were other offspring; Harmonia, the unhappy mother of a strife-rent family, was borne to him by Aphrodite; and the Theban dragon slain by Kadmos was also his issue. Prior to the great assault against the city of Thebes, the Seven Generals of the Argive host took the oath binding them to a united cause by dipping their hands in bull's blood caught in the hollow of a shield as they pronounced the names of Ares, Enyo, and Phobos. The ethical influence of Ares was negative and therefore slight, and depended entirely on the inference that his scant popularity must indicate general disapproval of his works and character.

Ares in Art. — An ideal type of Ares in art was apparently never definitely established. In the earlier period he is generally shown on vases as a fully armed and bearded warrior; there are several types in extant statuary bearing the influence of the later period, the best known being the so-called Borghese Ares of the Louvre, where he is a nude youth wearing a helmet and gazing dreamingly before him.

CHAPTER V

THE GREATER GODS — HERMES

THE *Origin and the Name of Hermes.* — Hermes was found in all Hellenic communities, but the part which he played was relatively inferior. Only in two or three localities had his cult any deep foundation in the history and thought of the people, and in Arkadia alone was he accounted a divine ancestor. Although his name seems to be Greek in external form, it has not yielded to investigators any radical connexion with the Greek language, and, *a fortiori*, any meaning consistent with the character of Hermes. Scholars are practically unanimous in their belief that the deity is not Hellenic, and most of the theories which they venture to make point to the east, a very recent theory,[1] supported, as it is, by the tangible evidence of the monuments, making it almost certain that Hermes and his distinctive attribute, the caduceus, came to Hellas, apparently by a circuitous path, from the Mesopotamian valley.

Hermes in Homer. — Homer alludes to Hermes as the son of Maia, but fails to state the name of his father. The god is already endowed with the individuality that marks him in later centuries. He is the herald and messenger of the gods; it is he who communicates to Kalypso the command of Zeus to free Odysseus and who bears the sceptre from Zeus to Pelops; and by him Priam is safely escorted to the encampment of the Greeks. His conduct of the slain suitors to the halls of Hades is the only instance in Homer of his function as the marshal of departed souls. The converse of this aspect is seen in the assistance which he gives to Herakles to return from the lower to the upper world. As the patron of thieves he confers on

Autolykos, the maternal grandfather of Odysseus, the allied gifts of thievery and falsehood, and he is, moreover, the special divinity of servants and the giver of wealth.

Myths of the Birth and Boyhood of Hermes. — A summary of the Homeric *Hymn to Hermes* will give us the best conspectus of the later Greek ideas of Hermes. After dalliance with Zeus "in love not quite legitimate," the nymph Maia bore Hermes in a cavern on Mount Kyllene in Arkadia. Even for a god the child was extraordinarily precocious, for, during the morning of the very day of his birth, he walked unaided out of the grotto, inquisitive to see what the world was like. Immediately he espied a tortoise, and, with divine intuition, perceiving in it possibilities as yet undreamed of, he killed the creature, removed its shell, and fitted it with a bridge and seven taut strings of sheep-gut. Thus he created the lyre.

> "When he had wrought the lovely instrument,
> He tried the chords, and made diversion meet
> Preluding with the plectrum, and there went
> Up from beneath his hand a tumult sweet
> Of mighty sounds, as from his lips he sent
> A strain of unpremeditated wit
> Joyous and wild and wanton — such you may
> Hear among revellers on a holiday." [2]

At the end of his song a strange desire for fresh meat tickled his infant palate, and descending quickly from Kyllene he came to the lands where the cattle of Apollo were grazing. Picking out fifty heifers, he cunningly reversed their hoofs, and, himself walking backward, drove them away through the night to the banks of the river Alpheios, where he invented the art of making fire by rubbing two sticks of laurel-wood together, after which he slew two of the heifers and offered a burnt sacrifice. At dawn he stealthily returned home, and wrapping his swaddling-clothes about him lay down in his cradle like a babe utterly innocent of all guile. Nevertheless, he could not deceive Maia, who was as watchful as any human mother, and at her words of rebuke he confessed his wrong-doing, but announced that it was only the first of a programme of acts which he had planned to carry out in order to achieve a place of distinction among the immortals. Soon afterward Apollo appeared, having traced, though with difficulty, the reversed footsteps to the cavern; but when he charged Hermes with the theft of the cattle, the infant blandly denied it.

"An ox-stealer should be both tall and strong,
And I am but a little newborn thing,
Who, yet at least, can think of nothing wrong:
My business is to suck, and sleep, and fling
The cradle-clothes about me all day long,
Or, half asleep, hear my sweet mother sing,
And to be washed in water clean and warm,
And hushed and kissed and kept secure from harm." [3]

His denial availed him nothing, however, for Apollo haled him away to the judgement-seat of Zeus on Olympos, where the king of the gods patiently listened to their statements, and highly amused at Hermes' transparent lies dismissed them both with the advice "to compose the affair by arbitration." Departing from Olympos, they came to the scene of Hermes' sacrifice. The evidences of the slaughter of his beasts enraged Apollo, but he was soon appeased by the unwonted strains of music which Hermes drew from the lyre. Thereupon they compacted an eternal friendship and sealed it with mutual gifts, Hermes presenting the lyre to Apollo and Apollo in his turn bestowing on Hermes the golden wand of wealth and a lash with which to exercise dominion over the flocks and herds of the field.

"Hermes with Gods and men even from that day
Mingled, and wrought the latter much annoy,
And little profit, going far astray
Through the dun night." [4]

Hermes Argeïphontes. — When Hermes was bidden to release the tethered Io, he approached her guardian Argos, and, after putting him to sleep with the music of the lyre, cut out his many eyes with his curved sword, earning for himself by this deed, it was popularly said, the title of Argeïphontes

("Argos-Slayer"). When he was taken before a court and acquitted of the charge of murder, the angry gods cast their voting pebbles at him, a detail which seems to be aetiological in character and designed to explain the origin of heaps of stones, dedicated to Hermes, which were often found beside frequented thoroughfares and to which each wayfarer added his contribution in kind as he passed by. Although it is customary nowadays to base the story of the slaying of Argos on a misunderstanding of Hermes' title, which seems really to mean "white-gleaming," it would probably be nearer the truth to base it on a folk-belief in an earth-born monster, who, under the control of Hermes, stood guard over souls in the lower world.

The Functions of Hermes. — Hermes is best known as the conductor of departed souls to Hades, and, conversely, he could also release them from the world below. Through the discharge of these duties he first of all became connected with necromancy, or conjuring of the dead, and later, in consequence of the popular classification of dream-oracles as necromantic, he was evolved into a god of sleep and of dreams, developing, in the end, out and out into a deity of magic. As the souls of the dead could be magically committed to him as they traversed the highway between the two worlds, so too could the souls of the living be guarded by him as they went their ways to and fro upon earth. Hence the images of Hermes at cross-roads were believed to avert evil from travellers, and here one can see the logic of his frequent association with Apollo, Artemis, and Hekate. As god of the highroad it was natural to suppose that he himself was immune from the perils of the way; he could, therefore, exercise the double duty of protecting heralds, the most sacred travellers among men, and of himself being the inviolate herald of the gods; and thus he was an important figure in the early stages of international law. Since the herald must have a fluent and persuasive tongue, Hermes became the god of oratory and speech in general. No one journeys as much as he who travels for gain, and hence Hermes

PLATE XLIV

Hermes and the Infant Dionysos

This famous statue apparently refers to the Theban legend which relates that Dionysos, just after his birth from the thigh of Zeus and prior to his sojourn with the nymphs of Mount Nysa, was put in the safe-keeping of Hermes. Praxiteles has seized on this brief period as the supreme moment in the career of Hermes for revealing him as the ideal protector of boys and youths. In looking upon this highly spiritualized creation one forgets that this god was the divine prince of knaves and liars. From the original marble of Praxiteles (fourth century B.C.), discovered in the Heraion at Olympia (Brunn-Bruckmann, *Denkmäler griechischer und römischer Sculptur*, No. 466).

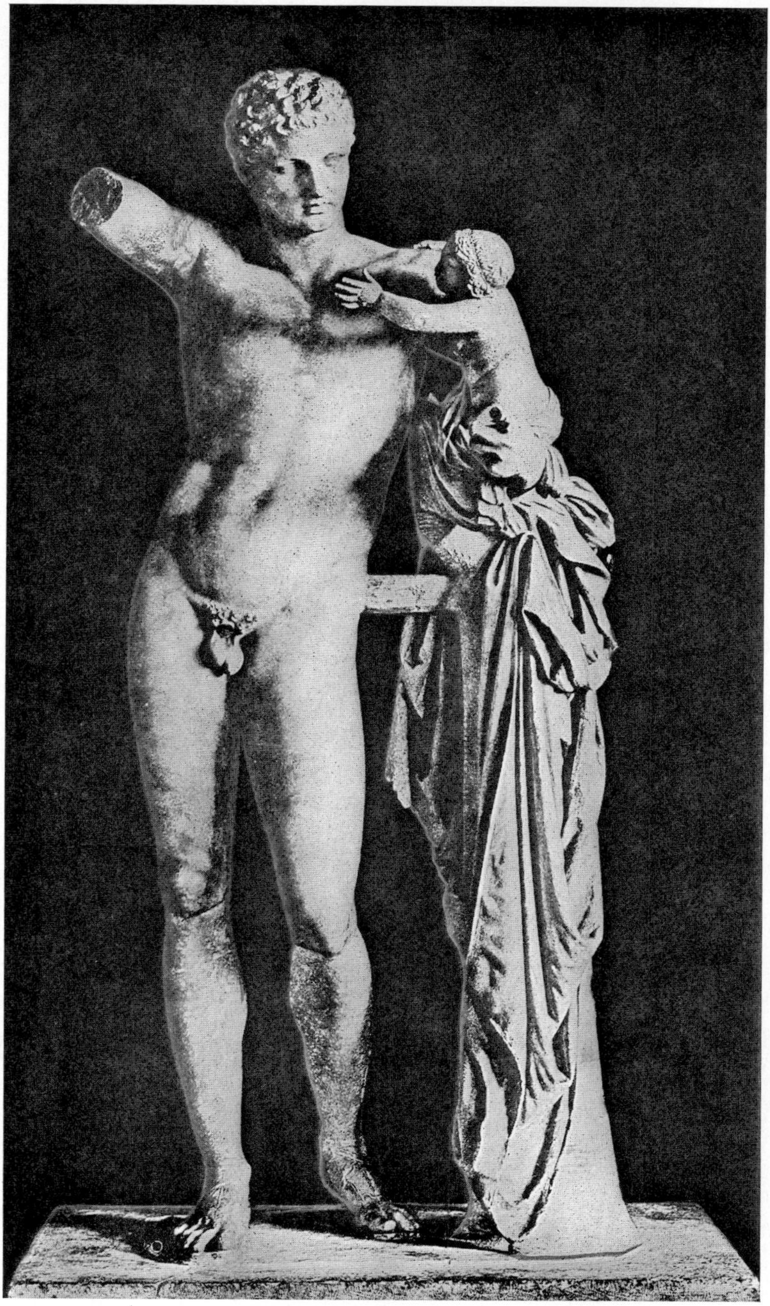

accorded a special protection to the itinerant trader and merchant. As, however, these folk were not noted, to say the least, for their straight dealing, it was not strange that their patron should acquire a reputation akin to theirs, or that the craft and cunning required for driving a profitable one-sided bargain, combined with Hermes' gift of flitting swiftly and safely here and there, should easily exalt him to the infamous position of divine prince of thieves and cutpurses, while it is equally intelligible that the invention, as well as the abuse, of weights and measures should have been assigned to him.

As a pastoral god Hermes became in Arkadian myth the father of Pan, and his peculiar alliance with Aphrodite and certain phallic features of his cult stamp him as the producer of fertility in males. The source of his association with luck may be traceable to his traditional success in the lists of love. Many tales connect him with instrumental music, although his *rôle* in this sphere is subordinate to that of Apollo. An account of the invention of the lyre unlike the one already related represents him as changing Chelone into a tortoise-shell and then into a lyre because she refused to come to the nuptials of Zeus and Hera. Finally, Hermes was the patron god of the palaestra and gymnasium and of all kinds of athletic contests, and was, moreover, to the young men the model of physical strength and agility, just as Apollo was their ideal of high intellectual attainment.[5]

Hermes in Art. — The herm, or developed fetish-form of Hermes, consists of a tall square column with stumps of arms and a phallos, and is surmounted by a bearded head, but we know next to nothing of the ideal Hermes of the fifth century, though he was sometimes shown as a well-matured young man with a short beard and clad in a chlamys. Not until the time of Praxiteles do we see him as a youth, nude or scantily garbed, shod with the winged sandals. The herald's staff is a constant emblem, other attributes being the chlamys and the travelling hat.

CHAPTER VI

THE GREATER GODS — APHRODITE AND EROS

APHRODITE

THE Origin and the Name of Aphrodite. — It is almost impossible to doubt that Aphrodite was a gift of the Semitic world to the Hellenic, so that the opinion, now entertained by a scant few, that the recent excavations in Crete show her to have been initially a purely Aegean creation is unfounded, since the discoveries prove no more than the great antiquity of a divinity who strongly resembled her; they do not at all remove the possibility of her having come at some incalculably early period to the Aegean isles as an emigrant from the Phoinikian coast. Many conceptions of Aphrodite bear marks of her Oriental nativity, and we may point out a few of them by way of example. Her main functions were the same as those of the great Astarte, or Ishtar, and substantially the same objects in nature were sacred to them both, while each was represented in the heavens by the planet Venus, and Aphrodite's epithet Ourania ("Heavenly") seems to be an echo of the Eastern Queen of the Heavens. Further, the allusions in art and literature to Aphrodite's birth from a mussel-shell cannot but remind one that Astarte was the patroness of the industry which produced the famous purple. In her relations to the sea and to mariners Aphrodite bears a striking resemblance to the goddess of the Philistine city of Joppa, and her principal cult-centres, Cyprus, Crete, and Kythera, had direct communication with the eastern coasts through their situation on the main sea-highways. In Thebes alone of Greek cities, a place peculiarly connected with the East in legend, was she venerated as ancestress. Unhappily, the name of Aphrodite tells us nothing concerning her origin. The first half is surely connected with the Greek ἀφρός, "foam," but as to the meaning of the second we must admit ignorance, although, in conformity with certain legends of her birth, the name was popularly interpreted as "Foam-Born." [1]

Aphrodite in Homer. — Homer accepts Aphrodite as the daughter of Zeus and Dione (the earth goddess of Dodona), and numbers her among the Olympians. She is the wedded wife of Hephaistos, but is notoriously unfaithful to her vows. In an amour with Ares she was caught *flagrante delicto* by her husband, whose wits were not as halting as his feet; and by another *affaire du cœur*, with Anchises, she became the mother of Aineias. She is the golden goddess who smiles bewitchingly on both mortals and immortals, and her loveliness is the ideal of all beauty. She is the supreme divinity of love and as such is not suited for strife, yet she essays to take a small part in the great war. Since it was she who had put it into the heart of Helen to leave her husband and go with Paris to Troy, she favours the arms of the Trojans for the sake of being consistent, and snatches both Paris and Aineias from the sword-point of the enemy, although in saving her son she is wounded by the hand of Diomedes.

Birth and Family Relationships. — In Hesiod, Aphrodite is said to have sprung into being from the contact of the severed sexual parts of Ouranos with the sea and to have been afterward washed ashore on Cyprus, the evident purpose of this myth being to account in one breath, as it were, for her simultaneous relation to the life of the sexes and to the sea. Even after Homer she was considered as the wife of Hephaistos, and one old story alludes to Eros and Hermes as the issue of the union, although Harmonia and Aineias were, at all periods of myth, the most famous of her children. She had a close affinity with the Horai ("Seasons," "Hours") and the Charites

("Graces").[2] Ariadne, Leukothea, Galateia, and even her daughter Harmonia, as well as certain other women of myth, are to be regarded as her doubles.

Aphrodite as the Goddess of Love. — While Demeter and Dionysos were associated with the productive potencies of nature, Aphrodite was concerned with, in fact was embodied in, the reproductive powers. She was the divine personality who brought together in procreating love not only human beings but the beasts of the field and the fowls of the air, and, moreover, was responsible for the appearance of fresh growths and new generations of plants.[3]

In the Plant World. — It is in the story of Adonis, which the Greeks borrowed from the East (the name Adonis being only a Greek adaptation of the Semitic form of address *ădhônī* "lord"), that Aphrodite most clearly appears as the force which promotes vegetation. A certain Assyrian king, the tale runs, had a daughter named Smyrna (or Myrrha), whom, because of her continued disdain for Aphrodite, the goddess in anger drove to commit a dreadful sin upon her father. When he learned of her wickedness, he drew a sword and pursued her, and would have thrust her through had not the gods changed her into a myrrh-tree, whose bark burst open nine months later, revealing the infant Adonis. Aphrodite hid him in a chest and entrusted him to Persephone, but when the latter had beheld his beauty, she refused to surrender him, whereupon the two goddesses laid their dispute before Zeus, who decreed that Persephone was to possess the youth for one third of the year and Aphrodite a second third; during the remaining four months Adonis was to be free to do as he would, but as soon as he heard of the verdict, he gave this period of freedom to Aphrodite and became her favourite. While yet in the flower of youth he was slain in the chase by a wild boar, and when Aphrodite grieved beyond consoling, from his blood grew the blossom of the red anemone. This graphic portrayal of the cycle of conditions through which vegetation passes in the course of a year was the theme of certain dramatic acts in the worship of Aphrodite.

Among Men. — Aphrodite would brook no disobedience to her commands to love. We have just seen how she punished Smyrna, and it was through spurning her that Hippolytos was sent to his death. So imperiously did she sway Medeia, Hippodameia, and Ariadne that they abandoned or betrayed their parents to cleave to their lovers, and with alluring promises she bribed the allegiance of the hesitating Paris, paying the bribe with Helen and her gold, while even the frigid heart of Atalante was melted to love at the glitter of Aphrodite's golden apples. The stories of others who yielded to her spell must now engage our attention.

The author of the *Homeric Hymn* to Aphrodite relates how the goddess was taken with a great desire for the mortal Anchises of Troy. Entering her temple-home in Cyprian Paphos, she donned a robe more glittering than the flame of fire and, bedecking herself with her loveliest jewels, she set out for Mount Ida, the very sight of her subduing to love the hearts of even the fiercest beasts of the wild as she made her way up the green slopes. She found Anchises alone in the sheepfolds and through the eloquence of her beauty quickly won his affection, Aineias being the offspring of their union. For many years Anchises observed the injunction of Aphrodite to tell no man of their son's divine descent, but one day, in his cups, he made the secret known to his companions and was stricken dead by a bolt of Zeus. Certain others say that he slew himself with his own hand, while Vergil, as we shall see, has still another tale to tell. Beside this story of Aineias it is interesting to place one of Aphrodite's cult-titles, viz., Aineias, a term whose meaning is lost to us. It may perhaps be an allusion to the hero, and, further, the original Aineias may have been a priest of Aphrodite whose long and tiresome journeying from land to land as he spread the cult of his goddess finally became crystallized into a great myth.

The legend of Pygmalion and Galateia belongs to the cycle of Aphrodite. Pygmalion, a sculptor of Cyprus, failing to see any good in women, vowed himself to lifelong celibacy. Yet, like most misogynists, he still cherished in his heart a high ideal of womanhood, and to embody this in physical form he fashioned a beautiful statue of ivory which fell short of perfection only in its lack of spiritual traits. By constant gazing on the work of his heart and hands he at last fell in love with it and would fain believe it was actually of flesh and blood, and when the festival of Aphrodite came around, offering the customary sacrifices to the goddess and standing by her altar, he raised a prayer: —

"O Aphrodite, kind and fair,
That what thou wilt canst give,
Oh, listen to a sculptor's prayer,
And bid my image live!
For me the ivory and gold
That clothe her cedar frame
Are beautiful, indeed, but cold;
Oh, touch them with thy flame!"[4]

At these words Aphrodite made the flame of the incense shoot aloft in three tongues — an omen of her good will, and when, after the sacrifice, Pygmalion returned to his house, he found his image endowed with the endearing charms of a living woman. She was given the name of Galateia, and with the favour of Aphrodite was wedded to the man whose loving heart had conceived her, their marriage being afterward blessed with a son Paphos, after whom the famous city of Cyprus was named.

This cycle also includes the story of Phaon, who used to ferry travellers back and forth between the islands of Lesbos and Chios. One day Aphrodite, in the guise of an old woman, entreated of him to give her in her poverty a free passage, and so ungrudgingly did he comply with the request that she bestowed a magic philtre upon him. Anointing himself with this, he became a beautiful youth who wakened love in the

PLATE XLV

Eros

"He is springing forward, lightly poised on the toes of his right foot. The left arm is extended forward and holds the socket of a torch; the right is lowered and held obliquely from the body with fingers extended. He is nude and winged, the feathers of the wings being indicated on the front side by incised lines. His hair is curly and short, except for one tuft which is gathered about the centre of the head and braided.

"This famous statue is one of the finest representations of Eros known. The artist has admirably succeeded in conveying the lightness and grace associated in our minds with the conception of Eros. Everything in the figure suggests rapid forward motion; but this is attained without sacrificing the perfect balance of all parts, so that the impression made is at the same time one of buoyancy and of restraint. The childlike character of the figure is brought out in the lithe, rounded limbs and the smiling, happy face" (Miss G. M. A. Richter, *Greek, Etruscan and Roman Bronzes in the Metropolitan Museum of Art*, pp. 85–86). From a Hellenistic bronze in the Metropolitan Museum of Art, New York (*photograph*). See pp. 203–04.

hearts of all the women of Lesbos, and to him, legend says, Sappho addressed some of her tenderest and most beautiful songs.

The Eastern tale of Pyramos and Thisbe, borrowed by the Greeks, also reveals the old belief in the invincible power of Aphrodite. Pyramos was the most handsome youth in the kingdom of Semiramis, and Thisbe the most beautiful maiden, and their families lived in houses separated only by a party-wall. Aphrodite put a mutual love in their hearts, but their parents forbade their marriage, and, what is more, even tried to prevent them from conversing with one another. Their passion, however, would brook no obstacle, and, discovering a crack in the wall between the two houses, unknown to their parents they spoke sweet messages through it, until at length, filled with resolve to wed at all costs, they arranged that they should each slip out of their homes and meet that evening at a certain trysting-place. Thisbe came first, but while she was awaiting her lover, a great lioness, her jaws dripping with fresh blood, suddenly approached to drink from a neighbouring spring. In fear Thisbe turned and fled, dropping her veil, which the lioness tore and left smeared with blood. Reaching the spot a few minutes later, Pyramos recognized the blood-stained veil as Thisbe's and, thinking that it was a token of her death, he drew his sword and pierced himself through the heart, while the blood from his wound sank into the ground and passing upward to the white berries of a near-by mulberry-tree turned them to a deep red. As Pyramos writhed on the ground in the throes of death, Thisbe returned, the sight of her veil and her lover's empty scabbard at once telling the reason of the dreadful deed. Drawing the sword from his heart, she plunged it into her own and passed away at his side; and ever since the fruit of the mulberry has been of the hue of blood.

The story of the love of Hero and Leandros (Leander) belongs to a late period when the making of myths was a more conscious and arbitrary process than formerly and was less closely connected with religious thought; yet it deserves consideration here by reason of its implied association with Aphrodite and its fame in literature. In Sestos, on the Hellespont, lived a beautiful maiden called Hero, who used to tend the sacred birds in Aphrodite's shrine; and in Abydos, on the opposite shore of the strait, dwelt a handsome youth named Leandros. When the time came for celebrating the festival of the goddess of love, Leandros crossed to Sestos to take part in it. In the midst of the rites it chanced that he and Hero came face to face, and at the first glance each became enamoured of the other; but the modest maiden would allow no more than words to pass between them, for she had vowed to go through life unwedded. Love, however, is always stronger than discretion, and Hero's resolution at last weakened so far that she allowed her lover to meet her regularly at an appointed place. By night she would stand on an eminence and hold a torch aloft to guide Leandros as he swam across the Hellespont. But one evening a tempest arose, and though the youth plunged into the water as usual, undaunted by the high seas, his strength gave out before he could reach the other side and he was drowned. His body was flung by the waves upon the shore before the eyes of Hero, who in the frenzy of her sorrow threw herself upon his lifeless frame and died of a broken heart.

Two of the cult-epithets of Aphrodite in Athens were Ourania and Pandemos, the first apparently marking a transplantation of the worship of the Semitic Queen of the Heavens, while the second was probably a manner of recording the worship of Aphrodite by the united townships of Attike, although as early as Solon it was understood to designate the goddess as the one who presided over popular love.[5]

Aphrodite in Art. — Through three or four centuries the Greeks were slowly evolving an ideal type of Aphrodite. In archaic art she appears fully clothed, generally with a veil and head-cloth, and with one hand either outstretched or pressed on her bosom and holding some attribute — the apple, pomegranate, flower, or dove — while the other hand either falls at her side or grasps a fold of her garment. Up to the middle of the fourth century the full clothing of her figure predominates, although even as soon as the later half of the fifth century parts of her body were bared. At this period she is depicted as without passion, though capable of it; but it was only in the hands of the Hellenistic sculptors that she lost her dignity of pure womanhood and became sensuous and conscious of her charms.

EROS

Eros, the frequent companion of Aphrodite, and known to the Romans as Cupido (Cupid), does not appear at all in Homer. This, however, is not to be taken as an indication that he was a later creation, for his prominence in the theogonic literature, notably that of Hesiod, points to his existence in the old daemonic stratum of religious thought. His parentage is variously given: he is the issue of Chaos, or is hatched from the egg of Night; he is the son, now of Ouranos and Gaia, now of Hermes and Artemis, now of Iris and Zephyros; again, he was begotten by Kronos, or born of Aphrodite. As far back as Hesiod he was the intimate associate of the goddess of love, and he is said to have been the lover of the ocean-nymph Rhodope.

Both in worship and in the popular mind Eros, whose opposite was Anteros, was the god of sexual love, and in several places his nature became coarsened through the influence of the cult of Priapos. He was attributed, especially in the later period, with the power of firing men with the passion of love by means of his sharp shafts and stinging tongues of flame, but his personality remained practically unchanged for many centuries, except in the field of philosophy, where he was held to be the cosmic force of attraction. Although Apuleius's story of Cupid and Psyche was based on a developed form of an old Greek folk-tale possessing a religious significance, its excessive literary elaboration excludes it from our pages.

Eros is generally shown by the artists as a winged boy bearing bow and quiver; and among his commonest attributes are the dolphin, the swan, the lyre, and the mussel-shell.

CHAPTER VII

THE GREATER GODS — HEPHAISTOS AND HESTIA

HEPHAISTOS

THE Origin and the Name of Hephaistos. — Whatever may have been the precise initial conception of Hephaistos, he was certainly held by the Greeks at the period of which we have clear records to be the god of fire, and as such we purpose to classify him here, his connexion with the manual arts being apparently derived from the many uses which they made of fire. Whether he was Hellenic or not in origin, we cannot venture to say, but the most plausible explanation of his name tentatively links it with the bases *ϝαφ* and *αιθ*, which would yield the meaning "quivering flame."

Hephaistos in Homer. — Homer knows Hephaistos only as the son of Zeus and Hera, and in the epics he is unequivocally the god of fire, and at times, by a figure of speech, is fire itself, while partly as an instrument in the hands of Achilles and partly as a free agent he consumes the waters of the raging Skamandros. In one passage he is married to one of the Graces, but in another he is the husband of the amorous Aphrodite, who openly manifests her preference for the more human Ares. Two of his characteristics stand out above all the others — his physical appearance and his trade. He is everywhere the lame god, and his limp is a constant source of laughter among his fellows on Olympos. Homer is aware of two accounts concerning the cause of this disability, one of which he puts into the mouth of Hephaistos himself. "Once," he says warningly to Hera, "he [i. e. Zeus] caught me by the foot and hurled me from the heavenly threshold; all day I flew, and at the set of sun I fell in Lemnos, and little life was in me. There did the Sintian folk tend me for my fall." [1] The other version is that which will be given under the next heading. Hephaistos has the distinction of being the only craftsman on Olympos, and the works of his hands are many and wonderful. The greatest of these was, perhaps, the aegis of Zeus, although he also built the houses of the gods and wrought in his forges the sceptre of Agamemnon, the armour of Diomedes and of Achilles, and the golden tripods, which, unguided and unsupported, could enter and depart from the hall of Zeus. Through a combination of disposition and disability he takes but little part in the strife of the Greek and the Trojan.

The Character and Functions of Hephaistos. — Mythology makes a much larger contribution to our mosaic portrait of Hephaistos than does cult, for the bold outlines of his physical appearance and the concrete nature of his activities made him a ready theme for the myth-maker and myth-monger, although these same characteristics debarred him from those phases of worship which demanded some measure of abstract thought, so that he was, in fact, the least abstract and the most concrete of all the gods.

In a myth which seems to belong to a very old stratum Hephaistos had no blood-relationship at all to Zeus; instead, like Typhon, he was merely the son of the unpaired Hera, but after she had borne him, she observed that he was a weakling and cast him down from Olympos, the fall making him lame ever after. Below he took refuge with Thetis and Eurynome in their sea-home and spent his time in training his hand in the cunning of the crafts. Harbouring a grudge against his mother for her cruelty, he fashioned and sent to her a golden chair fitted with invisible snares, so that when she sat in it she was held so fast that not even the strength of the gods could release her. Ares went to Hephaistos to beg him to come and loosen the snares, but Hephaistos drove him back home with

PLATE XLVI

The Return of Hephaistos to Olympos

Hephaistos, crowned with the festive ivy and holding a pair of smith's tongs, rides unsteadily on a spirited mule. In front of him walks Dionysos carrying his special emblems, the *thyrsos* and the *kantharos*. The short and merry procession is led by a Satyr with a horse's tail and pointed ears, who as he goes along seems to be dancing to the accompaniment of his own lyre. From a red-figured *krater* of about 440 B.C., in Munich (Furtwängler-Reichhold, *Griechische Vasenmalerei*, No. 7). See pp. 206–07.

fire-brands, although after a time Dionysos put Hephaistos under the spell of wine, and bringing him to Olympos had him free his mother, from whom, in the end, he received full forgiveness. His lameness (humorously contrary to the modern theories of heredity) was inherited by his sons Periphetes and Talos, and is observable in his doubles, Typhon and Anchises. Some students see the origin of the lameness in the unsteady movements of flame, although it has recently been suggested that a brotherhood of warriors who needed a smith-god as patron accepted Hephaistos in this capacity and made him lame to prevent him from running away.[2]

To such an extent was Hephaistos the chief god of fire that when the hearth-fire crackled, men said, "Hephaistos laughs," just as they said of a shower, "Zeus rains." He was concerned principally with terrestrial fire, the lightning being outside his province and the conception of him as the god of the sun's heat, who rides on a glowing car by day and falls to earth at evening, was by no means general. He manifested his power in volcanoes, burning gases, and hot springs. In his relation to artificial fire he is associated with Prometheus, and the torch-race at Athens was dedicated to these two gods in conjunction with Athene. His chief volcanic centre was the island of Lemnos.

In his almost primeval *rôle* as worker in metal Hephaistos, along with Athene, was the instructor of the Kyklopes in their trade. He himself was the maker of the golden maidens endowed with life and human faculties, the brazen giant Talos, Europe's brazen dog, the brazen-footed bulls with which Iason ploughed, and the gold and silver dogs that guarded the house of Alkinoös, while of inanimate objects he wrought the arms of Memnon, the sickle of Demeter, the arrows of Apollo and Artemis, the curved sword of Perseus, the cup of Helios, and many other things. It may be that Hephaistos was very early identified with the demon of magical powers supposed by most primitive peoples to reside in metals both before and after forging.

Apparently from the idea made current by certain physical philosophers that fire was the substance out of which life was produced, Hephaistos came to be conceived as the creator of men. Pandora, we remember, was moulded by his hand out of clay, and a hint of this function may also be read in the account of his strange fathering of Erichthonios in union with Athene. Invocations supported by magical rites were often addressed to him to bring fertility to barren women.

Hephaistos in Art. — The artists consistently represented Hephaistos as a smith holding a hammer. Many statues of the sixth century grossly caricatured his lameness, but others merely hinted at it or almost entirely suppressed it. In the late period he became a rare theme of art, and where he was represented at all it was as the serious artisan.

HESTIA

The Origin and the Name of Hestia. — Hestia undoubtedly belonged to an old stratum of Greek life, and unlike most of the other gods she was herself the object for which her name stood — the hearth — for that she was not the fire, nor the spirit of the fire burning on the hearth, is clear from the lack of daemonic characteristics in her person. As the hearth itself she was originally a product of the preanimistic stage of thought, and from this stage she never advanced far, a circumstance which was due to her static nature. The other gods could exercise their activities over broad ranges of territory and peoples, but her virtue would have vanished with movement, and, like home-keeping youths, she had homely wits. Her importance rested on the imperative need of fire in the primitive home and in the immense difficulty of procuring it in event of sudden demand.

The Genealogy and Functions of Hestia. — The earliest statement of Hestia's parentage is to be found in Hesiod, where she is the eldest daughter of Kronos and Rhea, although not a word is said of her duties as a goddess. In a *Homeric Hymn* [3] addressed to her we find merely the remark that she dwells in Apollo's sacred house at Delphoi, and it is to the *Homeric Hymn to Aphrodite* [4] that we must look for the fullest delineation. There her inviolate purity is enhanced by contrast with the easy abandon of the goddess of love, for the works of Aphrodite, says the hymn in substance, are displeasing to Hestia, the modest daughter of Kronos whom both Poseidon and Apollo wooed in vain. With a mighty oath sworn on the head of Zeus she declared that she would remain a virgin all her days, wherefore her father granted her a gift instead of marriage, and she took her place in the midst of the dwelling and was accorded high honour in the temples of the gods, and from mortals received the greatest homage. Pindar sings of her as the divine guardian of the integrity of the state.

These few myths are transparent views of the functions of Hestia, who was the divine symbol of the purity of the home. As the hearth-fire burned unceasingly, so was she the protectress of the continuity of the family life; but while Hera stood for the government of the household, Hestia typified rather the intimate daily relations of its members. Oaths sworn upon the hearth and suppliants beside the hearth were sacred to her, and all liturgical acts in both public and private life were prefaced by a special recognition of her, while there are some reasons for thinking that they were also thus closed. Nevertheless, despite her formal importance, Hestia never showed a strong directing hand in the moulding of the social organization.

In art Hestia appears as a sedate matron without distinguishing attributes, the flowers and fruit with which she was sometimes shown having apparently been added solely as ornaments.

CHAPTER VIII

THE GREATER GODS — POSEIDON AND AMPHITRITE

POSEIDON

THE Origin and the Name of Poseidon. — If we consult only the geographical register of the distribution of Poseidon's cult, we shall incline to classify him as a god of northern origin introduced into Hellas by immigrating Greeks. If, on the contrary, we have regard principally for his chief cult-centres, such as Corinth and Boiotia, and accept a recent demonstration that his inseparable emblem, the trident, was in origin the lightningbolt of a Mesopotamian divinity, we cannot well help believing that he, too, came from the east,[1] in which event his cult would first have reached Crete and thence have been spread by sailors to Hellenic ports on the Aegean and Mediterranean. Whatever his initial functions may have been, he became among the Greeks the supreme master of the sea; and to explain his name as connected with πόσις ("lord") and Ἴτανος or Ἴτωνος, a name of Crete, makes the suggestion as to his Eastern origin very plausible.

Poseidon in Homer. — Homer knows Poseidon as the son of Kronos and Rhea. When the new kingdom was divided, the dominion of the sea was put into his hands, while earth and Olympos were set aside as common territory for all the gods. His home is understood to be in the sea somewhere near Aigai. In the war at Ilion he displays no great partisanship, although his sympathies incline toward the cause of the Greeks, yet he saves Aineias from Achilles because the hour of the former's doom has not yet struck. He was the father of Polyphemos, for whose death he viciously harassed Odysseus by raising storm-winds and billows in his ship's path; and because the lesser Aias boasted of his power to escape the perils of the sea, he brought him to a watery grave. He is the ancestor of Alkinoös, king of the Phaiakians, and turns one of his ships to stone in midsea. He is the mighty supporter of the earth, which he causes to quake by rocking the waters which bear it up; and the trident, apparently by this time conceived as a fish-spear, is uniformly the emblem of his power. In appearance he is grim, and his head is covered with heavy locks of sea-green hair; in disposition he is moody and imperious, and resents those commands of his elder brother, Zeus, which seem to encroach on his sphere of authority. The horse and horsemanship come under his special patronage.

The Family Relationships of Poseidon. — Poseidon is everywhere accorded the honour of being the son of Kronos, and he fought with Zeus against his kinsfolk, the Titans, wielding the trident which the Kyklopes had forged for him. His wedded wife was Amphitrite, but he had scant regard for the moral obligations of marriage, for his intrigues with women both divine and mortal almost defy counting, among them being those with Tyro, Amymone, Chione, and Libye. His offspring were still more numerous, and practically all of them were in some way associated with the sea, Aiolos, Nereus, Pelias, Glaukos of Potniai, Sinis, Bousiris, Antaios, Boiotos, Polyphemos, and, if we may credit one account, Theseus, all being his sons by many mothers. Not a few of his offspring were of a monstrous nature, for instance, the terrible creatures which he raised up from the sea to harass Aithiopia and Troy, the dragon of Thebes, the ram of the Golden Fleece, the bull of Marathon, and the bull which maddened the horses of Hippolytos.

The Functions of Poseidon. — In myth and cult alike Poseidon was pre-eminently the god of the sea, though all significant bodies of fresh water also came under his sway. The greater number of his epithets record his sundry relations with the sea and with things pertaining to the sea; nor, indeed, can it be doubted that whenever he was invoked in worship by the average Greek, his association with the sea was present before the mind, no matter how many other aspects he bore. Inland lakes or springs of brackish water were held to be of his creating; for instance, the so-called Sea on the Acropolis of Athens; and he was the chief deity of sea-faring communities like Iolkos, Troizen, and Corinth. While he gave no specific encouragement to the building of ships and to the technicalities of navigation, he was looked up to as the most reliable protector of ships and sailors amid the perils of voyage. No wonder that his shrines were very frequently located in harbours — he could calm or trouble the sea as he would.[2] A certain myth represents the award of the Isthmus of Corinth to Poseidon by Briareos as the source of his patronage of that region, and it was here that Iason so suitably dedicated to Poseidon the ship of ships, the Argo. Finally, the doubles of Poseidon reflect his marine character; Aigeus, Theseus, Peleus, and Achilles all stand in some distinctive relation to the sea.

Inasmuch as the sea appeared to hold up the land, it was natural to attribute the otherwise inexplicable phenomena emanating from the depths of the earth to the activities of the powerful god of the ocean. It was he who caused the great upheaval which in some remote geological age drained the plains of Thessaly through the Vale of Tempe and left the face of nature scarred and wrinkled; and some of the Greeks even went so far as to say that the shocks of earthquakes were due to Demeter's resistance to the embraces of Poseidon, just as a turbulent sea was attributed to a similar brawl between Thetis and Peleus, a duplicate of Poseidon. The roaring and rumblings of earthquake and billow were explained as proceeding from prodigious raging bulls or horses living in the deep hollows of earth and sea, these creatures being understood now

PLATE XLVII

Poseidon

This conception of Poseidon is infinitely nobler than that appearing on p. 6, although the two portraits endow him with the same attributes. Here the god seems to have just emerged from his home beneath the waves, and now, standing as on an eminence and surveying his vast domains, is about to cry out to the elements to obey his will. From a late Hellenistic marble (second or first century B.C.), found in Melos and now in Athens (Brunn-Bruckmann, *Denkmäler griechischer und römischer Sculptur*, No. 550).

as animate emblems of Poseidon, now as identical with the god himself.[3]

By striking his trident on a Thessalian rock, Poseidon is said to have produced the first horse, and he it was who gave to Pelops the chariot that could fly over land and sea drawn by the immortal horses Balios and Xanthos. Moreover, he himself drove swiftly over the waves in his own chariot, nor do we need to be reminded that he was the father of the winged Pegasos and of Areion, the horse of Adrastos. The sacrifice of a horse in connexion with his cult distinguished his ritual from that of the other divinities, and at Corinth he even went by the title Hippios ("Equestrian"). That the horse-god should become the deity of horse-racing, and finally of the breeding and breaking of horses, involves a very easy process of thought.

The god who operated in the unseen depths of the earth was very naturally held to be the giver of springs and spring-fed streams and lakes, the famous fount of Hippoukrene being created with a stroke of the hoof of Poseidon's Pegasos. The springs of Lerne were revealed by Poseidon to Amymone, and prior to the arrival of the family of Danaos in Argolis he had withheld water from the fountains and rivers so that the land had become parched and barren. So far, then, as water from these sources promotes the growth of plant life, Poseidon is rightly to be designated a god of fertility.

Poseidon uniformly appears in myth as a god of little intellectual and still less ethical character.

Poseidon in Art. — Art received its model of Poseidon from Homer. From the best period onward he appears as a well-matured man not unlike the type of Zeus, but distinguishable from it by his heavier musculature and his less lordly manner. Ordinarily he is nude or lightly clad, either standing on a dolphin or a rock, or in the act of taking a step forward, and his frame stoops slightly, as if peering into the distance. He is shown bearded and with the hair of the head variously long or short and very often dishevelled. He generally holds a trident in his hand, but if this and the dolphin are absent, identification is often difficult.

AMPHITRITE

Amphitrite does not strictly belong to the circle of the great gods, but owing to her formal association with Poseidon she may not improperly be brought to our attention here. As the wife of Poseidon she received many of the honours accorded as a matter of course to the superior divinities. In myth she was the Queen of the Sea, and in reality she seems to have been the sea itself in its aspect as the vast flood of waters which envelops the earth. As to the meaning of her name, we can merely divine, rather than prove, that it refers to this feature of her nature. In the *Iliad* she is scarcely more than an allegorical figure, while in the *Odyssey* she has become invested with at least the pattern of a personality, being here regarded as the divine being who sends the monsters of the sea and drives waves against the rocks.

Amphitrite was either one of the many daughters of Okeanos or the daughter of Nereus and Doris. Poseidon first saw her, runs the myth, in the company of her sister-nymphs in Naxos. Of all those fair ones she was the fairest, and powerless to resist her charms he seized her and bore her away to be his wife. In the sea she sat upon a throne at Poseidon's side and with Thetis led the chorus of sea-nymphs in their dances. In art she is depicted as a Nereid of queenly mien with moist, flowing hair bound in a net.

CHAPTER IX

THE GREATER GODS — DIONYSOS

THE *Origin and the Name of Dionysos.* — We need only direct evidence to demonstrate visually that the home of Dionysos was outside of Hellas, for the circumstantial evidence favours that contention as strongly as arguments of this kind can support one side or another of a problem of religious origins. The orgiastic character of the rites of Dionysos was assuredly un-Greek, and the early legends which depict hostility to him in various parts of Hellas must embody the historical fact — if they contain any history at all — that certain communities resisted the introduction of his worship. Perseus fought against Dionysos; the daughters of Proitos were driven mad for their contempt of his rites, although it was these very ceremonies by which they were finally healed; the daughters of Minyas were likewise afflicted with madness for the same sin; and Pentheus of Thebes was killed for his resistance. Lykourgos, the king of the Edonians, also paid dearly for his foolish attack on the god. Homer [1] puts the story into the mouth of Diomedes: — "Dryas' son, mighty Lykourgos, was not for long when he strove with heavenly gods, he that erst chased through the goodly land of Nysa the nursing-mothers of the frenzied Dionysos; and they all cast their wands upon the ground, smitten with murderous Lykourgos' ox-goad. Then Dionysos fled and plunged beneath the salt-sea wave, and Thetis took him to her bosom, affrighted, for a mighty trembling had seized him at his foes' rebuke. But with Lykourgos the gods that live at ease were wroth, and Kronos' son made him blind, and he was not for long, because he was hated of the immortal gods."

Yet the evidence does more than point away from Hellas; it indicates Thrace with some degree of definiteness. Many Greeks of the historical period were firmly convinced of Dionysos's Thracian origin, and, moreover, what little we know of the old Thracian religion shows that it had characteristics very similar to those of the cult of Dionysos, while, further, the scene of action and the mad votaries of Dionysos in the Lykourgos-myth are Thracian.

The route of Dionysos's approach to Greece presents more difficulties than the question of his nativity. Few believe that he came directly from Thrace, at least at first, although one must admit the possibility of a late current of his cult sweeping into Greece through a straight channel. The prevailing opinion is that Dionysos was first carried by Thracian immigrants to Phrygia, where his nature as a god of fertility bound him intimately with the earth goddess of the region, who seems to have been known as Zemelo, a name strikingly similar to that of Semele, the mother of Dionysos in Theban legend. From Phrygia the god made his way to Crete, and thence to those parts of Greece which were in close marine contact with Crete, notably Argos and the Boiotian coast. The myths of these places involving Dionysos show that here were situated his oldest establishments in Greece. He seems to have reached Athens under the kings by way of the Marathonian tetrapolis, and his advent is celebrated in a legend which probably goes back to the eighth century, the period of the Boioto-Euboian influence. This alleges that Dionysos came to Ikarios, who dwelt on the northern borders of Attike, giving him a shoot of the vine and instructing him in its culture. Wishing to bestow a boon upon men, Ikarios gave some unmixed wine to a band of shepherds, but they, having partaken of it too freely, became drunk, and believing that they had been poisoned set upon Ikarios and killed him. Later, coming to their senses, they buried his body, but Erigone, his daughter, with the aid of her dog, found his grave and hanged herself on a tree which overhung it. As a penalty for the death of Ikarios Dionysos sent upon the people an epidemic which was appeased only when they had publicly offered him the phallic emblem; and to make amends for the death of Erigone the Attic maidens began hanging themselves, the baneful practice being carried to such an extent that for it was substituted a festival in which the young girls swung from trees. This last feature of the story probably arose when the original purpose of this ritual swinging, the excitement of sexual passion, had been forgotten. Another cult-practice[2] seems to embody as an historical fact a second and later introduction of Dionysos into Attike by way of the town of Eleutherai.

The word "Dionysos" is divisible into two parts, the first originally Διος- (cf. Ζεύς), while the second is of unknown signification, although perhaps connected with the name of the Mount Nysa which figures in the story of Lykourgos.

Dionysos in Homer. — Dionysos plays a very subordinate *rôle* in Homer, for he is not yet exalted to the circle of the Olympians. The poet regards him as the son of Zeus and Semole and is acquainted with the tale of his persecution by Lykourgos, besides making him the witness of Theseus's departure from Crete with Ariadne, and recording that it was he who gave to Thetis the golden jar, the handiwork of Hephaistos, in which she placed the ashes of Achilles.

The Birth of Dionysos. — After the birth of Dionysos, of which we have read in an earlier passage, shoots of twining ivy sprang from the ground to give a protecting shade to the infant god, and remained to deck the shrine of his mother Semele, which was afterward erected on the spot where she died, its roof being supported by pillars which fell from heaven with the bolts of lightning by which she was slain. When Dionysos had been reborn from the thigh of Zeus, Hermes entrusted him to the nymphs of Mount Nysa, who fed him on the food of the gods and made him immortal.

The Functions and the Cult of Dionysos. — The ecstatic orgies of the Dionysiac rituals and the prominence of the vine in myths relating to Dionysos are altogether responsible for the very common notion that he was primarily the god of wine, although, on the contrary, he was in reality the deity who embodied in his single being the sum total of all those unseen powers which produce all kinds of plant life. Naturally he was given most consideration in his relation as producer of those plants on which human life most depended, and the vine, as one of these, readily became his popular symbol. Dionysos's character as a divinity of vegetation is revealed in a number of myths where, like the Lakonian Hyakinthos, he appears as alternately dying and coming to life, this being apparently the signification of his fall with Semele and of his subsequent rebirth. Under the title of Zagreus he was thought to be torn asunder and revived, and the idea is also present in that part of the Homeric story of Lykourgos which we have reviewed. Lykourgos represents those elements which at a certain season cause the death of all vegetation, but since these factors cannot always prevail, Lykourgos is subdued and Dionysos lives on to enjoy immortality. The continuation of this legend beyond the point to which Homer carries it is in the same vein. Dionysos, it recounts, smote Lykourgos with madness, and while in this condition the king, in an attempt to cut the trunk of a vine with an axe, accidentally killed his own son. Still out of his senses, he foully mutilated the boy's body, but the land then withheld its fruits, and an oracle declared to the people that this state of things would continue until they had brought about the death of Lykourgos. Thereupon the Edonians seized him and bore him off to Mount Pangaion, where he was drawn asunder by horses,[3] thus satisfying Dionysos, who caused the land to bear.

It was in the character of producer of those forms of vegeta-

PLATE XLVIII

The Enthroned Dionysos

Dionysos is seated on an elaborate marble or ivory throne, studded with jewels, and behind him rises a sacred pillar. The god, with his emblems (garland, *thyrsos*, and *kantharos*) is depicted as a bibulous-looking celebrant of his own rites. On the ground at his right is a *tympanon* supported in an oblique position, and at his left a panther, highly suggestive of the Oriental associations of the Dionysiac cult. The painting is remarkable for its blending of soft flesh-tints, dainty blues of the drapery, and the delicate white of the throne, against an unrelieved background of rich red. From a wall-painting in the Casa del Naviglio, Pompeii (Hermann-Bruckmann, *Denkmäler der Malerei des Altertums*, No. 1).

tion useful to men that Dionysos and his worship were spread abroad not only within Greece, as the story of Ikarios demonstrates, but also without. A *Homeric Hymn* to Dionysos [4] consists entirely of the narrative of his introduction to a seafaring folk of the west. Once as he was standing in the guise of a youth in his prime on a promontory overlooking the sea, some Tyrrhenian sea-rovers espied him, and capturing him took him into their vessel, where they bound him with fetters. When with the utmost ease he burst his bonds asunder, the pilot perceived that he was a god and warned his fellows against doing him any evil; but since they would have none of his words and trimmed their sails to make haste to the high sea, Dionysos began to show his might. First he caused wine to pour into the ship's hold, and next he made a vine laden with clusters of grapes to clamber over the sail and an ivy plant to ascend to the peak of the mast. In their fear at these wonders the sailors tried to put to shore, but Dionysos, becoming a lion, seized their captain and forced them to leap into the sea, where they were changed into dolphins, only the pilot who had recognized his divinity being spared.[5] Of much the same order is the account of Dionysos's wanderings after the jealous Hera had made him mad because of his discovery of the uses of the vine. From one land of the East to another he went triumphantly spreading his cult and his gift of wine, until at last he reached distant India; [6] but in the end he returned to Greece and took up his abode in Thebes, where he became the idol of a horde of women votaries. He is again seen as a wine-god in the person of his duplicate, Oineus of Kalydon, whose name is obviously connected with οἶνος ("wine"), and, moreover, in one source it was Dionysos, not Oineus, who was the wife of Althaia ("Nourishing Earth").

It is, therefore, not at all surprising that this god entered into certain affiliations with Demeter,[7] the earth goddess of Eleusis, the Thracian origin of Eumolpos, the founder, according to legend, of the Eleusinian priesthood, adding plausibility to the union, while Iakchos, whose name is etymologically akin to Bakchos, one of the divine personages of the mysteries, was a form of Dionysos. That feature of the rites in which Persephone, Demeter's daughter, was redeemed from Hades as the personal representative of the initiates, was such as to attract Dionysos in his capacity as releaser from Hades, a function which he derived, perhaps, from the power of wine to release the mind from care and worry, and myth records that he liberated both Ariadne and Semele from the eternal bondage of the underworld.

Although the fountain-nymphs are often said in legend to be his ministrants, this is not to be taken to imply that he was a water-god. If the easiest interpretation is to be followed, it means, rather, that the Greeks regarded the watercourses as aiding him in the production of an abundant growth.[8]

To count the god of fertility as the deity of wealth is an easy transit for the imaginative mind, and a late, and uncanonical myth, as we may term it, depicts him in this guise. After Midas, the Mygdonian king, had been given the ears of an ass for having preferred the music of Marsyas to that of Apollo, Dionysos chanced to pass through the kingdom on his way to India. Entertaining him liberally, Midas gave him a guide for his journey, and in gratitude Dionysos bestowed upon the king the power of turning to gold whatever he touched. This boon, however, proved to be only a bane, for even the food which Midas would convey to his lips became gold, so that he was in a fair way to starve to death. At last he begged to be delivered from his ruthless gift, wherefore Dionysos bade him wash himself in the river Paktolos, whose waters took on the tinge of gold as soon as his body touched the stream.

The relation between Dionysos and the Muses goes back to the Thracian period of his worship. From the earliest times in Hellas his special rituals consisted of songs and dances designed magically to stimulate the growth of useful plant life and to avert such influences as threatened it. At first these performances were merely crude, spontaneous outbursts of religious emotion, but in time the orderly mind and the creative fancy of the Greek moulded them, as it were, out of the dust of the earth into those sublime figures of literary and musical art, the dithyramb (or independent choral song), tragedy, and comedy. The divine mission of Dionysos "to mingle the music of the flute and to bring surcease to care" [9] is transparent through the text of any of the works of the great dramatists.

Space allows us to draw attention only to the more important festivals of Dionysos. In Sikyon, Corinth, and Attike these were made special occasions for musical performances, but only in the last of these three places did they attain to monumental distinction. Here they were four in number, beginning, if we follow the order of our months, in January with the Lenaia, the feast of wild women (Λῆναι). The Anthesteria, combining ceremonies attendant on the opening of the new wine with a primitive "all souls'" festival, came next in February, and in connexion with this there took place a symbolic marriage of the wife of the king Archon to Dionysos. In March followed the Greater, or City, Dionysia, at the beginning of which the introduction of Dionysos into Attike by way of Eleutherai was processionally represented; and finally, in December, the people of the country districts celebrated locally the uncouth and unrestrained Rural Dionysia. The connexions established between Dionysos and professional actors and musicians in the organized festivals led to his adoption as the patron deity of the brotherhoods or the guilds of these performers, societies which continued to thrive until a late date.

Sufficient remark has already been made on the general significance of the Dionysiac rituals, but it remains to speak of the ecstasy of the votaries. This was not induced wholly by the use of wine, as is almost universally supposed, for it arose in the first place through the potent suggestiveness of the mere idea that it was possible for the individual mortal, by the observance of certain forms, to become spiritually one with the immortal god, the potency of the concept being immeasurably increased when it possessed a company of people of like mind, even though they remained static. With the aid of dancing, music, drinking, shouting, and participation in the raw flesh and blood of victims in which the god was thought to dwell, the idea threw the votaries into an uncontrollable frenzy akin to madness in its external demonstration, whence the madness of the daughters of Proitos and Minyas, and of Dionysos himself.

To the field of morals Dionysos made no new contributions, nor, contrary to the common belief, with all the seeming licence of his rites did he add to general immorality. His gift was mainly religious, although it had a salutary social reaction. To countless thousands whose individualities had been submerged in the primacy of state interests he brought a stimulating hope and a buoyant faith in the possibility of attaining to an immortal existence, as free from worldly care as was the divine ecstasy of his ritual.

Dionysos in Art. — After Dionysos came to be represented in fully iconic form, two distinct types were developed. In the first, seen on Attic vases of the sixth century, he is generally shown as a bearded man becomingly clothed, and to distinguish him from a similar type of Hermes, a branch of vine or of ivy is put into his hand. In the second aspect, doubtless given vogue through Pheidias, he appears as a youthful god of inspiration. The *kantharos*, a kind of drinking vessel, the *thyrsos*, a ceremonial wand, and a fawn-skin are his most common emblems. He is sometimes surrounded by Maenads, and his whole bearing is one of ecstasy, so that occasionally he is even shown as intoxicated; it is not, however, until after the fourth century B.C. that excessive sensuality and effeminacy were attributed to him so frequently as to be regarded as essential features.

Myths of Alexander the Great. — Alexander the Great was variously said to have been a direct descendant of Dionysos, a reincarnation of Herakles, and a son of Ammon. After his victorious march to the Orient the story of the wanderings of Dionysos acquired many new features and a new meaning, although the best known myths of Alexander relate him to Ammon. It is said that the last of the native kings of Egypt, Nektanebos, fled in disguise from Egypt to Pella and there became an astrologer in the court of Philip. As it happened, Olympias, the queen, came to him for a reading of her future, and he told her that by the god Ammon she would conceive a son who would rule the world and avenge her on the king for his cruelty. Just as he said, the god approached her in the form of a serpent, and in due time she became the mother of a son whose birth was accompanied by earthquake, lightning, and thunder — signs which proved him to be divine. Moreover, his very appearance and manner marked him as one not of the common order of kings, for his right eye was as black as night, and his left was as blue as the heavens, while his hair and teeth, and likewise his spirit, resembled those of a lion. Although he bore no resemblance to Philip, yet the latter accepted him as his son and was pleased to account for his divinity by tracing his own descent back to Okeanos and Thetis and that of Olympias to Kronos and Poseidon.

On the death of Philip, Alexander marshalled a great army and at its head marched through many lands. Through Thrace he went, through Italy and Sicily, Carthage and Libya, until he came to the shrine of the great Ammon, where he offered due homage and left a votive inscription bearing the words: "Alexander to his father, the god Ammon." Thence he passed on through Egypt, Syria, Persia, and the lands about the Euxine, and at last reached Greece. At the shrine of Delphoi he demanded an oracle concerning his destiny, but the priestess refused him, whereupon, burning with anger, like Herakles before him, Alexander seized the sacred tripod and threatened to carry it away. The priestess then made haste to speak, calling him Herakles Alexander and prophesying that he would be greater than all mortals. Emboldened by these words, Alexander marched to the conquest of the golden East, where, one after another, the great kings and kingdoms fell before him — Persia, Media, Baktria, India — until there were no more lands to conquer. On his homeward march he fell ill and died, and took his rightful place in heaven among the gods.

PLATE XLIX

1

Dionysos in the Ship

Dionysos, crowned with ivy, leans back at his ease in the middle of his ship. Springing from beside him, two stout vine-stalks clamber up the mast, at the peak of which they send out spreading branches laden with grapes and leaves. The dolphins indicate that the ship is afloat in the sea, but the painter gives no hint whether they represent the transformed pirates of the literary myth. From a black-figured *kylix* by Exekias (latter part of the sixth century B.C.), in Munich (Furtwängler-Reichhold, *Griechische Vasenmalerei*, No. 42). See p. 219.

2

Kastor and Polydeukes at Home

The figures in this composition can be identified by means of the inscriptions. They represent all the family of Tyndareos, excepting Helen, in their Spartan home; proceeding from right to left they are Tyndareos himself, a boy slave, Kastor, Leda, and Polydeukes. The whole scene is eloquent of a domestic harmony which includes even the animals of the household. From a black-figured *amphora* by Exekias (latter part of the sixth century B.C.), in the Vatican (Furtwängler-Reichhold, *Griechische Vasenmalerei*, No. 132). See pp. 24 ff.

CHAPTER X

THE GREATER GODS — DEMETER, KORE, HADES

DEMETER AND KORE (PERSEPHONE)

THE *Origin and the Name of Demeter.* — The goddess Demeter, the daughter of Rhea and Kronos, is an exceedingly important figure in the history of religions on account of the numerous phases of her character in cult and myth, and also because of the powerful influence which she exerted on the whole Greek world after a certain period. It is impossible to say more in reference to her origin than that, when we go back as far as we can, she still seems to be a Hellenic divinity. Parallels to her cult found among barbarians remain parallels and nothing more, and the fact that she was acknowledged as the chief divinity of the northern Amphiktyony is proof positive of her very ancient establishment as a goddess common to many Hellenic tribes. While she is obviously a form of Gaia (Ge), she was in function the soil goddess rather than the broadly generalized earth goddess. In the light of her character it is very attractive to interpret her name Δημήτηρ as a dialectic variant of γῆ-μήτηρ, but the suggestion will not stand etymologically. A more novel way, and one which conforms to known caprices of folk-speech, is to explain the name as an alliterative form, invented half deliberately, half unconsciously, to correspond to the antithetical Διεὺς πατήρ, thus giving the co-operating divine pair, Mother Earth and Father Sky; and still another interpretation which is worth considering makes the name signify "Barley Mother," a meaning quite consonant with the scope of her operations.

Demeter in Homer. — Demeter is more of a symbol in Homer than a personality. She is the divinity of the corn, and Thessalian Pyrasos is known as her sacred field, owing, no doubt, to its productivity. She has no place as yet in the group of the Olympians, nor has she any part to play in the action of either *Iliad* or *Odyssey*. Homer is not acquainted with her as the mother of Persephone, and the story of her amour with Iasion as related in the epic will be referred to under the next heading.

Demeter as the Goddess of the Soil. — The nature of Demeter is brought out by an admittedly ancient myth found both in Homer and in Hesiod, the latter's account [1] being richer in details. "Demeter, divine one of goddesses, mingling in love with the hero Iasion in a thrice-ploughed fallow field in the fat land of Crete, bore Ploutos, a goodly son who goeth everywhere upon earth and upon the broad ridges of the sea. Whatsoever man he meeteth and into whose hands he cometh doth he make rich, and to him doth he vouchsafe abundant happiness." Homer adds that when Zeus learned of the deed of Iasion, he smote him dead with a thunderbolt. This myth, although not cast in the form of an explanation, seems to be in reality an attempt to solve the origin of, and to supply a divine sanction for, the performance of rites involving the actual or symbolic cohabitation of a man and a woman in a field about to be sown, these ceremonies fertilizing the earth so that she would bring forth her increase and confer wealth and happiness upon mankind.[2] Though the bounty of Demeter comprehended every product of the soil which was of use to men, the cereal fruits came to be regarded as the special objects of her care. All operations on the farm, all parts of the farm, such as barn and field and so forth, which had to do with the cultivation of the grain, the crops in all stages of their growth, the cut grain in the sheaf and on the threshing-floor, all these things too came under her surveillance. The first loaf of the newly harvested crop was dedicated to her, and all of her festivals, no matter at what time of the year they occurred, were cereal celebrations suitable for the season.

It has been very happily suggested that from Demeter's *rôle* as producer of wealth was directly evolved her peculiar character as Θεσμοφόρος, the maintainer of political and social stability. If this be so, Demeter is here simply the personified recognition of the fact, so strongly emphasized by modern economists, that the real prosperity of a country varies directly with its agricultural conditions. If Demeter was propitious, social relations were not disturbed, but if unpropitious, the altered ability to sell, purchase, or barter effected a general upheaval. Under this same appellative Θεσμοφόρος, Demeter had also an intimate relation to the institution of marriage and thereby to the family, this being a consequence of the natural evolution of the central idea contained in the field-rites. Children were therefore just as much her gifts as were the fruits of agriculture, and on the assurance of a steady birth-rate depended proportionately the continuity of the social order.[3]

Demeter and Kore (*Persephone*). — It will be easier to understand the mystic meaning of the bond between Demeter and Persephone when we have reviewed in its entirety the legend which constitutes the theme of the so-called *Homeric Hymn* to Demeter. This Eleusinian story,[4] doubtless through its superior artistic presentation, ultimately overshadowed every other local tradition of the two divinities and came to be the canonical version for all the Greeks. Persephone, the daughter of Demeter by Zeus, was playing in the meadows of Mysia with nymphs of the sea and plucking the wild flowers of the springtime — roses, crocuses, irises, violets, and hyacinths — when she spied an especially beautiful and fragrant stalk of narcissus and hastened to pick it. Alas! this was a snare devised by Zeus and Earth to entrap her, for just as her fingers closed on the stem, the ground opened beneath her, and Hades, leaping forth in his golden chariot, seized her and bore her swiftly away. Only the Sun and Hekate, the moon-goddess, saw her capture, but her mother heard her cries and instantly rushed forth to seek her, going about the earth for nine days and nine nights, without tasting food or drink, and bearing in her hands blazing torches to light up the darkest recesses. During this time neither the gods who had been witnesses of Persephone's seizure nor any omen came to the mother's aid with a word of information, but on the tenth day Hekate led her to the Sun, who told her where the maiden was. Again the distracted mother betook herself to wandering, and having passed unrecognized through many lands in the guise of an old woman, she came at last to Eleusis in Attike, where she sat down by the public well, known as the Fountain of Maidenhood. Hither came the four daughters of Keleos, the king of the country, to draw water. Won by their gracious willingness to listen to her, Demeter told them a fictitious tale of her escape from pirates who had enslaved her, and then asked them to obtain for her a place as nurse in some family, whereupon they took her to their own home, putting their infant brother Demophon in her care. By day Demeter anointed the child with ambrosia and by night bathed him in fire, as Thetis did with Achilles, and he was like to become immortal when his mother Metaneira discovered the performance of the magic rites and snatched him away. Instantly the goddess threw aside her disguise and, revealing herself in all her divine freshness and beauty, she announced her name and bade the people of Eleusis build her a temple in which she would teach them the ceremonial of her worship. Keleos did as she had commanded, and in the temple she took up her abode; but so great was her grief for her daughter that she withheld her blessings from the soil, so that men began to die for need of food, and the altars of the gods lacked sacrifices. At length Zeus sent Iris and the other gods one after another to plead with her to relent, but she would not hear of it until her daughter should be given back to her, wherefore Zeus dispatched Hermes to the underworld to bid Hades release Persephone. Unable to resist the command of his elder brother, Hades yielded, but before letting Persephone go shrewdly gave her a pomegranate seed to eat,

FIG. 8. TRIPTOLEMOS

Triptolemos is setting forth on his mission to bring the cereal fruits and the knowledge of agriculture to mankind. In the version followed by the painter the car is not drawn by dragons, but flies through space on winged wheels. Perhaps the wheel was originally the sun's disk. From a red-figured *lekythos* of the fifth century B.C., found at Gela (*Monumenti Antichi*, xvii, Plate XIX).

and by tasting of it she magically bound herself to return to Hades after a time spent above. In the golden chariot she was conveyed to Eleusis, where her mother welcomed her with an outburst of joy, and when a message from Zeus came to Demeter announcing that Persephone could thenceforth remain with her during two parts of the year, spending only the third part below, she forgot her sorrow and consented to rejoin the gods on Olympos. Moreover, summoning the rulers of the land, Triptolemos, Eumolpos, Diokles, and Keleos, she made them the ministers of her worship and revealed to them the manner of performing her secret holy rites, rites which would confer upon initiates a peculiar blessedness in the after-life beneath the earth.

Demeter and Triptolemos. — The story explaining the significance of Demeter in agricultural pursuits may be reconstructed by combining several sources. Triptolemos was the son, according to the variant versions, now of Okeanos and Ge, now of Eleusis, and now of Keleos, ranking, as son of this last named, either as the oldest, or as the youngest whom Demeter nursed on her coming to Eleusis. In her affection for him she taught him to yoke oxen and to till the soil, and gave him the first corn to sow. In the rich plains about Eleusis he reaped the first harvest of grain ever grown, and there, too, he built the earliest threshing-floor. In a car given him by Demeter and drawn by winged dragons, he flew from land to land, scattering seed for the use of men, and for this Keleos ordered his death, but Demeter, hearing of the intention, removed the king and gave the throne to Triptolemos. It is said that when he found that a pig had rooted up his first sowing, he took the animal to the altar of his benefactress, and, placing grains of corn on its head, slew it as an offering, whence, ever afterward, the pig was sacrificed in this same manner in the worship of Demeter.

The Nature of Persephone. — Persephone, who was generally known in cult as Kore ("Daughter"), was obviously an offshoot of Gaia, the earth goddess, and, therefore, a duplicate of Demeter. The mother and daughter represented two phases of the vegetative power of the soil, the first standing for the entire power, latent or active, at all seasons of the year; and the second typifying rather the potency in its exuberant youthful aspect, manifested chiefly in the renewed growth of

PLATE L

Mystic Rites at Eleusis

The proper order of analysis of this scene proceeds from left to right. First, one observes a gnarled and twisted tree, the sacred laurel which keeps evil influences away from the sanctuary. Next, there is an altar from which rises a flame surrounded by a circle of fruits. The first two human figures are the youthful Iakchos and Demeter, the latter seated on a fawnskin spread over the so-called mystic chest, about which a serpent has wound its coils. The headless female figure next in order is Kore, in the *rôle* of divine hierophant, who with lowered torches is cleansing the soil just as Demeter purifies the air with a flame held aloft. On the throne of expiation sits the initiate with veiled head and resting his feet on the sanctifying fleece of a ram, while before him a male hierophant bows over a low altar on which the flesh of the ram is being burned, and with his right hand pours water on the fire. On the opposite side stands Dionysos grasping a torch, and at the same time pouring a liquid, probably wine, from a *kantharos* upon the flame of the altar. Behind the god is a female divinity who is doubtless to be identified as Hekate. From a relief on a marble sarcophagus found at Torre Nuova (*RMitt.* xxv, Plate I). See pp. 231–32.

spring. As may readily be gathered, the seizure of Persephone as it occurred in the myth, and her subsequent espousal to Hades for four months of each year, are but graphic representations of the annually recurring period during which vegetation practically ceases. Our knowledge of the meaning of the name Persephone is incomplete; the second part is certainly related to the base of the verb φαίνειν, "to show," but of the first we are entirely ignorant.

The Mysteries of Eleusis.—Like the nature cult of Dionysos, that of Demeter developed, in the consciousness of the worshipper, along two different lines. Working along the one, it aimed to supply physical needs, and along the other, spiritual wants, the first touching society in the mass, while the second affected the individual. It is with the latter influence that we are most concerned, although in reality the two lines were but one; the difference was a matter of interpretation.

The Eleusinia, or Mysteries of Eleusis, took place just prior to the autumn sowing. They began on the fifteenth day of the month Boëdromion (roughly, September) and lasted for ten days, or a few more according to the historical period, the entire festival being divided into four distinct ceremonial acts. The first, which covered four or five days, consisted in the assembling of the properly qualified *mystai*, i. e. candidates for initiation, in impressing upon them the duties of silence, secrecy, and purity, and, finally, in giving them a ritual purification. In the second the *mystai*, departing from Athens at daybreak and usually reaching Eleusis late at night, advanced in procession, dancing, singing hymns, sacrificing at the shrines by the way-side, swinging torches, and bearing the image of the infant Iakchos, or Dionysos. The next act involved concerted efforts of the *mystai* to awaken in themselves the emotions that stirred the heart of Demeter in her search for her daughter. At night, with torches in their hands, they would roam about the sea-shore, as she had done, haunting those places which tradition still associated with her. As each candidate beheld his neighbour doing the same thing as himself, and presumably through the same motives, the meaning of the ceremony was driven deeply into his soul, giving a thousandfold intensification to his belief in the reality of Demeter's power, drawn from her own sorrow, to sympathize with the heartbreak of mortals. When the *mystai* had all become one with the god, and therefore with one another, they appropriately partook of food and drink in common and together handled certain sacred objects. Concerning the last act we are told only the barest outline, so sacredly did the initiates keep their vows of secrecy. Substantially all we know is that the votaries gathered together in the great Hall of Initiation and there witnessed certain performances, probably of a dramatic character and based on the experiences of the divine mother and daughter. They listened, too, to weird sounds produced by the hierophant and his associates, and into both sight and sound the spectators, with their fancy quickened by long and intense contemplation of holy things, read meanings which were not at all warranted in fact. When the secret rites were over, the festival terminated with public games.

There can be no doubt that the Mysteries of Eleusis effected much good in Greece. While the bare substance of their teaching was practically the same as that of the cult of Dionysos, they were much superior as a spiritual tonic, so to speak, in that they strengthened the finer feelings and relied less upon wanton extravagance of action; and many a despondent man became filled with a saving hope at the thought that he, too, could know the immortal joy of Demeter.

Demeter and Kore in Art. — Prior to the fourth century art had not devised two distinct types for the mother and the daughter, and in many cases inscriptions are necessary to identify them severally. Both goddesses were shown with that serious air which, reflecting a past sorrow, has become a part of their character. In the later art Demeter appeared as a matron, seated or standing, her head crowned with the lofty *polos* or covered with the folds of her robe, her emblems being the torch, sceptre, bowl, and sheaf. In function she was now the bestower of grain, and now the grief-worn mother. Persephone became distinctively maidenly in form, face, and dress; as a chthonic divinity she held a torch, and as a queen a sceptre.

HADES

When the kingdom of the universe wrested from Kronos was divided, the dominion of the invisible realm beneath the earth was given to his son Hades. He was, therefore, not a place, after our modern way of thinking, but a person, and his name, which to the Greek signified "the unseen," betrayed at once his dwelling-place and his general functions. These simple statements of myth seem to disclose at a single glance the complete story of Hades from the very inception of his career as a divinity, but in reality, as we shall see later on, they are deceptive, for the manner and stages of his growth are by no means certain.

While Homer generally speaks of this nether god as Hades, in one passage he knows him as "Zeus of the underworld," yet, although suggestions of royal power accompany mentions of him, real kingly attributes are lacking. His chief function is to put into effect the curses uttered by men against their fellows, and the practice, which continued to a late day, of invoking his name in oaths was a recognition of his power to discharge this duty, for, when one bound himself to destruction at the hands of Hades in event of failure to keep a solemn pledge, he was giving utterance to a conditional curse.[5] From this most unlikely source the god derived what little moral significance he had, although at the best it was of a negative character. His relation to the principle and to the enforcement of retribution is seen in a rather moralizing genealogy which makes him the father of the Erinyes.

The various appellations and titles of Hades throw light

upon his nature, and, indeed, the commonest form of his name, which we have just used, had much to do in shaping his character. Through its obvious reference to the unseen abode of the dead and because of its formal association with curses, which are nothing else than injury by magic, the word became so foreboding of ill that men could not take it easily upon their lips. It was very natural to deny to such a name the beneficent power that gave increase to the crops and herds, so that, as a consequence, the worship of Hades dwindled away and the enlargement of his personality was arrested. Only in Elis did he have a temple and a cult under this name, although as the earth god Trophonios he dispensed oracles in his cave at Lebadeia in Boiotia, while his title, Zeus Eubouleus, with its evident suggestion of the wisdom of his counsel, is a distinct echo of his oracular functions. As Plouton (Pluto) or Plouteus he is the divinity who enriches men with the abundance of the field and the fecundity of the flocks, whence Ploutos, the son of Demeter and Iasion, is apparently none other than a double of Hades.

With the data available it is impossible, as has already been hinted, to state in just what form Hades first emerged. It may be that it was in the aspect in which he was known to Homer, as the lord of the departed, but if so, he could scarcely have been a product of the worship of ancestors, for nowhere do we find any Greek stock tracing its descent back to him. A much more probable theory is that Hades was given a being in the mind of the Greek worshipper in answer to the demand that, for the sake of absolute uniformity in the divine government of the universe, the lower world, like the upper, should have its own separate ruler. Hence Hades was a nether Zeus, and exercised over the assembled souls a dominion akin to that of his greater brother over the hosts of the living, both human and divine.

Hades in Art. — One need not go far to find a reason for the fact that Hades was comparatively neglected by the artists.

Except in Etruscan paintings, he is generally shown in his beneficent aspects, the cornucopia placed in his hands stamping him as the bestower of abundance, the eagle sometimes perched on his sceptre or on his cap marking him as the Zeus of his own special realm. His nether functions are suggested by a dense mass of hair, which generally falls forebodingly over his forehead.

CHAPTER XI

THE LESSER GODS — OF THE CIRCLE OF ZEUS, OF LIGHT, AND OF HEAT

OF THE CIRCLE OF ZEUS

EURYNOME. — We have already met with Eurynome, the beautiful daughter of Okeanos, as one of the wives of Zeus, and there is a story concerning her to the effect that, long before her marriage, she and the Titan Ophion together ruled the universe from the summit of Olympos, but were at length forced to give place to Kronos and Rhea. If she was actually, as is reasonably to be suspected from her parentage, a personification of the "wide-ruling" element of moisture, this legend may record a very old belief that in the beginning the earth was entirely covered with water and afterward emerged from it by degrees. Eurynome holds an inconspicuous place in myth, and remains little more than a symbol of the far-reaching dominion of her husband.

Charites ("*Graces*"). — Eurynome is best known through the Charites, the lovely daughters who blessed her marriage with Zeus, and who were at first conceived as gracious divinities that caused the soil to bring forth flowers and fruit for the use of man, although they were not yet endowed with the joyful spirits and unaffected charms which have made them a favourite study of poet and artist. A brief legend testifies to the sombre character of their worship in the island of Paros. Minos was offering sacrifices to them here when word came to him that his son Androgeos had been killed, whereupon, distraught with sorrow, he commanded the flute-players to cease their music and tore the garlands from his head. From

PLATE LI

1

Helios

Helios, with radiate head, ascends in his car, drawn by four winged horses, out of the eastern sea, and the stars (the small boyish figures) disappear one by one in the water or beneath the horizon. From a red-figured *krater* of the first part of the fifth century B.C., in the British Museum (Furtwängler-Reichhold, *Griechische Vasenmalerei*, No. 126). See pp. 241 ff.

2

The Horai

The Horai (thus named by the artist) are here represented in their original character as divinities of vegetation and fruitfulness. The first carries what seems to be a fig-branch; the second bears two branches, the larger of which is laden with pomegranates; and the third holds a plucked fruit on the tip of her hand. From a red-figured *kylix* of the fifth century B.C., in Berlin (Furtwängler-Reichhold, *Griechische Vasenmalerei*, No. 123). See pp. 237–38.

1

2

that day, the legend explains, flutes and garlands were no longer used in the worship of the Charites, this suggesting that their rites took place during that gloomy season of the year when vegetation had disappeared. In contrast to their worship was their gladdening bounty of springtime, this irresistible infection touching their personalities, and in time transforming them from elemental into spiritual forces. Thenceforth they were divorced from natural objects as such, and stood for those subtle qualities in persons and in things pertaining to the social life of man which beget the purest joy and happiness. They were associated, for instance, with tasteful dress, with the various forms of art, and with personal and household ornaments, and this connexion throws light on their relations to Aphrodite and to the craftsman-god in the well-known spring-song of Horace: —

> "Now Cytherea leads the dance, the bright moon overhead;
> The Graces and the Nymphs, together knit,
> With rhythmic feet the meadow beat, while Vulcan, fiery red,
> Heats the Cyclopian forge in Aetna's pit." [1]

The Charites are generally held to be three in number, Hesiod giving their names as Aglaia ("Splendour"), Thaleia ("Luxuriant Beauty"), and Euphrosyne ("Good Cheer").

Themis. — The second wife of Zeus, according to the account in the *Theogony* of Hesiod, was Themis ("Justice"), and, as we have pointed out elsewhere, she is a form of the great earth goddess. Her primary *rôle* apparently was that of controlling the cycle of the seasons, and so regularly did she bring about the periods of productiveness that men came to look upon her as a power to whom they could appeal for the elucidation of matters in which human arbiters failed. In brief, she became an oracular goddess, and the righteousness of her deliverances established her as the personification of justice and equity.

Horai ("Hours"). — The Horai who, according to Hesiod, were Eunomia ("Order"), Dike ("Law"), and Eirene

("Peace"), inherited in name the social traits of their mother Themis, but, in respect to their origin, her terrestrial characteristics. They seem at the outset to have had to do with the seasonal stimulation of plant life; it was they who adorned the newly-created Pandora with garlands of vernal blossoms, and every spring and autumn they were honoured at Athens with a procession and were given offerings of the fruits of the earth. We are told that here these divinities were called Thallo ("Bloom"), Auxo ("Growth"), and Karpo ("Fruitage"), but we cannot be sure that these are the official names. In late times the Horai were often regarded as the hours of the day.

Mnemosyne; The Muses. — By her union with Zeus, Mnemosyne ("Memory") did more than serve as a living reminder of his power; she brought him the nine comely daughters, the Muses, who by their many and varied gifts have done much to give charm to the life of mankind. It has been suggested that they sprang from the same stratum of elemental powers as the Graces and the Hours, and it certainly appeals to one's poetic sense to find personified in them the musical voices of the rivulet and of the foliage of the forest, although we are probably much nearer to real fact if we assign to them the psychic origin which is claimed for their mother. One modern writer [2] advances the very acceptable explanation that they were "the mental tension that relieves itself in prophecy and song," the stress to which Tennyson [3] alludes when he says that

> "For the unquiet heart and brain
> A use in measured language lies."

As men became more and more conscious of this state of mind, they tended to dissociate it from themselves and to attribute an independent existence to it; how it became pluralized we cannot outline, but may only fancy.

The native abode of the Muses was in the extreme north of

Hellas; hence their kinship with the Zeus of Olympos and their association with Orpheus.[4] At Delphoi they became attached to Apollo, and in the south Mount Helikon in Boiotia was

FIG. 9. MNEMOSYNE AND KALLIOPE

Mnemosyne, a beautiful and dignified matron, stands holding a scroll as she gazes sympathetically on her daughter, the Muse Kalliope, who is seated before her playing on a seven-stringed *kithara* (zither). This is the first recorded instance in which Mnemosyne is definitely identified by the presence of her name in the vase-paintings. From a red-figured *lekythos* of the fifth century B.C., found at Gela (*Monumenti Antichi*, xvii, Plate XXVI).

their permanent centre. We know of many Greek states in which Mouseia, or schools under the patronage of the Muses, were established for the advanced education of the youth.

The Muses were recognized in groups of various numbers;

but that in which nine were enumerated became fixed as the standard, although the differentiation of their functions and personalities took place only late and not always along logical lines. The nine were formally divided, as shown in the appended table, into three classes corresponding to the great departments of literature.

	Name	Sphere	Attribute
Epos	Kalliope ("Sweet-Voiced")	Heroic Epic	Writing-tablet
	Kleio ("Praise")	Historical Epic	Scroll or writing-tablet
	Ourania ("Heavenly")	Astronomical Epic	Globe
Lyric	Erato ("Loveliness")	Love-lyric	Zither
	Terpsichore ("Delight in the Dance")	Choral lyric	Lyre
	Euterpe ("Delight")	Flute music	Flute
Drama	Melpomene ("Song")	Tragedy	Tragic mask
	Thaleia ("Luxuriant Beauty")	Comedy	Comic mask
	Polymnia ("Many Hymns")	Religious hymns and pantomime	No definite attribute

Ganymedes. — The story of Ganymedes, the beautiful son of Tros of Ilion, is found in its most attractive form in the persuasive words of Aphrodite addressed to Anchises in the *Homeric Hymn* to Aphrodite.[5] "Indeed counselling Zeus snatched away golden-haired Ganymedes for his beauty's sake that he might dwell with the immortals and in the home of Zeus be a cup-bearer to the gods, a marvel to look upon, held in high honour as he pours the ruddy nectar from a golden bowl. And inexorable grief possessed the soul of Tros, nor did he know whither the divine whirlwind had hurried his dear son. Then indeed did he mourn him unceasingly day after day. And Zeus had pity on him and gave him as a recompense for his son swift steeds, such as draw the immortals. These he gave him as a gift, and Hermes at the behest of Zeus told him clearly that, like the gods, he should never die nor know old age." In the most widely known form of the story Ganymedes was borne aloft by an eagle, or by Zeus in the guise of an eagle. He seems to stand for the healthy beauty and joy of youth, and is a male counterpart of Hebe in her later aspects.

Hebe. — In origin Hebe ("Youth") seems to have been more than the mere personification of the charms of youth or of the well-preserved beauty of her mother, Hera, for she was, rather, a spring divinity of flowers akin to the Horai and Charites, or perhaps she was the earth goddess herself, regarded as in the prime of maidenhood. The legend which makes her the child of Zeus is undoubtedly not so old as that in which she is born of a strange union between Hera and a leaf of lettuce, and the not improbable suggestion has been advanced that Hebe was in a very early period the equivalent of Dione, the spouse of Zeus at Dodona, and that with the amalgamation of the two stocks whose chief deities were Zeus and Hera, Hebe was thrust from her place and a myth was created to give her legitimate standing as a daughter in the new family. Like the other children of Zeus and Hera, she never enjoyed any great distinction; her *rôle* was always that of an attendant. In the *Iliad* she is the maiden cup-bearer to the Olympians, and on one occasion she helps Hera get her chariot and horses ready for a journey, while at another time she performs the rather menial task of preparing the bath for the dust-begrimed Ares on his return from a battle.

Iris. — Iris is no more than a personification of the rainbow. Like the rainbow, she comes and goes without warning, while her speed of movement and her pathway across the heavens fit her for the post of messenger of the gods. She is clothed in the bright colours becoming to youth, and on golden wings she flits from place to place, performing the errands of her greater companions, notably Zeus and Hera. In her representations in art she is scarcely to be distinguished from other winged figures, except when she is shown as bearing a herald's wand.

OF THE GREATER LUMINARIES

Helios ("*Sun*"). — From a remote time many phases of the sun's power had been observed by the Greeks with an attention which was akin to adoration, but only in a few places did this develop into genuine worship; for the sun was altogether too corporeal an object to appeal strongly to the religious fancy. Yet it must have aroused in the mind some feeling of divinity, inasmuch as it was the daily practice of the Greek to rise at dawn and greet the sun with a kiss of the hand; and very early this luminary became a frequent theme in myths, although little by little these legends lost their distinctive solar characteristics in the popular consciousness.

In myth, Helios is the son of Hyperion and Euryphaëssa ("Far-Shining"), both of them Titan children of Ouranos and Gaia, and Hyperion ("High-Going") being transparently another name for Helios himself. Helios took as his wife Perse ("Gleaming"), the daughter of Okeanos, their children being Kirke, the sorceress of the West, and Aietes, the father of Medeia, the sorceress of the East. Pindar relates the story of another marriage which is of prime importance in our study, having to do, as it does, with the chief centre of the sun-cult among the Greeks. When the jurisdiction of the various departments of the world was apportioned, it happened that Helios, being absent, was forgotten, but although, on discovery of the error, Zeus wished to make a new division, Helios dissuaded him from so doing, stating that he was willing to receive as his share an island which he beheld rising from the sea. This Zeus granted him, and wedding the nymph Rhodos (or Rhode), the daughter of Amphitrite, Helios gave her name to the island and named the three cities of Rhodes after three of their sons. Helios is also said to have had as wives Leukothoë, Klytia, and Neaira, the last of whom, according to Homer, bore him two daughters, Lampetië, who tended her father's cattle, and Phaëthousa, who shepherded his sheep. There were seven herds of cattle and seven of sheep, each comprising fifty animals; that is, there were three hundred and fifty of each kind; and Aristotle is probably right in seeing in these a reference to the days and nights of a lunar year. The herds were generally located either in Sicily or Crete.

The appearance of the sun in the heavens reminded the

PLATE LII

Ganymedes and the Eagle

"Though the copy is but an inadequate rendering of the original, it serves to show the originality and power of the composition, which almost transcends the bounds of sculpture in its addition of surroundings and accessions to enhance the effect. A high tree-trunk forms the background and support for the whole, which is most skilfully constructed, so that the feet of the boy do not touch the ground, and the wonderful upward sweep of the whole composition is enhanced by the contrast with the dog, who sits on the ground and looks upward after his master. The outspread wings of the eagle form a broad summit to the group from which it gradually narrows down to the feet of Ganymede, and thus the effect is further increased. Eagle and boy alike strain upward in an aspiration like that which Goethe expresses in his poem of Ganymede. There is no hint of sensual meaning in the treatment of Leochares; the eagle is merely the messenger of Zeus; and we can see in his grip of the boy the care which Pliny mentions" (E. A. Gardner, *A Handbook of Greek Sculpture*, p. 376). From a Roman marble copy, now in the Vatican, of a fourth century original by Leochares (Brunn-Bruckmann, *Denkmäler griechischer und römischer Sculptur*, No. 158). See p. 240.

TI·P·M

Greeks of a variety of objects — a ball of fire, a head with streaming golden hair, an eye, a bow bristling with arrows, or a spoked wheel — but the most commanding and persistent likeness which they saw was that of a chariot and horses. Poets gave the four steeds names suggestive of the sun's outstanding properties and had them feed on the same ambrosial herb which made Glaukos immortal. Homer follows Helios's course across the heavens from his ascent out of the stream of Okeanos in the east to his descent in the western reaches of the same stream, describing each stage with a wealth of epithet. The puzzle of the sun's nightly return from the west to the east the Greeks lightly dismissed with legendary explanations. Some said that there was a land of light whose boundaries embraced both east and west, and whose inhabitants — a good and kindly folk — stabled Helios's steeds each evening and led them out each morning. Others declared that Helios, chariot and all, was conveyed eastward every night in a golden goblet, although one poet, more appropriately, understands that the conveyance was a bed instead of a drinking-vessel.

Helios had genuinely ethical functions, and as one who took in the whole world at a glance he was invoked in oaths. After the murder of Klytaimestra, Orestes appealed to him as a witness of his mother's establishment of a precedent in crime, and together with Hekate he was a witness of the seizure of Persephone. Not only did he make clear the path of goodness and purity to those who sought to walk in it, but he was pure himself, as he showed when he shrank from the slaughter of the house of Atreus.

On Rhodian coins Helios is shown as in the full bloom of youth, from whose head, covered with a thick growth of hair, radiate streams of light.

Phaëthon. — In Phaëthon ("Gleaming One") we cannot fail to recognize once more the person of Helios, but he has no standard genealogy, being in one myth the youthful son of Eos and Kephalos whom Aphrodite seized and set to guard her temple by night, while elsewhere he is the son of Helios, either by the sea-nymph Klymene or by Rhode. The most famous legend which grew up about his name recounts that he coaxed his father until he obtained permission to drive the fiery chariot of the sun for a single day, but since he lacked his parent's skill in handling the reins, the swift horses soon got beyond his control. In their mad career they descended too low, and the flame of the car caused such great heat and so terrible a drought upon earth that Libya became forever a desert, the people of Aithiopia took on a black hue, and the channels of mighty rivers were dried; but at length Zeus smote Phaëthon with a thunderbolt and he fell from his car into the river Eridanos. His seven sisters, weeping over his body, were turned into poplars (or poppies) and their tears became beads of amber (or rubies), while the Eridanos was given a place among the constellations. One version states that, in order to put an end to the drought and the conflagrations raging upon earth, Zeus filled the channels of the rivers to overflowing and the Great Flood of Deukalion came to pass. The story of Phaëthon probably had its roots in an ancient festival in which the death of vegetation in the heat of midsummer was celebrated by mourning.[6]

Selene. — Selene ("Moon") was too transparently a definite material body to become invested with the many and varied traits which go to make up a great personality. She was, in consequence, generally conceived merely as a planet with feminine characteristics, for the softness of her light appealed to the Greeks, as it does to us, as very feminine in comparison with the more virile light of the sun. Homer never fully deified her, and even in the later period, when her divinity was somewhat enlarged, she yielded up all her moral attributes to Artemis and Hekate. The regularity of her phases was altogether too mechanical to give to the Greek religious imagination that freedom of action which could create an entire circle of gods out of phenomena only vaguely comprehended or out of pure illusion. The family relationships of Selene are confused. In one passage she is the daughter of Zeus, but, again, she is the sister, or daughter, or wife of Helios, and as his wife she bore to him Pandia, "a daughter of surpassing beauty among the immortal gods." From her association with Helios she was conceived as riding across the heavens in a car drawn by horses or bulls, but very often poetical allusions to her car are patently metaphors.

The classic legend of Selene is that which tells of her love for Endymion, the son of Aëthlios. One night she looked down from the clear heavens upon this youth as he was sleeping near his flocks on the slopes of Mount Latmos in Karia, and at the sight of his beauty a tide of affection rose in her heart which her will was unable to stem. Coming down from heaven, she stooped and kissed him and then lingered near him till dawn as he slept on, repeating these visits night after night until her absences excited suspicion among her divine companions. When at length the cause of them became known, Zeus gave Endymion the choice between death and an endless sleep, and, choosing the latter, he may still be found asleep on the mountain-side, visited each night by his pale lover, who keeps a careful watch over his flocks.

OF PHASES OF LIGHT

Eos. — Eos ("Dawn"), the Roman Aurora, was very early considered the equal of the great luminaries, this being clear evidence of the importance of the return of the day to a primitive people lacking the means of producing strong and steady artificial light. Eos not only brought the dawn, but she *was* the dawn. She slept in her home among the Aithiopians, and, wakening when her hour came, rose from the stream of Okeanos; or, again, she was thought to keep watch at the frontiers of Day and Night, driving Night to the underworld and letting Day go forth after the morning star had heralded the return of the light. According to Homer, the sun spent the hours of darkness near her so that at his appointed time she could call forth his gleaming chariot. It was she who roused the breeze of morning and sprayed the grass with refreshing dew. Sometimes, like the sun, she was conceived as riding in a car drawn by two or by four horses, but often she was thought to move by running, or by flying with wings growing from her shoulders and feet. She is commonly represented in art as winged and with her hair streaming behind her as she speeds forward.

Eos was uniformly the daughter of Hyperion, and, therefore, the sister of Helios and Selene. She had a notorious *penchant* for beautiful young hunters, for example, Kephalos and Orion, and another of her lovers was Tithonos, a brother of Priam of Troy. Enamoured of his beauty, she carried him off in her chariot to the land of the Aithiopians, and, inasmuch as he was a mere mortal, she besought Zeus to grant him endless life. Zeus granted her request, but she had forgotten to ask also for the boon of eternal youth, so that, after many years, Tithonos wasted away with the steady advance of old age, and became only a burden to himself and to Eos. To get him out of the way she enclosed him in a room from which only the faint cry of his voice could emerge, and finally, to end his misery, she changed him into a cicada. Their children were Memnon, who fell at Troy, Emathion, and Hemera. It is customary to account for Tithonos as the regular return, the waxing, and the waning of the day, and to explain Memnon, the dusky Aithiopian, as the darkness between evening twilight and the dawn, while Emathion (cf. ἦμαρ, "day") and Hemera are masculine and feminine conceptions of the day.

Helen and the Dioskouroi. — Helen, in myth the wife of Menelaos and Paris, has been considered by a number of scholars as originally a divinity of light, being identified now with the moon, now with the red of dawn, and now with the phenomenon of a single orb of St. Elmo's fire. This last was held to be fraught with evil, while the appearance of the twin globes, represented by Helen's brothers, the Dioskouroi, was regarded as favourable. Some scholars believe that the Dioskouroi were at first daemons of the morning and evening twilight.[7]

OF SINGLE STARS AND CONSTELLATIONS

Astraios, Phosphoros, Eosphoros. — Astraios ("Starry Heaven") was accounted the son of the Titan Krios and Eurybia, but any lustre that attached to his name was a reflection of that of the children whom Eos bore him — Eosphoros, or Phosphoros, and the winds Argestes, Zephyros, Boreas, and Notos. The allegorical character of this parentage is clear at a glance.

Eosphoros ("Dawn-Bearer") and Phosphoros ("Light-Bearer") are two names for the morning star, the planet Venus, whose Latin name, Lucifer, is a translation of Phosphoros. In the myths, Eosphoros was united in marriage with Philonis (or Kleoboia), by whom he became the father of Philammon, a son, and Stilbe ("Flash"), a daughter whose name is a manner of recording the fact of the unusual brilliancy of the morning star.[8] He was conceived as the forerunner of the sun and the dawn, speeding forward on a white horse, or a chariot. Like Phaëthon, he was taken away by the love-smitten Aphrodite to be night-watcher in her temple — an aetiological explanation of the absence of his star from the heavens until just before daybreak — and he was considered to have the power of fructifying the crops. Art portrayed him in the company of other divinities of light as a youthful rider bearing a torch.

Hesperos. — Not until a comparatively late day was Hesperos (Latin Vesper), the evening star, identified by the ancients with the morning star. In the field of myth he was called the son, and again the brother, of Atlas, and he had a daughter Hesperis, who as the wife of Atlas bore the seven Atlantides (or Hesperides). For an obvious reason he was always associated with the west, but when he scaled the lofty peak of Atlas to gaze at the stars, a storm-wind suddenly snatched him away, and he was seen no more. Nevertheless, he was honoured as divine, and the brightest stellar body in the western heaven was given his name, while the memory of his piety and loving nature lived after him among men, so that his orb was known as the star of love, that is, of Aphrodite, or Venus, its religious importance lying in the ease with which the dates of festivals could be determined from its periodic movements.

Pleiades and Hyades. — Owing to their conspicuous character, constellations received much more attention among the ancients than did single stars, and two groups, one of seven stars and the other of five, which appear in the constellation of Taurus, were known to the Greeks — in fact, are still known to us — by the names of Pleiades and Hyades respectively, these belonging among the earliest attested star names. In Homer, Hephaistos depicts the Pleiades on the shield of Achilles, and by them Odysseus holds his course for Scheria. They and the Hyades were said to have been originally the daughters of Atlas through a union with Pleione or Aithra, but when their brother Hyas was killed by some creature of the wild, all twelve died of grief, and Zeus accorded them places among the stars. One ancient author, however, mothered them on the queen of the Amazons. As for the Hyades as a separate group, a well-known legend identifies them with the attendants of Dionysos who were pursued by Lykourgos, but who, after they had safely delivered their ward to Ino, fled to their grandmother Tethys and were appointed a constellation by Zeus. The names of the individual Pleiades and Hyades vary to such an extent that no purpose would be served by their recital here.

Very early the Greeks fancied that they saw in the Pleiades

PLATE LIII

The Death of Aktaion

Artemis, carrying a quiver on her back and wearing a fawn-skin over her shoulders and breast, braces herself to draw her bow as she places an arrow on the string. Before her Aktaion is falling to the ground overpowered by his four maddened dogs, which leap upon him and tear his flesh. From a red-figured *krater* of the fifth century B.C. (Furtwängler-Reichhold, *Griechische Vasenmalerei*, No. 115). See p. 252.

a swarm of wood doves, and, indeed, many scholars seriously entertain the belief that their name was derived from the word πέλειαι ("doves"). The ancients themselves ranged widely in their attempts to find the source of the name of the Hyades. To some the peculiar resemblance of the form of the stellar group to a capital Υ supplied at once an initial impulse and an initial letter for the formation of Ὑάδες, although, because of the Hyades' relations to fertility, others discovered a connexion between their name and that fertile animal, the pig (ὗς). The most popular derivation, however, was apparently that which linked the appellation with the verb ὕειν ("to rain"), for the seasons of their early rising and their early setting were notoriously rainy. A certain type of vase-picture shows the influence of this traditional association, since it depicts Alkmene as being saved from a burning pyre by the arrival of two Hyades, who extinguish the flames with water. The rising and the setting of both Hyades and Pleiades divided the year into two parts, the portion between May and November marking the period of safe navigation.

Orion. — In treating of Orion one must bear in mind that the name stands both for a constellation and for a mythical personage, and although the frequent confusion of the two makes it impossible to say with certainty which was the original, it can scarcely be doubted that some of the sagas of Orion developed without reference to the stellar group. Homer, for instance, knows the two forms as distinct, although he does not always treat them as such. Were we to rely solely upon him, we should incline to the conclusion that the Orion of myth came first in point of time and was afterwards imported into the realm of the stars; but, on the other hand, late Greek and Roman writers allude only to the constellation.

This stellar group is situated near Taurus and, therefore, near the Pleiades and Hyades, and owing to its peculiar shape it was also called the Cock's Foot, or the Double Axe. The period of the early rising of Orion and Sirius, the dog-star

(i. e. June), marks the end of the rainy season and ushers in the heat of summer, while the Pleiades and Hyades at the time of their early setting (November) disappear from the western sky ahead of Orion and Sirius, as if driven away by them. In these astronomical facts one can read without further commentary the meaning of some of the myths which concern these constellations.

In the Homeric epic Orion, the meaning of whose name is unknown, was a hunter of remarkable beauty and of a stature that exceeded even that of the giants Otos and Ephialtes. Eos cast looks of love upon him and carried him away to her dwelling, but her inordinate happiness over her good fortune aroused the anger of the gods, and Artemis, deceived by a trick of Apollo, with her noiseless shafts gave Orion an early death in the island of Ortygia (Delos). Together with Leto she set him among the stars, while in Hades his shade, armed with a brazen club, continued to pursue and kill the wild beasts which he had hunted in life.

In the legends of Boiotia, Orion was a hero born of the soil in Tanagra or Thebes. Once, when Pleione and her large family of daughters were passing through Boiotia, he accosted them, and although they immediately turned and fled, for five continuous years he relentlessly pursued them until, moved by the unhappy plight of the women, Zeus exalted them all to the heavens, where the pursuit still goes on. Side, the wife of Orion, dared to vie in beauty with Hera, and for her boldness was consigned to Hades.

In other cycles of myth Orion was the son of Poseidon and Euryale, the daughter of Minos, and his father endowed him with the gift of moving swiftly over the sea, either by striding across it, or by walking through it with his head high and dry above the waves, or, again, by using the islands as gigantic stepping-stones. From Boiotia he made his way to Chios, where he married the daughter of King Oinopion, but, partaking too liberally of the vintage of his father-in-law, he became intoxicated and attempted a serious crime against hospitality, whereupon Oinopion put out his eyes and drove him out of his home. As Orion wandered about, he chanced to reach Lemnos and there he found Hephaistos, one of whose servants guided him to the sunrise, where the light of the solar rays made his eyes whole again. He then gave himself over to searching for Oinopion that he might punish him for his cruel deed, but failing to find him, he at last joined Artemis in the chase in Crete and there was killed by the sting of a scorpion.

Ursa Major, or Great Bear; Boötes. — The peculiar arrangement of the stars in the constellation known as Ursa Major has always attracted the attention of the peoples of the northern hemisphere. Homer knew it both as the Bear and as the Chariot, and the suggestion of its appearance as a vehicle is perpetuated in a couple of its English names — Charles's Wain, or the Great Wain — whereas the utilitarian American eye sees it as the Great Dipper. The Greeks explained its designation as the Bear by the story of the Arkadian Kallisto, near whom in the heavens was placed her son Arkas in the form of the stellar group sometimes known to the ancients as Arktophylax ("Guardian of the Bear"), but generally as Boötes ("Ox-Driver").[9]

OF MIDSUMMER HEAT

Aristaios, Sirius (Greek *Seirios*), *Aktaion.* — As the legends which follow more than hint, Aristaios was an agricultural god of the primitive inhabitants of Greece, and in spite of his frequent confusion with Apollo, he seems to have been originally not a sun-god, but a personification of the period of cooling Etesian winds which gave relief to man and beast and crop during the burning dog-days.

Apollo is said to have espied the beautiful nymph Kyrene hunting amid the foothills of Mount Pelion, and overcome by his passion, he bore her away in his golden car to Libya, where he wedded her. In process of time she became the mother of Aristaios, and Hermes took the child to his great-grandmother Gaia, who in her turn entrusted him to the Hours. These maidens nurtured him on nectar and ambrosia, thereby making him an immortal, and later he was trained by Cheiron in the arts of manhood, while the Muses instructed him in healing and prophecy, and from certain nymphs he learned the culture of the olive, dairying, and bee-keeping, fable declaring that he visited almost every land in the Mediterranean basin in his successful efforts to establish these rural industries among men. On one occasion he went to the island of Keos when the heat of Sirius was causing a plague to spread among the Aegean islands, and raising an altar to Zeus Ikmaios, a divinity of moisture, he put an end to the plague by the regular offering of sacrifices to him and to Sirius. Zeus sent the Etesian winds to blow for forty days and cool the atmosphere, thereby acquiring for himself the title Aristaios ("Best"), and by following the example of Aristaios in offering sacrifices the people of the island were thenceforth able each year to mitigate the extreme heat of midsummer. Aristaios married Autonoë, a daughter of Kadmos, and by her became the father of Aktaion, of whose unhappy fate we have read in the stories of Thebes. Aktaion personified the strong plant growth of spring withered by the parching heat of the summer weeks, and the madness of his dogs is a graphic representation of the supposed result of the heat upon these animals, an effect which is still popularly recorded in the expression "dog-days."

Linos. — The story of Linos affords an excellent illustration of the manner in which a myth and a personality could be evolved from religious rites. The name seems to have been derived from the sad refrain *ai lĕnū* ("woe to us"), occurring in Semitic ritual songs in which the parching of vegetation under the summer sun was lamented, while the ceremonies rested on the wide-spread belief that daemons of heat and drought run about like ravening dogs.

The parentage of Linos varied according to the localization of his story. In Argos he was the son of Apollo and the princess Psamathe, and, exposed by his mother for fear of her father, he was found by the king's hounds and torn to pieces. In anger at his child's death, Apollo dispatched a monster called Poine ("Punishment") to tear children from the wombs of the Argive women, but when the people rose up and slew the creature, they only brought on themselves a plague from which they suffered until they gave Apollo a temple in their city. Another version, however, relates that the plague was sent because the king killed Psamathe, and that it was ended only when the women of Argos appeased the souls of Linos and his mother with ceremonial prayers and dirges. Elsewhere in Hellas Linos was the son of Apollo and the Muse Kalliope, or again, of Amphiaraos and Ourania. As the son of the latter pair he was killed by Apollo because in a song he rashly likened his gifts to those of the god, and was buried on the slopes of Mount Helikon nearest to Thebes. From the song developed the singer and lyre-player, and in this capacity Linos became the music-teacher of Herakles, although, as we have recorded among the deeds of that mighty hero, he met a violent death at the hands of his choleric pupil. To the musical gifts of Linos myth gratuitously added others of an allied nature, crediting him with having been the first to use in the writing of Greek the letters brought from Phoinikia by Kadmos, and also declaring that he was a grammarian, and, like Orpheus, the author of philosophical works.

Lityerses. — The personality of Lityerses ("Prayer for Dew"), who was, according to the legends, a son of Midas, also grew, in part, out of a midsummer song. Under the pretence of hospitality, he made a practice of luring passers-by into his palace, but once they were in his power, he would take them to the harvest fields, wrap them in sheaves, and cut off their heads, until at length Herakles came on the scene and, killing him, threw his body into the Maeander River. Another form of the story represents Lityerses as engaging in mowing contests in the fields. On achieving victory in each contest he would cruelly scourge his defeated competitor, but in the end he was himself defeated by a stronger mower. In these stories a combination of several features may be observed. The scourging is an allusion to the primitive practice of whipping up laggard mowers, and the treatment accorded to the last mower reflects an ancient custom which was designed to insure successful reaping on the following day, while the disposal of the prince's body in the river seems to be a fanciful portrayal of a magic rite to produce dew.

PLATE LIV

Linos Slain by Herakles

Linos, the kneeling figure, has been knocked down by Herakles with a fragment of a chair, which can be partly seen lying on the floor in the background, and, as he attempts to defend himself with his lyre, is in danger of being struck again by another piece of the chair brandished in the hand of his pupil. The youthful comrades of Herakles, some thoroughly terror-stricken, others manifesting a desire to help their master, stand helplessly looking on. High in the background to the left is a writing-tablet. From a red-figured *kylix* of the style of Douris (early fifth century B.C.), in Munich (Furtwängler-Reichhold, *Griechische Vasenmalerei*, No. 105). See pp. 79, 252–53.

CHAPTER XII

THE LESSER GODS — OF WATER, WIND, AND WILD

> "And hark, below, the many-voicèd earth,
> The chanting of the old religious trees,
> Rustle of far-off waters, woven sounds
> Of small and multitudinous lives awake,
> Peopling the grasses and the pools with joy,
> Uttering their meaning to the mystic night."

THESE words of Pyrrha in Moody's *Fire-Bringer* interpret for us the peculiar appeal of terrestrial nature to the Greek far better than a multitude of well-turned periods of the most logical prose, and, moreover, through suggestion they subtly reveal that the sources of the appeal are as numerous as are the departments of nature. It is hopeless for us to think of obtaining for this presentation a just and adequate classification of these departments; if only we obtain a convenient one, we must be content.

OF THE WATER

Okeanos and the Okeanides. — When Pausanias [1] makes the statement that Okeanos "is not a river, but the farthest sea that is navigated by men," he is assuming the *rôle* of the enlightened teacher and is consciously correcting an ignorant public, for from the age of Homer, and doubtless before, men had no other thought than that it was a deep refluent stream of fresh water. Homer distinguishes clearly between it and the salt sea, the Mediterranean, and deems it the father of all being, human and divine, and the source of all mundane waters. Hesiod accounts Okeanos as the son of Ouranos and Gaia, and the husband of his natural counterpart, Tethys, by whom he begat the rivers, brooks, and springs of earth — three thousand divine daughters, the Okeanides, and three thousand divine sons. Nine parts of the water of Okeanos, says Hesiod, flow about earth and sea, while the tenth part becomes the Styx and flows underneath the earth, bursting out again through a rocky opening.

As to the location of Okeanos, we are told that it is the outer boundary of the upper world and also the border between the nether world and the heavens. The Kimmerians dwelt on its northern shore, the Aithiopians on the eastern and the western, and the dwarflike Pygmies on the southern; but nowhere in Greek literature is it even hinted that people believed in the existence of a further and outer shore.

In art Okeanos is shown reclining like the river-gods, but he can be distinguished from them by his possession of a steering oar or by the presence of sea animals near him.

Rivers. — The belief in the divinity of rivers was general among the Greeks, this doubtless arising from the speed and strength of their currents down the steep mountain valleys as well as from their stimulating influence upon vegetation. They usually passed as the sons of Okeanos, but sometimes as the sons of Zeus; their relations to Poseidon are not clear. They were conceived as being now of human form, now of animal shape, now of a combination of the two. The Acheloös, for example, appeared to men with the body of a bull and the head of a man bearded and horned, while in human shape the Skamandros talked and fought with Achilles, and was in turn attacked by Hephaistos. In Homer the river-gods are found in the great council of Zeus.

The chief function of the rivers was the bestowal of fertility, and so important was this to the growth and even to the existence of many communities that rivers were often worshipped as the founders both of the local stocks and of the local culture. The Asopos occupied this high place in Phlious and Sikyon, the Inachos in Argos, the Peneios in Thessaly, the Eurotas in Sparta, and the Kephisos in Boiotia, while the *rôle* of the Acheloös is obvious in his gift of the Horn of Plenty to Herakles, and such rivers as the Kaïkos of Mysia and the Himeros of Sicily were thought to possess powers of healing disease and of averting harm. The many early stories which tell of the union of human maidens with river-gods apparently go back to rites, partly religious, partly magical, in which young women just prior to marriage were made fertile by bathing in the waters of a river.

A pretty story is told of the river Alpheios of Elis. At first Alpheios was a huntsman who fell in love with Arethousa, a huntress maiden, but she refused his advances and crossed over the sea to the little island of Ortygia before the harbour of Syracuse, where she was transformed into a fountain of fresh water. In despair Alpheios became a river, but since his love remained unchanged, he made his way beneath the sea until he came to Ortygia and there mingled with the outflow of the spring.

Springs (*Nymphs*). — The first nymphs were the Naiads, who dwelt

"By deep wells and water-floods,
Streams of ancient hills, and where
All the wan green places bear
Blossoms cleaving to the sod." [2]

That is to say, they were spirits of the springs, and from them developed, by very natural processes, the marks and functions of the nymphs of hill and forest. In the life-giving element of the springs the Greeks fancied that they saw a kind of female fruitfulness, whence the fundamental meaning of the name *νύμφη* ("bride") embodies the idea of pregnancy, although by long usage the word became less and less strict in its application until at last it could be appropriately used to designate also the Nereids and Okeanids, who essentially belonged to the larger waters; the Oreads, or mountain-spirits; and even the Dryads and Hamadryads. In their proper sphere, which included all places, like caves and marshes, where moisture gathered, the nymphs were as potent as was Poseidon over the sea or Demeter over the earth, and from their conception as feminine powers in the bloom of youth they acquired all sorts of maidenly characteristics. They danced and sang, and ceaselessly made merry in their woodland retirement; they were the nurses of the infants Dionysos and Zeus; and, again, they were the chaste attendants of Artemis; while through their fresh charms they won many lovers from among both gods and men.

In myth the nymphs are as a rule simply the daughters of Zeus; the name of a mother is seldom mentioned, although the Melian nymphs come into being from the blood of Ouranos, and in the Orphic hymns all nymphs are the offspring of Okeanos. Once in Homer the nymphs appear upon Olympos, and they plant elms about the tomb of Andromache's father. A group of Naiads inhabits the island of Ithake. In various places the divinities of many of the famous springs were reputed to have originally been women, most of whom had been drowned, the stories of the fountains of Peirene and Glauke at Corinth and of Kirke at Thebes being excellent illustrations of this manner of myth-making. There were also nymphs of cities who were the daughters of the important rivers of the neighbourhood and who were in many instances wedded to the local eponymous hero. Some of these divinities were credited with the gift of foretelling the future, a belief which was derived not so much from the poetic fancy that running water talks as from the conviction that the drinking of certain waters produced a state of inspiration. Indeed the epithet of "nymph-smitten" was applied to persons wrought up to prophetic ecstasy.

The worship of the nymphs was generally limited to special

spots in the open air, as in groves, on the slopes of hills, or beside streams and natural fountains. Garlands of flowers were the common offerings of the worshippers, but very often cereals and animal victims were also given.

The Sea. — Owing to their proximity to the sea and to their manifold interest in it as a source of life and as a highway, the Greeks were from the remotest times much attracted by its numerous phases. Calm and storm and the various gradations between these conditions meant to them safety or danger. The countless forms of marine life opened a wide field for the free play of their fancy, while the uncertainty of the sea's depths and shallows and reefs kept them in a constant state of wonder. The only feature of the sea about which there was any assurance was its aqueous character and this was so obvious that, like Selene, the sea never became sufficiently divinized to be the proper material for myth. Those phases, on the other hand, which were marked by vagueness or vastness, or were susceptible of limitless variation, were eagerly seized by the myth-making mind. Pontos, for instance, was the sea in its aspect as a boundless barren tract, whereas Phorkys, the grey son of Plouton and Gaia, together with his wife, Keto, represented in themselves, and, in part, in their offspring (Skylla, the Graiai, and the Gorgons), the monstrous elements of the sea, while the many arms of the Aegean, reaching far into the recesses of the mainland and islands, were personified by the hundred-handed Briareos, or Aigaion. Atlas, "who knoweth the depths of every sea, and himself stays the towering pillars which keep earth and sky apart,"[3] is really not a mountain, but rather the sea-billow on which the heavens seem to rest.

Triton. — Triton is a figure of the roaring of the sea and the larger bodies of fresh water. He was known as the son of Poseidon and Amphitrite and dwelt with them in a golden palace beneath the waves, although his special home seems to have been in Lake Kopaïs of Boiotia. The Greeks pictured him as driving a horse-drawn chariot over the sea and as holding a trident, or a dolphin, or a drinking-horn in his hand; but his chief attribute was a sea-shell, on which he used to blow loudly or softly according as he desired to arouse or to calm the sea. The artists delineated him as of human form above but of animal shape below the waist, the line of union being concealed by a garment. In the later centuries, however, his lower parts were shown as those of a fish.

A Boiotian tale narrates that the women of Tanagra, who had gone down to the sea to be purified in preparation for a festival of Dionysos, were attacked by Triton while they were in the water, but the god heard their cries for help and beat their assailant off. In another tale, Triton was charged with raids on the herds and shipping of Tanagra until at last the people set out a bowl of wine as a trap, whereupon, drinking the wine, Triton fell asleep on the shore of the sea, and a man of the city chopped off his head with an axe. That is why the Tanagran image of Triton was headless.

Nereus. — Nereus, "the Ancient of the Sea," portrayed in his person and family the multiform beauties of the sea. He was the issue of Pontos and Gaia, and by his wife Doris he begat a host of daughters, the Nereids, the beautiful nymphs of the inner sea as opposed to the Okeanids, the nymphs of the outer sea. He was a benevolent old man always ready to help those who were in trouble, his great age being marked by the hoary foam of the breaking waves. Like certain other gods of the sea, he was an unerring prophet and gifted with marvellous powers of transformation, but in spite of his changes into many animal forms, he was forced by Herakles to point out the road leading to the golden apples of the Hesperides. In his true form he was conceived as an old man with a thick beard and a heavy tangled mat of hair. His emblem was the trident.

The Nereids seem to have stood for the ripples and waves of calm weather, those most famous in myth being Amphitrite and Thetis.

PLATE LV

Odysseus and the Sirens

Odysseus stands on tiptoe, lashed faceforward to the mast. In front of him is a Siren perched on a branch and singing to the accompaniment of a *tympanon* which she is beating, while behind him is another Siren, similarly seated, holding a *kithara* (zither) in her left hand and a *plektron* (pick) in her right. The four companions of Odysseus are working distractedly at their oars as they gaze spellbound at the alluring creatures above them. From a design, done in white and three colours, on a Lucanian *krater* of the third century B.C., in Berlin (Furtwängler-Reichhold, *Griechische Vasenmalerei*, No. 130). See pp. 262–63.

Proteus. — Proteus, the son and underling of Poseidon, was so far the master god of elusive "sea change" that the epithet Protean has become a synonym of the sophistical and dissimulating mind. His two sons, Polygonos and Telegonos, met Herakles at Torone as the latter was returning from the country of the Amazons, and challenged him to a wrestling bout, but the hero threw and killed them both. According to Homer and Euripides, Proteus was the king of the Egyptian island of Pharos [4] and the husband of a Nereid nymph. He was the herder and guardian of the seals and knew everything that took place in the depths of the sea, and also, like Nereus, all that had happened or was to come to pass upon earth. Through the connivance of his daughter, Eidothea, he was seized by Menelaos and forced to reveal to him the state of affairs at Sparta and to direct him on his homeward voyage.

Glaukos. — The sea-god Glaukos was said to have been at first an ordinary human being, the son of Anthedon and Alkyone, this being a mythological way of saying that he was a native of the Boiotian city of Anthedon. By trade he was a fisherman, and one day, when reclining on the shore after landing his catch, he observed that some of the fish, eating of a certain herb, came back to life and leaped into the sea. After tasting the herb himself, he, too, sprang into the water at a spot which the Anthedonians later called "Glaukos's Leap" and was transformed into a deity, being admitted into the circle of the sea-gods after Okeanos and Tethys had purged him of all human imperfections, and becoming so skilled in prophecy that in this art he gave instruction to Apollo and Nereus. The artists were wont to sketch him as a fisherman equipped with fish-traps and a fish-basket and as wearing the skin of a fish on his head. This story is, without doubt, essentially related to the more widely known legend of the search for the Fountain of Youth.

Ino (Leukothea). — We are already aware of the *rôle* played by Ino, the daughter of Kadmos, in those events of the early history of Thebes which culminated in the great tribal movement known in mythology as the Voyage of the Argonauts. Her function as guardian of the sailor folk, which she exercised under the new name of Leukothea, is exemplified most clearly in the Homeric episode where she comes to the aid of the shipwrecked Odysseus. Seeing the hero exhausted by his efforts to save himself, she rose from the sea and sat beside him on his raft, giving him a magic veil and bidding him bind it about his breast, cast himself into the raging water, and endeavour to swim to the Phaiakian coast. Following her counsel, Odysseus was kept afloat by the veil for two days and two nights, and on the morning of the third day he set foot upon land.

Seirenes (*Sirens*). — By nature the Sirens ("Bewitching Ones") were akin to the Keres and Erinyes, being winged daemons of death who haunted graves and the underworld. The belief in them was deeply rooted in the minds of the common people, and Homer must have been aware of their special attributes, although he seems to have chosen only such of them as would serve his literary purposes. He is the creator of their musical gifts and is responsible for their association with the sea.

The descent of the Sirens was not definitely fixed. They were reputed to be the children of Phorkys, or, again, they were born of the drops of blood that fell upon Earth from the broken horn of Acheloös, while another genealogy accounts them the children of this same Acheloös and one of the Muses. In Homer they are two in number, though the vase-painters generally represent them as three; but in the sphere of popular religion their number is unlimited by reason of their very nature, and any names that attach to them are invariably suggestive of meretricious wiles and charms. Hesiod locates these beguiling divinities in the flowery island of Anthemoëssa in the western sea.

Kirke thus describes the Sirens to Odysseus: "To the Sirens first shalt thou come, who bewitch all men, whosoever come to them. Whoso draws nigh them unwittingly and hears the sound of the Sirens' voice never doth he see wife or babes stand by him on his return, nor have they joy at his coming; but the Sirens enchant him with their clear song, sitting in the meadow, and all about is a great heap of bones of men, corrupt in death, and round the bones the skin is wasting." To the description Kirke added directions for defeating their witchery, and by following these Odysseus and his companions passed safely by. "But do thou drive thy ship past," she said, "and knead honey-sweet wax, and anoint therewith the ears of thy company, lest any of the rest hear the song; but if thou thyself art minded to hear, let them bind thee in the swift ship hand and foot, upright in the mast-head, and from the mast let rope-ends be tied that with delight thou mayest hear the voice of the Sirens. And if thou shalt beseech thy company and bid them to loose thee, then let them bind thee with yet more bonds." [5]

The Sirens are often represented in tombstone reliefs and in vase-paintings as birds standing or flying, and with human heads, which are occasionally bearded.

Skylla and Charybdis. — Among the most formidable monsters known to Greek mythology were Skylla and Charybdis, the former of whom regularly passed as the daughter of Phorkys and Krataiïs ("Mighty"). Up to the age of womanhood she was a divinity of such beauty as to awaken love for her in the breast of Poseidon, but when Amphitrite discovered her husband's waywardness, she jealously threw magic herbs into the spring in which Skylla was wont to bathe, after which her rival became the horrible ravening creature against whom Kirke warned Odysseus. She dwelt in a dim cave in the face of a cliff hard by his course, and as the vessel passed by, she reached out her six long and snakelike necks, with each head snatching a sailor from his bench, and crushing him in her pitiless jaws.

Over against Skylla was Charybdis, a less repulsive but no

less cruel monster, who, too, had been born a goddess, being the daughter of Poseidon and Gaia. Her chief characteristic was an insatiable voracity, and, because of repeated thefts of cattle from Herakles, Zeus, with the stroke of a thunderbolt, hurled her into the sea, where, in the very path of ships, she sucked down black water three times a day, and thrice daily spouted it forth. Beginning with the fifth century B.C., Skylla and Charybdis were localized in the Straits of Messina.

OF WINDS AND STORMS

A little knowledge of the meteorological conditions of Greece and of the manner of life to which the ancient Greek was bound by the very nature of things makes it plain why Hesiod [6] called the winds "a great trouble to mortals." One who is well acquainted with modern Greece writes: "In the winter the winds blow from every point of the compass and cannot be relied upon from one day to the next," [7] while in strong contrast is the regularity of direction of the summer winds. In all this variety of air-currents, sometimes humouring, sometimes thwarting the plans of man, it was not at all strange to see the operations of beings of independent will and of those motley traits which go to make up personality. It was inevitable that the mountain hurricanes, which without warning swooped down on the sailor or fisherman who thought himself safe as long as he hugged the shore, should seem to be daemons of destruction; and it was equally axiomatic that the useful trade-winds should be credited with peaceful and benevolent dispositions. Owing to their importance the winds were very early given a place in cult or in those magic ceremonies which can be differentiated from cult only with difficulty; and, consequently, as there were rain-charms, so were there wind-charms to avert or to arouse the winds as necessity required. With the continuous development of chthonic elements in Greek ritual the tendency gained momentum to identify the violent winds with malignant daemons of the earth; yet, on the other hand, many of them were thought to reside in birds of prey, such as the sea-hawk, while in the kingfisher dwelt the spirit of midwinter calm, whence we still speak of "halcyon (kingfisher) days."

Boreas, Euros, Notos, and Zephyros. — The most important winds, Boreas, Euros, Notos, and Zephyros, were classified in myth as the sons of Astraios and Eos. The character which Boreas, the north wind, exhibits in Attic myth holds good everywhere else. He is lustful, cruel, and strong, and with a decided bent for thievery; he is a cold, blustering, and uncouth Thracian; he leaps swiftly down from the peaks of the hills, uprooting the oaks and shattering the ships which lie in his path; according to his caprice, he brings clear sky or cloud. Homer tells us that Achilles besought Boreas and Zephyros to fan the flames of Patroklos's pyre, and the Athenians of the fifth century attributed to Boreas's connexion with them by marriage the destruction of the fleet of Xerxes off Chalkis. They habitually thought of him as a shaggy-haired and heavy-browed man, equipped with wings on both shoulders and feet, while at Thourioi he was regarded as so nearly human that he was given the rank of citizen and was assigned a domicile. Homer relates, however, that in the form of a horse he begat by the mares of Erichthonios twelve foals that could race over the sea without sinking and over the tilled lands without leaving a footmark or the trail of a wheel behind them.

The remaining winds are devoid of the sharp individuality of Boreas. From the southland comes Notos in autumn and winter, his beard heavy with clouds, and his grey poll dripping great drops of moisture, while from his wings a leaden mist falls over glen and hill, and men and beasts and herbage become sluggish and sickly. Over the sea he spreads a dense mist so that sailors despair of making port, and, in Horatian phrase, he is the wind "than whom there is no greater ruler of the Adriatic." [8] Along with Euros he hindered Odysseus's departure from Thrinakia and drove him back upon Charybdis. In the south-east is the home of Euros, at whose warm breath the snows melt and rains fall. Zephyros is the gentle wind of the west which gives strength to plants, and in a very childish allegory myth makes him the husband of Chloris ("Verdant Herbage"), by whom he became the father of Karpo ("Fruitfulness").

Aiolos. — In the *Odyssey* Aiolos, the steward of the winds, inhabits the floating island of Aiolia in the western sea along with his family of six convivial sons and six convivial daughters. The story of how he packed the winds in a bag and gave them to Odysseus we need not repeat here. The person of Aiolos seems to represent the mobility and variability of the winds, and his children, living as they did "*in Saus und Braus*," their rapacity; while his method of controlling them is paralleled in a primitive Germanic custom of bagging the winds in order to quell them.

Harpies. — The hated and destructive squalls that burst suddenly from the mountain valleys on the coastal shipping were well described in the appearance and the actions of the Harpies (Ἅρπυιαι, "Snatchers"), whom popular epithet styled "the dogs of Zeus," and with good reason, as their treatment of Phineus has already demonstrated. These loathsome creatures had the arms and breasts of a woman, but all their remaining parts were those of a bird. The talons of their hands and feet were long and sharp, and with their wings they flew about with the speed of the wind, their names, Aëllopous ("Storm-Foot") and Okypete ("Swift-Flying"), being accurate registers of their nature. To account for such marvellous beings mythology derived them from some monstrous sire like Thaumas, or Typhon, or Poseidon; and, since like begets like, they in their turn became the mothers of the swift steeds of Achilles, Erechtheus, and the Dioskouroi. Their home was in the Strophades, a group of islands in the Aegean, or, according to Vergil, at the very gates of the underworld.

PLATE LVI

Oreithyia and Boreas

Boreas, well characterized as a thick-set and bristly-haired man of cruel countenance, has grasped Oreithyia around the waist, and, lifting her off her feet, is on the point of flying away with her through the air. A sister of the maiden, Pandrosos, is hastening away in fear, while Herse, another sister, runs forward to lend aid. From a red-figured *amphora* of about 475 B.C., in Munich (Furtwängler-Reichhold, *Griechische Vasenmalerei*, No. 94). See pp. 73–74, 265.

Typhon and the Kyklopes. — Apparently Typhon and all the forms of the Kyklopes — the Homeric, the smiths of Zeus, the spirits of the volcano, and the mythical builders of city walls — were originally storm-daemons.[9]

OF THE WILD

Pan, Silenoi, and Satyroi (*Satyrs*). — Pan has about him the unmistakable marks of a native of the hills and the grazing lands of Arkadia, his name (a contraction of Πάων) denoting "the grazier." It was in the Arkadian mountain, Lykaion, where he was born a son of Hermes and Dryope, or of Zeus and Kallisto, and only among the pastoral Arkadians was his cult of national importance. On his favour to flock and herd hung the existence and the prosperity of the inhabitants, and with the spread of the story that in the battle at Marathon he reinforced the Greek cause by driving the Persians into a mad rout, his cult extended into every part of Greece. Nevertheless, with the exception of his exaltation in certain philosophical circles to the position of the All-God (a conception born partly from the false derivation of his name from the adjective meaning "all"), he had no contact with the spiritual life of the people — he always remained, as he is portrayed in the *Homeric Hymn* in his honour, the unconventional, if not wanton, divinity of the wilderness and country-side.

As the "goat-footed, two-horned lover of the dance" he haunts "the snowy height, the mountain peaks, and paths amid the crags. Hither and thither he fares through the thick copses, now enticed by the gentle streams, and now, climbing an exceeding lofty height overlooking the herds, he makes his way among the rocks. Often he runs over the long white ridges of the mountains, and often, again, over the foot-hills, slaying wild beasts and glancing sharply about him. Then at evening, returning from the chase, he sings alone and plays a sweet song upon the pipes. Not even the bird which pours forth her sweet lays amid the leaves of flowery spring can excel him in song. With him then join in the melody the sweetly singing nymphs of the highlands thronging round the darkling fountain, and echo resounds about the summit of the mountain." [10]

At the outset Pan was simply a generative daemon of the flocks and herds, but the concept of his being a sort of ideal shepherd and protector was a natural sequel of this function, and in time his powers were so enlarged that he was held to exert an influence on the growth of forage plants, although he never became a full-fledged deity of vegetation. In the foregoing spheres his emblem was the phallos. So far as wind and weather affected the condition of the cattle, Pan was a weather-god, and doubtless his fabled skill on the pipes is a reminiscence of the primitive magical practice of endeavouring to control the winds by whistling or by playing on wind-instruments. As the chief divine inhabitant of the solitudes Pan contrived the special perils that beset hunters, herdsmen, travellers, and others who invaded his domains. The mirage was a device created by him to mislead and perplex, and panic, named after himself, was his *coup de maître* for suddenly dispersing great hosts.

The Satyrs and the Silenoi can best be comprehended, perhaps, in the statement that they are a plurality of Pans, although in them this playful and lustful character stands out in exaggerated relief. They combine the elements of human, brute, and inanimate nature more successfully than any other creatures of myth. By virtue of their connexion with fertility they frequently appear in the circle of Dionysos as well as in that of Pan.

The representations of Pan and his lesser congeners in art are, in more than the ordinary sense, myths in pictorial or graphic form. Two periods of their development may be observed, the dividing line being drawn, roughly, at about 400 B.C. In the first the human element predominates, all of the divinities being regularly shown as possessing the heads and bodies of men and the members of animals, such as horns, tail, pointed ears, shaggy hair, and the legs of goats or of horses. Toward the end of this time types appear which represent them as beautiful youths, bearing here and there upon their persons mere hints of their semi-bestial nature. In the second period the animal element becomes more prominent, but more smoothly fused with the human, and the types of Pan, the Satyrs, and the Silenoi now begin to diverge along their own

FIG. 10. SATYRS AT PLAY

In the centre of the lower band is a Maenad holding a *thyrsos* (ritual wand) and looking at a group of four Satyrs, two of whom, riding on the backs of the others, are waiting to catch the ball about to be thrown by the old Satyr at the extreme left of the picture. Between the old Satyr and the Maenad is a boy Satyr lightly leaning on a hoop which he has just been trundling. The upper band shows a pantomimic dance of maidens (*JHS* xi, Plate XII).

separate lines. Pan is now practically always seen with goat's legs and has a leering, sensual countenance, while the flute of reed, the goatherd's staff, and the goatskin are his common attributes. All these characteristics are gradually taken over by the Satyrs.

Maenads and Bacchantes. — The Maenads and Bacchantes were the spirits of the wild conceived as feminine. Although they were much less gross than their male companions whom we have just described, in that they were devoid of the bodily attributes of the animal kinds, nevertheless, they counted the beasts of the wild among their chief associates, and, despite their human form, they were distinctly unhuman in spirit.

They had their birth in the belief, common to many primitive peoples, that the storms of the latter part of the winter release the daemons which put life into herb and tree; in fact, they were these storms themselves, wanton, wild, and free. Their natures brought them into an intimate alliance with Dionysos, and the *rôle* which they played in his rites has made their names synonyms of unrestraint and revelry. Wrought to a state of ecstasy by the shrill music of the flute and the clash of cymbals, they would shout and sing as they ran wildly to and fro, waving burning brands and *thyrsoi* (ritual wands). As Agave tore her unbelieving son Pentheus asunder, so the Maenads were said to rend the young of wild animals and then to eat their flesh raw.

Dryads and Hamadryads. — The spirits which were thought to inhabit trees were known as Dryads or Hamadryads, and they became classed as nymphs, as we have previously pointed out, by a very easy extension of terms. Under the name of Dryad the Greeks seem to have comprehended a female spirit dwelling among the trees, whereas a Hamadryad, on the other hand, was the spirit of an individual tree whose life began and ended with that of her host. Stories which bring out the individuality of Hamadryads — for example, that of Daphne and Apollo — are simply the devices of mythology to explain the marked peculiarities of single trees or of single species of trees.

Kentauroi (Centaurs). — Of all the monsters put together by the Greek imagination the Centaurs constituted a class in themselves. Despite a strong streak of sensuality in their make-up, their normal behaviour was moral, and they took a kindly thought of man's welfare. The attempted outrage of Nessos on Deianeira, and that of the whole tribe of Centaurs on the Lapith women, are more than offset by the hospitality of Pholos and by the wisdom of Cheiron, physician, prophet, lyrist, and the instructor of Achilles. Further, the Centaurs were peculiar in that their nature, which united the body of a horse with the trunk and head of a man, involved an unthinkable duplication of vital organs and important members. So grotesque a combination seems almost un-Greek. These strange creatures were said to live in the caves and clefts of the mountains, myth associating them especially with the hills of Thessaly and the range of Erymanthos.

CHAPTER XIII

THE LESSER GODS — OF THE EARTH

I. GAIA (GE)

IF a poet of this utilitarian day and generation can sing, with such happy fancy,

> "The earth that is the sister of the sea,
> The earth that is the daughter of the stars,
> The mother of the myriad race of men," [1]

why should we wonder at the Greeks' imputation of personality to the various features of the material world? This modern conception of Earth, i. e. Gaia or Ge, is almost textually, we may safely say, that of the most ancient Greeks of whom we have even the vaguest knowledge. At Dodona Zeus, the sky-god, was coupled with the earth goddess, a union long consummated even then. In Homer's time she was held to be a sentient being, although perhaps not quite personal enough to be a goddess, but later, in Hesiod, we find her consciously exercising the functions of parenthood. As we have seen in the chapter on the beginning of things, she was the mother, first of Ouranos, and afterward, by him, of the Titans, of the Kyklopes, and of the Giants, and, by the indirect process of descent, of gods and men; while in the local myths we learned that men like Pelasgos, Kekrops, and Alalkomeneus sprang straight from her bosom. When she had brought all these into the world, she nourished them, enriched them, and gave them the mysterious power to reproduce their kind, whence at Athens she was venerated under the title "Nourisher of Youths."

PLATE LVII

A Maenad

This vigorously drawn figure represents a Maenad at the height of her orgiastic frenzy. Her slightly raised foot and the flutter of her garments show that she is dancing wildly rather than moving swiftly forward. She wears a girdle of fawn-skin, and is crowned with a wreath of ivy from beneath which flow long loose tresses of her hair. Behind her and to one side her *thyrsos* (ritual wand) stands obliquely in the ground. In each hand she holds a part of the fawn which in her madness she has just rent asunder, as the blood still dripping from the wounds testifies. From a red-figured *lekythos* of about 475 B.C., from Gela (*Monumenti Antichi*, xvii, Plate LV a). See pp. 269–70.

Under the name of Gaia, however, the development of the goddess stopped, for Gaia was too obvious a suggestion of the material earth to stir the constructive Greek fancy into action, although certain of her epithets descriptive of different concepts of the earth-power survived and took on attractive forms. Thus, as Pandora ("All-Giver") she became the theme of a significant myth, and as Pandrosos ("All-Bedewing") she plays a *rôle* in early Athenian religious history, while, partly from the righteousness of her oracles, as delivered, for instance, from her pre-Apolline shrine at Delphoi, she became Themis ("Justice"), although it was under the name of Demeter that she attained her highest and loveliest attributes of divinity.

Yet there is another side to the nature of Gaia, for after death men were laid away in her deep bosom, whence they had first come, so that she presided over the host of departed spirits, and it was only natural that, under the name of Persephone, she ultimately came to be known as the queen of the lower world. She was associated with the Genesia, a festival in which ancestors were honoured, and with the latter part of the Anthesteria, while in public oaths that bound treaties and alliances she was invoked, along with Zeus and Helios, as an ever-present witness of the solemn obligation.

II. RHEA-KYBELE (GREAT MOTHER)

Beginning with the fifth century, the names Great Mother or Mother of the Gods, Rhea, and Kybele were employed indifferently to designate a single divine being, a great earth goddess, and it is altogether probable that historically also they represented only one being. At Athens her official title was the first of the foregoing names, or its alternative form, and there, as early as the sixth century, she was accorded a shrine, known as the Metroön, which served as the depository of the state archives, an honour which seems to have come to her through her likeness to Demeter, who had already been naturalized. The name Rhea belonged rather to the circle of myth, being seldom used as a formal religious designation, while the mention of Kybele always called to mind the peculiar manner of cult connected with the Asiatic form of the mother goddess of earth.

Rhea was primarily the Cretan conception of the maternal principle resident in the earth, and as with the other gods her functions increased with her recognition, until many were included which in reality had only a remote relation to her actual nature. In some quarters her name is explained as being possibly a Cretan form of *γέα* (*γῆ*), "earth," while in others it is connected with *ῥεῖν*, "to flow," a relation which seems to put emphasis on her function as a producer of rain. In the Orphic genealogy Rhea is the daughter of Okeanos and Tethys, but in the Hesiodic the offspring of Ouranos and Gaia. Becoming the sister-wife of Kronos, she bears Hera, Zeus, Poseidon, Hades, Demeter, and Hestia, and in this way she plays a very important part in the early scenes of the world's history as set forth in myth. The story of her giving birth to Zeus in Crete is a mirror of her functions and cult, Zeus representing the herbage of spring emerging from the fertile bosom of mother earth, and the nymphs attending him being the countless kindly spirits which cherish the tender plants of earth. The Kouretes, who later become an organized priesthood, are none other than the early Cretans engaged in the performance of magical ceremonies designed to encourage the productivity of earth, while the stone which Rhea gives Kronos to swallow must surely be a rain-stone to bring rain upon earth. Finally, the death of Zeus as reported in Crete is, in the language of myth, the annual decline of vegetation, the fall of leaf and flower upon the breast of earth.

In the fifth century the name and worship of Kybele were introduced into Greece and spread abroad, largely through the influence of freed Phrygian slaves. The personality of this goddess included, without doubt, traits of many other local earth goddesses whom she had assimilated from time to time, and, as one may clearly observe in the legend which we are about to relate, she and her youthful favourite, Attis, are parallel cult-figures to Aphrodite and Adonis.

An almond-tree wedded to the Phrygian river Sangarios became the mother of a handsome lad named Attis, who spent his childhood in the wilds among the beasts and birds, and became a herdsman when he grew to manhood. His beauty attracted the attention both of Kybele and of the princess of the realm, so that they became rivals for his love, but when his marriage with the princess was about to be celebrated in the presence of a large gathering, Kybele suddenly appeared and smote the guests with madness. Attis, fleeing to the highlands, killed himself, and though Kybele entreated Zeus to restore the boy to life, all that she could obtain was the consent that his body and hair were to remain as in life, and that he could move his little finger.

The legend just narrated seems to be an attempt to follow back to its sources the ritual in which the yearly death and re-birth of the young god of wild vegetation were symbolized by a fir-tree. But Kybele was also associated with the vegetation of the tilled lands, this being suggested, first, by the legends which make her the wife of Gordias, the first king of Phrygia, and by him the mother of Midas, whom she generously blesses with the wealth of the earth; and, secondly, by the myths where the daughter whom she has borne to the river Sangarios is joined in wedlock to Dionysos. The dependence of Phrygia upon her bounty for its well-being made her the chief divinity both of the separate cities and of the entire country.

Kybele was attended by the lion and other wild animals and by bands of priests known as Korybantes and Daktyloi. The former might be characterized as male Maenads, so wild and abandoned were their rites, and, in fact, they surpassed the Maenads in this respect, even going so far as to practice mutilation of their bodies. The aim of their ritual was twofold — to advance the growth of vegetation, and to free themselves from eternal death by mystic union with the immortal goddess. Owing to the highly emotional and unreflective character of this cult, it was never thoroughly acceptable to the Greek temperament.

During the fifth and fourth centuries art did not succeed in elaborating a strictly Greek type of Rhea-Kybele, who was often portrayed in a manner which suggested the Artemis of the wild beasts — a matronly figure seated, crowned, and accompanied by lions. Her later type was an amplification of the earlier, although barbarian traits now predominated.

III. LESSER DIVINITIES OF THE UNDERWORLD

Erinyes (Latin *Furiae*). — After the murder of Abel, we are told in Genesis,[2] God said to Cain: "The voice of thy brother's blood crieth unto me from the ground," and from the same idea of the appeal of murdered souls for vengeance the Erinyes were born. The Hebrew and the Greek differed, however, in the extent to which they severally elaborated the idea, since the former put the avenging power into the hands of God, and the latter into the hands of the injured souls themselves. The soul of the murdered man, according to Greek belief, could rise from the ground and as a free agent hound the murderer night and day until he made proper expiation for his crime, this avenging soul being an Erinys. In time, through the influence of a common tendency to pluralize daemonic conceptions, it was expanded into a number of beings of a like nature; and as these became established in popular thought, they acquired an ever-enlarging endowment of attributes, the most important being those which they acquired from the earth out of which they came. As Earth was generally conceived as feminine, so were they, and at times men even entreated them, as they would Earth, for the blessing of a good harvest. Strange to say, the Erinyes did not pursue every murderer; their vindictive fury was reserved especially for him who had committed the sin of sins, the slaughter of a kinsman, and herein lies the significance of their pursuit of Orestes and Alkmaion — each had slain his mother. Once established as defenders of the family, to the Greek mind the mainstay of the social order, their powers to enforce justice were broadened, and they now became the champions of the right of the first-born, and of strangers, and of beggars. In Homer we find them depriving Achilles' horses of the gift of speech in order to correct an offence against the just laws of nature. They are generally, but not always, represented as being three in number and named respectively Alekto, Megaira, Tisiphone. In imagination men painted them as repulsive caricatures of women; for hair they had a tangle of serpents; instead of running, they flew about like birds of prey; in their hands they brandished scourges with which they threatened the victim of their pursuit; and the Taurian herdsmen reported to Iphigenia Orestes' description of the Erinys who assailed him:

> "A she-dragon of Hell, and all her head
> Agape with fangèd asps, to bite me dead.
> She hath no face, but somewhere from her cloak
> Bloweth a wind of fire and bloody smoke:
> The wind's heat fans it: in her arms, Ah see!
> My mother, dead grey stone, to cast on me
> And crush." [3]

Eumenides, Semnai Theai, Maniai. — Small wonder that the Greeks shrank from pronouncing the name of such dire beings as the Erinyes. Since a name has a happy way of cloaking realities, they called them in Athens Semnai Theai, "Revered Goddesses," and at Kolonos, the Eumenides, "Benevolent Ones," but in time they forgot that these epithets were only substitutes and built up new divine characters to suit them, such being the pliability of the myth-making mind. The Maniai ("Madnesses") of Megalopolis seem to have been of identical nature.

Miscellaneous. — Besides the Erinyes, there was a host of inferior hellish creatures popularly located in the underworld. The Keres passed now as the souls of the dead, now as malevolent death-dealing daemons of an independent origin and existence; the Stringes ("Vampires") were horrid winged creatures in the form of night-birds who brought evil dreams and sucked the life-blood of sleepers; and Empousa was a destructive monster with one foot of brass and the other of an ass. Lamia, who still lives in modern Greek superstition, was said to have been a woman of Libya whose children, begotten by Zeus, were slain by Hera, and who in revenge gave herself over to the perpetual task of killing strange children.

In the underworld there also lived Hypnos ("Sleep") and Thanatos ("Death"), twin sons of Nyx ("Night") and Erebos ("Darkness"). Hypnos spent his time now on earth, now in the Island of Dreams, and now beneath the earth, exercising his power over men and gods as he willed; while Thanatos would come forth from below and clip a lock from the head of the dying to hasten the last breath.

PLATE LVIII

Hypnos

Hypnos, a beautiful, soft-fleshed, dreamy youth, seems originally to have held in his extended right hand a horn from which to pour sleep on reposing mortals; in his left he probably grasped a poppy-stem with which he cast over them a spell of forgetfulness. His appearance calls to mind the description of Sleep which Ovid puts into the mouth of Iuno: "Sleep, mildest of all the gods, thou art thyself sweet peace of mind, a soothing balm, an alien to care, and bringest rest and strength to mortals worn and weary with the toils of life" (*Metamorphoses*, xi. 623–25). A Roman marble copy of a bronze original (apparently of the fourth century B.C.), in the Prado, Madrid (Brunn-Bruckmann, *Denkmäler griechischer und römischer Sculptur*, No. 529). See p. 278.

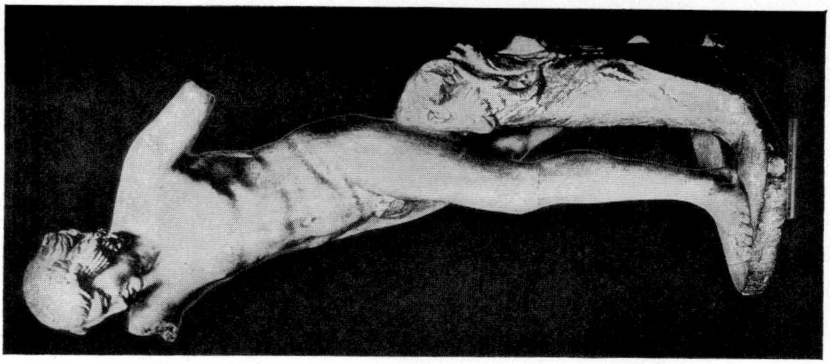
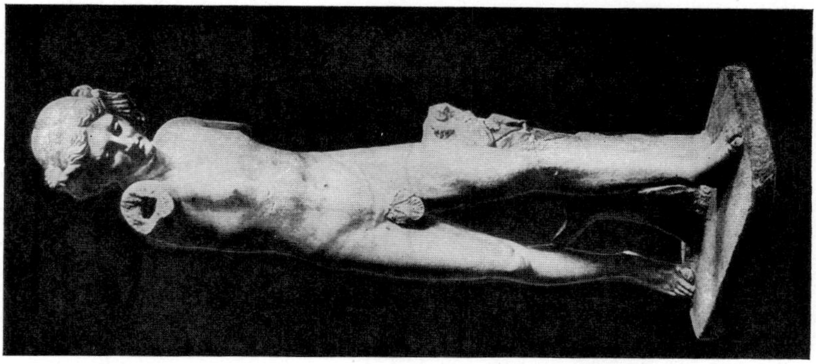
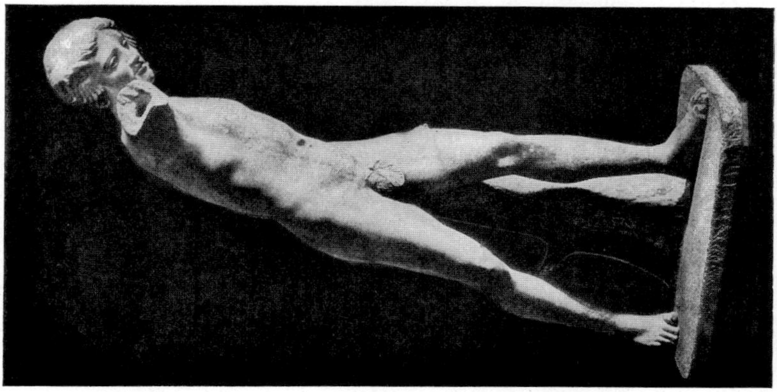

CHAPTER XIV

THE LESSER GODS — ASKLEPIOS, ABSTRACT DIVINITIES

I. ASKLEPIOS

ALTHOUGH, as we shall presently see, Asklepios was not, strictly speaking, an abstract divinity, yet the more or less abstract character of his function of healing affords some warrant for our present classification of him.

The Origin and the Name of Asklepios. — If the myths concerning the parentage of Asklepios are at all significant, he was the heir and successor of Apollo in the art of healing. This mythical relationship doubtless became established in some cult-shrine of Apollo, such as that in Epidauros or even that in Cretan Gortyna, where the two were affiliated and where, in the end, the younger divinity ousted the elder from the first place. Whatever may have been the initial nature of Asklepios, his mature form seems to reveal a combination of two natures, chthonic and solar, and of this there are traces in the myths that are to follow. Some scholars see in the first part of his name a root which embodies the idea of brightness, but, unfortunately, this is so uncertain that it is useless as a confirmation of the partly solar nature of the god. It is pretty generally agreed, on the other hand, that the second part of the name, -ηπιος, signifies "mild" or "soothing," a very appropriate quality for a dispenser of healing.

Myths of Asklepios. — Asklepios sometimes passed as the son of Arsinoë, the daughter of Leukippos, but generally as the son of Koronis ("Sea-Gull"), the daughter of Thessalian Phlegyas. Pausanias [1] tells the story of his birth and infancy with an attractive simplicity. "When he [i. e. Phlegyas] came to Peloponnese his daughter came with him, and she, all unknown to her father, was with child by Apollo. In the land of Epidauros she was delivered of a male child, whom she exposed upon the mountain which is named Titthion ('nipple'). . . . But one of the goats that browsed on the mountain gave suck to the forsaken babe; and a dog, the guardian of the flock, watched over it. Now when Aresthanas — for that was the name of the goatherd — perceived that the tale of the goats was not full, and that the dog kept away from the flock, he went up and down, they say, looking everywhere. At last he found the babe and was fain to take it up in his arms. But as he drew near he saw a bright light shining from the child. So he turned away, 'For surely,' thought he, 'the hand of God is in this,' as indeed it was. And soon the fame of the child went abroad over every land and sea, how that he had all power to heal the sick and that he raised the dead." Another account relates that while Asklepios was still in the womb of his mother, a raven came to Apollo with the tidings that Koronis was unfaithful to him, whereupon Apollo straightway cursed the raven, which, in consequence, was changed forever from white to black, and, hastening to Koronis, he slew her and burned her body on a pyre. Snatching the child from the midst of the flames, he took him to Cheiron, who trained him in the chase and in the mysteries of healing, whereby Asklepios became so skilful as a physician that he not only kept many men from death, but even raised to life some who had died, for instance, Kapaneus, Hippolytos, Tyndareos, Glaukos the son of Minos, and others. Zeus, however, fearful lest men, too, might learn how to revive the dead, slew Asklepios with the thunderbolt, whereupon, in reprisal, Apollo killed the Kyklopes and for this act had to make expiation by serving Admetos as a slave. The legend also tries to explain the healing means employed by Asklepios, saying that, through Athene, he secured blood from the veins of

Medousa. With that which came from her left side he destroyed men, while with that which was derived from the right he brought them back to life.

The people of Epidauros said that Asklepios was first known as Epios, but after he had healed King Askles of a grievous malady, he assumed the longer and traditional name. In Epidauros his wife was Epione, but elsewhere she was Lampetië, a daughter of Helios. Machaon, the hero-physician, was always held to be a son of Asklepios and sometimes Epione and Hygieia ("Health") were said to be his daughters.

The serpent is the constant symbol of Asklepios in both legend and worship, the burghers of a certain Epidauros in Lakonia claiming that their shrine of the god was built on a spot where a snake had disappeared beneath the earth. In his sacred precincts in the Argive Epidauros, and in those of Athens and Kos, which were offshoots of the former, the serpent was the living emblem of his presence and was thought to communicate means of healing to sufferers from disease as they slept in the holy place — the rite technically known as "incubation." [2] Asklepios was invariably attended by groups of priests who devoted themselves to surgery and other curative means, and many extant inscriptions tell of their wonderful successes. In the island of Kos in particular the priests of Asklepios laid the foundations of the modern scientific study and practice of medicine.

Asklepios in Art. — Owing to the failure of poetry to attribute any definite traits of face and form to Asklepios, the artists were thrown back upon their own ingenuity. They chose to represent him after the ideal of Zeus, but of milder countenance and of less majestic manner. He is shown seated or standing like the corresponding types of Zeus, though holding the sceptre not as a mark of might but as a staff on which to lean. The best representations of him are seen in the votive offerings of his shrine where incubation (sleep-cure) was practised.

II. ABSTRACT DIVINITIES

The same habit of thought which could clothe the mysterious operations of nature with all the features of personality could consistently treat in like manner the inscrutable processes of the mind and the qualities of things, whence we actually find the Greeks making these abstract conceptions over into divine beings. That this was not merely a late but a very early practice is demonstrated in the evident antiquity of Mnemosyne, Eunomia, and certain others of their kind in Hesiod. This entire class of divinities was treated in myth, when they were given any place at all, in the same way as were the more highly personalized nature-gods, although they were debarred from frequent appearance in this field, for temperamentally the Greek shrank from the bald literalness of their names, and some of the divinities recorded below are by nature perilously near the concrete. The list is of necessity far from complete and must be regarded as supplying little more than mere illustrations. It will be noticed that some of the names have been discussed in earlier chapters, but here we see them from another angle.

Of time: Eos, Hemera, Nyx, Chronos ("Time"; cf. "Father Time"), Hebe, Geras ("Old Age"), Kairos ("Opportunity," "Psychological Moment").

Of states of body: Hygieia, Hypnos, Thanatos, Limos ("Famine"), Laimos ("Pestilence"), Mania ("Madness").

Of states of mind: Phobos, Eleos ("Pity"), Aidos ("Modesty"), Eros, Himeros ("Longing"), Euphrosyne.

Of the spiritual faculties: Metis, Mnemosyne, Pronoia ("Forethought").

Of the virtues and vices: Arete ("Excellence" or "Virtue"), Sophrosyne ("Temperance"), Dikaiosyne ("Righteousness"), Hybris ("Offensive Presumption"), Anaideia ("Shamelessness").

Of sundry social institutions: Telete ("Rite of the Mysteries"), Litai ("Prayers"), Arai ("Curses"), Nomos ("Law"),

Dike ("Precedent"), Demos ("the People"), Eirene ("Peace"), Homonoia ("Unanimity").

To the foregoing catalogue we may add the personifications of the various phases of war and strife (e. g. Nike, "Victory") and of the several types of poetry.

III. THE ELEMENT OF CHANCE

Owing to the importance of the element of chance in legend and religious thought, it is well to treat this abstraction by itself.

Tyche. — Tyche ("Chance") was frankly the deification of the element of risk, and its relation to the plans and efforts of men to earn their daily bread and to better their conditions of life held it continually before the attention, so that men had to admit its existence as a real force. In the early days, when the Greeks had the self-reliant spirit of pioneers and a strong faith in the ability of men to bring to pass things which were not positively forbidden, Tyche received only meagre recognition, but in the later days of their religious degeneracy and enfeebled initiative they gratuitously endowed her with a power in contrast with which their own dignity as free agents entirely disappeared. Still more uncertain than the future of individuals is that of associations of individuals, and thus, from the sixth century onward, Tyche was exalted with gradually increasing frequency to the position of the goddess of the luck of the state, this development being doubtless aided in the Roman period by the influence of Fortuna.

Moira, Moirai, Ananke, Adrasteia. — Moira (or Aisa, "Fate") and the Moirai ("Fates") represented the order of chance, or, in other words, the determinative elements which seem to operate amid the vicissitudes of human life. Ethically, they imply a much healthier point of view than that implied in Tyche. In Homer, it will be remembered, Moira was an almost impersonal decree issuing from Zeus; that is, she was herself the will of Zeus, although the other gods limited her scope of action according to their respective degrees of greatness. Somewhat later than Homer she was conceived as an independent power to which gods as well as men must yield, and in this aspect she is Ananke ("Necessity"), or Adrasteia ("Inevitable").

In legend the Moirai, who were reckoned as three in number, were, appropriately, the daughters of Zeus and Themis [3] and bore the names Klotho, Lachesis, and Atropos. Plato may be following an old tradition when he states that into the ears of man Klotho sings of the present, Lachesis of the past, and Atropos of the future; and a late belief ascribed to them severally, in the order in which they have just been named, control over the birth, the life, and the death of mortals.

Nemesis. — The name of Nemesis[4] seems to have been first employed as an epithet of Artemis, intended to convey the idea that this goddess, as one who presided over birth, was also a dispenser of human lots. By the times of Homer and Hesiod, however, it had lost its character as a purely descriptive term and had become the name of a vague personality; while later it came to stand for the divinity who brought upon men retribution for their deeds and who was especially hostile to excessive human prosperity. "Pride breaks itself, and too much gained is gone." [5] We read in a fragment of the *Kypria* that Nemesis was a winged goddess who flew over land and sea and assumed the forms of many animals in order to escape the embraces of Zeus, but in the form of a swan he overtook her at Rhamnous and by her became the mother of Helen.

PLATE LIX

Nike

A winged Nike ("Victory"), clad in *chiton* and *himation*, and wearing a tongued diadem, pours out wine from an *oinochoë*, held in her right hand, into a saucer resting in the hand of an armed Greek warrior. The *kerykeion*, or *caduceus*, in the left hand of the goddess signifies that she is bringing a message of victory. From a red-figured Attic *lekythos* of the early fifth century B.C., found at Gela (*Monumenti Antichi*, xvii, Plate XIII). See p. 283.

PART III

THE MYTHOLOGY OF ANCIENT ITALY

THE MYTHOLOGY OF ANCIENT ITALY

INTRODUCTION

FOR the very good reason that the Italic mind and religious attitude were quite unlike the Greek, it is impossible to treat the mythology of the Italic peoples as we have considered that of the Greeks. Now, the mind of the Italian was not naturally curious and speculative, whence, since speculation is the motive power behind myth, the output of Italic myth was very small, and at the same time well-nigh barren of lively fancy. Furthermore, the Italian had not advanced to a stage of religious thought which would of itself favour the creation of a group of divine personalities specially adapted even for such imaginary genealogies and stories of marvellous achievement as his type of mind might be able to construct under certain circumstances. What, then, was the nature of his religion? We shall endeavour to compact a description of it into a paragraph or two.

Up to a point about midway between the animistic grade of religious thought and the stage of belief in personal divinities the Greek and the Roman seem to have developed in virtually the same way. Beyond this point, however, the lines of their progress diverged, for while the Greek mind easily and naturally emerged from animism into deism, as the moth from the chrysalis, the Roman found the utmost difficulty; and, indeed, so awkward was the metamorphosis that the great majority of the deities which it produced were and remained stunted and deformed as compared with the Greek divinities. In brief, the Roman seldom got farther than to regard the potency, or life-power, as a living will, a *numen*, as he termed it. Only the barest few of the *numina* did he endue with the many-coloured coat of personality; all others he left in the plain rustic garb of functional spirits of nature. The assignment of names to the favoured few and the establishment of their worships and priesthoods in definite localities added to the illusion of their personality in the popular mind. Although from the point of view of our classification the *numina* were scarcely gods, yet for the practical purposes of Roman private and public religion they were as much deities as were, for instance, the nobler figures of Iuppiter, Iuno, and Minerva.

By reason of the power of the gods to help or to harm it was to the best interest of the Roman to keep on good terms with them; in his own words, to secure and maintain a *pax deorum;* and, accordingly, every act of his worship was directed to this end. By rites, largely magical in character, by sacrifice, and by supplication he strove daily to ensure for himself, his family, his fields and flocks, and his state the favour of the benevolent divinities, and to avert the displeasure of the evil; but the fixed system of ritual which he evolved in a very early period so mechanized his religious thinking that he became incapable of imagining his gods as departing from the traditional conception of them, and hence was equally unable to invent myths.

In the dearth of Roman myth the Latin writers from Livius Andronicus onward were forced to draw for their literary material on the abundant store of Greek poetry, and with the poetry naturally went the Greek gods and the Greek mythology, although, in order to make the character of these beings intelligible to Roman readers, the authors had to equate or identify them with those of the accepted gods of the land whom they resembled most closely. In some instances they made use of identifications ready made in the popular belief, whence it came about that, for instance, Zeus was always represented by Iuppiter, Hera by Iuno, Artemis by Diana, and Demeter by Ceres. Practically all the myths of pan-Hellenic currency became common Roman property; only the narrowly local ones were untouched. Assuming this, we can read the

Greek myths of our preceding pages as Roman, if only we take the pains to change the names of the gods to those of their Roman equivalents.[1]

I. ETRUSCAN MYTHOLOGY

Unhappily we are unable to distinguish with exactness the Etruscan contribution to Roman religion, although Roman writers definitely labelled a few myths as from this source. According to an Etruscan cosmogony, the creator appointed twelve millenniums for the acts of creation and assigned to them severally the twelve signs of the zodiac. In the first millennium he created heaven and earth; in the second the firmament; in the third the land, sea, and lesser waters; in the fourth the sun, moon, and stars; in the fifth the creatures of air, earth, and water; and in the sixth man, whose race was to endure for the remaining six millenniums and then perish. A myth attributed the origin of the Etruscan religious system to a child named Tages, who took human form from a clod thrown up by a plough and in song delivered his holy message to a wondering throng. The nymph Begoë was said to have revealed the so-called sacred law of limitation to Arruns Veltymnius, while Mantus is recorded as the name of the Etruscan god of the underworld, and Volta as the appellation of a mythical monster.

II. NATIVE ITALIC GODS

(a) *Nature-Gods: Of the Sky, Atmosphere, and Time*

Iuppiter. — Iuppiter (Iovis, Diovis, Dius, Diespiter), the chief god of all the Italic stocks, was a personification of the sky and its phenomena, being, therefore, rightly identified with Zeus. His control over the weather and light made him of necessity the all-important divinity of a nation of shepherds and husbandmen, and his might was manifested in the thunder, lightning, and rain; in fact, legend reported him as coming to earth in bodily form with the thunderbolt. This is the origin of his epithets Fulgur ("Lightning"), Fulmen ("Thunderbolt"), and, doubtless, also of Feretrius, while as the rain-god he bears the names Pluvius, Pluvialis, and Elicius. From his lofty seat in the heavens he could behold all that happened upon earth; hence, as Terminus, he became the guardian of boundaries between properties, and, as Dius Fidius, the witness of men's fidelity to their oaths. Only a few of the Roman gods became thus moralized.

Mater Matuta. — Mater Matuta was the deity who, in the words of Lucretius,[2] "at a certain hour brings down the dawn through the tracts of air and diffuses the light of day"; but she was also a divinity of birth, and in these two capacities was likened by the Greeks to their Leukothea and Eileithyia respectively. As the former she became a goddess of the sea and of sailors, while Melikertes, or Palaimon, the son of Leukothea, was likened to the Roman Portunus ("Protector of Harbours").

The gods of the seasons were few. The explanations suggested by the ancients to account for the significance of the goddess Angerona are childish, and she seems really to have been, like Anna Perenna, a divinity of the winter solstice. As protector of plants through all their stages from blooming to fruit-bearing Vertumnus was perhaps aboriginally a god of the changing year. Ovid relates that, in the days of King Proca, Vertumnus fell in love with Pomona, a shy nymph who withdrew from the society of men to the retirement and duties of her orchard and garden, and although in many disguises he sought to make his way into her retreat, it was all in vain, until he presented himself in the form of an old woman. He then told her of his passion, but all his words could not avail to soften her heart. Only when he showed himself to her in his true likeness, as a youth of unblemished beauty, did she relent; and from that time on they were never seen apart.

PLATE LX

Genius and Lares

In the centre stands the Genius, presumably of the head of the household, in human form, while below he appears in the guise of a serpent approaching an altar to devour the offerings placed thereon. In his right hand the Genius holds a sacrificial saucer and in his left a box of incense, and on either side of him dance two Lares, each holding a *rhyton* (drinking-horn) and a small bronze pail. From a wall-painting in the House of the Vettii, Pompeii (Hermann-Bruckmann, *Denkmäler der Malerei des Altertums*, No. 48). See pp. 291, 298–99.

(b) *Nature-Gods: Of Human Life, Earth, Agriculture, and Herding*

Genius; Iuno. — If we adopt the Roman point of view, and regard the Genius of man and the Iuno of woman as functional powers originating outside of human life and employing men and women merely as fields of operation, we must place these two divinities among the nature-gods. Fundamentally Genius was the procreative power of each man and Iuno that of each woman, whence, finally, through a logical expansion the names came to stand severally for the two sexes and their respective life-interests. The ramifications of man's activities arrested the development of Genius as an individual *numen*, while the restricted sameness of woman's life intensified the individuality of Iuno. In Genius, however, was latent the germ of the man-worship of the Empire. Iuno presided over the conception of children and their development up to birth, while her Samnite epithet, Populona, marked her as the divinity who augmented the population. Her union with Iuppiter and her identification with Hera were late and greatly altered her personality.

Ceres. — Ceres and her male counterpart, Cerus (who was snuffed out early), were among the oldest of the Italic gods. Ceres was closely associated with Tellus. The purpose of all her festivals was to elicit her blessing on the crops in all their stages from seeding until harvest, and the fact that the staple grain foods were her gift to the people gave her a peculiarly plebeian standing. Myth represented her as very susceptible to offence and as prompt to punish the offender.

Tellus Mater. — Tellus, or Tellus Mater, seems to have belonged to the same ancient stratum as Ceres and to have been primevally affiliated with her. As her name implies, she was really Mother Earth, but in agriculture she was a personification of the field which receives and cherishes the seed. In time, however, she had to yield place to Ceres, as a double of the Greek Demeter, only to reappear later under the name Terra

Mater. In certain rites she was held to be a divinity of the underworld, for when the bodies of the dead were entrusted, like the seed-grain, to her care, she was simply taking back what she herself had given. In myth, she stood, of course, for Gaia (Ge).

Liber. — Liber first arose as an epithet of Iuppiter to designate the amplitude of his productive powers in the fertilization of the seed of plants and animals, but later the adjective became detached and invested with personality, the resulting divinity being then identified as Dionysos and appointed as the protector of the vine. Liber's female counterpart, Libera, was equated with Kore and was thus drawn into the circle of Ceres.

Saturnus.—From the ancient prominence of Saturnus ("the Sower"; cf. *serere*), or, in English, Saturn, Italy was often known in myth as Saturnia. The native function of Saturnus is transparent in his name, but this was gradually broadened so as to include practically all agricultural operations, his great December festival, the Saturnalia, having for its object the germination of the seed just sown, while the sickle, as his chief symbol, marked his intimate relation to harvesting. For some reason unknown to us he was given a high place in Italic myth, where he was the husband of Ops. Through his association with her he assimilated some of her chthonic traits, and, further, through her identification as Rhea, was in his turn identified with Kronos, thus coming to be exalted as the ruler of the Golden Age.

Consus and Ops. — The special province of Consus (cf. *condere*, "to store"), a purely Italic god, was the safe garnering of the fruits of the field, and the underground location of his altar at Rome is a sort of myth without words, symbolizing as it did the common custom of storing the grain in pits. His most intimate companion in cult was Ops, who seems primarily to have been the personal embodiment of a bountiful harvest, though she assumed the secondary function of protecting the private and public granaries against destruction by fire.

Mars. — The god Mars (Mavors, Marspiter, Maspiter) was known to all the primitive stocks. In his later career he was certainly the god of war, and in the Roman versions of Greek legends his name regularly replaced that of Ares, but that war was his *rôle* from the beginning is not generally admitted, for he may have been a god of vegetation and of the borderlands lying between the farmstead and the wild, and have possessed the double function of fostering the crops and herds and of defending them against the attacks of enemies from without. Just as the Greeks associated the horse and the bull with Poseidon, so the Italians variously connected the woodpecker, the ox, and the wolf with Mars.

Faunus. — No Roman god incorporated in his single person more features of terrestrial nature than did Faunus (cf. *favere*, "to favour"). There is no doubt that he had been established in the life of the people of the fold and the hamlet from a very remote age, and so familiar were they with him that they could take some of those liberties with his personality such as mythology allows. He was, their legends ran, the kindly spirit of out-of-doors who caused crop and herd to flourish and who warded off wolves, being Lupercus in this latter aspect. It was he who was the speaker of the weird prophetic voices which men heard in the forest, and late legend said that he cast his prophecies in the form of verse, and thus became the inventor of poetry. Yet there was a mischievous side to his nature as well as a serious, for he was the spirit who sent the Nightmare (Incubo). Fauna, a divinity of fertility, passed now as his wife, now as his sister.

Silvanus. — Silvanus seems to have sprung into being from the detached and divinized epithet of either Mars or Faunus, and his domain, true to his name, was the woodland. He bestowed his favour on hunter and shepherd and on all the interests of the husbandman who had won a title to his acres through clearing away the wild timber. He was himself mythologically conceived as a hunter or as an ideal gardener, and many stories of Pan were transferred to him.

Diana. — The earliest of the Italic divinities to be adopted by Rome was Diana, and her cult on the Aventine Hill was simply a transference of her cult at Aricia of Latium. The common belief of a later period that she was the same as Artemis obscured her original nature, but her affiliation at Aricia with the spring-nymph Egeria, and with Virbius, both divinities of child-birth, arouses the suspicion that her function was a similar one.

Venus. — The process which converted the native Italian Venus into a goddess of love and the Roman double of Aphrodite is very interesting. Her personality seems to have been an efflorescence of her name, which first denoted the element of attractiveness in general, then, as it narrowed, this quality in nature, and, in the end, the goddess who elaborated it. To the utilitarian Roman the chief field of her activity was the market-gardens on which the city depended for a large proportion of its food-stuffs, and it was in this capacity, no doubt, that she was recognized as the same as Aphrodite. With this identification she took over Aphrodite's attribute of love, but in so doing arrested her own development along its original lines. At an early date in Rome she was accorded special homage as the mother of Aeneas, and, later, as the divine ancestress of the Julian family, the temple of Venus Genetrix built by Julius Caesar and that of Venus and Rome constructed by Hadrian being material evidences of her high standing. Cupido became her companion in myth as Eros was that of Aphrodite.

Flora. — Flora was an ancient goddess of springtime and flowers, giving beauty and fragrance to the blossom, sweetness to honey, aroma to wine, and charm to youth. Her April festival was marked by the unstinted and varied use of flowers, and by the practice of pursuing animals often ritually associated with fertility.

PLATE LXI

1

Arethousa

The head of Arethousa may be distinguished from that of Persephone (see Plate IV, Fig. 4) in that it lacks the diadem of stalks and ears of grain. The dolphins indicate that the nymph dwells by the sea. From a decadrachm of Syracuse of the fourth century B.C. (enlarged two diameters). See p. 257.

2

Ianus Bifrons

This coin type delineates the Roman conception of the two-faced god of entrances. Each face is that of an old man with bushy hair and beard, and is in keeping with the idea recorded in Ovid that Ianus was the oldest of the gods. From a Roman bronze coin of the fourth century B.C. (G. F. Hill, *Historical Roman Coins*, Plate I, Fig. 1). See p. 297.

1

2

Fortuna. — If we follow the successive stages of Fortuna's growth, we must rank her as a nature-god. As far back as we can probe into her history, she was apparently the deification of that incalculable element which shapes the conditions of harvest, a time of great anxiety to an agricultural people, while her votaries at Praeneste believed that she controlled the destiny of women in child-birth. She was, in brief, a sort of independent predetermining force in nature. As Vergil represented her, however, she was the incorporate will of the gods, and submission to her decisions was always a moral victory. Her Greek counterpart was generally Tyche, rarely Moira.

(c) *Nature-Gods: Of the Water*

The importance of springs and streams in the life of the Italian sufficiently accounts for his belief in their individual *numina*. The *numina* of the springs appeared as kindly young goddesses gifted with song and prophecy and with the power of healing, but they were also, after a manner, sorceresses, though they used their magic to good ends. The best known of these at Rome was Iuturna who, the legends said, was the wife of Ianus and the mother of Fons ("Fountain"). The Camenae, nymphs of song and of child-birth, were known as the Roman muses, one of their number, Carmentis (or Carmenta), like a Greek Fate, singing to the new-born child its destiny. Egeria, the nymph brought in from Aricia, had gifts like those of the Camenae. The Romans imagined the *numina* of rivers to be benevolent and indulgent old men.

Neptunus. — Neptunus, as the divinity of the element of moisture, belonged to the oldest circle of the Roman gods, and only through his likeness to Poseidon did he become the lord of the sea. His nature confined the observance of his worship to the rural population, and the persistence of his festival, the Neptunalia, the purpose of which was to bring moisture to the land, into the fourth century of our era is one evidence of the tenacious power of nature-religion over the masses of the Roman people.

(d) *Nature-Gods: Of Fire, of the Underworld, and of Disease*

Volcanus. — The fire-god Volcanus was far less conspicuous than one would have expected him to be in the land of Vesuvius, and doubtless because the volcano had been quiescent for many centuries prior to 79 A.D. Although the god wore the mask of Hephaistos in the Latin renderings of Greek myth, he was by nature only partially qualified to do so. In the old Roman group of gods he was the spirit of destructive rather than of useful fire, and was reputed to be of an irascible disposition which always needed placation, whence the presence of many docks and valuable stores at Ostia led to the wide extension of his worship in that place.

Vediovis. — Left to himself, and with his imagination unprodded by the Greek spirit of wonder, the Roman gave little time to speculating on the lot of man after death. His chief interest was in the living and those yet to be born, so that one is not surprised to find his divinities of the underworld few and only vaguely outlined. The chief one was Vediovis (Veiovis, Vedius), who seems to have been given his place in the lower world largely for the reason that the logic of the Roman religious system called for a spiritual and physical opposite to Iuppiter. Little is known of him beyond the fact that he was invoked in oaths along with Tellus.

Febris. — The disease which the Romans feared the most was, of course, malaria, which was *the* fever (*febris*) *par excellence;* and so concrete and uniform were its manifestations that we utterly lose the Roman's point of view if we regard Febris, the divinity, as born of an abstraction. This holds equally true of the offshoots of Febris, Dea Tertiana and Dea Quartana, the one standing for the malarial chills which, according to our mode of reckoning, return every second day, the other for those which recur every third day.

(e) *Gods of Human Society*

Ianus. — So obscure was the origin of Ianus that the Roman poets took all manner of liberties with him, using the joint appearance of his head and of a ship on coins as data for a mythical history of this god. He was, said one of them, an aboriginal king who ruled on Mount Ianiculum, at first sharing his throne with a noble whose name was Camese, but later, when Iuppiter's divine *régime* began, being banished along with Saturnus and taking up his abode in Latium. In another account he was represented as having come to Latium from the land of the Perrhaiboians together with his sister-wife, Camese, who bore him three sons, one of them being Tiberinus, after whom the Tiber was named. The legends did not stint Ianus with wives. Besides Camese he is said to have married either the water-nymph Venilia and by her to have become the father of Canens, or the water-nymph Iuturna, who bore to him Fons (or Fontus). Again he is said to have conceived a passion for a certain divinity Carna, whom he seized in a grotto, after a long pursuit, promising to appoint her the Goddess of Hinges should she yield to him. Upon her compliance he renamed her Cardo, or Cardea ("Hinge"), and gave her the white thorn with which to banish evil from doorways.

Of all the theories to account for the origin of Ianus none is more probable than that which comprehends him as a personality gradually evolved from a private ritual of a magical order designed to drive evil influences from the doors of dwellings. "The very vagueness of this god, even with the Romans themselves, indicates that their interest was rather in the concrete values associated with the doorway and in the practical expedients necessary in guarding it." [3] As the state was simply an enlarged domestic circle, it was not unnatural that Ianus should be connected with the ancient gates or arches in the Forum which bore his name, and there, in the late Republican period, stood an image of the god with two faces, one of which was turned toward the east and the other toward the west. This intimation that his domain lay both before and behind him may have sprung from the very obvious fact that every entrance has two sides. From being a god of entrances it was not a far cry to become a deity of beginnings, and as such he was invoked at the beginning of each year, each month, and each day. The prominence of his name and of his epithet, *pater*, in ancient ceremonial formulae attests his great age.

Vesta. — By reason of her fixed character Vesta had no place in formal myth. She was the *numen* of the hearth, first of the home and then of the state, and since the functions and symbolism of the hearth never changed from century to century, neither could Vesta vary a jot or a tittle from her original conception — any alteration would have broken the thread of continuity in the religious sentiment of the Roman as a member of a family and as a citizen. In the home Vesta typified and protected the life of the family; the food in the larder, destined to be subjected to the heat of the hearth-flame, was under her care; the matron was her priestess. The Temple (or, better, the House) of Vesta in the Forum was nothing less than the home and fireside of the state, and on its hearth the six Vestal Virgins prepared sacrificial offerings in behalf of the state with food taken from the sacred larder, while the inviolability of the home and the integrity of the state were pictured in the purity of Vesta herself and of her Virgins. Her title, *mater*, was suggestive of her graciousness.

Di Penates; Lares. — Also closely connected with family life were the Di Penates, the numerous divinities of the *penus*, or larder, though they were so dimly conceived that they were endued with neither sex nor personality, their plurality being doubtless derived from the variety and the changing character of the stock of food-stuffs. From the time of Julius Caesar and Augustus the mythical idea of the Trojan origin of the Penates prevailed. The Lares are linked with the Penates in popular phrase, jointly constituting a synonym for household property, but at the outset, apparently, there was only one Lar to a household, and that the protecting *numen* of the allotment of land on which the actual building stood. At length its function was broadened so as to include the house, and in Imperial times the name became pluralized and acquired a character as a synonym of house. When Ovid wrote that the Lares were the children of the outraged Lara, or Dea Tacita, and Mercury, he was indulging his fancy; as a matter of fact, they were sometimes held to be the Roman counterparts of the Kouretes, the Korybantes, or the Daktyloi.

Minerva. — Any complexity there was in the personality of the static divinity, Minerva (Menerva), was due to the influence of Athene, with whom she was identified, for in her primitive estate she seems to have been merely the goddess of the few and simple arts of an undeveloped rustic community. The Romans probably got her from Falerii prior to its fall in 241 B.C. and after the institution of the so-called Calendar of Numa, and established her in a temple in the Aventine as the patroness of the crafts and the guilds. Her inclusion in the Capitoline triad beside Iuppiter and Iuno may have resulted from a conscious attempt to reproduce in Rome a group like that of Zeus, Hera, and Athene.

(f) *Abstract Gods*

The inelastic character of the Roman's religious thinking is nowhere more clearly brought out than in the circle of his abstract divinities, for Pavor ("Panic"), Pax ("Peace"), Concordia ("Harmony"), Spes ("Hope"), and the like, were each fixed personalities of one trait and one trait only, a circumstance which naturally shut them out from narrative myth. The field for which they were by nature suited was that of stereotyped symbolism, and only so far as an accepted religious symbol is a myth may they be considered as mythological personages. They and their several symbols are too numerous for us to discuss here.

(g) *Momentary and Departmental Gods*

The great host of the Roman's momentary and departmental divinities, commonly known to scholars as *Sondergötter*, seem at first glance to be an argument which disproves the lack of pliability in the Roman's habits of religious thought. As a matter of fact, however, they confirm the reality of this characteristic, for as a class they are nothing more than an aggregate of the most simply conceived units which sustain to one another the same immediate relations that exist between the practical interests and activities of a primitive people. Some of these divinities, such as Messor ("Harvester"), Convector ("Garnerer"), and Saritor ("Weeder"), spiritualize human acts, while others spiritualize certain processes of nature which are conspicuous either in themselves or in their results. A chosen few of this latter order will be ample for the purpose of illustration: Seia, Segesta, Nodutus, Patelana, and Matura are *numina* that preside successively over the sowing and sprouting of the corn, the formation of the joints on its stem, the unfolding of leaf and flower, and, finally, the ripening of straw and ear. Similarly each stage of a child's growth from conception to adult stature is guarded by a *numen* whose function is transparent in its commonly accepted name. In brief, no natural process of moment to the Roman's well-being fails to receive recognition as a divinity.

III. GODS OF FOREIGN ORIGIN

Apollo. — Apollo was from the beginning frankly a loan from the Greek world. He was brought to Rome in the fifth century by way of Cumae as a god of healing to put an end to a great plague which threatened to exterminate the populace, and in his train came the books of the Sibylline oracles. In the Augustan age the average Roman knew him only as the god of poetry and music, a *rôle* which was first assigned him in

PLATE LXII

Magna Mater

The image of Kybele, or, as known to the Romans, Magna Mater, is seated on a throne placed in a car drawn by lions. On her head is the so-called mural crown, on the back of which an end of her *himation* has been so caught up as to hang behind her like a veil. In her lap she holds a *tympanon* on edge. This group is commemorative of an annual Roman ritual in which the image of the Great Mother was conveyed in her car from her shrine in the city to a neighbouring stream, where both were ceremonially bathed. From a bronze of the second century A.D., found in Rome and now in the Metropolitan Museum of Art, New York (*photograph*). See pp. 273 ff., 303–04.

Rome, when translations of Greek literary works began to attain popularity. Augustus chose him as the divine patron of his *régime* and dedicated to him a beautiful temple on the Palatine.

Aesculapius. — The outbreak of a pestilence at Rome in 292 B.C. turned the Romans to a consultation of the Sibylline books, where they discovered directions enjoining them to send a deputation of citizens to the healing shrine of Asklepios at Epidauros, the envoys bringing back a serpent as a living symbol of the god, and at the same time instructions for establishing the new worship. It happened that when their ship reached the city, the serpent leaped overboard and swam to the island in the Tiber, where the new shrine was built, the god's name being given the Latin form of Aesculapius. When Salus, originally an abstract divinity of well-being in general, became recognized as the same as Hygieia ("Health"), the matter-of-fact Roman mind made her the official consort of the new god of healing.

Mercurius. — In the early fifth century, on the occasion of a failure of crops which necessitated the importation of foreign food-stuffs, the Romans borrowed one phase of the character of Hermes, and, exalting it to the dignity of godhead, used it to protect the maritime routes which the grain ships must follow. Naturally, this phase was the favour which Hermes accorded to trade and traders, and Mercurius, the name of the new god, connected as it is with the Latin words *merces* ("merchandise") and *mercator* ("tradesman"), served as a permanent register of his function. While Mercurius always took the place of Hermes in the Romanized Greek legends, his character in cult remained unaltered through the centuries. In art he was generally distinguished by the chief symbols of Hermes — the caduceus, the pouch, and the winged hat.

Castor and Pollux. — The worship of Kastor and Polydeukes, as Castor and Pollux, came to Italy at so early a date that when the Romans accepted it, apparently from Tusculum, they did so under the impression that it was of Italic origin; but the outstanding features of these divinities at Rome — their association with horses and lakes, and their power to give help in time of need — were brought with them from Greece. In myth it is recorded that they suddenly appeared at the battles of Lake Regillus, Pydna, and Verona just in time to bring victory to the Roman cause. After the battle of Lake Regillus they were seen to water their horses in the basin of the fountain of Iuturna, and on this spot the citizens erected a shrine known as the Temple of the Castors, or the Temple of Castor.

FIG. 11. MARRIAGE OF IUNO AND HERCULES

Zeus, seated on an altar-like throne between Iuno and Hercules, draws the two divinities toward one another, thus sanctifying their union. From the design incised on the back of an Etruscan bronze mirror of the fourth century B.C., now in the Metropolitan Museum of Art, New York.

Hercules.—Under the name of Hercules the Greek Herakles was admitted into the Roman family of gods as though he were a native Italic divinity. At his very ancient altar, the *Ara Maxima*, near the Forum Boarium, or the cattle-market, he was worshipped as a god powerful to aid commerce and other practical pursuits, whence, accordingly, tithes of profits in trade and of the booty of war were dedicated to him.

The popularity which Herakles enjoyed in Greece, owing to his unparalleled ability to bring things to pass, so inspired the Roman imagination that almost out of whole cloth it manufactured mythological forms to glorify the adopted Hercules. Not only did he have an intrigue with a certain Acca Larentia, but he was the husband now of Iuno, now of Evander's daughter, now of Rhea, now of Fauna; and by the last three in this order he became the father of Pallas, Aventinus, and Latinus. Among his mighty feats were numbered his retention of the waters of Lake Avernus in their basin by means of a dam, and his slaughter of some threatening giants at Cumae. When he was returning eastward through Italy with the cattle of Geryoneus, we are told, some of his herd were stolen by a native shepherd named Cacus (apparently an aboriginal fire-god) and driven backward into a cave; but, although at first puzzled by the inverted tracks, Hercules at length succeeded in locating and recovering the animals and in killing the thief. He then made himself known to Evander, an Arkadian refugee ruling on the Palatine, who received him with unbounded hospitality and dedicated to him the *Ara Maxima*, the ceremonies observed at this altar by Evander becoming the model of those used in the worship of Hercules through succeeding centuries.

Dis Pater. — Dis Pater — also known as Orcus — and Proserpina were both Greek, the name Dis being simply a translation of Πλούτων ("Wealthy") and that of Orcus a faulty transliteration of Ὅρκος, the "oath" sworn in the name of Hades, while Proserpina is obviously an adaptation of Persephone. To the Roman Dis Pater was the chief god of the lower world in his function as king of the departed, and Orcus was the same deity in his *rôle* as the inexorable reaper, or, occasionally, as that divinity who takes pity on suffering mortals and gently bears them away to their long rest, the nature of Orcus being so readily grasped by the Roman mind, in its slavery to fact, that he was the more popular of the two forms.

Magna Mater. — In the midst of the Romans' despair of receiving help against Hannibal from their accepted gods they turned, in obedience to a Sibylline oracle, to the Asiatic Magna Mater, the "Great Mother" of the gods. With the permission of Attalos of Pergamon they brought to Rome from Phrygia the meteoric stone which embodied her and then established a festival for the re-enactment of the rites which characterized her worship in the east. She accomplished the purpose for which she had been brought and drove Hannibal out of Italy, but in spite of his gratitude to her, the sedate Roman never became thoroughly accustomed to the wild abandon of her votaries.

IV. MYTHS OF THE EARLY DAYS OF ROME

The Aeneid of Vergil. — In their national epics Naevius and Ennius had made the glory of the city their central interest and had popularized the idea that the founders of Rome were of Trojan stock. Vergil took over these motives, and, by injecting into them his own deep love of his land and his broodings on the life and destiny of man, and by lavishing on them his chastened poetical skill, produced the greatest of all Roman epics, the *Aeneid*, which tells the story of the wanderings of Trojan Aeneas.

Aeneas (Greek Aineias), as we have read, was the son of Anchises and Venus (i. e. Aphrodite). Amid the confusion attendant on the sack of Troy, he made his way with his father and little son, Iulus, to the shelter of the wooded heights near the city, and there gathered about him a number of fugitives, whom he led in making preparations to sail away to a strange land and found a new home. After many busy weeks they set out, first crossing to Thrace and then steering southward to Delos, where, at the shrine of Apollo, they were bidden by the oracle to seek the motherland of their ancestors and there make their abode. Believing that this referred to Crete, Aeneas led his followers thither, but after the little colony had suffered many misfortunes he was warned in a dream to establish it instead in the western land of Hesperia (i. e. Italy). In the quest of this country he again set sail with his followers, and many were the vicissitudes of their long voyage. They came successively to the island of the Harpies, to the home of Helenus and Andromache on the coast of Epirus, and to the land of the Cyclops, where they saw the blinded Polyphemus. In an endeavour to avoid Scylla and Charybdis, they hugged the southern shores of Sicily with the intention of doubling the western extremity of the island, but Iuno espied them, and, unable to forget that they belonged to the Trojan race which she hated, roused a great storm that drove them on the coast of Carthage.

At this time Carthage was ruled by a Tyrian queen named Dido, who welcomed the fugitives into her court, entertaining them for many months as though they were a company of kings, and at her request Aeneas told the story of the fall of his city and of his perilous voyage from land to land in his search for a home. His personal charms won her love, and she offered to share her kingdom with him, but when, weary of wandering longer and despairing of finding his destined land, Aeneas was on the point of yielding to her passionate importunities, Iuppiter, through Mercury, roused him from his lethargy and turned his face once more toward the ships and the sea.

Re-embarking, the Trojans sailed northward and under the protection of Neptune reached the shores of Hesperia near Cumae, the home of the Sibyl. Here, like Odysseus in Kimmeria, Aeneas made the descent into Hades and saw many dire monsters and the shadowy troops of the dead. After conversing with the shades of some whom he had known in life, he turned to make his way upward to the light, his path leading him through Elysium, where he found the shade of his father, Anchises, who had died since the departure from Troy. By him he was led into the spacious Vale of Forgetfulness and was shown the vast assemblage of souls that were waiting to be implanted in some human body and given life upon earth, while Anchises also revealed to him the trials which he had yet to experience in establishing his colony in

Italy and the glories of the great nation into which the exiles were destined to grow. Pondering these things in his heart, Aeneas pursued his way back to earth.

From Cumae Aeneas sailed northward until he cast anchor in the mouth of the Tiber off the coast of Latium at a time when the king of this country was Latinus, the son of Faunus and a grandson of Saturn. Recognizing in Aeneas the man who, according to a prophecy, was to be the husband of his only daughter, Lavinia, he entered into a political alliance with him and promised to make him his son-in-law, thereby annulling Lavinia's betrothal to Turnus, the king of the neighbouring Rutulians. Through the interference of the implacable Iuno this led to a long war between Turnus and Latinus, but though the latter was killed in one of the early struggles, his forces, aided by Aeneas and his men, succeeded in winning a victory. Turnus, defeated but not discouraged, called to his assistance Mezentius, the Etruscan king, and to such an extent did he threaten the supremacy of the Trojans that the latter associated themselves with a band of Greek colonists who, under the leadership of Evander and his son Pallas, were living on the hills destined to be included in the city of Rome. In the conflicts that ensued, Pallas was slain by Turnus, and, later, Mezentius and Turnus fell at the hand of Aeneas, the Trojans achieving, through the death of this last foe, a victory which gave them undisputed possession of the land. At this point the narrative of the *Aeneid* ends, leaving the reader to infer that the nuptials of Aeneas and Lavinia were promptly consummated.

Events subsequent to those of the Aeneid. — After his marriage, Aeneas founded in Latium a new city which he called Lavinium after his wife, and when he died a short time later, his subjects, regarding him as a god, gave him the title of Iuppiter Indiges. About thirty years subsequent to the founding of Lavinium, Ascanius, the son whom Lavinia bore to Aeneas, withdrew a portion of its population and established

PLATE LXIII

Romulus and Remus

This archaic Italian bronze is commonly interpreted as representing the she-wolf suckling Romulus and Remus in the wild lands near the Tiber; it may have originally referred, however, to other legendary characters who were said to have been similarly reared. From a bronze in the Conservatory Museum, Rome (Brunn–Bruckmann, *Denkmäler griechischer und römischer Sculptur*, No. 318). See p. 307.

the colony of Alba Longa, over which he and his descendants ruled for several successive generations.

At length a quarrel arose between Numitor and Amulius, two brothers in the direct line of descent, as to which of them should reign, and Amulius, the younger and less scrupulous, getting the upper hand, banished his brother, and, in order to wipe out that branch of the family, forced his niece, Rea Silvia, to take the vows of a Vestal. But his wicked designs were frustrated by destiny, for the god Mars looked with favour on the maiden, and by him she became the mother of twin boys, Romulus and Remus. When Amulius learned of their birth, he cruelly had them set adrift in a basket on the flooded Tiber, but when the water subsided, they were left on dry land and were found and nursed by a she-wolf. As it happened, the king's shepherd, Faustulus, came across them in the wild lands and taking them to his home reared them as his own sons. When they had become men, they learned of their relationship to Amulius and of his wicked deeds, and, accordingly, with a band of youths they attacked him in his palace, slew him, and restored the kingdom of Alba Longa to their grandfather, Numitor. Unable to sever their connexions with the locality where they had spent their boyhood, they jointly founded a new city there, but when it became necessary to decide the question as to which of them should rule, they fell to quarrelling, until finally, in an outburst of anger, Romulus killed Remus, and, now without a rival, assumed the title and the powers of king. To perpetuate his own name he called his city Rome.

APPENDIX

APPENDIX

I. SURVIVALS OF ANCIENT GREEK DIVINITIES AND MYTHS IN MODERN GREECE

IN 1910 Mr. J. C. Lawson published at Cambridge a book entitled *Modern Greek Folklore and Ancient Greek Religion*, basing his treatise mainly on his own investigations, yet also taking into account those of his predecessors in the field, Polites, Hahn, Schmidt, Bent, and others. In undertaking his task he was more timely than he knew, anticipating as he did by only a small margin of years both the Balkan War and the present European War. In view of the rapidly changing conditions of life and thought in the peninsula since 1912, no one can entertain a doubt that Mr. Lawson has gathered together, just before it is too late, certain popular beliefs of undeniable antiquity which are of incalculable importance to the student of comparative religion in general and to the student of the ancient Greek religion in particular. It is generally regretted, however, that his book lacks the happy *multum in parvo* which would have made it more useful to scholars and would have ensured it a wider circle of lay readers; his prolix discussion, for instance, of Kallikantzaroi, and the protracted study of *revenants* among the Slavonic stocks, are, to say the least, *ennuyeux* as well as of doubtful profit, even for those thoroughly interested in such themes. Nevertheless, we overlook these faults in recognition of the true worth of the volume, and in the paragraphs which follow we shall present a summary of those features of the book which reflect most clearly the principal gods and myths discussed in our own study.

The objection is frequently urged that the strong Slavic strain in the population of modern Greece precludes the possibility of differentiating, with any degree of certainty, the purely Greek elements in the belief of the common people from those factors which have their origin in other sources. Mr. Lawson's reply to this is very convincing. He points out[1] that "even in the centre of the Peloponnese where the Slavonic element has probably been strongest, the pure Greek type is not wholly extinct," and also that in many of the islands the population is admittedly of an almost unmixed Greek descent. The probability of the continuity of Greek tradition, at least in certain districts, is therefore very strong. At any rate "the exact proportion of Slavonic and of Hellenic blood in the veins of the modern Greeks is not a matter of supreme importance."

Only in a few localities, notably in Crete, does any form of the name of Zeus survive, but the god still lives under the title *Θεός* ("God"), a title so conveniently equivocal that the Christian can use it without heresy and at the same time square perfectly with the ancient pagan belief. For instance, the modern Greek says, *βρέχει ὁ Θεός* ("God rains"), or, *ὁ Θεὸς ρίχνει νερό* ("God is throwing water"), just as the ancient said, *Ζεὺς ὕει* ("Zeus rains"). When it thunders, the modern exclaims, *βροντοῦν τὰ πέταλα ἀπὸ τ' ἄλογο τοῦ Θεοῦ* ("the hoofs of God's horse are resounding"), an expression which instantly calls to mind the story of Pegasos in the stables of Olympos or harnessed to the rolling car of Zeus. The lightning is God's peculiar prerogative and at times is even employed as an instrument of vengeance on offending mortals or devils as on the Titans and Salmoneus of old.

Poseidon survives in function and attribute only, though he can be identified as the divinity with the trident alluded to in a story of Zakynthos which Mr. Lawson[2] borrows from Bernhard Schmidt. "A king who was the strongest man of his time made war on a neighbour. His strength lay in three hairs on his breast. He was on the point of crushing his foes when his wife was bribed to cut off the hairs, and he with thirteen companions was taken prisoner. But the hairs began to grow again, and so his enemies threw him and his companions into a pit. The others were killed by the fall, but he being thrown in last, fell upon them and was unhurt. Over the pit his enemies then raised a mound. He found however in the pit a dead bird, and having fastened its wings to his hands flew up and carried away mound and all with him. Then he soared high in the air until a storm of rain washed away the clay that held the feathers to his hands, and he fell into the sea. 'Then from out the sea came the god thereof (*ὁ δαίμονας τῆς θάλασσας*) and struck him with a three-pronged fork (*μία πειροῦνα μὲ τρία διχάλια*)' and changed him into a dolphin until such time as he should find a maiden ready to be his wife. The dolphin after some time saved a ship-wrecked king and his daughter, and the princess by way of reward took him for her husband and the spell was broken." This story contains clear reminiscences of Nisos and Ikaros as well as of the ancient god of the sea.

To the Greek of today the Archangel Michael is as Hermes to the pre-Christian Greek, being the psychopomp, the divine escort of souls to the afterworld, which is still popularly located in the heart of earth. In the Maina, at the southern extremity of the Peloponnese, the belief prevails that, with drawn sword in hand, Michael keeps sentry on the mouths of the great cavern of Tainaros, which is still the best known approach to the underworld.

The character and functions of Dionysos are transferred to Saint Dionysios in a legend told in many places. "Once upon a time Saint Dionysios was on his way to Naxos: and as he went he espied a small plant which excited his wonder. He dug it up, and because the sun was hot sought wherewith to shelter it. As he looked about, he saw the bone of a bird's leg, and in this he put the plant to keep it safe. To his surprise the plant began to grow, and he sought again a larger covering for it. This time he found the leg-bone of a lion, and as he could not detach the plant from the bird's leg, he put both together in that of the lion. Yet again it grew and this time he found the leg-bone of an ass and put plant and all into that. And so he came to Naxos. And when he came to plant the vine — for the plant was in fact the first vine — he could not sever it from the bones that sheltered it, but planted them all together. Then the vine grew and bore grapes and men made wine and drank thereof. And first when they drank they sang like birds, and when they drank more they grew strong as lions, and afterwards foolish as asses."[3] A similar popular identification of this beneficent saint with Dionysos is also to be inferred from the fact that the road which skirts the south side of the Athenian Acropolis and the ancient theatre of Dionysos is at present known as the street of Saint Dionysios.

Of all the survivals of the greater goddesses, the most conspicuous is Demeter, who lives on in three forms. In one of these she retains her agrarian relations, but has changed her sex and taken on the name of Saint Demetrios, whereas at Eleusis she has well maintained her old character under the name of Saint Demetra. There is a popular myth concerning the saint, which, in spite of its many contaminations of ancient and mediaeval elements, is distinctly reminiscent of the sad wanderings of Demeter in her search for the lost Persephone. Along with Aphrodite and Pyrrha, Demeter contributes traits to the modern Goddess of the Sea and Earth. This hybrid divinity, the story runs, drowned all mankind by sending a flood upon the earth as a punishment of human sin, but on the subsidence of the waters she created a new race by sowing stones.

In Aitolia, the land of Atalante, the huntress Artemis survives as *ἡ κυρὰ Κάλω* ("Lady Kalo"), a title which seems to be more than a mere echo of the divine Kalliste and her mythic double, Kallisto. In some localities, however, Artemis, like Demeter, has gone over to the opposite sex and is now known as Saint Artemidoros, who, in his capacity as special patron of weakling children, is plainly the direct successor of the ancient *Ἄρτεμις παιδοτρόφος*.

At Eleusis Aphrodite (*ἡ κυρὰ 'φροδίτη*) has become the beautiful daughter of Saint Demetra, although she is also associated with Daphni and the heights of Corinth, at both of which places she had shrines in ancient times, while the people of Zakynthos still know her as the mother of Eros (Ἔρωτας). The chaste Athene, on the other hand, survives only in the recollection that the Parthenon was at one time converted into a church of the Blessed Virgin.

Although the Nereids were to the ancient Greeks a lesser order of divinities, they are perhaps the chiefest in the ill-co-ordinated pantheon of the modern. Their collective name, Νεράϊδες, appears in numerous dialectic forms, and this term, like the ancient designation Νύμφαι, is broadly inclusive of all types of female spirits of the wild — of water, wood, mountain, spring, and stream. The presence of the Nereids is suspected everywhere in the great out-of-doors, and they are conceived as "women half-divine yet not immortal, always young, always beautiful, capricious at best, and at their worst cruel."[4] In some districts they have borrowed from the satyrs the feet of goats or of asses. Human beings and animals alike are liable to fall under their spells, and like Thetis and her kindred folk of the sea they have the power of transforming themselves at pleasure. The Nereids of the springs sometimes steal children as the nymphs of old carried off Hylas, and when they pass over the land, their paths are marked by whirlwinds. So close are they still to the lives of the common people that they are believed to consort with men and to bear them children.

The grim grey ferryman Charon is now known as Charos, or, less frequently, Charondas, but in the process of centuries he has been almost utterly despoiled of his craft and oar, and, as the god of death, has assumed the sceptre of the underworld, Hades being no longer a person, but a place whither Charos receives the souls of the departed. Associated with Charos are his wife Charissa, or Charondissa, a merely nominal female counterpart, and a three-headed snake, although according to a Macedonian story, his animal companion is a three-headed dog, which can be none other than the hell-hound Kerberos. There exist only sporadic traces of the old custom of placing a coin in the mouth of a corpse as passage-money due to Charon. The prominent place occupied by Charos in the thought of the modern Greek suggests that his prototype was a much more important personage in the popular mythology of the ancient than the literature would lead one to believe, and it may be that among the rank and file of the people Charon, rather than Hades, was the Lord of the Dead.

The most monstrous of the mythical creatures living in the imagination of the modern Hellenes are the Kallikantzaroi, whose name, like that of the Nereids, appears in many dialectic forms, and is derived, Lawson believes and takes great pains to demonstrate, from that of the Centaurs. Be this as it may, at least a part of the bestial habits of the Kallikantzaroi have been drawn from the Centaurs. They are divided into two classes, according as they are of more than or less than human size, those of the former category being repulsive to look upon and generally malevolent, while those of the second type are given to frolic and mischief and are harmless to men, though not to animals.

In the faith of the populace the Moirai, or Fates, still possess a very real vitality and are endowed with a large measure of their primitive powers. In a story current in a certain district of Epeiros they are three in number, the first of whom spins the thread which determines the length of each human life, the second accords good fortune, and the third evil fortune. They are regarded as inhabiting caves and even artificially wrought openings in the sides of hills, such as the rock-dwellings in the Hill of the Muses at Athens. Women rather than men are their most constant votaries, matrons generally consulting them in reference to motherhood, and maidens in regard to matrimony. Offerings are made to them with the object of winning their favour and of influencing their decrees, which are inalterable when once they have been issued.

Pan is not yet dead, ancient legend to the contrary, and Lawson[5] gives the epitome of a story treating of him taken from Schmidt's collection of folk-tales. "Once upon a time a priest had a good son who tended goats. One day 'Panos' gave him a kid with a skin of gold. He at once offered it as a burnt-offering to God, and in answer an angel promised him whatever he should ask. He chose a magic pipe which should make all his hearers dance. So no enemy could come near to touch him. The king however sent for him, and the goatherd, after making the envoys dance more than once, voluntarily let himself be taken. The king then threw him into prison, but he had his flute still with him, and when he played even houses and rocks danced, and fell and crushed all save him and his. 'The whole business,' concludes the story, 'was arranged by Panos to cleanse the world somewhat of evil men.' . . . If the tale be a piece of genuine tradition [i. e. not a scholastic revival], the conclusion of it is remarkable. The moral purpose ascribed to the deity seems to indicate a loftier conception of him than that which is commonly found in ancient art and literature."

II. SURVIVALS OF DIVINITIES AND MYTHS OF THE ETRUSCANS AND ROMANS IN THE ROMAGNOLA

Although Charles Godfrey Leland's book, *Etrusco-Roman Remains*, first appeared as long ago as 1892, it is still the best compilation of the modern survivals of any ancient Italian religion. It must, however, be used with great caution. In the first place, it treats merely of one small district in the north of Italy, the Tuscan Romagna, or Romagnola, whose inhabitants speak a rude form of the Bolognese dialect, so that one must refrain from applying the author's remarks and deductions to the whole Italian people of today. In the next place, Leland was not a scholar in the best sense, for his knowledge of the ancient religion and mythology was only superficial, and his judgements are, consequently, very far from safe. His book is written throughout in a journalistic style, intimate and spirited, but careless and uncritical. Nevertheless, Leland must be given credit for having been an enthusiastic and enterprising investigator, and for having shown a remarkable faculty in winning the confidence of the simple but suspicious folk of the Romagnola and in inducing them to yield to him the secrets of *la vecchia religione*, whence scholars should be grateful to him for blazing a trail for them through a wilderness hitherto almost unknown. It is to be hoped, as Professor W. Warde Fowler says, that the pioneer work of Leland will lead some really qualified investigator to undertake a study in Italian survivals similar to that made by Lawson in the vague traces of Greek myths still existing in modern times.

The religions of the Etruscans and the Romans appear today merely as *disjecta membra*, and even when the divinities can be recognized, they have lost the sharp definition of character and function which distinguished them of old, because of the utter disappearance of some traits and through the obscuration of others. An explanation may be readily seen if one reflects that this *vecchia religione*, or "old religion," is really much less a religion than a system of magic, a *stregería*, as indeed it is frankly called by the people whom it serves, the tendency of magic being to narrow down the functions of divinities as far as possible.

In name Iuppiter is dead, but his prerogative of control over the phenomena of lightning, thunder, and hail is still held by the great *folletto* ("spirit") Tinia, who cannot well be other than Tina (or Tinia), the head of the Etruscan pantheon, and the people dread this spirit's power of destruction on home and field and flock as their primitive ancestors feared Iuppiter and Tina. Terminus, the god of boundaries, born of an epithet of Iuppiter, survives under the name of Sentiero, the spirit of the boundary-stone, and those who wantonly remove such landmarks expose themselves to the vindictive attacks of the Sentieri.

In Jano with his two heads, one human and the other animal, we may easily recognize the ancient Ianus *bifrons* of the Forum and the coins, and Jano's function of presiding over chance is simply a natural development of Ianus's oversight of incipient undertakings.

Maso, "a very great *folletto*" who protects the crops, may derive his name and office from those of the primitive Mars, who is believed by many to have been a deity of the fields and marchlands before war became his special sphere of operations.

There can be no doubt that Fanio is the successor of Faunus in the latter's *rôle* of the practical joker of the woodland sprites. Fanio suddenly comes on peasants in the thickets, frightening them out of their wits and laughing at the consternation he has caused, while at weddings he often anticipates the bridegroom in his embraces, and when the young husband bursts into a rage, he interrupts him with a laugh, saying:

> "Who am I? — if you would know,
> I'm the spirit Fanio!
> What in life once gave me bliss,
> Pleases me as much as this;
> And I think that thanks are due
> Unto me for helping you!"[6]

As Faunus had Silvanus for his double, so Fanio has Silvanio, who is good-natured, but very sensitive to offence. He is the special bogey of the charcoal-burners, whose piles of wood he scatters when moved by caprice so to do.

The Lassi, or Lassie, as spirits of ancestors who are heard or seen in a house after the death of a member of the family, must surely be in origin the Lares (the Lasa of the Arval Brethren). They are regarded as both male and female. Larunda, the mythical mother of the Lares Compitales, is now Laronda, the spirit of the barracks, who manifests a special fondness for soldiers.

The two peculiarly Etruscan divinities, Tages and Begoë, reappear in Tago and Bergoia. Tago, who remains a *spirito bambino* and is invoked to bring healing to afflicted children, is said to emerge from the ground at times and predict the future. Bergoia retains Begoë's power over the thunder and the lightning, but seems to have lost her gift of augury, although this diminution of her power is offset by her ability to assume human form and thus mingle with men and women.

Of the deities which to the ancient Romans were frankly Greek a few are still found in forms not difficult to recognize. Aplu (cf. the Etruscan Aplu, Aplun, Apulu) possesses not only traits of his original, Apollo, but also some borrowed from Artemis. "Aplu is the most beautiful of all the male spirits. He is also a spirit of music, and when any one would become a good hunter, or good musician, or a learned man — *un uomo dotto e di talento* — he should repeat this:

'Aplu, Aplu, Aplu!
Thou who art so good and wise,
So learned and talented,
Aplu, Aplu, Aplu!
Thou who art so good
And through all the world renowned;
And spoken of by all,
Aplu, Aplu, Aplu!
Even a spirit should be generous,
Granting us fortune and talent.
Aplu, Aplu, Aplu!
I (therefore) pray thee give me
Fortune and talent!'"[7]

The knavish and nimble Mercurius is represented in the Romagnola by Téramó (Etruscan Turms). He is not only notorious as a deceiver of innocent maidens, but is also — and primarily — the friend of thieves, traders, and messengers; in fact, he is himself a *spirito messagiero* who can flit with news from place to place in the twinkling of an eye. A constant companion of his, Boschet by name, may be in origin a form of Apollo.

The spirit of the vines is no longer Liber, but Faflon (Etruscan Fufluns, Fuflunu), who is probably the equivalent of Dionysos. At the vintage he often scatters the gathered grapes, and if the vintagers become angry at his pranks, he utterly destroys the fruit; but if they take his mischief good-naturedly, he puts the grapes back in the baskets. Leland thus renders into English a prayer offered to Faflon for a good vintage:

"Faflon, Faflon, Faflon!
Oh, listen to my prayer.
I have a scanty vintage,
My vines this year are bare;
Oh, listen to my prayer!
And put, since thou canst do so,
A better vintage there!

"Faflon, Faflon, Faflon!
Oh, listen to my prayer!
May all the wine in my cellar
Prove to be strong and rare,
And good as any grown,
Faflon, Faflon, Faflon!"[8]

Pano, undoubtedly the ancient Pan, is a whimsical spirit who favours the crops in their growth, or, if so minded, beats them down with a high wind.

Orcus, of the nether world, now lives in the person of Orco, who, in the thought of the people, was once a great wizard.

The functions and attributes of the goddesses of the old mythology have become much attenuated in the gradual process of transmission to their modern descendants. Esta is surely Vesta, although her office is the converse of that of her original, for "when a light is suddenly and mysteriously extinguished or goes out apparently of its own accord, especially when two lovers are sitting together, it is commonly said in jest that 'Esta did it.'"[9]

Through their kinship with Hekate, Diana and Artemis (the latter under the amplified epithet of Artemisia) have entirely gone over to the realm of witchcraft and goblinism, the first being now more potent for evil than Satan himself, while the second has become a vampire who sucks the blood of the newly buried dead.

The combined functions of Aphrodite, Venus, Mater Matuta, and Aurora (Eos) are represented by a group of divinities who cannot easily be distinguished except in name, and even in this respect there is a certain overlapping. They are Turanna (Etruscan Turan), apparently to be connected historically with Téramó (cf. the association of Aphrodite and Hermes), Tesana (Etruscan Thesan), Alpena (Etruscan Alpan), Albina, and La Bella Marta (Mater Matuta). Exceptional beauty, connexion with the dawn, and interest in human love characterize them all in varying degrees.

Floria presents in her single person a contamination of Flora and Pomona. None of the goddesses has changed less than Carmenta, for under her ancient name she is still besought to grant motherhood to the barren and to render aid in child-birth. Feronia is generally regarded by mythologists as being originally a spring-nymph, but now the people of the Romagnola conceive her as a spirit who wanders about the country in disguise and who haunts market places. To those who receive her hospitably she is kind and generous, but those who neglect her she requites by casting evil spells on their children and domestic animals, this belief being very possibly based on conceptions of Feronia which have failed to find their way into the ancient literature. Indeed, it may well be that many, or even most, of the traits of the divinities whom Leland has rescued from oblivion were possessions of these same divinities as they lived in the religious fancy of the common people of ancient Rome and Italy.

NOTES

NOTES

The complete titles and descriptions of the works cited in the Notes will be found in the Bibliography.

INTRODUCTION TO THE GREEK MYTHS

1. Cf. W. G. Sumner, *Folkways*, Boston, 1907, *passim*.

2. For extended discussions of the nature and development of primitive religion special recommendation may be made of Marett, *The Threshold of Religion;* King, *The Development of Religion;* S. A. Cook, "The Evolution of Primitive Thought," in *Essays and Studies presented to William Ridgeway*, pp. 375 ff.

3. Gruppe, *Gr. Myth.*, p. 1061; cf. A. B. Cook, *Zeus*, i. 9–14.

4. Murray, *Four Stages of Gr. Rel.*, p. 99.

5. Gruppe, p. 989.

6. S. A. Cook, *The Found. of Rel.*, p. 17.

7. *Republic*, 377A ff.

8. ll. 451 ff.

9. The question whether Homer was one or many does not affect the influence of the Homeric poems.

10. *Amores*, III. vi. 17–18 (as translated by E. K. Rand, in *Harvard Essays on Classical Subjects*, Boston, 1912).

11. Lang, *Custom and Myth*, p. 21.

PART I

Chapter I

1. Milton, *Paradise Lost*, vii. 211–12.

2. F. Solmsen, in *Indogermanische Forschungen*, xxx. 35, note 1 (1912), claims ancient lexical authority for regarding the name Τιτήν as an early Greek word for "king." A. B. Cook (*Zeus*, i. 655) accepts the explanation. While the present writer is ready to admit that the word once had this meaning, he is strongly inclined to believe that in origin it was non-Greek, possibly Semitic.

3. E. S. Bouchier, *Life and Letters in Roman Africa*, Oxford, 1913, p. 82.

4. Milton, *Paradise Lost*, vi. 211–14.

5. Preface to the *Prometheus Unbound.*

6. *Prometheus Unbound*, Act I.

7. A. B. Cook (*Zeus*, i. 325–30) regards Prometheus as essentially a god of fire.

8. It is more in accord with Pandora's origin as a form of the Earth Goddess to interpret her name as meaning "All-Giving."

9. Euripides, *Iphigeneia in Tauris*, ll. 414–15 (translated by Gilbert Murray, New York, 1915).

10. Strictly, *λαοί* means the subjects of a prince.

Chapter II

1. Gruppe, pp. 918–20, suggests that this myth is based on the belief that a man who had offered a human sacrifice and made himself one with the god by partaking of human flesh was himself a wolf, i. e. he was banished from the society of men and became a wanderer like a wolf. The similar but much more penetrating explanation offered by A. B. Cook (*Zeus*, i. 70–81) is too elaborate and detailed to be even summarized here.

2. *Description of Greece*, VIII. xxviii. 6.

3. This cannot be the flower which we know as the hyacinth.

4. Stephen Phillips, "Marpessa," in *Poems*, London and New York, 1898, pp. 26–29.

5. Friedländer, *Arg.*, pp. 5 ff.; Gruppe, pp. 168 ff.

6. See *infra*, p. 193.

7. The name of the Kimmerian (i. e. Crimean) Bosporos was similarly explained. As far as the Thracian strait is concerned the derivation is wrong. Βόσπορος is really a dialectical form of Φωσφόρος ("Light-Bearer"), a title of Hekate.

8. A. H. Sayce (*The Religions of Ancient Egypt and Babylonia*, Edinburgh, 1903, p. 55) derives Aigyptos from *Ḥa-ka-Ptaḥ* "the temple of the *ka* of *Ptaḥ*," the sacred name of the city of Memphis. In the Tell el-Amarna letters this is *Khikuptakh.*

9. See Gruppe, pp. 831–32; Friedländer, pp. 15–16, 25–30. "If we may trust Eustathius, it was the custom to place 'on the grave of those who died unmarried a water jar called *Loutrophoros* in token that the dead had died unbathed and without offspring.' Probably these vases, as Dr. Frazer suggests [i. e. on Pausanias X. xxxi. 9], were at first placed on the graves of the unmarried with the kindly intent of helping the desolate unmarried ghost to accomplish his wedding in the world below. But once the custom fixed, it might easily be interpreted as the symbol of an underworld punishment" (Harrison, *Prolegomena*, p. 621).

10. See Friedländer, pp. 36–37.

11. In other versions the weapon employed by Perseus was a stone, or a sword, or his scimitar (sickle-sword).

12. The story of Perseus in its bearings on primitive folk-tale and religion is exhaustively treated by E. S. Hartland, *Legend of Perseus*, 3 vols., London, 1894–96.

13. Homer, *Odyssey*, xi. 593–600 (translated by S. H. Butcher and A. Lang, London, 1900).

14. Fick (*Hattiden und Danubier in Griechenland*, pp. 43 ff.) suggests that the name and person of Sisyphos are derived from Tišup (or Tishub, Teshub), the principal male deity of the Hittites so often depicted on their monuments.

15. For a similar story see that of Kyknos and Tennes in Pausanias, X. xiv.

16. One is probably nearer the truth in connecting it with πηγός (cf. πήγνυμι), "strong."

Chapter III

1. Christopher Marlowe, *Dido*, Act II.

2. For a discussion of the problems involved consult T. G. Tucker, *Aeschylus, The Seven against Thebes*, Cambridge, 1908, Introd.; Gomme, "The Legend of Cadmus," etc.; and "The Topography of Boeotia," etc.

3. For the story of Aktaion see *infra*, p. 252; of Ino, p. 262; of Semele and Dionysos, p. 217.

4. Sophokles, *Oidipous Koloneus*, ll. 1611 ff. (translated by E. H. Plumptre, Boston, 1906).

5. Allinson, *Greek Lands and Letters*, p. 332.

6. Cf. Tucker, pp. xxxiv–xxxvii; Allinson, p. 292.

7. Homer, *Iliad*, ix. 573–99.

Chapter IV

1. "In Cretan myth the sun was conceived as a bull. On the other hand, in Cretan ritual the Labyrinth was an *orchestra* of solar pattern presumably made for a mimetic dance. . . . It would seem highly probable that the dancer imitating the sun masqueraded in the Labyrinth as a bull" (A. B. Cook, *Zeus*, i. 490–91).

2. Pausanias, II. iv. 5 (translated by J. G. Frazer).

3. Miss Harrison (*Myth. and Mon.*, pp. xxxiii, xxxv) advances the very probable suggestion that this story is primarily aetiological in character, being intended as an explanation of the ritual of the Arrephoria (or Hersephoria). The fate of the disobedient sisters is a detail

added for the purpose of frightening officiating maidens into strict observance of the rules governing the ritual.

4. Another etymology derives the word from ἀρῶν πάγος, "hill of curses"; cf. pp. 102, 189.

5. I. xxx. 3.

Chapter V

1. For the development of Herakles as a mythological character see especially Friedländer, *Herakles*.

2. xix. 90–133.

3. The order of the labours which we shall follow is that given by Apollodoros.

4. For discussions of the identity and character of the Amazons see especially the articles by Adolphe Reinach listed in the Bibliography.

5. Pindar, *Olympian Odes*, xi. (x.) 44 ff.

Chapter VII

1. Apollonios of Rhodes, *Argonautika*, i. 113–14.

2. ib. i. 544–45.

3. ib. ii. 79–80.

4. The writer is tempted, in agreement with A. B. Cook (*Zeus*, i. 723–24), to see in the person of Talos a reference to the *cire perdue* method of hollow-casting in bronze.

Chapter VIII

1. A. B. Cook (*Zeus*, i. 414–19) is strongly inclined to believe that both this golden lamb and the golden ram of Phrixos are epiphanies of Zeus.

2. The most accessible collection of the fragments and ancient summaries of the Cyclic Epics is to be found in the *Scriptorum Classicorum Bibliotheca Oxoniensis*, *Homeri Opera*, v. (Oxford, 1911). The fragment of the *Kypria* just quoted appears on p. 118.

3. Euripides, *Trojan Women*, ll. 892–93 (translated by Gilbert Murray, New York, 1915).

4. ib. ll. 924–33.

5. Euripides, *Iphigeneia in Tauris*, l. 15 (translated by Gilbert Murray).

6. i. 52 (translated by A. Lang, W. Leaf, and E. Myers, London, 1907).

7. vi. 486–89 (translated by Lang, Leaf, and Myers).

8. xix. 67–70 (translated by Lang, Leaf, and Myers).

9. See Oxford text of Homer, v. pp. 125–27.

10. See Oxford text of Homer, v. pp. 127–40.

11. Euripides, *Trojan Women*, ll. 1160–61 (translated by Gilbert Murray).

12. ib. l. 75 (translated by Gilbert Murray).

13. Oxford text of Homer, v. 140–43.

14. Aischylos seems to have made Argos and not Mykenai the scene of the *Agamemnon* in order to please the Argive allies of Athens.

15. Euripides, *Iphigeneia in Tauris*, ll. 79 ff. (translated by Gilbert Murray).

16. Tennyson, *The Lotos-Eaters*.

17. Oxford text of Homer, v. 143–44.

Chapter IX

1. Euripides, *Trojan Women*, ll. 632–33 (translated by Gilbert Murray).

2. Swinburne, *Atalanta in Calydon*.

3. It was customary to explain as Charon's fee the obol which the Greeks put into the mouth of a corpse, but the account is plainly aetiological, for the custom is really a survival of the belief that the metal of the coin had power to avert evil influences. Allegorically the obol might be interpreted as a ferry fare.

4. Can the howling of the wind at the cavernous entrances to the underworld have helped in giving rise to the canine conception of Kerberos?

5. Pausanias, III. xxv. 5.

6. "The mythical Ixion, if I am not mistaken, typifies a whole series of human Ixions, who in bygone ages were done to death as effete embodiments of the sun-god" (A. B. Cook, *Zeus*, i. 211). By this argument the wheel is the circle of the sun.

7. "Men say that he by the music of his songs charmed the stubborn rocks upon the mountains and the course of rivers. And the wild oak-trees to this day, tokens of that magic strain, that grow at Zone on the Thracian shore, stand in ordered ranks close together, the same which under the charm of his lyre he led down from Pieria" (Apollonios of Rhodes, *Argonautika*, i. 25–31, translated by R. C. Seaton, London and New York, 1912).

8. Ovid, *Metamorphoses*, x. 41 ff. (modified translation).

9. Homer, *Odyssey*, iv. 563–68 (translated by Butcher and Lang).

PART II

Chapter I

1. Gruppe, p. 1102.

2. See A. B. Cook, *Zeus*, i. 1–8.

3. In time this process of generalizing the personal characteristics of the gods practically neutralized all other processes of their development.

4. Hera's power in this sphere was doubtless derived from her union with Zeus, while that of Poseidon came from his traditional association with the sea.

5. The unqualified use of the epithet Ὀλύμπιος in Homer invariably designates Zeus.

6. Porphyrios, *Life of Pythagoras*, 17; cf. Tatian, Πρὸς Ἕλληνας, 27 (Migne, *Patrologia Graeca*, vi. 865).

7. Most of these mythical marriages can probably be explained as attempts to secure sanction for the recognition of Zeus in localities into which he was newly introduced and in which the chief native divinity was a goddess. The identification of the new god as the husband of the old goddess immediately gave the former a standing with the local worshipper.

8. *Idylls*, iv. 43; cf. xvii. 78.

9. Only in this sense can he be regarded as the Creator; in the Orphic philosophy he was life itself.

10. This school would see the same earth goddess in the original of the Eleusinian Demeter. For a discussion of the problem see Farnell, *Cults*, i. 192, and *The Higher Aspects*, etc., p. 14.

11. A. B. Cook, "Who was the Wife of Zeus?" in *CR* xx. 365–78, 416–19 (1906).

Chapter II

1. If this derivation is correct, it may possibly go back to a myth which set forth one or other of these characteristics of Athene.

2. *Homeric Hymn to Athene*, xxviii. 9–16.

3. Euripides, *Trojan Women*, ll. 801–02 (translated by Gilbert Murray).

Chapter III

1. *Homeric Hymns*, iii.

2. Cf. πίθεσθαι, "to become rotten, to rot."

3. See Swindler, *Cretan Elements*, etc.

4. Through its famous enigmatic reference to wooden walls, which Themistokles interpreted to mean ships, the oracle foretold the successful defence of Greece against the Persians.

5. The statement that Apollo "is the solar word of Zeus conceived as the eternal and infinite god and through him the revealer of the archetypes of things" (Schuré, "Le Miracle hellénique. L'Apollon de Delphes et la Pythonisse," in *Revue des deux Mondes*, 6th pér. vii. 344–45 [1912]) ignores the progressive development of Apollo from a simple to a complex personality.

6. Occasionally Artemis was a goddess of counsel, that is to say, of health of mind, an extension of her function as the goddess of health of body.

7. Hekate's association with sorcery is ample explanation of the fact that she figured more prominently in private than in public cult.

Chapter IV

1. The same kind of magical imprisonment seems here to be involved as that to which the genie was subjected in the story of Aladdin and the Wonderful Lamp.

Chapter V

1. This was presented by Professor A. L. Frothingham in a paper read before the Archaeological Institute of America at its annual meeting held at Haverford College, Dec. 1914. So far as the present writer knows, the paper is not yet in print.

2. Shelley's translation of the *Homeric Hymn to Hermes*, ix.

3. ib. xlv.

4. ib. xcvii.

5. The union of Hermes with both Herse and Pandrosos in Attic legend probably signifies that at least in Athens he had a connexion with certain phases of the weather, but such an association does not seem to have been general.

Chapter VI

1. Since the manuscript has left the author's hands he has come to the conclusion that Farnell is right in regarding the name as wholly foreign. In the forthcoming volume of the *Transactions and Proceedings of the American Philological Association* the writer presents a preliminary statement of what he believes to be the correct derivation, and later he hopes to publish an article supporting the etymology in detail.

2. The affinity is due to Aphrodite's primitive connexion with vegetation.

3. The matter-of-fact mind can easily detect an overlapping of the

functions of Aphrodite on those of other divinities of fertility. Yet this need disturb no one, for the Greek gods were not mechanical creations. To insist upon a precise differentiation among the Greek divinities is to miss the Greeks' religious point of view and to be insensitive to the myth-making spirit.

4. A. Lang, *The New Pygmalion*.

5. In philosophical circles the epithets Ourania and Pandemos were thought to signify the relations of Aphrodite to pure celestial love and degrading sensuality respectively; and common knowledge of the licentious character of certain rites of the goddess gave colour to this interpretation of the second epithet.

Chapter VII

1. *Iliad*, i. 591 ff.
2. Murray, *Four Stages of Gr. Rel.*, p. 66.
3. xxiv.
4. v. 21 ff.

Chapter VIII

1. See Blinkenberg, *The Thunderweapon;* Powell, *Erichthonius and the Three Daughters of Cecrops*, p. 12.

2. The tidal wave which submerged Helike in the fourth century B.C. was regarded as a demonstration of Poseidon's power.

3. If the name of Poseidon's son Boiotos means anything at all in this connexion, it implies that Poseidon was in the form of a bull when he begat this son.

Chapter IX

1. *Iliad*, vi. 130 ff. (translated by Lang, Leaf, and Myers).

2. See *infra*, p. 221.

3. This myth contains unmistakable evidence of human sacrifice in certain of the earlier Dionysiac rites.

4. vii.

5. It is still a moot point whether the appearance of the ship in this myth of Dionysos reflects the influence of certain Oriental vegetation-rites in which a ship was a prominent feature.

6. See *infra*, p. 224.

7. The use of the phallic emblem in the rites of Demeter to arouse fertility in the earth was one of a number of factors in bringing about an association of Demeter and Dionysos.

8. To regard Dionysos unqualifiedly as a rain-god is to exaggerate the influence of Osiris on his development.

9. Euripides, *Bacchai*, ll. 379–81.

Chapter X

1. *Theogony*, ll. 969 ff.

2. Whether Demeter was originally connected with these rites or whether they were a product of sympathetic magic primarily unrelated to any divinity, it is clear that during the height of the Demeter-cult the woman was the representative of the goddess.

3. Demeter's power to fructify human beings was the thought underlying the ceremonies of the Thesmophoria, a festival in which only matrons of good civic standing took part.

4. See *Homeric Hymns*, ii.

5. For the invocation of Hades (or Plouton) in curses see A. Audollent, *Tabellae Defixionum*, Paris, 1904, Index, pp. 461 ff.

Chapter XI

1. *Odes*, I. iv. 5–8 (translated by J. Conington, London, 1909).

2. Farnell, *Cults*, v. 434.

3. *In Memoriam*, v. 5–6.

4. "In early days the Muses were to Zeus what the mountain-roaming Maenads were to Dionysos" (A. B. Cook, *Zeus*, i. 111). J. Wackernagel (*Zeitschrift für vergleichende Sprachforschung*, xxxiii. 571–74 [1895]) expresses his belief that the relation of the Muses to mountains was original, and accordingly he would trace their name back to *μοντ-, "mountain."

5. v. 202 ff.

6. Those who see in the fall of Phaëthon and his car the sun's approach to earth at sunset ignore those details of the myth which emphasize the effect of the sun's heat.

7. For the most recent discussions of the Dioskouroi consult A. B. Cook, *Zeus*, i. 760 ff., and Harris, *Boanerges*.

8. In the clear air of the east Venus shines so brightly as to cast a faint shadow and to render her successive phases visible to the naked eye.

9. The stars of this group seemed to outline the figure of a man driving a yoke of oxen in the Great Wain. It is difficult for us modern city-dwellers, who seldom really see the stars and for whom they have little or no practical significance, to understand how the Greeks and their neighbours could find a world of living creatures in the night heavens.

Chapter XII

1. I. xxxiii. 4.

2. Swinburne, *Atalanta in Calydon*.

3. Homer, *Odyssey*, i. 52–54.

4. This association of Proteus with Egypt is secondary; his native habitat seems to have been Chalkis.

5. Homer, *Odyssey*, xii. 39–54.

6. *Theogony*, l. 871.

7. A. E. Zimmern, *The Greek Commonwealth*, Oxford, 1911, p. 35.

8. *Odes*, I. iii. 14.

9. A. B. Cook (*Zeus*, i. 302 ff.) holds the one-eyed Kyklopes to be monstrous incarnations of the disk of the sun.

10. *Homeric Hymns*, xix. 6–21.

Chapter XIII

1. Charles L. O'Donnell, *Ode for Panama Day.*

2. iv. 10; see also vs. 11.

3. Euripides, *Iphigeneia in Tauris*, ll. 285–91 (translated by Gilbert Murray).

Chapter XIV

1. II. xxvi. 4–5 (translated by Frazer, 1st ed.).

2. On this rite see L. Deubner, *De incubatione*, Leipzig, 1900, and Mary Hamilton, *Incubation*, London, 1906.

3. So in Hesiod, *Theogony*, l. 904; but ib. l. 217 they are the daughters of Nyx.

4. So Usener, *Götternamen*, p. 371. A. B. Cook (*Zeus*, i. 273), however, holds Nemesis, like Diana, to have been first of all a goddess of the greenwood (cf. *νέμος*, "glade," *νέμειν*, "to pasture").

5. Swinburne, *Atalanta in Calydon.*

PART III

1. It has long been the practice to assume that virtually all Italic myths were corruptions or adaptations of Greek myths. Now, however, there is a growing tendency to account for them as independent products of Italian religious experience. See especially Ettore Pais, *Ancient Legends*, etc.

2. *De Rerum Natura*, v. 655–56.

3. King, *Devel. of Rel.*, p. 130.

APPENDIX

1. p. 27.
2. Lawson, p. 75.
3. ib. p. 43.
4. ib. pp. 132–33.
5. ib. pp. 77–78.
6. Leland, p. 101.
7. ib. pp. 37–38.
8. ib. p. 69.
9. ib. p. 61.

BIBLIOGRAPHY

BIBLIOGRAPHY

I. ABBREVIATIONS

AA . . . Archäologischer Anzeiger (see *JBAI*).
ABSA . . The Annual of the British School at Athens.
AJA . . . American Journal of Archaeology.
AJP . . . The American Journal of Philology.
AM . . . Mittheilungen des kaiserlich deutschen archäologischen Instituts: athenische Abtheilung.
AR . . . Archiv für Religionswissenschaft.
AtR . . . Atene e Roma.
BAAR . . Bolletino dell' associazione archeologica romana.
CP . . . . Classical Philology.
CQ . . . . The Classical Quarterly.
CR . . . . The Classical Review.
diss. . . . dissertation.
DL . . . . Deutsche Literaturzeitung.
DR . . . . Deutsche Rundschau.
E . . . . Eranos, Acta philologica Suecana.
ERE . . . Encyclopaedia of Religion and Ethics. James Hastings, editor.
H . . . . Hermes, Zeitschrift für classische Philologie.
JBAI . . Jahrbuch des kaiserlich deutschen archäologischen Instituts mit dem Beiblatt Archäologischer Anzeiger.
JHAI . . Jahreshefte des österreichischen archäologischen Institutes in Wien.
JHS . . . The Journal of Hellenic Studies.
JP . . . . Jahrbücher für classische Philologie (see *NJ*).
JRS . . . The Journal of Roman Studies.
MAH . . Mélanges d'archéologie et d'histoire.
MB . . . Le Musée belge.
Mnem. . . Mnemosyne, Tijdschrift voor classieke Litteratuur.
MVG . . . Mitteilungen der vorderasiatischen Gesellschaft.
NJ . . . Neue Jahrbücher für das klassische Altertum, Geschichte und deutsche Literatur und für Pädagogik (Continuation of Jahrbücher für classische Philologie).
OL . . . . Orientalistische Literaturzeitung.
Phil. . . . Philologus, Zeitschrift für das klassische Altertum.

RA . . . Revue archéologique.
REA . . . Revue des études anciennes.
RHLR . . Revue d'histoire et de littérature religieuse.
RHR . . . Revue de l'histoire des religions.
RM . . . Rheinisches Museum für Philologie.
RMitt . . Mittheilungen des kaiserlich deutschen archäologischen Instituts: römische Abtheilung.
SIFC . . Studi italiani di filologia classica.
S . . . . Socrates, Zeitschrift für Gymnasialwesen.
SSAC . . Studi storici per l'antichità classica.
WS . . . Wiener Studien.

II. GENERAL WORKS

DAREMBERG and SAGLIO, *Dictionnaire des antiquités grecques et romaines d'après les textes et les monuments.* Paris, 1892 ff.

FORRER, R., *Reallexikon der praehistorischen, klassischen und frühchristlichen Altertümer.* Berlin and Stuttgart, 1907 ff.

HASTINGS, *Encyclopaedia of Religion and Ethics.* Edinburgh and New York, 1908 ff.

LICHTENBERGER, *Encyclopédie des sciences religieuses.* Paris, 1877–82.

PAULY-WISSOWA, *Real-Encyclopädie der classischen Altertumswissenschaft.* Stuttgart, 1901 ff.

ROSCHER, W. H., *Ausführliches Lexikon der griechischen und römischen Mythologie.* Leipzig, 1884 ff.

SCHRADER, O., *Reallexikon der indogermanischen Altertumskunde.* Strassburg, 1901.

SMITH-MARINDIN, *A Classical Dictionary of Greek and Roman Biography, Mythology, and Geography.* London, 1899.

III. SPECIAL WORKS

(a) Greek

ADAM, J., *The Religious Teachers of Greece.* London, 1908.

ALLEN, T. W., "The Date of Hesiod," in *JHS* xxxv. 85 ff. (1915).

ALLEN, T. W. and SIKES, E. E., *The Homeric Hymns.* London, 1904.

ALLINSON, F. G. and A. C. E., *Greek Lands and Letters.* Boston, 1909.

ALPERS, J., *Hercules in bivio.* Göttingen, 1912 (diss.).

ALY, W., *Der kretische Apollokult.* Leipzig, 1908.

Aly, W., "Zur Methode der griechischen Mythologie," in *DL* xxxi. 261–67 (1910).

——— "Ursprung und Entwickelung der kretischen Zeusreligion," in *Phil.* lxx. 457–78 (1912).

Ancey, G., "Questions mythiques," in *RA* xxi. 209–13, 376–82 (1913).

Andres, F., *Die Engel- und Dämonlehre der griechischen Apologeten des 2. Jahrhunderts und ihr Verhältnis zur griechisch-römischen Dämonologie.* Breslau, 1913 (diss.).

Aubert, H., *Les Légendes mythologiques de la Grèce et de Rome.* Paris, 1909.

Baker, E. K., *Stories of Old Greece and Rome.* New York, 1913.

Bapp, K., *Prometheus, Ein Beitrag zur griechischen Mythologie.* Oldenburg, 1896 (Osterprogramm des Gymnasien).

Bassi, D., *Mitologia greca e romana ad uso delle scuole e delle persone colte.* Florence, 1912.

Baumeister, A., *Denkmäler des klassischen Altertums zur Erläuterung des Lebens der Griechen und Römer in Religion, Kunst und Sitte.* 3 vols. Munich and Leipzig, 1885–88.

Baur, P. V. C., *Centaurs in Ancient Art, the Archaic Period.* Berlin, 1912.

Bender, W., *Mythologie und Metaphysik.* Stuttgart, 1899.

Bennett, Florence M., *Religious Cults associated with the Amazons.* New York, 1912.

Bérard, V., *De l'origine des cultes arcadiens* (*Bibliothèque des écoles françaises d'Athènes et de Rome*, lxvii). Paris, 1894.

——— *Les Phéniciens et l'Odyssée.* 2 vols. Paris, 1902–03.

Berge, R., *De belli daemonibus qui in carminibus Graecorum et Romanorum inveniuntur.* Leipzig, 1894 (diss.).

Berger, E. H., *Mythische Kosmographie der Griechen* (Supplement to Roscher's *Lex.*). Leipzig, 1904.

Bethe, E., *Homer, Dichtung und Sage*, i (*Ilias*). Leipzig, 1914.

Blinkenberg, C., *The Thunderweapon in Religion and Folklore.* Cambridge, 1911.

Blum, G., "ΜΕΙΛΙΧΙΟΣ," in *MB* xvii. 313–20 (1913).

Bodrero, E., *I Giardini di Adonide.* Rome, 1913.

Boehm, J., *Symbolae ad Herculis historiam fabularem vasculis pictis petitae.* Königsberg, 1909 (diss.).

Boetticher, K., *Baumkultus der Hellenen und Römer.* Berlin, 1856.

Boetzkes, R., *Das Kerykeion.* Münster, 1913 (diss.).

Bouché-Leclerq, A., *Histoire de la divination dans l'antiquité.* 4 vols. Paris, 1879–82.

Bouché-Leclerq, A., *L'Astrologie grecque*. Paris, 1899.

——— *Leçons d'histoire grecque*. Paris, 1913.

Braun, E., *Griechische Mythologie*. Hamburg and Gotha, 1850.

Bréal, M., *Mélanges de mythologie et de linguistique*. Paris, 1877.

Brinton, D. G., *Religions of Primitive Peoples*. New York, 1899.

Brown, R., *Semitic Influence in Hellenic Mythology*. London, 1898.

Bruchmann, C. F. H., *Epitheta deorum quae apud poetas Graecos leguntur* (Supplement to Roscher's *Lex.*). Leipzig, 1893.

Bubbe, Gualterus, *De metamorphosibus Graecorum capita selecta*. Halle, 1913 (diss.).

Bursian, C., *Ueber den religiösen Charakter des griechischen Mythos*. Munich, 1875.

Buttmann, P. K., *Mythologus, Gesammelte Abhandlungen über die Sagen des Alterthums*. 2 vols. Berlin, 1828–29.

Campbell, L., *Religion in Greek Literature*. London and New York, 1898.

Carolidis, P., *Bemerkungen zu den alten kleinasiatischen Sprachen und Mythen*. Strassburg, 1913.

Cerquand, J. F., *Études de mythologie grecque: Ulysse et Circé; Les Sirènes*. Paris, 1873.

Chadwick, H. M., *The Heroic Age*. Cambridge, 1912.

Clarke, Helen A., *Ancient Myths in Modern Poets*. New York, 1910.

Collignon, M., *Manual of Mythology in Relation to Greek Art* (translated and enlarged by J. E. Harrison). London, 1899.

Constant, B., *De la religion considerée dans sa source, ses formes et ses développements*. Paris, 1831.

Conze, A., *Heroen- und Göttergestalten der griechischen Kunst*. Vienna, 1875.

Cook, A. B., *Zeus*, i. Cambridge, 1914.

Cook, S. A., "The Evolution of Primitive Thought," in *Essays and Studies presented to William Ridgeway*, pp. 375 ff. Cambridge, 1913.

——— *The Foundations of Religion*. London, 1914.

Corbellini, Caterina, "Gli Eroi argivi nella Boiotia e l'intreccio del ciclo troiano col tebano," in *SIFC* xix. 337–49 (1912).

——— "Gli Eroi del ciclo eracleo nel catalogo omerico delle navi," in *SIFC* xix. 350–59 (1912).

Cornford, F. M., "Hermes, Pan, Logos," in *CQ* iii. 281–84 (1909).

——— *From Religion to Philosophy*. London, 1912.

CORNFORD, F. M., "The Origin of the Olympic Games," in J. E. Harrison, *Themis* (q.v.), pp. 212–59.

——— *The Origin of Attic Comedy*. London and New York, 1914.

CORSSEN, P., "Der Mythos von der Geburt des Dionysos in den Bakchen des Euripides," in *RM* lxviii. 297–306 (1913).

——— "Apollons Geburt," in *Verhandlungen der philologischen Versammlung zu Marburg am Lahn*, lii. 163–64 (1914).

COURCELLE-SENEUIL, J. L., *Les Égéens sur les côtes occidentales de l'Europe vers le xvie siècle avant notre ère*. Paris, 1914.

COX, G. W., *Mythology of the Aryan Nations*. London, 1870.

——— *An Introduction to the Science of Comparative Mythology and Folklore*. London, 1883.

CROISET, M., "Observations sur la légende primitive d'Ulysse," in *Mémoires de l'Académie des Inscriptions*, xxxviii. 171–214 (1899).

CUMONT, F., *Astrology and Religion among the Greeks and Romans*. London and New York, 1912.

CURTIUS, A. W., *Das Stiersymbol des Dionysos*. Cologne, 1892.

CURTIUS, E., *Ueber den religiösen Charakter der griechischen Münzen*. Berlin, 1869.

DÄHNHARDT, O., *Natursagen*. Leipzig and Berlin, 1907.

DAVIS, GLADYS M. N., *The Asiatic Dionysos*. London, 1914.

DECHARME, P., *La Critique des traditions religieuses chez les Grecs des origines au temps de Plutarque*. Paris, 1904.

DIETERICH, A., *Mutter Erde*. Leipzig, 1913.

DIETZE, J., "Zur kyklischen Theogonie," in *RM* lxix. 522–37 (1914).

DOMASZEWSKI, A. VON, *Die Hermen der Agora zu Athen*. Heidelberg, 1914.

DRERUP, E., *Die Anfänge der hellenischen Kultur*, i *Homer*. Mainz, 1915.

DURKHEIM, ÉMILE, *The Elementary Forms of the Religious Life* (translated from the French by J. S. Swain). London and New York, 1915.

DUSSAUD, R., *Les Civilizations préhelléniques*. Paris, 1914.

——— *Introduction à l'histoire des religions*. Paris, 1914.

DYER, L., *Studies of the Gods in Greece*. London, 1891.

EHRENREICH, P., *Die allgemeine Mythologie und ihre ethnologischen Grundlagen*. Leipzig, 1910.

EITREM, S., "Hermes und die Toten," in *Christiania Videnskabsselskabs Forhandlingar*, No. 5 (1909).

——— "Die Hera mit der Schera," in *Phil.* lxii. 444–47 (1914).

Engelmann, R., *Bilder-Atlas zum Homer.* Leipzig, 1889.

Evelyn-White, H. G., "The Myth of the Nostoi," in *CR* xxiv. 201–05 (1910).

——— "Hesiodea," in *CQ* vii. 217 ff. (1913).

Fairbanks, A., *A Handbook of Greek Religion.* New York, 1910.

——— *The Mythology of Greece and Rome.* New York, 1912.

Farnell, L. R., *Cults of the Greek States.* 5 vols. Oxford, 1896–1908.

——— "Evidence of Greek Religion in the Text and Interpretation of Attic Tragedy," in *CQ* iv. 178–90 (1910).

——— *Greece and Babylon.* Edinburgh, 1911.

——— *The Higher Aspects of Greek Religion.* New York, 1912.

Ferrabino, A., *Kalypso: Saggio d'una storia del mito.* Turin, 1914.

Fick, A., *Vorgriechische Ortsnamen.* Göttingen, 1905.

——— *Hattiden und Danubier in Griechenland.* Göttingen, 1909.

Fiske, J., *Myths and Myth-Makers.* Boston, 1896.

Foster, B. O., "The Duration of the Trojan War," in *AJP* xxxv. 294–308 (1914).

Foucart, P., *Les Mystères d'Éleusis.* Paris, 1914.

Fox, W. S., "The Johns Hopkins Tabellae Defixionum," in *AJP* Supplement xxxiii, part 1 (1912).

Frazer, J. G., *The Golden Bough*, 3rd ed.:

Part i. *The Magic Art and the Evolution of Kings.* 2 vols. London, 1911.

Part ii. *Taboo and the Perils of the Soul.* London, 1911.

Part iii. *The Dying God.* London, 1911.

Part iv. *Adonis, Attis, Osiris.* 2 vols. London, 1914.

Part v. *Spirits of the Corn and of the Wild.* 2 vols. London, 1912.

Part vi. *The Scapegoat.* London, 1913.

Part vii. *Balder the Beautiful.* 2 vols. London, 1913.

——— *Pausanias's Description of Greece*, translated with a commentary by J. G. Frazer. 2nd ed. corrected. 6 vols. London, 1913.

Friedländer, P., *Argolica.* Berlin, 1905 (diss.).

——— *Herakles: Sagengeschichtliche Untersuchungen.* Berlin, 1907.

——— "Kritische Untersuchungen zur Geschichte der Heldensage: (1) Argonauten; (2) Der Krieg um Theben; (3) Οἰχαλίας ἅλωσις," in *RM* lxix. 299–341 (1914).

Fries, C., "Babylonische und griechische Mythologie," in *NJ* ix. 689 ff. (1902).

——— "Studien zur Odyssee, i Das Zagmukfest auf Scheria und der Ursprung des Dramas," in *MVG* xv. (1910).

FRIES, C., "Studien zur Odyssee, ii Odysseus der bhikshu," in *MVG* xvi. (1911).

FRIES, C., *Die griechische Götter und Heroen vom astralmythologischen Standpunkt aus betrachtet.* Berlin, 1911.

FROTHINGHAM, A. L., "Medusa, Apollo, and the Great Mother," in *AJA* xv. 349–77 (1911).

——— "Medusa, the Vegetation Gorgoneion," in *AJA* xix. 13–23 (1915).

FÜRTWÄNGLER, A., "Charon," in *AR* viii. 191 ff. (1905).

GARDINER, A., *Tales of Old, being Myths and Legends of Greece and Rome.* London, 1909.

GARDNER, E., *Religion and Art in Ancient Greece.* London and New York, 1910.

GARDNER, P., *Origins of Myth.* Oxford, 1896.

GAYLEY, C. M., *The Classic Myths in Literature and in Art,* based originally on Bullfinch, *Age of Fable.* Boston and New York, 1911.

GELDART, E. M., *Folklore of Modern Greece.* London, 1884.

GENNEP, A. VAN, *La Formation des légendes.* Paris, 1910.

——— *Rites de passage.* Paris, 1911.

——— "De la méthode à suivre dans l'étude des rites et des mythes," in *Revue de l'Université de Bruxelles,* xvi. 505–23 (1910–11).

GERHARD, E., *Griechische Mythologie.* Berlin, 1854–55.

GERLAND, G., *Der Mythus von der Sintflut.* Bonn, 1912.

GILBERT, O., *Griechische Götterlehre in ihren Grundzügen dargestellt.* Leipzig, 1898.

——— *Griechische Religionsphilosophie.* Leipzig, 1911.

GIRARD, J., *Le Sentiment religieux en Grèce d'Homère à Eschyle.* Paris, 1869.

GOMME, A. W., "Topography of Boeotia and the Theories of M. Bérard," in *ABSA* xviii. 189–210 (1911–12).

——— "The Legend of Cadmus and the Logographi," in *JHS* xxxiii. 53–74, 223–45 (1913).

GOW, A. S. F., "Elpis and Pandora in Hesiod's Works and Days," in *Essays and Studies presented to William Ridgeway,* pp. 99 ff. Cambridge, 1913.

GRUPPE, O., *Die griechische Kulte und Mythen.* Leipzig, 1887.

——— *Griechische Mythologie und Religionsgeschichte* (*Handbuch der klassischen Altertumswissenschaft,* herausgegeben von Dr. Iwan von Müller, v. Band, 2. Abteilung). 2 vols. Munich, 1906.

GRUPPE, O., *Die mythologische Literatur*, aus den Jahren 1898–1905 (*Jahresbericht für Altertumswissenschaft.* Suppl. 1907). Leipzig, 1908.

——— "Die eherne Schwelle und der thorikische Stein," in *AR* xv. 359–79 (1912).

GUERBER, G., *The Myths of Greece and Rome.* London, 1907.

GUMMERE, F. B., *Myth and Allegory.* Haverford College Studies, 1892.

GUNNING, P. G., *De Ceorum fabulis antiquissimis quaestiones selectae.* Amsterdam, 1912 (diss.).

HABERT, O., *La Religion de la Grèce antique.* Paris, 1910.

HAHN, J. G. VON, *Sagenwissenschaftliche Studien.* Jena, 1876.

——— *Griechische und albanesische Märchen.* 2 vols. Leipzig, 1864.

HALLIDAY, W. R., *Greek Divination.* London, 1913.

HARRIS, J. R., *The Cult of the Heavenly Twins.* Cambridge, 1906.

——— *Boanerges.* Cambridge, 1913.

——— "The Dioscuri in Byzantium and the Neighbourhood," in *Essays and Studies presented to William Ridgeway*, pp. 547 ff. Cambridge, 1913.

HARRISON, JANE ELLEN, *Mythology and Monuments of Ancient Athens.* London and New York, 1890.

——— *Religion of Ancient Greece.* London, 1906.

——— *Prolegomena to the Study of Greek Religion.* 2nd ed. Cambridge, 1908.

——— *Themis, A Study of the Social Origins of Greek Religion*, with an excursus on the ritual forms preserved in Greek tragedy by Professor Gilbert Murray, and a chapter on the origin of the Olympic games by Mr. F. M. Cornford. Cambridge, 1912.

HARTLAND, E. S., *Mythology and Folk-Tales.* London, 1900.

HARTMANN, W., *De quinque aetatibus Hesiodeis.* Freiburg-im-Breisgau, 1915.

HARTUNG, J. A., *Die Religion und Mythologie der Griechen.* 4 parts. Leipzig, 1865–73.

HAURY, I., *Das eleusinische Fest ursprünglich identisch mit dem Laubhüttenfest der Juden.* Munich, 1914.

HEDÉN, E., *Homerische Götterstudien.* Upsala, 1912.

HEIDEMANN, L., *Zum ethnischen Problem Griechenlands.* Berlin, 1914.

HEINEMANN, K., *Thanatos in Poesie und Kunst der Griechen.* Munich, 1913.

HEPDING, H., *Attis seine Mythen und sein Kult.* Giessen, 1903.

HERMANN, G., *De mythologia Graeca antiquissima.* Leipzig, 1817.

——— *Ueber das Wesen und die Behandlung der Mythen.* Leipzig, 1819.

HERMANN, K. F., *Lehrbuch der gottesdienstlichen Alterthümer der Griechen.* Heidelberg, 1858.

HOORN, G. VAN, "De origine cistophorum," in *Mnem.* xliii. 233–37 (1914).

HÜBNER, F., *De Pluto.* Halle, 1914 (diss.).

IMMERWAHR, W., *Die Kulte und Mythen Arkadiens.* Leipzig, 1891.

JACOBI, E., *Handwörterbuch der griechischen und römischen Mythologie.* Koburg and Leipzig, 1835.

JACOBSTHAL, P., *Der Blitz in der orientalischen und griechischen Kunst.* Berlin, 1906.

JAISLE, K., *Die Dioskuren als Retter zur See bei Griechen und Römern und ihr Fortleben in christlichen Legenden.* Tübingen, 1907.

JEVONS, F. B., *Introduction to the Study of Comparative Religion.* New York, 1908.

KAISER, J., *Peleus und Thetis, eine sagengeschichtliche Untersuchung.* Munich, 1912.

KANNE, J. A., *Mythologie der Griechen.* Leipzig, 1805.

KERN, O., "TITΥPOI," in *H* xlviii. 318–19 (1913).

KING, I., *The Development of Religion.* New York, 1910.

KIOCK, A., "Athene Aithyia," in *AR* xviii. 127–33 (1915).

KJELLBERG, L., "Die Giganten bei Homer," in *E* xii. 195–98 (1914).

KNIGHT, R. P., *An Inquiry into the Symbolical Language of Ancient Art and Mythology.* London, 1836.

KÖRTE, A., "Zu den eleusinischen Mysterien," in *AR* xviii. 116–26 (1915).

KRANZ, W., "Die Irrfahrten des Odysseus," in *H* l. 93–112 (1915).

KRICHENBAUER, A., *Theogonie und Astronomie.* Vienna, 1881.

KUHN, A., *Mythologische Studien.* Gütersloh, 1912.

KÜSTER, E., *Die Schlange in der griechischen Kunst.* Heidelberg, 1913 (diss.).

KUTSCH, F., *Attische Heilgötter und Heilheroen.* Giessen, 1913 (diss.).

LAGOSTENA, A., *Il Mito degli Argonauti nella letteratura greca.* Genoa, 1914.

LAISTNER, L., *Das Rätsel der Sphinx.* Berlin, 1889.

LANG, A., *Myth, Ritual and Religion.* London, 1899.

LANG, A., *Custom and Myth.* New York, 1910.

——— *The World of Homer.* London, 1910.

——— "Mythology," in *Encyclopaedia Britannica* (11th ed.) xix. 128 ff.

LAQUEUR, R., "Zur griechischen Sagenchronographie," in *H* xlii. 513–32 (1907).

LAWSON, J. C., *Modern Greek Folklore and Ancient Greek Religion.* Cambridge, 1910.

LEAF, W., *Troy, A Study in Homeric Geography.* London, 1912.

LE CLERC DES SEPT-CHÊNES, *Essai sur la religion des anciens Grecs.* Paris, 1787.

LEONHARD, W., *Hettiter und Amazonen. Die griechische Tradition über die Chatti und ein Versuch zu ihrer historischen Verwertung.* Leipzig and Berlin, 1911.

LOBECK, C. A., *Aglaophamus sive de theologiae mysticae Graecorum causis.* 2 vols. Königsberg, 1829.

LOISY, A., "Dionysos et Orphée," in *RHLR* iv. 130–54 (1913).

——— "Cybèle et Attis," in *RHLR* iv. 289–326 (1913).

LORENZ, F., "Das Titanen-Motiv in der allgemeinen Mythologie," in *Imago* ii. 22–72 (1913).

LÖWY, E., "Zur Aithiopis," in *NJ* xxxiii. 81–94 (1914).

LUNG, G. E., *Memnon, archäologische Studien zur Aithiopis.* Bonn, 1912 (diss.).

MCDANIEL, W. B., "Some Greek, Roman and English Tityretus," in *AJP* xxxv. 52–66 (1914).

MALTEN, L., *Kyrene, Sagengeschichtliche und historische Untersuchungen.* Berlin, 1911.

——— "Hephaistos," in *JBAI* xxvii. 232–64 (1912).

——— "Elysion und Radamanthys," in *JBAI* xxviii. 35–51 (1913).

——— "Das Pferd im Totenglauben," in *JBAI* xxix. 179–255 (1914).

MANNHARDT, W., *Antike Wald- und Feldkulte.* 2 vols. Berlin, 1904–05.

MARETT, R. R., *The Threshold of Religion.* London, 1909.

MATZ, F., *Die Naturpersonifikation in der griechischen Kunst.* Göttingen, 1913 (diss.).

MAURY, A., *Histoire des religions de la Grèce antique.* 3 vols. Paris, 1857–59.

MAYER, M., *Die Giganten und Titanen in der antiken Sage und Kunst.* Berlin, 1887.

MÉNARD, R. J., *La Mythologie dans l'art ancien et moderne.* Paris, 1878.

MENRAD, J., *Der Urmythus der Odyssee und seine dichterische Erneuerung: Des Sonnengottes Erdenfahrt.* Munich, 1910.

MEYER, E., *Geschichte des Altertums.* 2nd ed. Vol. i, part 2. Stuttgart and Berlin, 1909.

MEYER, E. H., *Indogermanische Mythen.* 2 vols. Berlin, 1883–87.

MICHEL, C., "Le Culte d'Esculape dans la religion de la Grèce ancienne," in *RHLR* i. 44 ff. (1910).

MOMMSEN, A., *Feste der Stadt Athen im Altertum.* Leipzig, 1898.

MÖSSNER, O., *Die Mythologie in der dorischen und altattischen Komödie.* Erlangen, 1907 (diss.).

MUELDER, D., "Das Kyklopengedicht der Odyssee," in *H* xxxviii. 414–55 (1903).

MÜLLER, F. M., "Comparative Mythology," in *Chips from a German Workshop.* Vol. ii. London, 1858.

MÜLLER, H. D., *Mythologie der griechischen Stämme.* 2 vols. Göttingen, 1857–61.

MÜLLER, K. O., *Prolegomena zu einer wissenschaftlichen Mythologie.* Göttingen, 1825.

MÜLLER, P. F., *Die antiken Odyssee-Illustrationen in ihrer kunsthistorischen Entwicklung.* Berlin, 1913.

MÜLLER, V. K., *Der Polos, die griechische Götterkrone.* Berlin, 1915.

MÜLLER, W. M., "Marsyas," in *OL* 433–36 (1913).

MURRAY, G., *The Rise of the Greek Epic.* Oxford, 1907.

——— *Four Stages of Greek Religion.* New York, 1912.

NAEGELSBACH, C. F. VON, *Die nachhomerische Theologie des griechischen Volksglaubens bis auf Alexander.* Nürnberg, 1857.

——— *Homerische Theologie* (3rd ed. revised by G. Autenrieth). Nürnberg, 1884.

NEUSTADT, E., *De Iove Cretico.* Berlin, 1906.

NICHOLSON, W., *Myth and Religion.* Helsingfors, 1892.

NILLSON, M. P., *Griechische Feste von religiöser Bedeutung.* Leipzig, 1906.

——— "Die älteste griechische Zeitrechnung, Apollo und der Orient," in *AR* xiv. 423–48 (1911).

——— "Der Ursprung der Tragödie," in *NJ* xxvii. 609 ff., 673 ff. (1911).

NOCERA, V., *I Simboli mitologici negli stemmi ed emblemi greci e romane.* Terranova, Sicily, 1913.

Ohnefalsch-Richter, M., *Kypros, the Bible and Homer.* 2 vols. London, 1893.

Oldfather, W. A., *Lokrika.* Munich, 1908 (diss.).

Orelli, C. von, *Allgemeine Religionsgeschichte.* 2nd ed. 2 vols. Bonn, 1913.

Osthoff, H., "Etymologische Beiträge zur Mythologie und Religionsgeschichte," in *AR* x. 44–74 (1907).

Overbeck, J., *Griechische Kunstmythologie.* Leipzig, 1871 ff.

——— *Ueber die Grundlagen des idealen griechischen Götterbildes.* Leipzig, 1875.

Pascal, C., *Studi di antichità e mitologia.* Milan, 1896.

Penka, K., *Die vorhellenische Bevölkerung Griechenlands.* Hildburgshausen, 1911.

Philpot, Mrs. J. H., *The Sacred Tree, or The Tree in Religion and Myth.* London, 1897.

Poerner, J., *De Curetibus et Corybantibus.* Halle, 1913 (diss.).

Powell, B., *Erichthonius and the Three Daughters of Cecrops.* New York, 1906 (diss. Cornell University).

Preller, L.-Robert, C., *Griechische Mythologie,* i. 4th ed. Berlin, 1894.

Premerstein, A. von, "Kleobis und Biton," in *JHAI* xiii. 41–49 (1910).

Quandt, G., *De Baccho ad Alexandri aetatem in Asia Minore culto.* Halle, 1913 (diss.).

Radermacher, L., "Mythica," in *WS* xxxiv. 28–36 (1912); xxxvi. 320–28 (1914).

——— "Zur Hadesmythologie," in *RM* lx. 584–93 (1915).

Radet, G., *Cybébé, Étude sur les transformations plastiques d'un type divin.* Bordeaux, 1909.

——— "Quelques remarques nouvelles sur la déesse Cybébé," in *REA* xiii. 75–78 (1911).

Ramorino, F., *Mitologia classica illustrata.* Milan, 1911.

Reichel, W., *Ueber vorhellenische Götterkulte.* Vienna, 1897.

Reinach, A., "L'Origine des Amazons," in *RHR* lxviii. 277–307 (1913).

——— "L'Origine de deux légendes homériques," in *RHR* lxix. 12–33 (1914).

Reinach, S., "Aetos Prometheus," in *RA*, 4th series, x. 59–81 (1907).

——— *Cultes, mythes et religions.* 4 vols. Paris, 1908–12.

——— "Le sacrifice de Tyndare," in *RHR* lxviii. 133–45 (1913).

——— *Orpheus.* Paris, 1914.

Reinach, S., "Essai sur la mythologie figurée et l'histoire profane dans la peinture italienne de la Renaissance," in *RA*, 5th series, i. 94–166 (1915).

Reitzenstein, R., *Die hellenistischen Mysterienreligionen, ihre Grundgedanken und Wirkungen.* Leipzig, 1910.

Riaille, G. de, *Mythologie comparée.* Paris, 1878.

Ridgeway, W., *The Origin of Tragedy.* Cambridge, 1910.

Robert, C., "Archäologische Nachlese," in *H* xlvi. 217–53 (1911).

——— "Pandora," in *H* xlix. 17–38 (1914).

——— *Oidipous.* 2 vols. Berlin, 1915.

Roberts, D. G., "Theseus and the Robber Sciron," in *JHS* xxxii. 105–10 (1912).

Rohde, E., *Psyche.* 6th ed. Tübingen, 1910.

——— *Der griechische Roman und seine Vorläufer.* 3rd ed. Leipzig, 1914.

Roscher, W., *Iuno und Hera.* Leipzig, 1875.

Rothe, C., *Die Ilias als Dichtung.* Paderborn, 1910.

——— *Die Odyssee als Dichtung und ihr Verhältnis zur Ilias.* Paderborn, 1914.

Rubensohn, O., "Triptolemos als Pflüger," in *AM* xxiv. 59–71 (1899).

Rühl, C., *De Graecis ventorum nominibus et fabulis quaestiones selectae.* Marburg, 1909 (diss.).

Samter, E., *Die Religion der Griechen.* Leipzig, 1915.

Savignoni, L., "La purificazione delle Pretidi," in *Ausonia* viii. 145 ff. (1915).

Scheuer, G., *De Iunone Attica.* Breslau, 1914.

Schmidt, K., *Das Geheimnis der griechischen Mythologie und der Stein von Lemnos.* Gleiwitz, 1908.

Schredelseker, P., *De superstitionibus Graecorum quae ad crines pertinent.* Heidelberg, 1913 (diss.).

Schuré, E., "Le Miracle hellénique. L'Apollon de Delphes et la Pythonisse," in *Revue des deux Mondes*, 6th pér. vii. 340 ff. (1912).

Schwartz, E., "Prometheus bei Hesiod," in *Sitzungsberichte der königlich preussischen Akademie der Wissenschaften*, pp. 133–38 (1915).

Schwartz, F. L. W., *Der Ursprung der Mythologie.* Berlin, 1860.

Schwenk, K., *Die Mythologie der Griechen.* Frankfort, 1855.

Scott, J. A., "Paris and Hector in Tradition and in Homer," in *CP* viii. 160–71 (1913).

——— "Phoenix in the Iliad," in *AJP* xxxiii. 68–69 (1912).

——— "Two Homeric Personages," in *AJP* xxxv. 309–25 (1914).

SEIFFERT, O., *Die Totenschlange auf lakonischen Reliefs.* Breslau, 1911.

SEYMOUR, T. D., *Life in the Homeric Age.* New York, 1908.

SHEWAN, A., "The Waterfowl Goddess, Penelope and her Son Pan," in *CR* xxix. 37–40 (1915).

SIECKE, E., *Mythus, Sage, Märchen in ihren Beziehungen zur Gegenwart.* Leipzig, 1906.

——— *Drachenkämpfe: Untersuchungen zur indogermanischen Sagenkunde.* Leipzig, 1907.

SMITH, S. C. K., *The Elements of Greek Worship.* London, 1915.

SOMMER, L., *Das Haar in Religion und Aberglauben der Griechen.* Münster, 1912 (diss.).

SOURDILLE, C., "Une Théorie récente sur la formation du mythe d'Épaphos," in *REA* xiv. 267 ff. (1912).

STEUDING, H., *Griechische und römische Mythologie.* Leipzig, 1911.

STORCK, K., *Die ältesten Sagen der Insel Keos.* Giessen, 1912 (diss.).

SWAIN, J. S. See DURKHEIM, ÉMILE.

SWINDLER, M. H., *Cretan Elements in the Cults and Ritual of Apollo.* Bryn Mawr, Pa., 1913 (diss.).

SYBEL, L. VON, *Die Mythologie der Ilias.* Marburg, 1877.

THOMPSON, J. A. K., *Studies in the Odyssey.* Oxford, 1914.

TÖPFFER, J., *Attische Genealogie.* Berlin, 1889.

TOSI, T., "Il Sacrificio di Polissena," in *AtR* xvii. 19–38 (1914).

TOUTAIN, J., *Études de mythologie et d'histoire des religions antiques.* Paris, 1909.

USENER, H. K., *Götternamen.* Bonn, 1896.

——— *Die Sintfluthsagen.* Bonn, 1899.

——— "Mythologie," in *AR* vii. 6 ff. (1904).

VIGNIOLI, T., *Myth and Science.* London, 1882.

VOLLGRAFF, W., "Dionysos Eleuthereus," in *AM* xxxii. 567–75 (1907).

VÜRTHEIM, J., *De Aiacis origine cultu patria, accedunt commentationes tres: de Amazonibus, de Carneis, de Telegonia.* Leyden, 1907.

——— *Teukros und Teukrer.* Rotterdam, 1913.

WARD, W. H., "The Greek and the Hittite Gods," in *Essays presented to C. A. Briggs.* New York, 1911.

——— "Asiatic Influence in Greek Mythology," in *Studies presented to C. H. Toy.* New York, 1912.

WASER, O., "Uber die äussere Erscheinung der Seele in den Vorstellungen der Völker, zumal der alten Griechen," in *AR* xvi. 336–83 (1914).

WASER, O., "Theseus und Prokroustes," in *AA* xxix. 32–38 (1914).

WEBER, W., *Ägyptisch-griechische Götter in Hellenismus*. Groningen, 1912.

WEICKER, G., *Der Seelenvogel in der alten Literatur und Kunst*. Leipzig, 1902.

WELCKER, F. G., *Griechische Götterlehre*. 3 vols. Göttingen, 1857–63.

WELLMANN, M., "Beitrag zur Geschichte der attischen Königsliste," in *H* (1910) xlv. 554–63.

WIDE, S., *Lakonische Kulte*. Leipzig, 1893.

——— Article on "Greek Religion," in Gercke and Norden's *Einleitung in die Altertumswissenchaft*, iii. 191–255. Leipzig, 1910.

WILAMOWITZ-MOELLENDORFF, U. VON, *Greek Historical Writing* and *Apollo*, Two lectures delivered before the University of Oxford. Oxford, 1908.

WUNDT, W., "Märchen, Sage und Legende als Entwicklungsformen des Mythus," in *AR* xi. 200–23 (1908).

——— *Völkerpsychologie*. Leipzig, 1909.

WÜNSCH, R., "Griechische und römische Religion 1906–1910," in *AR* xiv. 517–602 (1911).

(b) Roman

AGAHD, R., "M. Terentii Varronis antiquitatum rerum divinarum libri i, xiv, xv, xvi," in *JP* Supplementband xxiv. 1–220 (1898).

ALBERT, M., *Le Culte de Castor et Pollux en Italie*. Paris, 1883.

ALLEN, KATHARINE, *The Treatment of Nature in the Poetry of the Roman Republic*. University of Wisconsin, 1899 (diss.).

ANZIANI, D., "Démonologie étrusque," in *MAH* xxx. 257–77 (1910).

AUST, E., *Die Religion der Römer*. Münster, 1899.

AXTELL, H. L., *The Deification of Abstract Ideas in Roman Literature and Inscriptions*. Chicago, 1907.

BINDER, J., *Die Plebs*. Leipzig, 1909.

BIRT, T., *Kulturgeschichte Roms*. Leipzig, 1911.

BOISSIER, G., *La Religion romaine*. 2 vols. Paris, 1906.

CARTER, J. B., *De deorum Romanorum cognominibus quaestiones selectae*. Halle, 1898 (diss.).

——— *Epitheta deorum quae apud poetas Latinos leguntur* (Supplement to Roscher's *Lex.*). Leipzig, 1902.

——— "The Cognomina of the Goddess 'Fortuna'," in *Transactions and Proceedings of the American Philological Association*, xxxi. 60–68 (1900).

CARTER, J. B., *The Religion of Numa*. London, 1906.

——— *The Religious Life of Ancient Rome*. Boston and New York, 1911.

——— "Die Etrusker und die römische Religion," in *RMitt.* xxv. 74–88 (1910).

CIACERI, E., *Culti e miti nella storia dell' antica Sicilia*. Catania, 1911.

——— "Sulla pretesa origine cretese del culto di Venere erecina," in *SSAC* v. 164–80 (1912).

CORSSEN, P., "Die Sibylle im sechsten Buch der Aeneis," in *S*, new series, i. 1–16 (1913).

CUMONT, F., *Les Religions orientales dans le paganisme romain*. Paris, 1909.

——— *La Théologie solaire du paganisme romain*. Paris, 1909.

DE MARCHI, A., *Il Culto privato di Roma antica*. 2 vols. Milan, 1896–1903.

DEUBNER, L., "Lupercalia," in *AR* xiii. 481–508 (1910).

——— "Zur Entwicklungsgeschichte der altrömischen Religion," in *NJ* xiv. 321–35 (1898).

DOMASZEWSKI, A. VON, "Eigenschaftsgötter der altrömischem Religion," in *Festschrift zu Otto Hirschfeld*, pp. 243 ff. Berlin, 1903.

——— *Abhandlungen zur römischen Religion*. Leipzig, 1909.

DOUGLAS, E. M., "Iuno Sospita of Lanuvium," in *JRS* iii. 61–72 (1913).

FORNARI, F., "Lavatio Matris Deum," in *BAAR* ii. 87–89 (1912).

FOWLER, W. W., *The Roman Festivals of the Period of the Republic*. London, 1899.

——— *Social Life at Rome in the Age of Cicero*. New York, 1909.

——— *The Religious Experience of the Roman People*. London, 1911.

——— "The Oak and the Thunder-God," in *AR* xvi. 317–20 (1913).

——— *Roman Ideas of Deity*. New York, 1914.

FRIEDLÄNDER, L., *Sittengeschichte Roms*, 8th ed. 3 vols. Leipzig, 1910.

——— *Roman Life and Manners under the Early Empire* (English translation of the 7th ed. of the foregoing by L. A. Magnus). 3 vols. London and New York, 1908–09.

GALIETI, A., "Sul serpente genio di Giunone Sospita," in *BAAR* iii. 10–11 (1913).

GERCKE, A., "Fetischismus im alten Rom," in *DR* clx. 268–78 (1914).

GLOVER, T. R., *Conflict of Religions in the Early Roman Empire*. London, 1909.

Graillot, H., *Le Culte de Cybèle, mère des dieux, à Rome et dans l'empire romain* (*Bibliothèque des écoles françaises d'Athènes et Rome*). Paris, 1912.

Grupp, G., *Kulturgeschichte der römischen Kaiserzeit.* 2 vols. Munich, 1903–04.

Kienzle, H., *Ovidius qua ratione compendium mythologicum ad Metamorphoses componendas adhibuerit.* Basel, 1903 (diss.).

Krampf, F., *Die Quellen der römischen Gründungsage.* Leipzig, 1913 (diss.).

Krassowsky, W., *Ovidius quomodo in isdem fabulis enarrandis a se ipso discrepuerit.* Königsberg, 1897 (diss.).

Kretschmer, P., "Remus and Romulus," in *Glotta*, i. 288 ff. (1909).

Lafaye, G. L., *Les Métamorphoses d'Ovide et leurs modèles grecs.* Paris, 1904.

Marchesi, C., "Leggende romane nei 'Fasti' di Ovidio," in *AtR* xiii. 170–92 (1910).

Mommsen, T., *Römische Geschichte.* 5 vols. Berlin, 1881–85 (English translation, London and New York, 1911).

Neri, F., *Le Tradizione italiane della Sibilla.* Turin, 1913.

Otto, W. F., "Juno, Beiträge zum Verständnisse der ältesten und wichtigsten Tatsachen ihres Kultes," in *Phil.* lxiv. 161–223 (1905).

——— "Religio und Superstitio," in *AR* xiv. 406–22 (1911).

——— "Römische Sagen," in *WS* xxxiv. 318–31 (1912); xxxv. 62–74 (1913).

——— "Die Luperci und die Feier der Lupercalien," in *Phil.* lxxii. 161–95 (1913).

Pais, E., *Ancient Legends of Roman History.* New York, 1905.

Pansa, G., *L'Officina monetaria di Lanuvio e gli attributi di Giunone Sospita.* Milan, 1913.

Preller, L.-Jordan, H., *Römische Mythologie.* 3rd ed. 2 vols. Berlin, 1881–83.

Reid, J. S., "Human Sacrifices at Rome and other Notes on Roman Religion," in *JRS* ii. 34–52 (1912).

Rose, H. J., "Italian 'Sondergötter'," in *JRS* iii. 233–41 (1913).

Seeck, P., "Zur Geschichte des lavinatischen Kultus," in *RM* lxviii. 11–15 (1913).

Soltau, W., *Die Anfänge der römischen Geschichtsschreibung.* Leipzig, 1909.

Soltau, W., "Die Entstehung der Romuluslegende," in *AR* xii. 100–25 (1909).

Toutain, J. F., *Les Cultes païens dans l'empire romain.* Paris, 1907.

Usener, H., "Italische Mythen," in *RM* xxx. 182 ff. (1875).

Vaccai, G., *Le Feste di Roma.* Turin, 1902.

Vollgraff, W., *De Ovidio mythopoeia.* Berlin, 1901 (diss.).

Wide, S., Article on "Roman Religion," in Gercke and Norden's *Einleitung in die Altertumswissenschaft*, iii. 256–88. Leipzig, 1910.

Winter, J. G., *The Myth of Hercules at Rome* (University of Michigan Studies, Humanistic Series iv, part 2). New York, 1910.

Wissowa, G., "Römische Sagen," in *Philologische Abhandlungen Martin Hertz zum siebzigsten Geburtstag dargebracht*, pp. 156–68. Berlin, 1888.

——— *Gesammelte Abhandlungen zur römischen Religion- und Stadtgeschichte.* Munich, 1904.

——— *Religion und Kultus der Römer.* 2nd ed. Munich, 1912.

Zeller, E., *Religion und Philosophie bei den Römern.* Berlin, 1872.

IV. ARTICLES ON GREEK AND ROMAN RELIGION IN THE ENCYCLOPAEDIA OF RELIGION AND ETHICS (vols. i–viii)

Bethe, E., "Agraulids," i. 225–26.

——— "Amphiaraus," i. 393–94.

——— "Cecrops," iii. 270.

——— "Danaïds," iv. 392–93.

Bevan, E. R., "Deification (Greek and Roman)," iv. 525–33.

Blakiston, H. E. D., "Graiai," vi. 384–85.

Bloomfield, M., "Cerberus," iii. 316–18.

Bosanquet, R. C., "Minotaur," viii. 674–76.

Burns, I. F., "Charites," iii. 372–73.

——— "Cosmogony and Cosmology (Greek)," iv. 145–51.

——— "Cosmogony and Cosmology (Roman)," iv. 175–76.

——— "Faith (Greek)," v. 694–95.

——— "Faith (Roman)," v. 697.

——— "Holiness (Greek)," vi. 741–43.

Campbell, L., "God (Greek)," vi. 279–82.

CARTER, J. B., "Ancestor-Worship and Cult of the Dead (Roman)," i. 461–66.
——— "Arval Brothers," ii. 7–11.
——— "Love (Roman)," viii. 178–80.
CURTIS, C. D., "Initiation (Roman)," vii. 327–28.
DEUBNER, L., "Charms and Amulets (Greek)," iii. 433–39.
——— "Fleece (Greek and Roman)," vi. 51–52.
DUFF, J. W., "Communion with Deity (Greek and Roman)," iii. 763–71.
FAIRBANKS, A., "Amazons," i. 370–71.
FARNELL, L. R., "Greek Religion," vi. 392–425.
FOWLER, W. W., "Fortune (Roman)," vi. 98–104.
GARDNER, E. A., "Centaur," iii. 306.
GARDNER, P., "Images and Idols (Greek and Roman)," vii. 133–38.
GRAY, L. H., "Incubation," vii. 206–07.
HALL, F. W., "Abode of the Blest," ii. 696–98.
HARRISON, J. E., "Gorgon," vi. 330–32.
——— "Harpies," vi. 517–19.
——— "Initiation (Greek)," vii. 322–23.
——— "Kouretes and Korybantes," vii. 758–60.
——— "Mountain-Mother," viii. 868–69.
HERBIG, G., "Etruscan Religion," v. 532–40.
HOGARTH, D. G., "Aegean Religion," i. 141–48.
HOPKINS, E. W., "Hyperboreans," vii. 58–59.
KROLL, W., "Momentary Gods," viii. 777–79.
LATTE, K. and PEARSON, A. C., "Love (Greek)," viii. 168–73.
MAIR, A. W., "Hesiod," vi. 668–71.
——— "Life and Death (Greek and Roman)," viii. 25–31.
PEARSON, A. C., "Achelous," i. 73.
——— "Achilles," i. 73–74.
——— "Demons and Spirits (Greek)," iv. 590–94.
——— "Heroes and Hero-Gods (Greek and Roman)," vi. 652–56.
——— "Human Sacrifice (Greek)," vi. 847–49.
——— "Mother of the Gods (Greek and Roman)," viii. 847–51.
REID, J. S., "Demons and Spirits (Roman)," iv. 620–22.
——— "Light and Darkness (Greek and Roman)," viii. 56–60.
ROSE, H. J., "Festivals and Fasts (Greek)," v. 857–63.
SAYCE, A. H., "Chaos," iii. 363–64.

SCOTT, W., "Giants (Greek and Roman)," vi. 193–97.
SHOREY, P., "Hope (Greek and Roman)," vi. 780–82.
SHOWERMAN, G., "Attis," ii. 217–18.
——— "Cybele," iv. 377–78.
SIKES, E. E., "Hearth and Hearth-Gods (Greek)," vi. 562–63.
SMITH, K. F., "Ages of the World (Greek and Roman)," i. 192–200.
——— "Hecate's Suppers," vi. 565–67.
——— "Magic (Greek and Roman)," viii. 269–89.
STOCK, ST. G., "Fate (Greek and Roman)," v. 786–90.
——— "Fortune (Greek)," vi. 93–96.
——— "Incarnation (Greek and Roman)," vii. 192–93.
THRÄMER, E., "Health and Gods of Healing (Greek)," vi. 540–53.
——— "Health and Gods of Healing (Roman)," vi. 553–56.
WISSOWA, G., "Divination (Roman)," iv. 820–27.
——— "Hearth and Hearth-Gods (Roman)," vi. 563–65.
WOODHOUSE, W. J., "Aphrodisia," i. 604–05.
——— "Apollonia," i. 608–09.
——— "Cimmerians," iii. 655–57.
——— "Keres," vii. 687–88.
WOODS, F. H., "Deluge," iv. 545–57.
WÜNSCH, R., "Charms and Amulets (Roman)," iii. 461–65.
——— "Cross-Roads (Roman)," iv. 335–36.
——— "Human Sacrifice (Roman)," vi. 858–62.